THE CAMBRIDGE COMPANION TO
ANCIENT GREEK AND

This book provides a comprehensive overview of the key themes in Greek and Roman science, medicine, mathematics, and technology. A distinguished team of specialists engage with topics including the role of observation and experiment, Presocratic natural philosophy, ancient creationism, and the special style of ancient Greek mathematical texts, while several chapters confront key questions in the philosophy of science such as the relationship between evidence and explanation. The volume will spark renewed discussion about the character of 'ancient' versus 'modern' science, and will broaden readers' understanding of the rich traditions of ancient Greco-Roman natural philosophy, science, medicine, and mathematics.

LIBA TAUB is Director of the Whipple Museum of the History of Science and Professor of History and Philosophy of Science at the University of Cambridge. She is the author of *Ancient Meteorology* (2003), *Aetna and the Moon: Explaining Nature in Ancient Greece and Rome* (2008), and *Science Writing in Greco-Roman Antiquity* (Cambridge, 2017).

OTHER VOLUMES IN THE SERIES OF CAMBRIDGE
COMPANIONS

continued at the back of the book

The Cambridge Companion to

ANCIENT GREEK AND ROMAN SCIENCE

Edited by

Liba Taub
University of Cambridge

CAMBRIDGE
UNIVERSITY PRESS

CAMBRIDGE
UNIVERSITY PRESS

University Printing House, Cambridge CB2 8BS, United Kingdom

One Liberty Plaza, 20th Floor, New York, NY 10006, USA

477 Williamstown Road, Port Melbourne, VIC 3207, Australia

314–321, 3rd Floor, Plot 3, Splendor Forum, Jasola District Centre, New Delhi – 110025, India

79 Anson Road, #06-04/06, Singapore 079906

Cambridge University Press is part of the University of Cambridge.

It furthers the University's mission by disseminating knowledge in the pursuit of education, learning, and research at the highest international levels of excellence.

www.cambridge.org
Information on this title: www.cambridge.org/9781107092488
DOI: 10.1017/9781316136096

First published 2020

Printed in the United Kingdom by TJ International Ltd, Padstow Cornwall

A catalogue record for this publication is available from the British Library.

ISBN 978-1-107-09248-8 Hardback
ISBN 978-1-107-46576-3 Paperback

Contents

Contributors

James Allen is Professor of Philosophy at the University of Toronto. He is the author of *Inference from Signs: Ancient Debates about the Nature of Evidence* (2001), articles on aspects of ancient scepticism, Stoicism, Aristotelian and pre-Stoic logic and dialectic, ancient ethical theory and medicine, among other subjects, and is the co-editor (with E. K. Emilsson, W. R. Mann, and B. Morison) of *Essays in Honour of Michael Frede* (2011).

Sylvia Berryman is Professor of Philosophy at the University of British Columbia. She is the author of *The Mechanical Hypothesis in Ancient Greek Natural Philosophy* (Cambridge, 2009).

Klaus Corcilius is Professor of Philosophy at the University of Tübingen. His most recent publications are *Aristoteles. De motu animalium.* New Greek Text and German translation with introduction and commentary (with O. Primavesi, 2018), and 'Ideal Intellectual Cognition in Timaeus 37a2–c5' (*Oxford Studies in Ancient Philosophy* 54.1 (2018), 51–105).

Patricia Curd is Professor of Philosophy Emerita at Purdue University. She is the author of *The Legacy of Parmenides* (1998), *Anaxagoras of Clazomenae* (2007), and numerous articles on the Presocratics, and co-editor (with Daniel Graham) of *The Oxford Handbook of Presocratic Philosophy* (2008).

David Ebrey is Research Fellow at Humboldt-Universität zu Berlin, part of the Research Training Group 'Philosophy, Science, and the Sciences'. He is the editor of *Theory and Practice in Aristotle's Natural Science* and the author of articles on Aristotle's logic and natural philosophy, and on Plato's ethics, epistemology, and metaphysics.

Thomas Kjeller Johansen is Professor of Philosophy at the University of Oslo. He is the author of *The Powers of Aristotle's Soul* (2012), *Plato's Natural Philosophy* (Cambridge, 2004) and *Aristotle on the Sense-Organs* (Cambridge, 1997).

Monte Ransome Johnson is Associate Professor of Philosophy at the University of California, San Diego, where he is also the Director of the Classical Studies Programme. He is the author of *Aristotle on Teleology* (2008), and of numerous articles on the influence of Greek philosophy on the history of philosophy and science, including contributions to *The Cambridge Companion to Lucretius* (Cambridge, 2007) and *The Cambridge Companion to Aristotle's Nicomachean Ethics* (Cambridge, 2014).

Massimo Raffa teaches Classics and is former Research Fellow at the Universities of Perugia and Calabria. He is the editor of Porphyry's *Commentary on Ptolemy's 'Harmonics'* for the Teubner series (2016) and the commentator of Theophrastus' sources on music for the *Philosophia Antiqua* series (2018).

David Sedley is Emeritus Laurence Professor of Ancient Philosophy, University of Cambridge. His books include *Creationism and its Critics in Antiquity* (2007).

Nathan Sidoli is Associate Professor of the History and Philosophy of Science at the School for International Liberal Studies, Waseda University, Tokyo. He is author (with Yoichi Isahaya) of *Thābit ibn Qurra's Restoration of Euclid's Data* (2018).

Liba Taub is Professor of History and Philosophy of Science at the University of Cambridge and a Fellow of Newnham College. Her books include *Science Writing in Greco-Roman Antiquity* (Cambridge, 2017), *Aetna and the Moon* (2008), *Ancient Meteorology* (2003), and *Ptolemy's Universe: the Natural Philosophical and Ethical Foundations of Ptolemy's Astronomy* (1993).

Laurence M. V. Totelin is Reader in Ancient History at Cardiff University and the author of *Hippocratic Recipes: Oral and Written Transmission of Pharmacological Knowledge in Fifth- and Fourth-Century Greece* (2009) and (with Gavin Hardy) *Ancient Botany* (2016).

Leonid Zhmud is currently Principal Scientific Researcher at the St Petersburg Branch of the Institute for the History of Science and Technology, Russian Academy of Sciences. His publications include *Pythagoras and the Early Pythagoreans* (2012), '*Physis* in the Pythagorean Tradition', *Philologia Classica* 13.1 (2018) 50–68, and (with A. Kouprianov) 'Ancient Greek *mathēmata* from a Sociological Perspective: a Quantitative Analysis', *Isis* 109 (2018): 445–72.

Acknowledgements

As editor of this volume, it is my pleasant duty to thank all of the contributors for their work, and also for their patience. Throughout the process, Hilary Gaskin was a helpful and robust commissioning editor for Cambridge University Press. I would also like to thank Sophie Taylor, Lisa Carter, Dawn Preston, Carol Fellingham Webb, Lizzie Evans, Amanda Kay, Auriol Griffith Jones, Toby Bryant, and Arthur Harris for their help preparing the volume for production.

Introduction

Liba Taub

One of the hallmarks of Herodotus' *Histories* (fifth century BCE) is the evidence that he offers of first-hand accounts from people living in various places, with different customs and points of view. However, regarding an explanation of the seasonal flooding of the river Nile, he complained that he could get no information from Egyptian priests, or ordinary Egyptians. Herodotus explained that:

> What I particularly wished to know was why the water begins to rise at the summer solstice, continues to do so for a hundred days, and then falls again at the end of that period, so that it remains low throughout the winter until the summer solstice comes round again in the following year. Nobody in Egypt could give me any explanation of this, in spite of my constant attempts to find out what was the peculiar property which made the Nile behave in the opposite way to other rivers, and why – another point on which I hoped for information – it was the only river to cause no breezes.[1]

Herodotus went on to report that while no one in Egypt could give any explanation about this, 'certain Greeks, hoping to advertise how clever they are, have tried to account for the flooding of the Nile' (2.20.1). In fact, he notes that those Greeks wishing to be thought clever had come up with three ways to account for the flooding. The somewhat detailed analysis he then presents of Greek explanations of the Nile's flooding indicates that he had a particular view as to what would constitute an acceptable explanation of this phenomenon. Here, Herodotus may have been articulating a view shared by many later historians, that Greeks who wished to be known for their cleverness had devised their own explanations of the world.

However, in discussing the three explanations offered by some Greeks, Herodotus immediately opines that 'two of the explanations are not worth dwelling upon'. He recounts that one of them maintains that 'the summer north winds cause the water to rise by checking the flow of the current towards the sea'. But he counters that in fact, 'these

1

winds on many occasions have failed to blow, yet the Nile has risen as usual; moreover, if these winds were responsible for the rise, the other rivers which happen to run against them would certainly be affected in much the same way as the Nile'. He notes that 'there are many such rivers in Syria and Libya, but that none of them are affected in the same way as the Nile'.[2] Herodotus rejects the first explanation because it does not accord with observation and experience of the world.

He objects to the second explanation as well, that the Nile behaves in the way it does because it flows from Ocean, the stream mentioned by Homer.[3] Here, Herodotus' objection is that this account is less intelligent, and seems to lack any factual basis; he complains that 'I know myself of no river called Ocean, and can only suppose that Homer or some earlier poet invented the name and introduced it into poetry' (2.23.1).

The final theory offered by the Greeks is that the water of the Nile comes from melting snow. For Herodotus, this theory is at the same time more plausible than the others, and yet it is also furthest from the truth. His objection is that the Nile flows from Libya through Ethiopia into Egypt, from a very hot climate to a cooler one. Since this is the case, how could the Nile possibly originate from snow? After rejecting the theories of the Greeks, Herodotus then goes on to offer his own detailed explanation, based on his view that the position of the sun (an important source of heat) is affected by storms: 'during the winter the sun is driven out of his course by storms towards the upper parts of Libya'. He argues that 'it stands to reason that the country nearest to, and most directly under, the sun should be most short of water, and that the streams which feed the rivers in that neighbourhood should most readily dry up' (2.24.1–2). Because the Nile is close to the course of the sun, it is more subject to the motions of the sun than are other rivers, and behaves in a way that is completely different from that of other rivers. Herodotus' original question about the Nile's behaviour linked it to astronomical events (namely, the summer solstice), and his own explanation of the Nile's flooding involves not only the river itself, but also the sun.

Herodotus' discussion of the flooding of the Nile is relevant for several reasons. First of all, in his opening paragraph, he refers to his work as *historia* (enquiry); he also talks about *aitiai* (causes). It is Herodotus' aim in his histories (enquiries) to identify causes. While, arguably, his primary objective was to explain the causes of events involving people (specifically, the Greco-Persian Wars), it is clear from his lengthy discussion here that he is also interested in explaining some natural phenomena (for example, he goes on to discuss winds in some detail). Rosalind Thomas has argued that Herodotus' work should be seen, at least partially, within the 'general milieu of debate, "scientific" and philosophical exposition, the *koine* [what is shared, or common] of Greek intellectual life in the second half of the fifth century' BCE.[4] While we may not normally think of Herodotus as a philosopher, he arguably shared something of the same intellectual environment as that of the Greek philosophers.[5]

Second, in his discussion of Greeks who wished to be thought clever, Herodotus criticises those explanations which do not accord with observation. Finally, Herodotus singles out Greeks as being the only ones who were interested in offering explanations about the flooding of the Nile. His positioning of Greek thinkers in this way may itself have been the start of a long tradition of emphasising a Greek desire to find causes, for natural phenomena as well as historical events.

Within the history of philosophy, the aim to explain and identify causes for phenomena such as the Nile's flooding has been regarded as a signal contribution of the ancient Greeks. Indeed, some ancient Greek authors were of the view that their predecessors were responsible for the invention of philosophy itself. Diogenes Laertius (probably first half of the third century CE) begins his account in the *Lives of Eminent Philosophers* by noting that 'there are some who say that the study of philosophy had its beginning among the barbarians. They urge that the Persians have had their Magi, the Babylonians or Assyrians their Chaldaeans, and the Indians their Gymnosophists; and among the Celts and Gauls there are the people called Druids, or Holy Ones' (1.1). However, he claims that 'these authors forget that the achievements which they attribute to the barbarians belong to the Greeks, with whom not merely philosophy but the human race itself began' (1.3); 'thus it was from the Greeks that philosophy took its rise'. He goes so far as to claim that 'its very name refuses to be translated into foreign speech' (1.4); the Greek *philo* and *sophia* together refer to the love of wisdom.[6]

Not all ancient Greek philosophers agreed about what the aims of philosophy should be, or upon what subjects it should focus. For some, as Diogenes Laertius indicates, philosophising about nature (*physis*) was a core activity. He described philosophy as having three parts, physics, ethics, and dialectic, and explained that 'physics is the part concerned with the universe and all that it contains' (1.18).

Herodotus, who singled out Greeks for offering explanations of the Nile's flooding, was himself from Ionia, home of the earliest Greeks who are credited with having invented philosophy: Thales and others from Miletus. Thales was also reputed in antiquity to have been the first to philosophise about nature. Simplicius (sixth century CE) explained that 'Thales is traditionally the first to have revealed the investigation of nature to the Greeks; he had many predecessors, as also Theophrastus thinks, but so far surpassed them as to blot out all who came before him'.[7] Clearly, at least some ancient Greek authors were invested in the idea that philosophy – and philosophy about nature – was the invention of their predecessors, other Greeks.

Plato (ca. 429–347 BCE) presented Socrates, in the *Phaedo*, as recalling that as a young man he had a strong interest in understanding nature.[8] There Socrates explains that he had been attracted to *historia* about nature (the phrase is *peri physeōs historian*):

> I thought it splendid to know the causes of everything, why it comes to be, why it perishes and why it exists. I was often changing my mind in the investigation, in the first instance, of questions such as these: Are living creatures nurtured when heat and cold produce a kind of putrefaction, as some say? Do we think with our blood, or air, or fire, or none of these, and does the brain provide our senses of hearing and sight and smell, from which come memory and opinion, and from memory and opinion which has become stable, comes knowledge? Then again, as I investigated how these things perish and what happens to things in the sky and on the earth, finally I became convinced that I have no natural aptitude at all for that kind of investigation.[9]

The Greek word *historia*, in a very basic sense, meant 'enquiry'. Some of the ancient 'histories' and ancient 'historians' (including Herodotus and Thucydides) aimed at offering explanations based on their enquiries.[10] Similarly, *historia* about nature can be understood as focused on not only enquiry but also explanation. Thomas has argued that by describing his work as *historie* (the Ionic form of *historia*), Herodotus was signalling to his contemporaries that 'his work belonged in the world of scientific enquiry, whether it be into nature, or the nature of man' or, as in Herodotus' own *Histories*, the 'nature of the conflict between Greeks and barbarians'.[11] The passage from the *Phaedo* provides a vivid sense of the sorts of enquiries that were part of *historia* about nature.[12]

ON 'NATURE'

In order to understand this activity aimed at explaining nature, it makes sense to try to understand the use of the word 'nature'. Etymologically, our English word derives from the Latin *natura*; *physis* is the Greek word translated as 'nature'. In his *Key Words: a Vocabulary of Culture and Society*, Raymond Williams argued that 'nature' is 'perhaps the most complex word in the [English] language'. He noted that while 'it is relatively easy to distinguish three areas of meaning: (i) the essential quality and character *of* something; (ii) the inherent force which directs either the world or human beings or both; (iii) the material world itself, taken as including or not including human beings', it is nonetheless evident that for the second and third meanings 'though the area of reference is broadly clear, precise meanings are variable and at times even opposed'. Williams highlighted difficulties involved in understanding the uses of the term 'nature' in contemporary English. He concluded his discussion of 'nature' by noting that '[t]he complexity of the word is hardly surprising, given the fundamental importance of the processes to which it refers. But since *nature* is a word which carries, over a very long period, many of the major variations of human thought ... it is necessary to be especially aware of its difficulty.'[13]

Perhaps following Herodotus' lead, G. E. R. Lloyd, in the 1989 Herbert Spencer Lecture delivered at the University of Oxford, argued that the concept of 'nature' was an invention of ancient Greeks.[14] The meanings and uses of the words *physis* in ancient Greek and *natura* in Latin have been studied in detail by a number of scholars and – perhaps unsurprisingly – histories of their usage demonstrate that they each had a range of senses and variety of referents, and that these were not static.[15] Lloyd emphasised that there was no single conception of 'nature' amongst ancient Greeks: 'to talk of such is to bracket the enormous differences between one philosophical position and another, and between philosophy and what passed as common opinions, as also the divergences between one period and another'.[16]

In Book 2 of the *Physics*, Aristotle distinguishes different ways in which the term 'nature' (*physis*) may be understood, sometimes referring to views of some of his predecessors. He explains that by one account, 'nature' is 'the primary underlying matter of things which have in themselves a principle of motion or change'; by another, it is 'the shape or form of things which is specified in the definition of the thing'.[17] Elsewhere in the *Physics*, Aristotle highlighted other ways of understanding 'nature'. For example, at the beginning of Book 3 he asserts that 'nature is a principle of motion and change, and it is the subject of our inquiry'; for this reason, he argues that 'we must therefore see that we understand what motion is; for if it were unknown, nature too would be unknown'.[18] Furthermore, for Aristotle identifying causes is fundamental to gaining knowledge: 'we think we understand a thing *simpliciter* (and not in the sophistic fashion accidentally) whenever we think we are aware both that the explanation because of which the object is is its explanation, and that it is not possible for this to be otherwise'.[19] In Book 8 of the *Physics*, he states that 'nature is everywhere the cause (*aitia*) of order'.[20] This identification of 'nature' itself as a cause provides a powerful theme throughout Aristotle's work,[21] and highlights the importance of finding causes (*aitiai*) when seeking to understand and explain.

As we have seen, ancient philosophers, including Plato and Aristotle, pointed to a range of questions that enquiries about nature might address. Nevertheless, modern historians and philosophers of science have not always agreed about what in antiquity would qualify as being called 'science'.[22]

THE PROBLEM WITH 'SCIENCE'

Issues involved in identifying and defining 'science' were addressed in September 2018, when the European Society for the History of Science met together with the British Society for the History of Science in London. One of the roundtable sessions asked a pointed question: 'What are we talking about when we talk about the history of science?' The programme noted that the organisers of the roundtable 'do not expect neat consensual answers, and … instead anticipate a diversity of responses in audience discussions that will illustrate the healthy pluralism among historians of science', and raised a number of further issues:

> While we all think we know (roughly) what science is … what
> really is the history of science the history of? One key issue
> is what relationship we see between history of science and
> other knowledge-generating/knowledge-based practices, such

as medicine, technology, mathematics, architecture, alchemy, crafts, music, literature, and the humanities. Another is: what kind of methodological perspectives can comprehend the history of such diverse practices – and whether conceived as a unified or disunified discipline? Previous generations had straightforward answers for such questions. When the history of science first became professionalized, many practitioners influenced by positivist philosophy of science focused on the unity and primacy of a monolithic 'Science'. We seem to have lost such ready answers by rejecting this positivist legacy and embracing instead sociological and anthropological perspectives across world cultures, and by recognizing diverse ways of knowing even within each science.

That historians of science are currently interrogating their own use of the word 'science' is an indication of the difficulties involved in using the term, recognised by many, including philosophers and anthropologists.[23]

The status of various human activities, as scientific, non-scientific, or even pseudo-scientific, is not always clear-cut. Some ancient Greeks were themselves very interested in classifying human activities. However, there was no one term, either in Greek or in Latin, which carried the meaning of the modern word 'science'. While some scholars have suggested that the Greek work *episteme* is equivalent to the Latin *scientia*, this is arguable; furthermore, neither the ancient Latin word *scientia* nor its nearest Greek equivalent, *episteme*, conveyed the same meanings as our modern word 'science'.[24] And, just as today there is no unanimity regarding what constitutes science and scientific practice, so in antiquity people were not agreed about the categories into which they placed those pursuits that might today fall under the historian's rubric of 'scientific'.[25]

Whether 'science' or the explanation of something understood as 'nature' was undertaken in other ancient cultures are questions that are debated. Francesca Rochberg, in *Before Nature: Cuneiform Knowledge and the History of Science*, has sought to 'raise and explore questions about observing and interpreting, theorizing and calculating what we think of as natural phenomena in a world in which there was no articulated sense of nature in our terms, no reference or word for it'.[26] Historians of science have been sensitised for some time to issues regarding what may be seen as a Hellenocentric view and the valorisation of ancient Greek science. In 1992, in a special section of *Isis*, a leading international history of science journal, David Pingree decried what he referred to as the 'Hellenophilia' of many historians of science, warning that the characteristics which define Greek science do not necessarily fit all scientific traditions.[27]

Using the word 'science' is a problem faced by many of the authors of this volume, especially as it appears in the title, *The Cambridge Companion to Ancient Greek and Roman Science*. In part the problem is due to changing understandings, by historians, philosophers, and modern practitioners, of what constitutes science. Furthermore, it is not at all clear that there was in the Greco-Roman world a unified conception of knowledge that was at all coextensive with the modern sense of 'science'. Recognising the use of the label 'science' is anachronistic, it is nevertheless a useful anachronism. For the purposes of this volume, science is understood to include a number of activities, which need not all be present or represented in any single work, or tradition. In addition to the sort of causal explanation identified by Herodotus and Socrates, the collection and organisation of information and knowledge, as well as prediction, are regarded as core activities of Greco-Roman scientific practice.[28]

Not only is the word 'science' somewhat anachronistic, the term 'scientist' itself is modern: William Whewell coined it in 1840, in his *The Philosophy of the Inductive Sciences Founded upon their History*.[29] Arguably, there is no exact analogue in other periods to that professional label. Nevertheless, there are a number of ancient authors and texts that few, if any, historians would question as being properly included in the study of ancient science. When we consider those who sought to explain nature (*physis*), many are usually considered to have been philosophers.[30] Yet, as Lloyd has noted, 'a distinction between "philosophers" and "scientists" is in general hard to draw in Greco-Roman antiquity. Natural science is a domain that straddles both those disciplines as *we* perceive them.'[31]

Aristotle set out his views about how we acquire and organise knowledge, including that concerning nature and also mathematics. In the *Metaphysics* (1025b25) he distinguished three kinds of thought: the practical (*praktike*), the productive (*poetike*), and the theoretical (*theoretike*). Furthermore, the theoretical is divided into three types: mathematical, physical, and theological.[32] Many others held similar views regarding mathematics as a type of knowledge, but as we will see in some of the chapters here, mathematics (and the various branches thereof) was not always only theoretical in aim. Arguably, other (non-theoretical) kinds of knowledge may be embedded in and derived from practice; however, the relationship between theoretical and practical knowledge may be difficult to analyse, and is debated.[33] Perhaps unsurprisingly, ancient understandings of what constitutes mathematics and philosophy were not always identical;[34] furthermore, they do not map on to modern conceptions in a straightforward manner.

This can be complicated because what is labelled as 'scientific' is often a matter of taste, sometimes personal, sometimes influenced by demarcations of modern disciplines and other factors.[35] There are those scholars, for example, who claim that the ideas of the Presocratic philosophers were not scientific, while there are numerous others who would counter that they represent the beginning of the scientific enterprise.[36] Ancient writings that are considered to be 'scientific' may look very different from the modern conception of such a work. There are many texts that have a form that the modern reader would regard as usual for a scientific work, including treatises, textbooks, introductions, and handbooks, but other forms and genres were also used to communicate scientific ideas. Poetry, including Aratus' *Phainomena* and Lucretius' *De rerum natura*, must be included, as must the dialogue form, exemplified by the writings of Plato; other types of texts include collections of 'questions' or 'problems', which were posed and answered (for example, the Pseudo-Aristotelian *Problems*), and astronomical tables (including Claudius Ptolemy's *Handy Tables*).

THE CAMBRIDGE COMPANION TO ANCIENT GREEK AND ROMAN SCIENCE

The Cambridge Companions to Philosophy is a long-established series covering areas of special interest, often focusing on particular philosophers, schools, or themes; the common thread throughout the series is the focus on philosophy. Much of Greco-Roman 'science' has been understood as being part of or closely related to ancient Greek philosophy. For this reason, the primary focus on Greek authors and texts here reflects the orientation of the series itself, and is not in any way meant to reflect a view that something that might be termed 'science' was not pursued in other ancient cultures.[37] Considering the Greco-Roman world, within this series, there have been a number of volumes with chapters relevant to natural philosophy and science,[38] but previously there has been no single volume which expressly addresses the need for more detailed treatment of a range of topics relevant to the study of ancient Greek and Roman science. The current volume, *The Cambridge Companion to Ancient Greek and Roman Science*, offers a broad framework within which both primary texts and the scholarly literature on science, mathematics, medicine, and technology can be studied. The aim has been to be representative, rather than comprehensive.

The chapters presented here can be understood broadly as being organised into two main groups. The first – including those by Patricia Curd ('Presocratic Natural Philosophy'), James Allen ('Reason, Experience and Art: the *Gorgias* and *On Ancient Medicine*'), Klaus Corcilius ('Towards a Science of Life: the Cosmological Method, Teleology, and Living Things'), David Ebrey ('Aristotle on the Matter for Birth, Life, and the Elements'), Thomas Kjeller Johansen ('From Craft to Nature: the Emergence of Natural Teleology'), and David Sedley ('Creationism in Antiquity') – for the most part are focused on philosophers and philosophical texts, primarily the Presocratics, Plato, and Aristotle. In several instances, a number of medical authors and texts are also brought to bear in these chapters, which highlight some of the 'big' questions that animate the study of ancient science: What is matter? How do we know? Is there a purpose? Was the world created? That medical authors as well as philosophers are treated here illustrates the richness of the broader cultural contexts in which such issues were contemplated and discussed. Readers will find many resonances between these chapters, which ideally will not be read in isolation. Serving together as an introduction to significant questions motivating ancient scientific inquiry, the approach in each of these chapters is primarily philosophical, and the contributors here present their own analyses and criticisms. The intention is to highlight some topics that were important for ancient philosophers, and also to present excellent examples of current research and scholarship on these ancient thinkers and topics.

The second group focuses on specific 'areas' of enquiry in antiquity, concerned with particular types of phenomena and explanations. Studies of plants, meteorological and astronomical phenomena, as well as mathematics, mechanics, and harmonics are discussed by this group of contributors, including Laurence M. V. Totelin ('What's a Plant?'), Monte Ransome Johnson ('Meteorology'), Nathan Sidoli ('Ancient Greek Mathematics'), Liba Taub ('Astronomy in its Contexts'), Sylvia Berryman ('Ancient Greek Mechanics and the Mechanical Hypothesis'), and Massimo Raffa ('Measuring Musical Beauty: Instruments, Reason, and Perception in Ancient Harmonics'). The authors emphasise that even terms such as 'meteorology', 'astronomy', 'mathematics', and 'harmonics' did not carry the same meaning in Greco-Roman antiquity that they do today. The areas of scientific study considered here were not only or always theoretical in orientation; practical applications and social contexts were often significant. Yet, it is not always clear what was primarily 'practical': some of the extant texts describe seemingly practical problems that were in fact didactic or recreational exercises.[39] And, to some extent, the various areas of Greco-Roman science – and the ways in which these have come to be categorised – have been determined by past scholarship, as well as by those scholars who today study what they regard as scientific or technical fields. In a number of these chapters, the issues that were highlighted by the first group of contributors reappear, for example, the role of reason, and that of experience.

The first chapter of the volume, by Patricia Curd, focuses on those who are traditionally regarded as the first Greeks to have philosophised about nature, the Presocratics. Curd also highlights questions about the relationship between philosophy and science. The final chapter, by Leonid Zhmud ('Ancient Greek Historiography of Science'), considers the writing of the history of science in antiquity. This seems a fitting end to the section centred on specific areas of scientific study, and also to the volume as a whole: Zhmud presents a study of the work of those ancient authors who engaged in a version of what we today think of as history of 'science'.

Amongst the contributors to this volume are scholars who consider themselves to be primarily philosophers, and others who consider themselves to be primarily historians. That work by both philosophers and historians is featured here emphasises that *historia* and *philosophia* are both necessary to the project of studying ancient science.

ABOUT THE COVER IMAGE

The cover image reproduces a small portion of a third-century CE Roman mosaic, currently in the Rheinisches Landesmuseum Trier, Germany. A man is depicted, seated and holding a sundial. While there is no inscription, some have accepted the suggestion that he represents Anaximander of Miletus (sixth century BCE), one of the early Ionian philosophers.[40] Diogenes Laertius credited Anaximander with having been the first to invent or discover the *gnomon*, a shadow caster, which he set up in Sparta, to mark the solstices and equinoxes (the latter point duly credited by Diogenes Laertius to Favorinus' *Miscellaneous History*). However, Herodotus (2.109) had reported that the Greeks had gained knowledge of the *polos* (sundial) and the *gnomon* and the twelve parts of the day from Babylon. The much later tenth-century CE work known as the *Suda* credited Anaximander with having written *On Nature* and also with having introduced the *gnomon*.[41] The type of sundial shown here, consisting of two vertical plane surfaces folded in a dihedral angle, is anachronistic for Anaximander's time, and was popular in Roman areas in the second and third centuries CE, sometimes depicted on sarcophagi.[42] The mosaic reminds us that not all of our evidence about Greek and Roman science is textual, and also that not all of the scientific work credited to ancient Greeks was theoretical, even when those Greeks were primarily identified as philosophers.

NOTES

I am grateful to Nick Jardine, Laurence Totelin, and Niall Caldwell for their comments and suggestions on this Introduction.

1 Hdt. 2.19.2–3, trans. de Selincourt and Marincola 2003, 102. This translation is used in what follows as well.
2 Hdt. 2.20.1–3.
3 See, for example, Hom. *Iliad* 18.607; *Odyssey* 20.65.
4 Thomas 2000, 26.
5 Myres 1953, 43 suggested that 'in the collection of facts about *Man*, and in the interpretation of them, Herodotus is the only "presocratic" writer who is preserved in full'.
6 Translations of Diogenes Laertius here and in what follows from Hicks 1925.
7 Simpl. *in Phys.* 23, 29; trans. Kirk in KRS 1983, 86 (text 81).
8 Socrates (469–399 BCE), the Athenian public figure, was roughly a contemporary of Herodotus.
9 Pl. *Phd.* 96a–c, trans. Grube (ed. Cooper 1997), 83.
10 Hunter 1982/2017.
11 Thomas 2000, 167, see also 263.
12 There were, apparently, many ancient works titled *Peri physeōs* ('about nature'), although few survive; however, in some cases the title would have been assigned to works by later readers/writers. See Kahn 2003; Naddaf 2005, 16–17; Taub 2017, 11–15.
13 Williams 1976/83, 219, 224. See also Lovejoy 1948/60, ch. 5, ' "Nature" as Aesthetic Norm', on the difficulties of understanding the diversity of meaning of the term, particularly in the seventeenth and eighteenth centuries.
14 The lecture, entitled 'Greek Antiquity: the Invention of Nature', was published as Lloyd 1991c. This view has not been universally agreed; see, for example, Grant 2007, 1.

15 For example, on *physis*, see Pohlenz 1953; Pellicer 1966 (who discusses *natura* at length); Peters 1967, s.v. 'physis'; and Naddaf 2005, 1–4, 11–35. See also Collingwood 1945/78.

16 Lloyd 1991c, 417.

17 Arist. *Ph.* 193a28–31, trans. Hardie and Gaye (ed. Barnes 1984), I: 330. Acknowledging these different understandings of the term 'nature' (194a12), Aristotle states that it is for natural science to 'know nature in both its senses' (194a26–27).

18 Arist. *Ph.* 200b12–15, trans. Hardie and Gaye (ed. Barnes 1984), I: 342.

19 Arist. *An. post.* 71b9–12, trans. Barnes (ed. Barnes 1984), I: 115.

20 Arist. *Ph.* 252a12, trans. Hardie and Gaye (ed. Barnes 1984), I: 421.

21 See Lang 1998. Aristotle's own studies of nature were extensive, as evidenced by his surviving works.

22 See, for example, Cunningham and Williams 1993 on the origins of science.

23 www.bshs.org.uk/eshs-2018. See, for example, the chapters in Lloyd and Vilaça 2019.

24 See also Zhmud and Kouprianov 2018, esp. 451–3. Furthermore, modern uses of the word 'science' are not always indicative of a single agreed meaning.

25 On the classification of knowledge and expertise, see Kühnert 1961; Tatarkiewicz 1963; Lloyd 2009.

26 Rochberg 2016, 1.

27 The articles included in the section on ancient science in *Isis* 83 (December 1992) are Bernal 1992; Lloyd 1992; Pingree 1992; Rochberg 1992; von Staden 1992.

28 See Jones and Taub 2018, Introduction.

29 Whewell 1840, I: cxiii (cited in the *Oxford English Dictionary*, s.v. 'scientist'). See also Ross 1964, and now Miller 2017.

30 Aristotle referred to many of the earlier philosophers as *physikoi* (e.g. at *Ph.* 184b17, 187a12, 205a5), which we might translate as 'enquirers into *physis*'. See Lloyd 1991c, 417–18 caution about understanding *physikē* as physics.

31 See also Lloyd 1991a, 301–2, who distinguishes 'between those who engaged in detailed empirical work, and those who did not'. Zhmud and Kouprianov 2018 restrict their study to what he regards as a group of established disciplines that, since the fourth century BCE, were called *mathēmata*, including mathematics, mathematical astronomy, harmonics, mechanics, and optics; he also includes geography.

32 Arist. *Metaph.* 1026a6–32.

33 On these and related issues, see, for example, the chapters by Berryman, Johnson, Raffa, Sidoli, and Taub in this volume.

34 For example, whilst Aristotle gave theology primacy (*Metaph.* 1026a6–32), Claudius Ptolemy (*Syn. Math.* 1.1) argued that mathematics was the highest form of philosophy.

35 Judgements about what counts as science today are reflected in research funding and in educational curricula, for example.

36 For example, Cunningham and Williams 1993 date the origin of science to the Age of Revolutions, approximately 1760–1848; on the work of the Presocratics as scientific, see Curd 2016 and Chapter 1, in this volume.

37 For an introduction to science in the Old World, see Jones and Taub 2018; the chapters there trace the principal scientific traditions in antiquity that left substantial textual evidence, namely, the Mesopotamian, Egyptian, Greek, Roman, Indian, and Chinese.

38 See, for example, the chapter by Hankinson, 'Philosophy and Science', in Sedley 2003.
39 See, for example, the arithmetical problem-poems in the *Greek Anthology*, discussed by Taub 2017, 39–49.
40 Rheinisches Landesmuseum Trier identification number 1898.29. On the mosaic, see Evans 2016, 151–3; Rood 2017.
41 *Suda*, s.v. 'Anaximandros' (Adler α 1986), www.stoa.org/sol-entries/alpha/1986. Hannah 2009, 70 and A. B. Lloyd 1988, 34–5 have noted that it is possible to imagine Anaximander, on the western shore of present-day Turkey, having been credited with introducing knowledge from Babylon. On Anaximander, Herodotus, and sundials, see Hannah 2009, 68–75.
42 Evans 2016, 151–4, also with an image of a frieze from a Roman sarcophagus ca. 140–60 CE, showing putti with a dihedral sundial, Musée du Louvre, Paris (MA1341).

1 Presocratic Natural Philosophy

Patricia Curd

Recent studies have revived interest in the early Greek philosophers as both scientists and philosophers. This chapter explores the relation between these kinds of activity, suggesting that early Greek interests in the possibility of human knowledge and in science support each other. The early philosophers' analyses of knowledge included developing new views about the nature of human intellect and of divinity, making room for human knowledge about the world that does not rely on traditional divine inspiration or warrant.

PRESOCRATIC PHILOSOPHY? PRESOCRATIC SCIENCE?

Who are the Presocratics? And does it make sense to speak of either philosophy or science in connection with them?

'Presocratic' is a label used for identifying early Greek philosophical thinkers of the sixth and fifth centuries BCE. It was coined in the late eighteenth century, and originally was meant to contrast these figures with Socrates (d. 399 BCE), who supposedly was the first to consider philosophical problems in ethics. It is an inexact expression, both because it is chronologically inexact – some of the so-called Presocratics were contemporaries of Socrates – and because not a few of these figures had things to say about ethics. Nevertheless, it is a useful historiographic expression for referring to the earliest period of Greek philosophy before the classical philosophers Plato and Aristotle, and it will be used here in that sense.[1] A line from Heraclitus presents us with what may be the earliest reference to philosophers as such: "those men who are lovers of wisdom (*philosophoi*) must be inquirers into very many things" (DK22B35).[2] This use links being a literal lover of wisdom with curiosity and the activity of inquiry. In the *Phaedo* (96a4–5), Plato's Socrates says, 'When I was young I was an enthusiast for that sort of wisdom (*sophia*) that is called inquiry into nature: I thought it was magnificent to know the causes of each thing, why it comes to be, why it perishes, and why it is.' Here is Heraclitus' inquiry into very many things. The Greek words for 'philosopher' and 'philosophy' begin to characterise distinct kinds of human activity through their use by Plato (who contrasts Socrates with the earlier inquirers into nature and with the Sophists) and Aristotle. That it is appropriate to link philosophy and the Presocratics is indicated by Aristotle's discussions in Book I of the *Metaphysics*. Moreover, in Aristotle's physical treatises (on physics, biology, meteorology, coming-to-be, and passing-away, etc.), he treats his Presocratic predecessors as scientists like himself. They were not (in Aristotle's view) successful; nevertheless, he sees them as engaged in the same activity because they are trying to give an account of nature. Some contemporary historians of science fret about using 'science' to describe this endeavour, given current concerns about demarcating genuine scientific from pseudo-scientific activity, but we shall not worry too much about the terminology.[3] We will consider the natural philosophy of the Presocratics: their inquiry into the world and their views about nature.

'Nature' (*physis*) is another term about which there is scholarly disagreement. It seems to have its roots in the Greek verb *phuō* (to grow), and it occurs just once in Homer, at *Odyssey* 10.302–6. To aid Odysseus' escape from Circe's enchanted island, Hermes gives him a charmed plant, moly, and in explaining how it will work, 'showed [him] its *physis*: it was black at the root with a blossom like milk'. While Homer stresses the outward appearance, in Presocratic philosophy, *physis* comes to include at least some reference to the basic character of a thing, what is responsible for (or is the cause of) its being what it is, with a strong hint of order and regularity. After all, the way a plant or animal grows or develops is primarily determined by the sort of thing it is; different individuals of a species (say, monarch butterflies) will have slightly different characteristics, yet they all will share a certain pattern of growth and change because they are of the same kind.[4] The Presocratics differ in many ways, but they share a commitment to the idea that the world of nature is orderly in fundamental ways (that is, a *kosmos*, an arrangement rather than a random collection of items), and so subject to explanation: an account or *logos* of it can, in principle, be given. Thus, Aristotle is right to call them *physiologoi*, no matter how unlike modern scientific claims their theories may seem to us. The discussion here will concentrate on early Greek theories of cosmology, meteorology, and astronomy, although during this period interest in mathematics and harmonics also developed.[5] Study of the Presocratics is limited by how little material survives. For Thales of Miletus, traditionally listed as the first of the Greek philosopher-scientists, there is no surviving written material: indeed, Thales may not have written a book at all (Aristotle seems to be relying on reports about Thales rather than any primary written material: at *de An.* 411a7–8 he attributes a view about soul to Thales on the basis of what has been reported about him[6]). Only scraps of sentences, quoted by later ancient scholars, remain from the works of Anaximander and Anaximenes. For the later Presocratics there is more material, but we have no complete work of any Greek philosopher before Plato.[7]

THE MILESIANS AND XENOPHANES: MEASURE, ORDER, AND INQUIRY

In the *Metaphysics*, Aristotle undertakes a study of 'first philosophy', the highest theoretical study of the principles of what there is. As is usual with Aristotle, he begins by looking to the views of his predecessors – 'let us take up those who went before us in the investigation of being and philosophized about the truth; for it is clear that they speak about certain principles and causes' – and he begins with Thales, as 'the founder of this sort of philosophy' (983b1–4, 20–1). He then says that Thales thought that the basic principle of all things is water; he interprets this as a commitment to water as the material cause and fundamental principle of everything that is, and asserts that most of his predecessors discussed only the material causes of things. Aristotle is proud of his distinctions among four types of cause/explanation: the material (the stuff from which something comes or is made), the formal (the shape or form/nature of a thing), the efficient (the moving cause), and the final (the end [*telos*] towards which a thing develops: the full manifestation of a thing[8]); in his view, earlier thinkers failed to offer adequate scientific and metaphysical theories because they overlooked or were ignorant of one or more of these causes.[9]

Aristotle gives his own treatment of the most general fundamental metaphysical questions; in his system, these questions are about the principles necessary for wisdom, the knowledge of *everything*. Aristotle's individual studies of nature are underpinned by these principles, but are not themselves part of metaphysics; in the first book of the *Metaphysics* Aristotle is not interested in his predecessors' scientific views as such. In turn, it seems that the earliest Presocratics were more interested in tracking, registering, and explaining natural phenomena than in doing more abstract metaphysics, and so one can sense a misfit between the projects described by Aristotle and the details (such as they can be recovered) of these thinkers' views. The accounts of nature that emerge will generate metaphysical and epistemological questions, and the answers that later Presocratics give to these questions will affect the scientific theories that they propose.

The Milesians may be said to have brought into the study of nature three important notions: close attention to and classification of empirical data about change, the idea of nature as an orderly cosmos, and a mechanism to maintain those orderly changes.[10] Although Thales is said to have predicted an eclipse of the sun, this is unlikely; nevertheless, the testimonia show that Thales was a keen observer of the skies. He seems to have measured the length of a solar year, refined measurements of star constellations used to mark weather seasons, and recognised and marked four seasons (rather than the traditional three) on the basis of close study of the stars.[11] What these activities have in common is a recognition of an orderly system of motions that is manifested by the regular movements of the constellations and the less uniform but predictable motion of the planets.[12] Aristotle notes that, according to Thales, the earth rests on water (this is one of Aristotle's reasons for claiming that Thales recognises water as the fundamental principle and cause); nevertheless, many of the ancient testimonia deal with his astronomical observations and measurements rather than with any thoughts about first principles.

Anaximander did leave at least one book (which is no longer extant); he too speculates about the heavens, but he also had views about the development of the cosmos (cosmogony) and its structure (cosmology). The cosmos developed from an indefinitely large mass of undifferentiated stuff: the testimonia refer to it as 'the boundless', the *apeiron*.[13] Simplicius (whose comment about Anaximander's language at the end of the passage indicates that he was familiar with a text) reports:

> Anaximander ... says that the *apeiron* is source and element of things that are, being the first to apply this name to the source. He says it is neither water nor any other of the so-called elements, but some other indefinite (*apeiron*) nature (*physis*), from which come to be all the heavens and the world-orders (*kosmoi*) in them. That from which is the coming-to-be of the things that are, into that

too is their passing-away, according to what must be; for they give justice [payment] and restitution to one another for their injustice, in accordance with the ordering of time, as he says in rather poetic language.

(DK12B1)

Although Anaximander recognises that the cosmos developed from an earlier stage, that development is neither a coming-to-be from nothing nor the result of a creation. In DK12A10, Pseudo-Plutarch reports that Anaximander 'says that something productive of hot and cold' was first separated off; it is from this that our world develops. In B1, Anaximander asserts that this order is maintained by time, and by this he means that the system (including the heavens and the activities of the seasons) is self-regulating, rather than being maintained or governed by anything external to the system itself (indeed, there is only the natural system itself). This notion of order, i.e. that the natural world is an orderly system (kosmos), is a crucial idea in the development of Presocratic views of nature. While it is implicit in Thales, it is this passage in Anaximander about justice, recompense, and the ordering through time that is our first written evidence of it. Here is a rejection of the mythical worlds of Homer and Hesiod with immortal gods driven by passions who erupt into and interfere with the natural world of mortal beings.[14]

Anaximander also had views about the details of the natural world. The evidence we have implies that he offered accounts of a wide range of phenomena: the earth stays put at the middle of the cosmos because there is no reason for it to move (one of the first arguments from sufficient reason); the sun, moon, and stars are open vents fixed on hollow rings of fire surrounding the earth. He estimates the sizes of the sun and moon rings in relation to the earth (the sun ring is twenty-seven or twenty-eight times larger than the earth[15]), and he is reported to have addressed meteorological phenomena: thunder, lightning, thunderbolts, firebursts, and hurricanes, according to the report in Aëtius (DK12A23), all result from wind reacting with cloud.[16] Anaximander also speculates about the origin and development of animals: they were 'engendered in the moist, surrounded by a thorny bark (or membrane), as they reached maturity they moved into drier places, and, breaking out of the bark, they lived a different sort of life for a little time' (DK12A30).

Anaximenes, the third of the Milesians, proposed a mechanism for some of the changes that Anaximander had studied. According to Simplicius (DK13A5), Anaximenes posited air as the unlimited (but not indeterminate) underlying nature and principle (in Aristotle's sense), and then suggested that different physical phenomena are produced from it by condensation (cooling) and rarefaction (heating). Testimonia suggest that, in explaining condensation, Anaximenes had in mind the process of producing felt from wool (DK13A7). Thus, when air is heated and so becomes highly rarified, it is fire; through progressive cooling and condensing, wind, cloud, water, earth, and stone are produced. In his view, motion and change are eternal; Anaximenes relies on both motion and the mechanisms of condensation and rarefaction to explain the phenomena of cosmogony, cosmology, and meteorology, covering many of the same subjects as Anaximander. The Milesians seem to have set an explanatory syllabus that the later Presocratics also follow.

While Thales is supposed to have said that 'all things are full of gods' (DK11A22 from Aristotle in *De anima*) and the other Milesians are reported to have asserted that certain of the heavenly bodies were gods, there is no clear active role for gods to play in these accounts of nature. Anaximander's view seems to exclude them from any sort of explanatory role in nature, and Anaximenes' world is equally remote from the worlds of Homer and Hesiod. The rejection of the traditional view of the gods becomes explicit in Xenophanes of Colophon, who proposed his own accounts of nature and natural phenomena, and is the first of the Presocratics to raise questions about the epistemic status of theories of nature.[17] In one fragment (21B18), Xenophanes denies the possibility of divine inspiration (such as Homer and Hesiod rely on in invoking the Muses), endorsing instead the efficacy of human inquiry. Trusting to human understanding and investigation is a far better path to knowledge:

> Indeed not from the beginning did the gods reveal all things to
> mortals, but, in time, inquiring, they discover better.[18]

In other texts (DK21B11, B12, B14, B15, B16), Xenophanes rejects and ridicules the traditional accounts of the gods.

While jettisoning the traditional views, Xenophanes proposed his own account of the nature of the divine:

DK21B23:   One god greatest among gods and men,
            not at all like mortals in body or in thought.

B24:   whole he sees, whole he thinks, and whole he hears.

B26:   always he remains in the same [state], changing not at all, nor is it fitting that he come and go to different places at different times.

B25:   But completely without toil he agitates all things by the thought of his mind.

This unchanging and unmoving divinity (line 1 of B26 addresses change in general; line 2 deals specifically with motion), aware of all things at all times, controls the cosmos by thought alone. Xenophanes replaces the traditional divinity-based accounts of meteorological events with his own naturalism:

> She whom they call Iris, this too is by nature cloud purple, and red, and greeny-yellow to behold ...
>
> (DK21B32)

> Xenophanes says that the star-like phenomena on ships, which some call the *Dioskouroi*, are cloudlets, glimmering because of their kind of motion.
>
> (DK21A39; also in Aëtius 2.18.1)

These fragments, together with B18, suggest that the cosmos is a rational system that humans can come to understand by using their innate capacities for reasoning based on evidence. As Mourelatos has shown, Xenophanes developed a full 'cloud-astrophysics' to explain a whole range of meteorological phenomena in a systematic way.[19] The only limit to the extent of the earth is its upper boundary 'here at our feet' (B28): the earth extends limitlessly downward and outward (horizontally). Things on the earth are 'of earth and water' (B29, B33), while the water of the great sea generates winds and mists that become the clouds of the heavenly phenomena (B30).

A summary of some of Xenophanes' views about the natural world shows the extent of his own inquiry and interpretation of evidence:

> Xenophanes says that the sun comes into being each day from the gathering together of small fires, and that the earth is unlimited and surrounded neither by the air nor by the heavens. And there are unlimited numbers of suns and moons, but that all things are from the earth. He says that the sea is salty because of the many mixtures flowing along in it ... Further, Xenophanes thinks that a mixture of the land with the sea comes about, but that in time

(the land) becomes freed from the moisture, and he asserts that there are proofs for these ideas: that shells are found inland and in mountains, and he says that in quarries in Syracuse imprints of fish and seals were found; and in Paros, the imprint of coral in the deep of the marble and on Malta slabs of rock containing all sorts of sea creatures. He says that these things came about when long ago everything was covered with mud, and then the imprint dried in the clay. And he says that all men will perish when the land sinks into the sea and becomes mud, and this change comes about in all worlds.

(Hippol. *Haer.* 1.14 = DK21A33; trans. Lesher)

Although Xenophanes exhibits great confidence in his recommendation of inquiry and in his own accounts of the divine and the natural world, B34 (quoted by the sceptic Sextus Empiricus) can seem to cast doubt on the reliability of his own methods:

and of course, the clear and certain truth [*to saphes*] no man
    has seen nor will there be anyone (1)
who knows about the gods and what I say about all things; (2)
For even if, in the best case, someone happened to speak what
    has been brought to pass, (3)
nevertheless, he himself would not know, but opinion is ordained
    for all. (4)

This fragment has generated much disagreement (about the scope of 'all things' in line 2, and about the status of seeming or opinion [*dokos*] in line 4, among other things).[20] Given his interest in inquiry and his claims about his own knowledge and expertise (B2.10–22), it is unlikely that Xenophanes is embracing universal scepticism. Rather, he notes a requirement to continue investigating and to be ready to revise in light of new evidence. The sort of certainty that was supposed by earlier poets to be guaranteed by divine inspiration through the Muses is not (and indeed never was) available to human beings. Xenophanes' claims raise new problems for those interested in explaining nature: now, in addition to attempting to explain how things are, natural philosophers face the question of whether any explanation can count as genuine knowledge, i.e. as clear and certain truth. This means that any acceptable theory must now also consider its own epistemic status.

HERACLITUS AND PARMENIDES: LOGOS, BEING, AND *DOXA*

Diogenes Laertius, who says that Heraclitus adopted fire as the principle (in the Aristotelian sense), also commented, 'but he sets out nothing clearly' (22A1.8). The fundamental driver of the Heraclitean system is change in accordance with what he calls the *logos* ('account'), which encompasses the principles of order (much like a set of laws of nature[21]). In B1 Heraclitus announces that he will speak of an account 'which holds forever' and which is independent of his utterance of it.[22] 'All things happen in accordance with this *logos*', and in presenting it Heraclitus says that he will be 'distinguishing each thing in accordance with its nature, and declaring how it is'. It is clear that Heraclitus treats fire as a symbol of this *logos* and of the ordered system (B30), but it is less likely that he saw fire as a fundamental element in the way that post-Aristotelian commentators suggest.[23] Instead, there is a systematic process of interchanging stuffs, and it is this interchange that produces the cosmos:

> 'The *kosmos*, the same for all, no one of gods or men made, but was, is, and will be, fire everlasting, kindling in measures (*metra*) and going out in measures (*metra*)' ... 'The turnings of fire: first sea, and of sea, half earth and half fiery waterspout.' For [Heraclitus] in effect says that fire, by the *logos*, i.e. god, that manages all things, is turned through air into moisture which, as a seed for the orderly arrangement, is called sea. From this again comes to be earth and the heaven and things surrounded by them.[24]
>
> (Clem. Al. *Strom.*. 5.14.104.2–5 containing B30 and B31a)

Heraclitus' use of measure (*metron*) as well as the range of changes that he discusses signal that the orderly processes governed by *logos* apply at all levels of the cosmos. The changes in living things can be subject to the *logos* insofar as soul, too, turns out to be part of the system, as a particularly hot and dry manifestation of the vaporous exhalations from the sea.[25] Diogenes Laertius says that 'he relates just about everything to vaporous exhalations from the sea', including day and night and meteorological phenomena, and gives some details of Heraclitus' accounts of the heavenly bodies.[26] Although he is unclear about what the surrounding atmosphere is (one assumes that Heraclitus would say that it, too, is constituted by the exhalations), he does say that there are bowls (or bowl-like formations) in those regions around the earth (with the hollow sides facing the earth). When the bowls fill with bright vapours, these ignite and produce the light of the moon, stars, and sun. The sun appears to be hottest and brightest because it is in a 'translucent and pure' area closer to the earth than the stars; the starts, being further away, are cooler and dimmer. Although the moon is closer to the earth than the sun, because its region of the atmosphere seems less pure, it is not as bright or hot as the sun. Eclipses and the phases of the moon are attributed to variations in the motions of the bowls. Diogenes Laertius concludes his discussion of Heraclitus' views this way (*Lives*, 9.11 = 22A1): 'He accounts for all the other phenomena in accordance with these [principles? the vapours?] but he does not make clear of what sort the earth is, nor anything about the bowls. And these were his opinions.'

The evidence suggests that while Heraclitus had some interest in the details of cosmology, he was most concerned with questions about the status and role of knowledge in human lives. He makes clear that understanding the *logos* is necessary for living well (and that this knowledge includes natural philosophy), but he claims that simply piling up empirical details through inquiry is not sufficient for understanding (he says at B40, 'much learning does not teach understanding', criticising Xenophanes by name, along with Hesiod, Pythagoras, and Hecataeus). Nevertheless, B35 implies that inquiry (in the Xenophanean sense) is necessary for wisdom. For Heraclitus nature is an orderly system, and genuine knowledge and understanding depend on grasping the system as a whole through understanding the *logos*. Unfortunately, although he is convinced that he himself has this understanding, Heraclitus does not explain how one attains it. Perhaps the point of his riddling teaching is to demonstrate the method without elaborating it.[27]

Parmenides presents a different problem. He argues that genuine knowledge is confined to that which neither comes to be nor passes away, is whole, unchanging, and complete. Only an entity that meets these criteria is genuinely real, and thus genuinely knowable. The difficulties in interpretation are compounded by Parmenides' presentation of his views in a poem written in Homeric hexameters. There are conventional names for the parts of Parmenides' poem: the opening fragment (B1) is the Proem, the arguments about the nature of what-is (B2–8.49) are referred to as 'Truth', and the remaining fragments (B8.50–19; using the DK collection) are called *Doxa* (Appearance). What-is-not (anything that is not what-is) is unreal and therefore unknowable.[28] This would seem to entail that nothing that belongs to the world of sense experience is genuinely real; yet Parmenides also makes important astronomical claims (found in both the extant texts and the testimonia) that must have resulted from study and discovery. How should we understand these astronomical claims in the *Doxa* and their relation to Parmenides' austere metaphysical requirements in *Truth*? Given his metaphysical arguments, natural phenomena cannot have the status of genuine being; yet although Parmenides claims that only what-is is genuinely knowable, he seems to suggest that nature, too, can be an object of knowledge. For example, in B10 the goddess promises,

> and you shall know the nature (*physis*) of the aether and all
> the signs in the aether, and the destructive works of the bright sun's
> pure torch, and from whence they came to be;
> and you will learn the wandering works of the round-eyed moon,
> whence it grew, and how Necessity led and bound it
> to hold the limits of the stars.

Further, while she states at B8.51 that 'the ordering of my words about the opinions of mortals' is deceitful, at B8.60–61 the goddess claims, 'I declare to you the whole likely-seeming ordering so that no opinion/ judgment (*gnōmē*) of mortals shall ever overtake you.' Again, one wonders how the claims about nature are to be understood. In 28B14 and B15, Parmenides states (a) that the moon does not produce its own light and (b) that the moon always faces the sun. The testimonia report that Parmenides claimed that the earth is spherical (Diogenes Laertius, following Theophrastus, 28A1) and that the morning star and the evening star are identical (Aëtius 28A40a; Diogenes Laertius A1).[29] These claims strongly suggest that the moon is illuminated by the sun (heliophotism), all the heavenly bodies are spherical, the orbit of the sun is further from the earth than that of the moon, the stars and planets are not new every day (as Xenophanes had claimed, followed by Heraclitus with respect to the sun), the heavenly bodies pass under the earth, and the heavenly bodies can affect one another.[30] Thus, his claims suggest the correct accounts of solar and lunar eclipses, but Parmenides apparently did not realise that.

In addition to these astronomical claims, the testimonia and the fragments of the *Doxa* include discussion of a dualistic cosmology including claims that the spherical cosmos consists of a series of alternating rings of fire (or light) and night (i.e. the rare and the dense), and that at the centre of the sphere is a goddess who rules all things. There are also claims about embryology and psychology. Parmenides uses the mixture of light and night to account for changes in the world that appears to the senses, and for human perception and thought. Although Parmenides follows a syllabus of topics much like that of earlier Presocratics, his arguments concerning the metaphysical status of the objects of the natural world, and the epistemic status of claims about that world, remain of permanent value.[31]

Aristotle is ambivalent about Parmenides. He treats Parmenides as a natural philosopher in *Metaphysics* 1.3 (984b), where he claims that Parmenides is not only a monist but also a dualist (in a way) about causes and principles. In *Metaphysics* 1.4 (986b27–987a2 = A24) he explains this: 'being forced to follow the appearances, and supposing that what is one according to reason is many according to perception', he posits the two principles/causes: heat and cold (fire and earth). Meanwhile, in *Physics* 1.2 he claims that neither Parmenides nor Melissus has an account of nature, since both claim that the fundamental principle is one and unchanging, and no such thing can be a principle of nature. At *Phys.* 1.3, he diagnoses the problem: Parmenides thinks that there is only one kind or way of being (cf. *Metaphysics* 986b18: 'Parmenides says that what-is is one in *logos* [definition or account], while Melissus says it is one in matter'). Then, in *Phys.* 1.5 (188a20–22) he says (as he does in the *Metaphysics*) that although Parmenides says the universe is one and unchanging, 'he makes the hot and the cold principles, but he calls them fire and earth'. Aristotle's difficulties in classifying Parmenides indicate the misfit between Aristotle's systematic divisions of knowledge among subjects, and the typical Presocratic mixed treatments of natural philosophy and meta-theoretical questions together. Aristotle supposes that 'the appearances' are where our explanations must start, but for Parmenides (and for other Presocratics as well as for Plato), the requirements of rational cosmology take precedence.

LATER NATURAL PHILOSOPHY: ANAXAGORAS AND EMPEDOCLES

In the later fifth century, Anaxagoras and Empedocles introduced complex accounts of the order of things, including both the natural world and questions about the status of scientific knowledge, as well as concerns with the metaphysical foundations of nature. Roughly contemporaries, Anaxagoras and Empedocles produced wide-ranging accounts of cosmology, meteorology, embryology, biology, and theories of perception.

From the evidence we have, Anaxagoras devoted most of his attention to natural philosophy, while Empedocles also gave an elaborate account of the best religious/ethical life (including a theory of metempsychosis).

In all Presocratic accounts of the natural world, there is no first moment of generation from what-is-not; rather the universe is eternal, developing from an earlier state. Parmenides' metaphysical arguments show that the entities of this state must meet his criteria for being (and indeed that only such a fundamental entity is genuinely real). This model appears in Anaxagoras; as he says in DK59B17,

> The Greeks are wrong about coming-to-be and passing-away, for no thing comes to be or passes away, but is mixed together and dissociated from the things that are; And thus they would be correct to call coming-to-be mixing-together and passing-away dissociating.

In Anaxagoras, there is an original mixture of ingredients (DK59B1): 'all things were together, unlimited both in amount and in smallness ... And because all things were together, nothing was evident on account of smallness.' The ingredients do not themselves come to be or pass away, but they can be moved; all things have a share of all else: there is some of everything in everything.[32] This original mixture of ingredients, a plenum, is put into rotation by *nous* (intelligence or mind), which itself is not an ingredient but an intelligent moving force. The ingredients then are rearranged through the force of the rotation, and their subsequent mixture and separation produce the cosmos that is familiar to us, with earth at the centre, populated by living things, and heavenly bodies moving around it (propelled by the force of rotation). The sun, a hot mass of molten metal, illuminates the 'earthy' body of the moon (Anaxagoras was probably the first to explain eclipses correctly).[33] In relying on mixture and separation of the unlimited ingredients as the mechanism for the emergence of the cosmos and the features of its contents, Anaxagoras seems to be following the example of Parmenides in the *Doxa* (where there is mixture and separation of light and night). Anaxagoras' great innovation is his explanation of the order and motion of the cosmos. *Nous* is radically different from the ingredients: it is not mixed with anything, although it can be in things that have soul – plants, animals, human beings. *Nous* sets the mass of ingredients in motion, and so orders and controls that motion. In the *Metaphysics*, Aristotle credits Anaxagoras with being the first to recognise intelligence as the reason that there is good order in the cosmos:

When someone said that *Nous* is present in nature just as it is in animals as the cause of the cosmos and of all its order, he appeared as a sober man among the random chatterers who preceded him. We know that Anaxagoras clearly held these views.

(Arist. *Metaph.* 1.3.984b15–19 = DK59A58)

Anaxagoras' *nous* is not a cause that is external to the cosmos; it is part of the cosmos, and its ordering is internal, on the same model as that in the Milesians and Heraclitus. Because, for the Presocratics, a cosmos just is, by its nature, an orderly system, they did not feel obliged to account for that order. Anaxagoras' *nous* is both a moving cause and an ordering principle (which Aristotle will see as Anaxagoras' conflation of efficient and final causes). Indeed, a few pages later in the modern edition of the *Metaphysics* (985a18–21 = 59A47), Aristotle transforms his compliment, complaining that 'Anaxagoras uses *Nous* as a contrivance (*mêchan*[34]) in worldmaking, and drags it in whenever he is puzzled about the reason why something is as it is necessarily, but in other cases he makes the causes of what happens everything except *nous*.'[35]

Aristotle's allegations about the limited role of *nous* overlook an important aspect of Anaxagoras' system. As with the other Presocratic natural philosophers, Anaxagoras is concerned with the order and repeatability of cosmic processes. Given the natures of the ingredients, and the continued presence of *nous* as ordering principle, heavenly and meteorological phenomena are generally predictable (just as in the Milesians and Xenophanes);[36] but, in addition, Anaxagoras explains biological regularities as well. That explanation relies on the seeds in the original mixture.[37] Anaxagoras twice says that the original mixture includes seeds (in DK59B4a and B4b). Moreover, in B4a, he links seeds with things that have soul, i.e. living things; B12 asserts (just as Aristotle says) that '*Nous* has control over all things that have soul, both the larger and the smaller.' This suggests that *nous* directs (and hence explains) the continued biological development of living things as well as sensation (in plants and animals) and thought (in human beings).[38] So, rather than dragging *nous* in at inconvenient explanatory moments, Anaxagoras relies on it throughout his account of nature.

After the austerity of Anaxagoras' prose and explanations, turning to Empedocles can be disorienting. He presents his views in flamboyant poetry, and his vocabulary includes a number of obscure terms (some of which appear nowhere else in the extant Greek corpus). In addition, he mixes discussions of topics that later thinkers will treat separately: physics and religious/ethical purification are connected in his thought.[39] The fundamentals of Empedocles' system include what he refers to as 'the roots of all things' – earth, water, air, fire – and two forces, Love (which separates likes and mixes unlikes) and Strife (which separates unlikes and mixes likes). There is a series of cosmic cycles between the complete mixture of the roots under the untrammelled reign of Love, in an entity called by Empedocles *Sphairos* or Sphere (a divine being with no biomorphic properties [B29], 'equal unto himself in every direction and wholly unlimited/a rounded sphere rejoicing in circular solitude' [B28]), and the complete segregation of the roots under the reign of Strife. In between, as Love and Strife wax and wane in strength, the resulting mixtures and separations of the roots will gradually produce and then destroy the natural world as the cycles move between complete integration and complete separation.[40] Empedocles describes the process using an analogy with wall-paintings (DK31B23):

> Just as when painters adorn votive offerings –
> men well taught by cunning in their craft –
> who when they take the many-coloured paints in their hands,
> mixing in harmony more of these but less of those,
> out of them make shapes resembling all things,
> bringing into being trees and men and women
> and beasts and birds and water-nourished fish
> and long-lived gods best in honours.
> So in this way do not let deception overcome your mind
> [to think] there is any other source for mortal things, as many as are
> seen, countless, perishable,
> but know these things clearly, having heard the story from a god.

The painters are Love and Strife, and the coloured paints are the roots; the mortal things (the products) are the living things and presumably the earth and the contents of the heavens. Although there are a number of fragments and testimonia that deal with cosmology,[41] Empedocles' main interest is in living things and how they are formed (some ancient biographies say that he was a physician).

Empedocles' cosmology and meteorology follow the patterns of other Presocratics. According to Aëtius (the doxographer who is the source of the claim) (A51), Empedocles 'says that the heaven is solid compacted by fire from air like crystal, surrounding the fiery and airy stuffs in each of the hemispheres'. The fixed stars are attached to this crystalline structure (A54), while the planets are unattached and so wander across the heavens. Empedocles, too, denies that the moon (which is compressed air, and disk-like in shape) has its own light, and agrees with Anaxagoras in his account of eclipses. He is most (wildly?) original in his accounts of the structure and generation of living things. Two fragments provide 'recipes' for bone (B96) and for blood and flesh (B98): they are combinations of the roots in certain ratios. Bone is two parts earth, two parts water, and four parts fire, 'joined by the marvelous glues of harmony [Love]'. Blood and flesh are more or less equal measures of all four roots (the slight differences would seem to account for the differences between blood and flesh and among the various types of animal flesh). The mixtures form only between the periods of the triumphs of Strife and Love, when the relative strengths of the opposing forces are less imbalanced. The account (so far as it can be reconstructed from fragments DK31B57, B59, B60, B61, B62 along with A70 and A72) is that first there are parts and limbs of living things formed, some of which fail to survive.[42] Others join with compatible surviving parts to form creatures capable of reproducing, and presumably, produce living things like those with which we are familiar. The roots mix in similar ways (although in different ratios or degrees of mixture), so that different animals and plants will have analogous parts (DK31B82 says that hair, leaves, feathers, and scales 'are the same'). This story of development suggests an equal story of disintegration later in the cycles, as the forces again become too unequal for mixtures to continue. Nothing that is formed from mixture of the roots between the alternating triumphs will survive those triumphs; hence all these mixtures are called 'mortal' by Empedocles.[43] Two long fragments describe the nature of the eye (B84) and the process of respiration (B100); in both of these Empedocles draws on everyday artefacts to explain how organs in the body (themselves constructed of earth, air, fire, and water) can filter other mixtures so that vision and breathing can occur. Empedocles' system maintains a remarkable consistency of metaphysical and physical explanation across all the many subjects he seeks to explain.

THE LATER FIFTH CENTURY: ATOMISM, DIOGENES OF APOLLONIA, PHILOLAUS

In the mid- to late fifth century there was a flurry of intellectual activity, involving both natural philosophy as well as medicine, mathematics, and harmonics. It is impossible to determine an exact chronology, and tantalising questions of influence remain open. Leucippus and Democritus of Abdera (the atomists), Diogenes of Apollonia, and Philolaus of Croton may have been contemporaries of Socrates.[44] Atomism, because of its later prominence in Epicureanism and Lucretius, is the best known of these later theories. Its fundamental entities, the full (atoms) and the empty (void), are eternal and eternally in motion (through vibration), according to testimonia from Aëtius.[45] All atomic stuff is the same; according to Aristotle's interpretation, atoms differ only in contour (shape), contact, and orientation (rotation).[46] All other things in the cosmos are constructions of atoms, produced by the intermingling of atoms and void as a result of motion and contact. How the world seems to us to be is the result of the mixtures of and interactions between the atoms that constitute us and all the other contents of the cosmos: 'By convention sweet, by convention bitter, by convention hot, by convention cold, by convention color; in reality atoms and void' (DK68B9 = B125). The atomists reject teleological explanations (in both the Platonic and the Aristotelian senses); the system is mechanistic, driven by the motions resulting from collisions of atoms. Leucippus (DK68B2) asserts, 'No thing occurs in vain [or: at random], but everything for a reason and on account of necessity.' The reason and necessity here do not include anything that resembles final causation. Although few fragments dealing with the details of the atomist theory survive, there are abundant testimonia showing that Democritus had worked out a comprehensive and extensive account of nature. Daniel Graham's collection of early Greek philosophical texts organises the atomist material into sections on cosmogony, cosmology, causation, astronomy, meteorology, geology, biology, physiology, embryology, anthropology, psychology and perception, epistemology, the almanac, geography, agriculture, geometry, the nature of language, and theology.[47] For the atomists, our cosmos is formed from a collection of atoms that rebound from each other and form a great vortex; the rotation then produces the earth and the heavenly bodies.[48] In all these cases, the ultimate explanations rest on atoms and the void, the arguments for which are ultimately metaphysical; there is no direct evidence for atoms or void, so their reality must be determined by reasoning.[49]

Diogenes of Apollonia is often overlooked in accounts of Presocratic philosophy; yet his views were widely known in fifth-century Athens.[50] He claims that everything is some form or other of air: 'It seems to me, to say it in its entirety, that all the things that are are alterations from the same thing and are the same thing' (DK64B2). These alterations are said to occur through condensation and rarefaction. Moreover, air is intelligent and self-organising: 'And it seems to me that the holder of intelligence (noēsis) is what humans call air, and everything is steered and controlled by this, for this very thing seems to be god and to reach everywhere and to arrange everything and to be present in everything.' Diogenes thus rejects Anaxagoras' separate nous and places the source of change (and soul) in the underlying intelligent air; but as with Anaxagoras, intelligence is the organiser and source of all things:

> For it would not have been possible for things to be distributed in this way without intelligence (noēsis) so that the measure of all things holds, of winter and summer, of night and day, of rain and of winds and of fair weather; and the others if one wished to take thought (ennoeisthai) one would find them disposed in the finest (kallista) way possible.
>
> (Diogenes DK64B3)

Although Diogenes adds here that the arrangement is the finest possible, his teleology seems more Anaxagorean or Aristotelian than Platonic.[51] His cosmology is conventional: the heavenly bodies are like fiery pumice stones (although because they are a form of air they have intelligence, unlike those in Anaxagoras' system); he also had meteorological, biological, and psychological views (including a theory of sensation). In a long fragment (DK54B6) he gives a detailed account, one of the earliest extant, of the human vascular system.[52]

The Pythagorean Philolaus of Croton, the last thinker to be considered here, was the first of the Pythagoreans to write a book.[53] He combines a Pythagorean interest in number with natural philosophy, arguing that 'Nature in the cosmos was fitted together (harmochthē) from the unlimited things and the limiters, both the whole of the cosmos and all the things in it' (DK44B1).[54] Here he makes clear that the form or pattern (the limiter that imposes a boundary) is as much a part of explanation as what is bounded.[55] Only what is limited can be known by humans, and Philolaus links limiters and number (B3); it is necessary, he says, that 'all things that are known have number' (DK44B4). This suggests that what is limited has measure and so can be grasped by the intellect, making the cosmos and its contents intelligible to human beings.

Although Philolaus seems to have covered many of the same topics as the other natural philosophers, there are some striking claims. Here is what he says about the sources of activity in living things:

> The head [is the seat] of intellect, the heart of life and sensation, the navel of rooting and first growth, the genitals of the sowing of seed and generation. The brain [contains] the origins of man, the heart the origin of animals, the navel the origin of plants, and the genitals the origin of all (living things). For all things both flourish and grow from seed.
>
> (Philolaus DK44B13, trans. Huffman)

This looks strikingly like Aristotle's (later) account of how psychic activity distinguishes various kinds of living things (plants, animals, humans); placing intellect (nous) in the head, and sensation in the heart, distinguishes thought from perception; similarly, the capacities for generation and nutrition are distinguished by placing their principle or origin (archê) in different parts of the body. Perhaps most innovative is Philolaus' removal of the earth from the centre of the cosmos, and replacing it with a central hearth or fire, the sun (B7). The earth moves, travelling around the sun 'like the stars' (as Aristotle puts it in De caelo). Philolaus also posits a counter-earth, which is not visible to us. Aristotle ridicules this as a Pythagorean move to have just the 'right' number of planets (Metaphysics A5.986a8). Yet, as Graham suggests, there may be another reason for the counter-earth: it allows Philolaus to adopt both heliophotism and the new account of eclipses, and could allow him to explain why lunar eclipses occur more often than solar eclipses.[56] The traditional Pythagorean interest in harmony is evident in B6a which gives accounts of the ratios in the musical scale, and in A7a Plutarch attributes to Philolaus the claim that 'geometry is the source and mother city' of other forms of knowledge.

CONCLUSION

In this brief account of Presocratic natural philosophy, I have focused on several main themes. There is the ambitious scope of Presocratic inquiry, unfettered by dogmatic claims grounded in popular religion, or depending on divine revelation. Related to this are the reliance on human reason and the recognition of core features of the world to be explained. It is further important to note the importance of metaphysical arguments to establish the basic ingredients of the explanations. Finally, there is a growing recognition that explaining the myriad features of the natural world (from stars and planets to human beings and plants) requires some force or power internal to the system itself. In most cases (excluding Presocratic atomism), this force includes some notion of intelligent guidance, albeit immanent rather than external, to account for the law-like regularities that Presocratic inquiry discovers.

NOTES

1 For discussions, see Long 1999b and Laks 2006. References to Presocratic texts are made through the standard classification system of Diels-Krantz, *Die Fragmente der Vorsokratiker* (DK) (Diels 1952). These texts in DK are listed in (roughly) chronological order; each entry classifies texts as either what the editors took to be testimonia, that is, reports of a figure's views from other, often very much later sources (identified by the letter 'A' and a number); genuine quotations (labelled 'B' with a number); and, in some cases, what the editors determined to be spurious attributions (labelled 'C'). Thus, each text has a unique identifier: DK22B35 (quoted in the next sentence) is the 35th fragment in Heraclitus who is number 22 in the DK order. Although there are several newer (and very useful) collections of early Greek texts, see especially Graham 2010 and Laks and Most 2016, the DK system of numbering is still, for the moment, the standard method for referring to texts.

2 The line comes from Clement, and scholars disagree about whether the word "philosophers" is from Heraclitus or belongs to the context of the fragment (in their editions of the text, Marcovich and Robinson reject it; in his edition, Kahn accepts it). In other fifth-century uses, Herodotus uses the verb *philosophein* in 1.30.2, and the Hippocratic author of *On Ancient Medicine* rejects the methods of the *sophistai*, i.e. those who practice *philosophia* (and mentions Empedocles).

3 See Kuhn 2012 on the general nature of scientific inquiry (the 4th edition contains an introduction by Ian Hacking who discusses the importance of Kuhn's work); G. E. R. Lloyd has written extensively on the question of ancient science (see especially 1979, 1987b, his Sather Lectures, and the papers collected in Lloyd 1991a). General discussions of Presocratic scientific inquiry are in Wright 1995 and Hankinson 2008.

4 As Aristotle puts it (in *Physics* 2), a thing has a nature (*physis*) if it has its own source of change and remaining unchanged; in a living thing that internal source is its form (the expression of its essence).

5 See also Chapter 3 by Corcilius, Chapter 5 by Johansen, Chapter 8 by Johnson, Chapter 9 by Sidoli, Chapter 10 by Taub, and Chapter 12 by Raffa, all this volume.

6 Barney 2012, 70, following Ross and others, suggests that Aristotle's account relies on Hippo as reported in Hippias' doxography.

7 For discussions of the various sources and the difficulties and problems of textual analysis and interpretation, see Mansfeld 1999; Runia 2008.

8 The notion of teleology, that there is an end or goal towards which each natural thing develops or which can be called on to explain an action or event, is often identified with Aristotelian final causes. We should be careful here, for teleological theories can include the notions of purpose, or design (for instance, Plato's account of the formation of the sensible world through the actions of the Demiurge in the *Timaeus* is such a theory). Not all teleological explanations are dependent on design or explicit purpose: Aristotle's own account of final causes is usually deemed to be a theory of immanent teleology, rather than teleological in the external sense as in the *Timaeus*.

9 For a nuanced account of Aristotle's view of his predecessors in *Metaph.*, see Cooper 2012.

10 Babylonian astronomers/astrologers also collected vast amounts of data involving the heavens over many centuries, but there is little evidence that these data were used outside religious practices.

11 See the articles by White (2002; 2008) for good accounts; he argues that 'Thales, it seems, pioneered the quantitative treatment of empirical data' (2002, 3). My claims here are indebted to White's studies.

12 The Greek for 'planet' (*planēs*) means 'wanderer'.

13 In Greek '*apeiron*' means literally 'without limit'. It comes to have the technical mathematical sense of 'infinite', but that is unlikely to have been what Anaximander meant (if indeed it is his term at all).

14 The status of 'the natural world' in Homer and Hesiod is a subject of debate. Here I contrast what seems to be the dependence of the Homeric and Hesiodic world on the sometimes capricious behaviour of individual gods (who may nevertheless be somehow identified with certain natural phenomena – Zeus with thunderbolt, Iris the messenger with rainbow, etc.) with the independent order of the system itself to be found in Presocratic natural philosophy.

15 Scholars disagree about how Anaximander reached these conclusions and the significance of the sizes. See, for instance, the views of Couprie and of Graham (in Graham 2008a).

16 See Graham 2010. See also Graham 2008a, 2013; Gregory 2013.

17 I have discussed Xenophanes on knowledge and divinity more fully in Curd 2013.

18 For a full discussion of this fragment, see Lesher 1992.

19 See Mourelatos 2008a.

20 A clear account of various interpretations is in Lesher 1992. In 21B35, a single sentence, Xenophanes says, 'let these things be accepted [believed] as like [resembling] the things that are true' (for good discussion of the various alternatives in interpretation of this fragment, see Bryan 2012).

21 What a law of nature is, and what counts as a law of nature, are subjects of much debate in the history and the philosophy of science. By using the term here, I mean something minimal: the seasonal and temporal regularities that the early Greek thinkers observed and measured in the heavens, as well as the uniformity of natural reproduction, were taken as indications of an orderly system within the natural world itself. Understanding this system (called the *logos* by Heraclitus) was one of the main interests of the earliest Greek philosophers, who in general took this system to be both descriptive and normative in the sense of describing and governing changes.

22 Thus, in 22B50 Heraclitus says, 'Listening not to me, but to the *logos*, it is wise to agree that all things are one.'

23 As with every other aspect of Heraclitus, there is disagreement about this among commentators. See Graham 2008a for this kind of interpretation.

24 Clement continues with a reference to *ekpyrosis* (and even quotes B31b), the Stoic process by which the cosmos is periodically consumed by fire and reborn. This is not Heraclitus' view, but later commentators often conflated the Heraclitean and Stoic accounts.

25 In B36, soul takes its place in the ordered transformations of fire, water, earth: 'it is death to souls to become water'; in B118, and B107, Heraclitus links soul with dry or hot and dry states. Aristotle asserts that Heraclitus links soul with exhalations in *De an.* 405a29 =22A15. It is not until late in the doxographical history that air appears as one of Heraclitus' elemental masses. For soul as exhalation, see Betegh 2013.

26 22A1; see also reports from Aëtius (22A12). There are also reports in one of the Oxyrynchus Papyri about Heraclitus' views on the appearances of the moon in its lunar month (*P. Oxy.* Vol. 53, no. 3110 col. Ii, fr. C, lines 43–47; col. Iii, lines 7–11 (cited in Graham 2010, 164–5).

27 The use of riddles and riddling language to conceal or obfuscate is pervasive in early Greek literature, e.g. in Homer, Hesiod, the classical tragedies, and myths, and the pronouncements of oracles. Heraclitus is part of that tradition, as he makes clear in B93: 'The lord whose oracle at Delphi [i.e. Apollo] neither speaks (*legei*) nor conceals (*kruptei*) but gives a sign (*sêmainei*).' The claim can be applied to Heraclitus himself as well as to Apollo.

28 For alternative interpretations of Parmenides' metaphysics, see Curd 2004; Palmer 2009.

29 The identity of the morning and evening stars was known to the Babylonians by the seventeenth century BCE (Graham 2008b, 182 n. 102), but the Greeks seem not to have been aware of this at the time of the Presocratics.

30 This list comes from Graham 2008a, 180–1. I follow Graham's account here. For fuller discussions of Parmenides' astronomy and the associated questions, see Popper 1998; Graham 2008a, 2013; Mourelatos 2008a, 2008b, 2013.

31 Johansen 2016 provides an interesting solution to the puzzle, relying on the notion of likelihood. Bryan discusses the connections among the claims of Xenophanes, Parmenides, and Plato's 'likely story' in the *Timaeus*. Other options appear in Palmer 2009; Curd 2004; Cordero 2010; Mourelatos 2014.

32 For discussions of 'everything in everything', see Graham 1994; Sisko 2005; Curd 2007; Marmodoro 2015 (which includes a discussion of the range of the ingredients); 2017.

33 The details of Anaxagoras' scientific system can be found in Curd 2007, and in Graham 2008a, 2013.

34 The word translated as 'contrivance' can refer to the elaborate machinery (a crane) used in Greek theatre when a god suddenly and miraculously appears at the end of a play to save the day or set things right (as Athena does at the end of Aeschylus' *Oresteia* trilogy). The present-day equivalent is the Latin *deus ex machina* (a 'god out of a machine').

35 Just before he complimented Anaxagoras, Aristotle introduced the need for a separate principle for the cause of order; it is unlikely, he says, that fire or any other (material) element can be the cause of things being in a good order, nor can such an important thing be left to chance. So, Anaxagoras appears (at first) as a hero. Plato's Socrates in the *Phaedo* (97b8–98c2 = A47) makes a complaint similar to Aristotle's: because Socrates expected a full-blown teleological explanation for why everything is as good as it can be (and also why it is good for Socrates himself to remain in prison), his delight at finding Anaxagoras' account of *nous* dissipated: 'I saw a man making no use of his Mind.'

36 Anaxagoras is supposed to have predicted the fall of a meteorite (he indeed had an account that would explain such a phenomenon, whether or not he predicted it), and according to Diogenes Laertius (A1.10), 'when he went to Olympia he sat down in a leather cloak, as though it were about to rain; and the rain began' (see also A6, A10, A11, A12). Whether or not the stories are true (and they probably are not), these and other stories of predictions by other early natural philosophers indicate how remarkable their accounts of regularities in nature could seem.

37 The account here draws on my discussion of seeds in Curd 2007.

38 In A16 (from Plutarch's *Life of Pericles*), Plutarch tells how Anaxagoras offered a natural account of a one-horned ram (by opening the skull and showing a developmental deformity) that others had treated as a political portent.

39 The ancient reports attribute a work 'On Nature' to Empedocles, and another called 'Purifications' (along with some other works that have probably not survived). Some scholars argue that there was only one poem (Osborne 1987; Inwood 2001); whether or not this is correct, recent scholarship is concluding that the content of the two works must be considered as related and not (as some earlier scholars suggested) as entirely different kinds of work that have no connection with one another. For discussions of this and other questions, see the collection in Pierris 2005. See also Martin and Primavesi 1999; Primavesi 2008. Overviews of Empedocles' system may be found in Inwood 2001; Wright 1995; Trépanier 2004.

40 All of this is governed by what Empedocles calls an oath of necessity, which makes the process orderly (see DK31B115).

41 DK31B38 and B39, B40, B41 A49a.

42 At this point heads without necks, shoulder-less arms, and forehead-less eyes wander about. They are followed by two-faced, two-chested monsters, ox-headed human-like creatures, and so on.

43 Some things can be long-lived (the gods and daimons), but they are not immortal in the sense of continuing through the periods of complete mixture and complete separation. The physical cycles are matched by (or include) a cycle in the lives of what Empedocles calls the daimons. These too are mixtures and so mortal, and they seem to appear as living things, and so may be what Anaxagoras would call a soul. The difference is that the daimons can be reincarnated during a cycle; as suggested by DK31B117, in which it is said that 'already I have been' a boy, a girl, a bush, a bird, and a fish. Compare with the lists of things in B17, B21, and B35: through mixture of the roots there come to be trees, men, women, beasts, birds, and fish. The range of reincarnations is apparently governed by the sort of life a creature has lived, and the roles of Love and Strife in that life.

44 These chronological claims should be taken lightly. Graham suggests that Diogenes' language resembles that of Melissus (and so may be slightly later than him). Melissus of Samos reportedly was admiral of the navy that defeated the Athenians under Pericles in about 440 BCE. For some of the most recent work on Melissus, see Mansfeld et al. 2016.

45 There is evidence that atomism developed partially as a response to paradoxes of plurality and motion in Zeno, and Melissus' denial of motion (because what-is – the One – is full and there is no void). Void in Democritus has been interpreted as empty space in which the atoms move, and also as that which is where the atoms are not, which itself moves relative to the atoms (see Graham 2008b on the former view, Sedley 1982 on the latter). See also Berryman 2002a on the importance of void.

46 Whether or not the Presocratic atomists accepted weight as an intrinsic property of atoms is a vexed question, which will not be discussed here. Aëtius says that Epicurus added weight as a property. The classic discussion is O'Brien 1981.

47 There is also a very large number of ethical fragments attributed to Democritus.

48 Details in Diogenes Laertius (DK67A1).

49 Sextus Empiricus, our source for a number of the fragments about knowledge, tries to recruit Democritus into the ranks of the sceptics. Scholars disagree about whether or not he was correct in this (see Curd 2001).

50 An excellent discussion of Diogenes and his place in accounts of Preplatonic philosophy can be found in Laks 2008. I discuss some of the metaphysical aspects of Diogenes' views in Curd 2004, ch. 6.

51 See Graham 2008a; Laks 2008.

52 McKirahan 2011, 349 comments, 'detailed but inaccurate'. Another early account is in the Hippocratic treatise, *The Nature of Man*, ch. 11.

53 Huffman 1993 is the most complete treatment.

54 There are complicated problems in determining what views early Pythagoreans actually held, and the nature of their interest in music and geometry. Good discussions are to be found in Riedweg 2005; Zhmud 2012; Cornelli, McKirahan, and Macris 2013; Huffman 2014.

55 Here I follow Huffman 1993 in thinking of the unlimiteds as continua, and the limiters as boundaries. See also Graham 2014 who suggests that Philolaus is the first who 'made limit or the class of limiting things a principle or element of reality' (53; italics omitted).

56 See Graham 2014 with diagram; also Graham 2013.

2 Reason, Experience, and Art: The *Gorgias* and *On Ancient Medicine*

James Allen

REASON VS. EXPERIENCE

The opposition between reason and experience is one of the legacies that we owe to ancient Greek philosophy and science, from which, via Latin, our terminology for it comes. The earliest plain statement of the distinction, if not in precisely these terms, is found in the *Gorgias*, which though set during Socrates' lifetime in the fifth century BCE, was composed by Plato in the following century (501a; cf. 465a; *Phdr.* 270b):

> I [Socrates] was saying that one of them, medicine (*iatrikê*), has investigated the nature of that for which it cares and the cause of the actions it performs, and is able to give an account (*logos*) of each of these, but the other [cookery (*opsopoiikê*)], occupied as it is with pleasure, towards which all of its care is directed, proceeds quite without art towards it, without having investigated the nature or the cause of pleasure, advancing altogether irrationally so to speak, having failed to distinguish and enumerate anything, merely preserving by routine (*tribê*) and experience (*empeiria*) the memory of what is accustomed to happen.

The contrast drawn here is between experience and the kind of knowledge or understanding apart from which, Socrates contentiously maintains, an art (*technê*) strictly and properly so called cannot exist. This understanding comprehends the nature of the objects on which the art operates and the causes over which it exercises an influence; its master is able to *explain* his artistic choices by giving a *logos* or account in terms of this nature and these causes. Experience, by contrast, is confined to recording 'what is accustomed to happen' – empirical regularities, as we would say; about their cause it remains unable to say anything (it is an *alogon pragma*) (*Grg.* 465a6).

Much the same distinction was drawn by Aristotle when he contrasted the experienced person's grasp of *the that* with the understanding of *the because*, or the grasp of causes, that distinguish the person with art (*technê*) or science (*epistêmê*) (*Metaph.* A 1, 981a28–30).[1] This person possesses a *logos*, in the sense of account or theory (981a15, 21, b5), and he 'knows the causes of the things that are done' (981b1–2).[2]

I shall dub this the classical opposition between reason and experience and speak of the classical framework in which it is at home. Part of this framework, explicit in Aristotle, but perhaps implicit in Plato, explains the inferiority of experience by appeal to the deficiencies of perception, whose deliverances preserved in memory are its material.[3] Perception is held to be defective in the relevant way not by being deceptive or false; within its limits, it is perfectly truthful. The problem is rather with the narrowness of those limits. As Aristotle observes, 'one does not regard the senses as wisdom (*sophia*), even though they give the most authoritative knowledge of particulars, because they never tell us the *why* of anything, e.g., *why* fire is hot rather than *that* it is so' (*Metaph.* I 1.1.981b10; cf. *An. post.* 1.31).

An important chapter in the long and influential history of the classical opposition, which has not yet ended, began in the third century BCE, approximately a century after Plato's death, when a school of self-styled Empiricists arose in the field of medicine. In effect, the medical Empiricists took the *Gorgias* as a challenge. They argued that a discipline enabling its practitioners to make systematic and effective use of all the available measures to its end, and which could be transmitted to students through teaching, was possible on the basis of experience apart from reason, i.e. that empirical medicine, and by implication other empirical disciplines, could satisfy all the demands that can legitimately be imposed on an art. They directed their arguments against a heterogeneous collection of medical schools on whose members they bestowed the, at first polemical, label 'rationalists' (*logikoi*).[4] In effect they – the Rationalists – upheld Socrates' position in the *Gorgias*. We owe the terms 'rationalism' and 'empiricism' to the ensuing controversy between these two medical persuasions.

My question is this: can the opposition between reason and the kind of knowledge it makes possible, on the one hand, and experience in the two corresponding senses, on the other, be traced back further than Plato, and, if the answer is 'no' or 'it's hard to say', what do we find instead?

THE LANGUAGE OF EXPERIENCE

Let us begin with the language of experience. The noun *peira* means a trial or test. The denominative verb *peirasthai* means to try, attempt, or, with an object in the genitive, to put to the test or make a trial of. It resembles one sense of the Latin verb *probare*, which is the source of the French *eprouver*, German *probieren* and *erproben*, and a now obsolete sense of English *prove*, found, e.g. in the King James version of the Bible (e.g. 1 Thess. 5:21 'Prove all things, hold fast that which is good'). Adding the prefix *en-* forms an adjective *empeiros*, which applies to someone who has profited from putting to the test, making trial of, or, if you will, *proving* many things; an adjective with the opposite meaning, *apeiros*, is formed by the addition of the alpha privative. Compare similar pairs like *empsychos* and *apsychos*, ensouled or animate versus without soul or lifeless; *ennomos*, lawful, legal versus *anomos*, lawless, and so on. The abstract noun *empeiria* means the state of the *empeiros*, the know-how or, at least in a broad sense of the term, knowledge that one has as the result of much *peira*, but sometimes also the activity that gives rise to it; *apeiria* is the opposite condition. The idea that learning begins with *peira* is an old one, possibly attested as far back as the seventh century BCE in a fragment of a poem by Alcman.[5]

Evidence about how this condition and the activities that give rise to it were understood includes testimonies containing compounds formed by combining *peirasthai* and *peira* with the prefixes *ana-*, *apo-*, *dia-*, and *ek-*.

Herodotus is full of examples. Candaules assures Gyges, who fears that nothing good can come of it, that it is not in order to test him (*diapeira*) that he has arranged for him to see his wife naked (1.9). Croesus sends emissaries to test (*diapeira*) the veracity of the better-known oracles, and, on the basis of the results, decides to put his faith in the Delphic oracle's response to the question whether he should go to war with Persia (1.46–7). And the famous linguistic experiment commissioned by the pharaoh Psammetichus, in which two children are brought up in isolation in order to discover whether, as he supposed, the Egyptians are the world's oldest people, is likewise described as a test (*diapeira*) (2.15; cf. 2.2).

It seems that one can learn a great deal from *peira*, e.g. that because the children's first word was *bekos* – Phrygian for bread – the Phrygians were an older people even than the Egyptians. If the knowledge one gains (though Herodotus does not put it this way himself) in this and other ways through *peira* is *empeiria*, it is not surprising that authors like Thucydides can treat *empeiria* as the opposite of *anepistêmosunê* (5.7.2; cf. 2.87.4–5), where we might expect *epistême*, which we translate as 'knowledge' or 'science' in deference to the superior standing assigned to it by Plato, Aristotle, and other ancient authors.[6]

The same linguistic tendency is on display in Xenophon's depiction of Socrates. In *Memorabilia* 4.7, he tells us that no one took more care than Socrates to discover about which subjects each of his students was already knowledgeable (was *epistêmôn*). Where he found gaps, if he had the knowledge himself and the subject was a fit study for a man both noble and good, he was eager to instruct his students. If he was relatively ignorant (*apeiroteros*), he sent his students to those who did know (to the *epistamenoi*). And he taught up to what point one should be *empeiros* in each field (cf. Thucydides 2.87.4–8). Even Aristotle sometimes uses the terms as though they were interchangeable in certain contexts, for instance when he suggests that the fact that experience (*empeiria*) in a particular sphere, e.g. of professional soldiers in war, may appear to be courage is the reason why Socrates held that courage is knowledge (*epistême*) (*Eth. Nic.* 3.8.1116b3–5; cf. *Eth. Eud.* 3.1.1229a14–16, 1230a4–10; [*Mag. mor.*] 1.20.1190b27–9).

Finally, there is a telling piece of evidence in the *Gorgias* itself. Early in the dialogue, Socrates' friend, Chaerephon, examines Polus in Socratic fashion, striving to elicit an answer to the question: 'what should we call Gorgias?' He explains his meaning with a pair of examples. 'If he were *expert* in the same art as his brother, Herodicus, we should call him a physician; if *expert* in the art in which Aristophon and his brother are, a painter.' 'Expert', however, first renders *epistêmôn*, then *empeiros* (448b4–c1).[7]

Plainly, in passages like these, it would be a mistake to understand either *epistême* or *empeiria* as though they had the contrasting meanings that Aristotle sometimes assigns to them. *Empeiria* is not being elevated above its station and *epistême* is not being demoted below its. A line is not drawn. Both terms remain available to specify much the same thing or range of things. To be sure, *epistême* and *empeiria* are not synonyms. The verbal counterparts of each term point in different directions: *peirasthai* to the activity of putting to the test that gives rise to expertise; *epistasthai*, which, like *savoir*, can take a dependent infinitive and mean 'to know how to', to the exercise of that expertise.

And the range of senses and applications they had were not perfectly coextensive.[8] But the assumption behind the uses that we have been exploring seems to have been that someone with a sufficient quantity of *peira* of the right sort will have and know how to use *epistêmê*, and that someone with *epistêmê* will owe it in some way or other to *peira*.

Compare the verb *historeô* and the abstract noun *historia*. The former means to inquire or investigate; the latter both the activity of inquiry and the knowledge won by means of it.[9] Later the medical Empiricists used it of the medical knowledge that a practitioner owes not to his own observation (*autopsia*), but to the learning of others, which is itself ultimately a result of their own observations. This resembles one of Aristotle's uses of the term: knowledge of particular facts that we gain through testimony (*Rhet.* 1.4.1359b32; *Poet.* 9.1451b7; *An. pr.* 1.30.46a24). But elsewhere and in other hands the knowledge called *historia* is not so restricted. The field by which the youthful Socrates was fascinated, according to the *Phaedo*, is the wisdom (*sophia*) called *peri phuseôs historia* (96a7–8). And the author of the Hippocratic treatise *On Ancient Medicine* speaks of *historia*, meaning the knowledge or science, about what the human being is, which his opponents claim must be grounded in foundational natural philosophy (20.2; cf. Aristotle, *Cael.* 3.1.298b2, *De an.* 1.1.402a4).[10] *Historia* acquires a sense meaning knowledge or science, the knowledge we have as a result of *historia* in the sense of inquiry.

The term *empeiria*, then, went some way down the path, fully traversed by *historia*, towards having the sense (among others) of 'knowledge', not restricted to inferior forms of the same. Had the contingencies that govern the emergence of new meanings been a little different, *empeiria* might have retained such a sense. It did not, and this insipient use of the term coexisted with others that were to prove hardier and more lastingly influential. Thus *empeiros* was used in the fifth century BCE to mean acquainted or familiar with that of which one has – as we would put it – *experience*. Hippocratic writers, for example, observe that women with experience of childbirth suffer less than those giving birth for the first time (*Morb.* 4.30.93). Sophocles writes of not being acquainted with marriage (*OC* 752) or being not unacquainted (*apeiros*) with evils (*Ant.* 1191). Euripides connects experience with age (fr. 619 Nauck; cf. Aristotle *Eth. Nic.* 6.11.1143b7–14).

The term *empeiria* was not always used to signal a contrast between experience, as it is understood in the classical framework, and superior forms of understanding; it came to do so. Was this a change in word-meaning alone or did it reflect more substantive developments? Put another way, to what extent was the opposition between mere experience and art or knowledge properly so-called – however expressed – there to be found, and to what extent did it have to be made?

EARLY MEDICINE

The idea that art emerges from experience, that an empirical precedes a rational phase, is an old one, used by ancients relatively nearer to us to understand their more distant predecessors. The pseudo-Galenic *Medicus* or *Introductio*, probably written in the second century CE, for instance, begins by citing the opinion of the Greeks, according to whom early humans did not yet have the medical art, but relied instead on experience of remedies and plants, of the kind possessed by Chiron the centaur and the heroes taught by him (1.1). In a less fanciful vein, the author goes on to maintain that the most ancient origin of medicine (and by implication of the other arts) is experience (*peira*) apart from reason (*logos*), as among the Egyptians and the barbarians (2.1). Aristotle describes a similar sequence of cognitive stages in *Metaphysics* A; the transition from *empeiria* to *technê* is part of the history of culture and not necessarily of every individual's acquisition of *technê* (981a3; cf. Alex. Aphr., *In Metaph.* 5.9–11). But did his and Plato's predecessors understand their own efforts or those of their predecessor in these terms? When did people begin to conceive of matters in this way?

It is natural to turn for illumination to the medical works of the Hippocratic corpus, which contain the first self-conscious reflections about artistic knowledge in medicine – or anywhere else – of which we have a written record, above all, of course, to *On Ancient Medicine*, the most methodologically sophisticated and reflective of them all. In a now century-old article, Max Pohlenz, while remaining properly cautious about *On Ancient Medicine* itself, argued nonetheless that Plato took the contrast between *empeiria* and *technê* from the discipline of medicine, where it may have been formulated by the great Hippocrates himself.[11] If he is right, not only was some early medicine – as we and later ancients can see – of an empirical character, but the reflective concepts of experience and reason, and perhaps the terminology for them, had their pre-Platonic origins in medicine. The implication of Pohlenz's suggestion is that these concepts not only serve to illuminate history, but have a history themselves.

Though the inference he draws is open to question, it is based on a penetrating observation. There is something more than a little odd about the contrast between *empeiria* and *technê* in the *Gorgias*. As presented by Socrates, it is already elaborately and tendentiously entangled with other distinctions (462b–465d). Experience is a false likeness of a true art, a form of flattery, occupied with a different and inferior object, pleasure, rather than the good of that for which it cares. Struck by the highly wrought complexity of this scheme, Pohlenz concluded that it must have presupposed an earlier and simpler form of the contrast, in which art and experience are opposed to each other as two ways of pursuing an activity directed to the same end.[12] This is how we find them contrasted in the *Laws*, in passages that use medicine as an example (4.720b–e; cf. 857c; cf. *Phaedrus* 270b). To be sure, if the medical authors did draw this distinction, it left remarkably few traces.[13] The words *empeiria* and *empeiros* are not of frequent occurrence in the Hippocratic corpus. *Empeiros* is used once in *On Ancient Medicine*, without receiving emphasis (18.1). More noteworthy there is the argument that medicine is an art because, were it not, everyone would be similarly inexperienced in, and ignorant of, it (*apeiroi* and *anepistêmones*) (1.2). Interpreters have plausibly taken the two terms to refer by implication to complementary aspects of an artist's expertise – experience and the know-how that results from it. Here too, however, it is assumed that the two go hand in hand.[14]

The fact that a view is not explicitly presented in terms of a named idea does not mean that it was not there. And many scholars have viewed *On Ancient Medicine* as, to one degree or another, empirical in character or hailed its author as an empiricist *avant la lettre*.[15] This line of interpretation has not gone unopposed, however. John Cooper goes so far as to argue, on the basis of the author's commitment to aetiology, that he 'belongs squarely to the rationalist wing of Greek medicine'.[16]

This scholarly disagreement suggests that interpretation is underdetermined by the evidence. But the problem may lie deeper still. Perhaps interpretations have diverged so sharply because, by themselves, the author's commitments do not constitute a form of either empiricism *or* rationalism, though they may contain germs of both. The most intriguing possibility of all is that the author's position lends itself – in addition or instead – to development in the direction of a view that cannot easily be accommodated by the classical opposition between rationalism and empiricism.

ON ANCIENT MEDICINE AND EXPERIENCE

The reasons that have led so many readers of On Ancient Medicine to regard its author as an empiricist of some kind are not far to seek. Both the hypothesis-based position described and rejected by the author in chapters 1–19, and the position that the author faults for tending towards philosophy in chapter 20, which demands that medicine take its start from knowledge (historia) of 'what the human being is', resemble rationalist positions. And some of the reasons he gives for rejecting them would not be out of place in an Empiricist polemic.

Interpreters are generally agreed that, for the author of On Ancient Medicine, a hypothesis is something that has been postulated arbitrarily or laid down by fiat.[17] The implicit contrast is with something established or discovered by the correct method or the proper procedure, whatever that might be. The author affirms that there are matters about which it is impossible to say anything except with the aid of a hypothesis conceived in this way.[18]

> I have deemed that medicine has no need of a newfangled
> hypothesis, as do nonevident and doubtful matters, about which, if
> someone is going to say anything at all, it is necessary to make use
> of a hypothesis, e.g., about celestial matters and those beneath the
> earth. If anyone should recognize and state how these things are,
> it would be clear neither to the speaker himself nor to his listeners
> whether what he says is true or not, for there is nothing by referring
> to which one would attain clear knowledge.

This remark at the end of the first chapter, which may echo a famous observation of Xenophanes (DK B 34), anticipates the Empiricists' attitude towards the non-evident entities and processes of which their rationalist opponents make free use in their theories. The Empiricists did not deny that such things exist, or that theories about them could be true, but argued that we will never be in a position to know and that, in any case, effective medical practice is possible without such knowledge (Galen, Subfig. emp. 87.7 Deichgräber; De sect. ingred. 3.10 Scripta minora (SM), On Medical Experience 105–6 Walzer).

The affinity with empiricism does not end here, but continues in the positive statement of the author's own method in the immediate sequel, which shows, he maintains, why medicine, in its true and ancient form, has no need for hypotheses (2.3).

> Above all, I believe, that in speaking about this art one must say things that can be understood by lay people. For it is not fitting either to investigate or to speak about anything other than the affections of these very people when they are sick and suffering. Now for them to learn about their own affections, how they come about and cease and on account of what causes they grow and diminish, is not easy, since they are lay people, but when these things have been discovered and stated by another, it is easy. For nothing is involved other than each person *being reminded* [undergoing *anamnesis*] of the things that are happening to him when he hears about them. But if someone misses the capacity of lay people to understand and does not put his listeners in such a state, he will miss the truth. And so for this reason, medicine has no need of a hypothesis.

If we assume a rough coincidence between lay knowledge and experience as classically conceived, this lends strong support to the idea of an affinity between the author of *On Ancient Medicine* and the medical Empiricists.[19]

Hans Diller seized on this passage's talk of recollection, *anamnêsis*, as an illustration of the broader thesis of his 1952 article, 'Hippokratische Medizin und attische Philosophie', according to which, contrary to the more usual tendency to detect Hippocratic influences on Plato and philosophy, Plato and philosophy exerted substantial influences in the opposite direction, not least on the treatise *On Ancient Medicine*. Diller argued that we should see the use of the idea of recollection in *On Ancient Medicine* as 'a translation of the Platonic conception of knowledge into empirical terms'.[20] According to him, the common assumption underlying the use of the term *anamnêsis* is 'the conviction that science can be erected only on the basis of knowledge that is assumed and acknowledged in the same way by all involved' and which, in the sphere of medicine at least, he plainly regarded as *empirical* in character.[21]

Diller's suggestion that Platonic influences are detectable here has not met with favour.[22] The author of *On Ancient Medicine* did not need to be influenced by Plato to have this thought. But a thesis like this does not cease to be of philosophical interest if it is not due to the influence of Plato or another philosopher. Of most importance for our present purpose is the idea, apparently shared by the author of *On Ancient Medicine* and the medical Empiricists, that the art of medicine must confine itself to matters that are objects of ordinary lay understanding.

But in speaking of recollection, the author is doing more than demanding that there be *some* relation between a doctors' physiological and pathological theories, on the one hand, and the patient's own perceptions, on the other, e.g. that the symptoms described by the patient somehow *confirm* the doctor's theory; his test requires that lay people be able to recognise the account of their illnesses as a description of what they know happens to them (2.3). The physician's knowledge differs from theirs by being more extensive, precise, and systematic, and in being the product of more sustained and diligent efforts to retain, augment, and impose order on the discoveries of generations past – and not by being occupied with entities and processes beyond the ken of lay people (cf. ch. 7). If – and I shall leave this 'if' hanging – that of which lay people are reminded is confined to the empirical realm, as Diller seems to have believed, there will be an affinity between the author of *On Ancient Medicine* and the medical Empiricists.

ON ANCIENT MEDICINE AND REASON

Evidence in favour of a rationalist interpretation is no less easy to find, however. When in chapter 20 the author takes aim at those who demand that medicine take its start from knowledge (*historia*) of 'what the human being is', derived from foundational natural philosophy, it is not in order to repudiate the need for, or the possibility of, knowledge of 'what the human being is'. This knowledge is possible and necessary, he maintains, but can be discovered only by the ancient and reputable art of medicine itself and not, as his opponents suppose, in natural philosophy. In a remark the intended scope of which has been much disputed, he turns the tables on his opponents, maintaining that knowledge about nature (*peri phuseôs*) is possible from no other source than medicine. Elsewhere the author speaks of the *nature* of human beings, the *causes* from which they come to be, the *causes* of disease, the *powers* or *potencies* of the stuffs that harm and benefit us, and the *reasoning* (*logismos*)[23] by which medicine gains knowledge of these matters.

Viewed from the perspective of later developments, these terms belong to the rationalists' vocabulary. According to Cooper's compelling 'rationalist' interpretation, the author of *On Ancient Medicine* is committed to 'the use of reason to discover hidden theoretical causes', he appeals 'to hidden theoretical entities as causes', uses explanations that 'deal with underlying and for the most part unobservable entities', and his method is 'deeply involved ... in making inferences to theoretical explanations'.[24]

REASON VS. EXPERIENCE RECONSIDERED

I have already hinted at the solution to this apparent paradox, namely that *On Ancient Medicine* does not yet operate with the classical opposition between experience and reason that was at the centre of the debate between rationalists and Empiricists. Therefore its author need not, as they did, conceive of lay abilities as coinciding with or approximating to experience as it is defined in the classical framework. As a result, the emphasis on the continuity between lay and artistic understanding, which is common to the author of *On Ancient Medicine* and the medical Empiricists, does not commit him, as it commits them, to an empirical conception of the abilities that artists share with lay people.

On Ancient Medicine's preferred explanation for, or causal theory of, health and disease is in terms of the myriad savours or humours, their blending, which is associated with health, and their excessive strength, which is associated with disease. These do not belong to a realm set apart from the one to which lay people have access through the use of ordinary capacities, but they are not for that reason strictly empirical in character and so robbed of explanatory power. Because it seems it is the causes of health and disease that the doctor induces his patients to recollect, the use of *anamnêsis* shows that lay people participate, imperfectly and unreflectively and no doubt to an inferior degree, in a kind of understanding that the classical framework would label 'rational' (cf. 2.3).

Rational knowledge as it is understood in the classical framework is defined in explicit opposition to empirical knowledge, but *On Ancient Medicine* betrays no awareness of this opposition. The rationalist interpretation is the position to which the author *would* be led were he explicitly to confront the classical opposition, and if he then agreed that he was committed to providing causal accounts of health and disease that went beyond the confines of experience as classically conceived. He might then be liable to the demand to explain how, on the basis of what can be known by observation, truths about the nature and causal powers of the human constitution and the humours or savours by which it is constituted and affected are inferred or otherwise established. His response to this demand could well take the form of a rationalist epistemology, in which inferences to theoretical explanations were at home.

In the same imagined circumstances, however, it would be open to the author to make different choices, which would yield an explicitly empirical position. In this scenario, the author would decide that the slow accumulation of medical lore to which he attaches so much importance is best viewed as a matter of grasping and systematising empirical regularities. He would then have to disavow claims to have discovered the nature of the human being and the causes of health and disease.

What I have said so far suggests that the position defended in *On Ancient Medicine* is, in a certain way, naïve. It could be held only by someone innocent of the crucial issues at the centre of the debate between rationalism and empiricism, issues that are in fact inescapable. Confronting them would spell the end of innocence, forcing decisions that required sacrifices. A decision in favour of rationalism would, perhaps, be at the cost of surrendering the affinity between lay and expert knowledge to which the author attaches much importance. A decision in favour of empiricism would make it necessary to renounce claims to have laid bare the nature of the human being and the causes of health and disease, by which he likewise sets much store.

But need this be so? At least one element of the outlook on display in *On Ancient Medicine*, which it shares with much fifth-century BCE natural philosophy, shows that enlisting the author in either camp might not be a perfectly straightforward business. The reliance on reasoning by analogy in fifth-century natural philosophical speculation and medicine has been much studied.[25] The main idea is to model explanations for things like the motions of the heavens, the behaviour of atoms, the inner workings of the human body, and the like on observable analogues. *On Ancient Medicine* contains a noteworthy statement of the principle. As he turns his attention to the body's internal structures, the author says: 'it is necessary to learn about these from evident items outside [the body]' (12.3). Compare the famous maxim, 'the phenomena are the vision of the nonevident', attributed to Anaxagoras and endorsed by Democritus (DKB21a).

Much attention has been devoted to the question of whether the analogies were seen as suggesting hypotheses – in our sense of the term – or already function as inferences that establish conclusions. Regardless of the answer, a successful application of the method of analogy will yield a *causal* explanation, i.e. one that specifies the nature or natures *because* of which the explananda must be as they are and behave as they do. If the procedure is to be effective, we must, within limits, have a causal explanation of the evident phenomenon that furnishes the model that is the point of departure for the analogy. If the behaviour, e.g. of billiard balls rebounding off one another is to serve as a model for the explanation of atomic motion, the knowledge of evident matters that we have on the basis of observation must already be explanatory so far as it goes. It will not be enough to know – as an empirical truth – *that* bodies in motion possessed of solidity and roundness behave in a certain way when they come into contact with one another on a flat surface; one must understand through observation why, *because* they have these properties, they behave as they do.

The example is, of course, due to Hume, whom it is fair to regard as a late but faithful exponent of the classical opposition. He maintains 'no object ever discovers, by the qualities which appear to the senses, either the causes which produced it, or the effects which will arise from it', and he says: 'we fancy that were we brought of a sudden into this world, we could at first have inferred that one billiard-ball would communicate motion to another upon impulse; and that we need not have waited for the event'. But this, he holds, is an illusion. It is custom based on experience that is the source of our expectations, not a grasp of causes (*An Enquiry concerning Human Understanding* I Sect IV, part 1).

This was not obvious to the author of *On Ancient Medicine* and his contemporaries: knowledge of the phenomena before inference to the unobservable is not necessarily empirical, at least as the classical opposition would have us understand empirical knowledge. What is missing, but will be supplied by the classical framework, is not a distinction between items that can be observed and those that cannot be, nor is it the idea that what we observe, the *phenomena*, sometimes require an appeal to unobserved causes for their explanation. Rather it is the decision to confine observation strictly to the revelation of brute facts so that the causes that explain these facts must always be sought, and can only be discovered, by going beyond it. Even now it is possible to doubt whether the line between observational language and concepts – what gets observed so to speak – on the one hand, and elementary causal notions, on the other, is as sharp as the classical framework insists.[26]

To be sure, when we go beyond the phenomena, we extend the scope of our explanations. The explanations that we are now in a position to give may be more fundamental than those from which we set out, they may throw light back on the phenomena that were our point of departure and help us to understand features of theirs that puzzled us, but to this way of thinking, it is not when we go beyond, or penetrate beneath, the phenomena that we first begin to have causal or explanatory understanding. Where the classical framework demands that we draw the sharpest and brightest of lines between the observable *explananda* grasped in experience and the hidden causes that explain them, we find at most a difference of degree that does not amount to a difference in kind.

A selective review of the evidence has not found the classical opposition between reason and experience in *On Ancient Medicine*, where it seemed most reasonable to expect it and where not a few scholars thought they had found it. If the argument sketched above is on the right lines, the distinction not explicitly drawn there is not obviously anticipated either, and the author's own position cannot easily be accommodated by the classical framework. There can be no doubt that the Hippocratic corpus is full of acute observations and that many treatises evince an appreciation of the value of what, from our perspective and that of our ancient predecessors, is rightly regarded as empirical research.[27] In these works, regularities established by observation are presented as such in implicit contrast with the grasp of their causes. But if I am right, recognising that we are often ignorant of the causes of what we observe is not enough to commit one to the classical opposition between reason and experience.

EXPERIENCE OUTSIDE MEDICINE

If fifth-century BCE medicine was not, as Pohlenz hypothesised, the home before Plato of the classical distinction, should we look elsewhere for its origins? The term *empeiria* is found in a number of tantalising contexts. Pittacus, one of the seven sages who flourished in the late seventh and early sixth century BCE, is said to have included experience (*empeiria*) in a list of qualities to be cultivated or esteemed, along with piety (*eusebeia*), temperance (*sophrosynê*), wisdom (*sophia*), truth (*aletheia*), faith (*pistis*), art (*technê*), friendship (*hetairia*), and dexterity (*epidexiotês*).[28] How the cognitive achievements among these are related to each other is anything but clear, however. Plutarch credits Anaxagoras, who was an older contemporary of Socrates', with the idea that, though inferior to the animals in other respects, we are able to make them serve us by experience (*empeiria*), memory (*mnêmê*), wisdom (*sophia*), and art (*technê*) (*De fortuna* 3.98 = DK21b). Scholars doubt whether this is a proper fragment as opposed to a testimony, so that we cannot be sure what words Anaxagoras used, let alone what he meant by them.[29]

What then of Polus?[30] In the *Gorgias*, his character responds to Chaerephon's question 'What should we call Gorgias?', i.e. 'Of what art is he the master?', with a rhetorical effusion, which heaps praise on Gorgias' art rather than saying what it is:

> There are many arts among men, Chaerephon, found by experience
> from experiences; for experience makes our age follow art,
> inexperience chance. Various men in various ways share in various
> of these arts, and the best men in the best. Amongst the best is
> Gorgias here, and he participates in the finest of the arts.
>
> (Pl. *Grg.* 448c, trans. Irwin, lightly modified)

It is not plain whether this is a quotation or a parody, but it is presumably either cited from or inspired by Polus' book about which we hear later in the dialogue and that scholars suspect was a rhetorical *technê* or handbook (462b). Part of the burden of my argument has been that *empeiria* and related words should not always, especially in the fifth century BCE, be understood in terms of the classical opposition. In his book Polus presumably emphasised the role of something that he called 'experience', which covered the kind of inquiry that would qualify as empirical according to the classical opposition. But in the light of what we have discovered about the use of the terms *empeiros* and *empeiria* in the fifth century, there is little reason to think that he confined *empeiria* to the empirical sphere as we understand it now, or that he was taking sides in the controversy between rationalism and empiricism rather than providing Plato with an occasion to draw his distinction between art and experience.[31]

I have been chiefly concerned to argue that the classical opposition between experience and reason is not inescapable, but may have been an innovation – sudden or gradual. Though we cannot be certain, the idea that Plato was not only the witness to its emergence, but also, perhaps with an assist from Aristotle and others, in some measure its author as well is plausible and attractive.[32]

Suitable comparative evidence is scarce. Like Plato and Aristotle, Isocrates contrasts *empeiria* with *technē* and *episteme*. But his is a different contrast. He distinguishes the factors that go in to the making of an accomplished orator in order to forestall charges brought against teachers like himself that are inspired by the fact that some of their students do not succeed or are no more successful than those who have not received instruction (*C. soph.* 17; *Antid.* 185). To this end, like Protagoras in Plato's dialogue of the same name, he emphasises the importance of a second factor, natural aptitude, without which students cannot hope to profit from study, but in whose presence teaching makes a real difference (cf. *Prt.* 327b). He also distinguishes a third factor, which he sometimes calls *empeiria* and which turns out to be practice applying the *technē or episteme* imparted by teaching (*Ad Nicoclem* 35; *Antid.* 187–92). Given the meaning of *peira*, Isocrates' use of *empeiria* in this way is not surprising – to become effective practitioners students must try out or test the precepts, the theory, or the method that are the subject of formal instruction. But it is not a cognitive state like *technē or epistēmē*, but an activity, and one moreover in which those with *technē or episteme*, in the sense of theory, engage; if it gives rise to a cognitive state of the same name, say a facility for applying general knowledge to particular cases, it will be one that is superadded to *technē or epistēmē*, not something with which those lacking *technē or epistēmē* make do.

In retrospect, from the perspective of the medical Empiricists and like-minded practitioners in other fields, *by demanding* more of an art than mere experience can supply, namely rational insight into the nature of the objects belonging to its domain, Plato was guilty of a tendentious innovation in the *Gorgias*. If my argument is sound, he broke new ground at least as much by erecting a divide between this kind of insight and everything that goes under the head of *empeiria*.

A development something like the following was necessary for the classical opposition to emerge. The test or trial, which is the original meaning of *peira*, comes down to an observation, which is an exercise of perception. What one knows as a result of *peira*, the *empeiria* that one has, comes to be restricted to matters that can be observed by perception, on a strict conception of perception, which may itself be an innovation. As a result, *empeiria* is confined to sequences and conjunctions of observable occurrences, what is accustomed to happen as Plato puts it, the *that* as Aristotle does, or empirical regularities as we say. The observations that contribute to the formation of *empeiria* are not restricted to cases of deliberate intervention – experiments – undertaken to see what will happen or, by repeating the experiment, to see if the same result can be reproduced, but can be spontaneous as well.

ARISTOTLE AND PLATO ON EXPERIENCE

So far Aristotle has appeared as an ally of Plato who is, like him, a proponent of the classical opposition between reason and experience, which, if I am right, superseded an earlier attitude. Yet it is customary to think that Plato was hostile to experience while Aristotle regarded it with favour, even if he reserved his highest accolade for superior forms of understanding. Let me conclude with a few speculative reflections about differences between them.

By contrast with Aristotle, Plato has remarkably little to say about the role of experience in the formation and development over time of an art or science. The experience through which doctors of the inferior sort learn in the *Laws* is observation of the practice of their betters (4.720b–e; cf. 857c). It is noteworthy how a view about the emergence of knowledge out of conditions inferior to it is given as an example of one of the natural philosophical questions for which Socrates says he has no talent in the *Phaedo* (96b): 'whether it is the blood with which we think or rather air or fire; or none of these, but the brain which provides the sense of hearing and sight and smell, and from these arise memory and opinion, and from memory and opinion, when they have taken on stability, knowledge comes to be in this way'.[33] As has often been noted, Aristotle holds a view that resembles this (*An. Post.* 100a3–9; cf. *Metaph.* 1.1.980b27–981a12). Aristotle, however, makes a place for *experience* in the development that he describes. He insists, as the author of the similar-seeming account in the *Phaedo* had not, that we must pass through an empirical phase on our way to art and knowledge, in this way distinguishing with a precision that is new between knowledge, strictly and properly so-called, and the conditions – perception, memory, and experience – that precede and help give rise to it. In this phase what has been grasped by observation through perception, retained in memory, and transformed into experience, amounts only to a grasp of the *that*, which falls short of, though it is an indispensable precondition for, genuine understanding of the *because*. If Aristotle rehabilitated experience in this role, it is nonetheless experience that he conceives of in much the same way that Plato had, a way of understanding 'experience' in opposition to reason that is then enshrined in the classical framework.

NOTES

1 On Aristotle's understanding of *empeiria*, see Gregorić and Grcić 2006; Cambiano 2012, 13–31; Hasper and Yurdin 2014.

2 This *logos* is mastered with the aid of *logos*, in the sense of reason. Though logos in the second sense is not used in the immediate context, see Bonitz, *Index Aristotelicus* 428b40–437a39 and n.b. *logismoi* 980b28.

3 On memory as a treasury of perception, cf. Pl. *Philebus* 34A.

4 See von Staden 1982

5 *Pêra toi mathêsios archa* (Alcman fr. 125).

6 Note, however, that Aristotle opposes the *empeiroi* to the *anepistēmones* at *Eth. Nic.* 10.9.1181b5–6).

7 Most but not all translations register a difference. Schleiermacher 1804–28, Irwin 1979, Zeyl 1997, and Dalfen 2004 do; Croiset and Bodin 1955, do not (*si … exerçait le même art … x 2*). Lamb 1932 has 'skilled' and 'expert'. Cf. Pl. *Resp.* 7.529e where, in a context in which the contrast between things that can be grasped by reason and intellect, on the one hand, and mere sight, on the other, is emphasised, Socrates speaks of the expert in geometry (*empeiros geometrias*). In general, nothing prevents one from being *empeiros*, i.e. it seems *expert*, in a *technê* (Ar. *Ran.* 811; Hippoc., *De arte* 8.7; Pl. *Plt.* 291c).

8 Like *technê*, *epistêmê* has a disciplinary sense, meaning a trade, metier, or science (cf. Pl. *Resp.* 7.522c). Though there are a few post-Platonic passages in which *empeiria* may have this sense (Arist. *Pol.* 1282a1, 1297b20), it is a fair question whether this sense is a polemical innovation in the *Gorgias* or an established usage implying no inferiority, put to a new pejorative use by Plato. There is evidence of a continuing dispute about the correctness of the terminological opposition between *technê* and *empeiria* in Sextus Empiricus (*Math.* 1.60–2).

9 The root of both is *histôr*, 'knower' or 'witness', which itelf derives from a verb of seeing. See Snell 1924, 59–71; on *historia* and its range of uses, Louis 1955.

10 Discussion in Schiefsky 2005, 310–13.

11 Pohlenz 1918, 409–14; viewed with favour by Festugière 1948, 29.

12 Pohlenz 1918, 411.

13 Already Capelle 1922, 264–5; Heinimann 1961, 144 with n. 50.

14 See Schiefsky 2005, 133, 354. Cf. *Flat.* 1.3 and n. ad loc. Jouanna 2003, 130–1.

15 Pohlenz spoke of an empirical tendency (1918: 412); others have been less cautious. J.-H. Kühn 1956 consistently refers to the author as an empiricist; Dunn 2005; Gregorić and Grcić 2006, 1–2.

16 Cooper 2004: 33, summarising the argument of 25–33.

17 For a full and illuminating discussion, see Schiefsky 2005, 111–15, 120–6.

18 This and the following translations are from Schiefsky 2005, lightly modified.

19 The medical Empiricists were later confronted with the charge that, by restricting the art to phenomena, which are accessible to observation of which everyone is capable, they abolished the distinction between expert and lay knowledge (Galen, *On Medical Experience* 98–9 Walzer; Galen, [*De optima secta*] 1.110.14–16 Kühn). Discussion in Allen 2001, 132–7.

20 Diller 1952, 56.

21 Ibid., 56–7.

22 See, e.g. Schiefsky 2005, 151.

23 Hippoc. *VM* 12.2, 14.2.

24 Cooper 2004, 26, 32.

25 E.g. in Diller's classic 1932 and Lloyd's magisterial 1966.

26 Cf. Anscombe 1971.

27 Studied by Bourgey 1953; Lloyd 1979. Cf. Diller 1964. (Note, Lloyd 1979, 50: 'to learn from[,] experience … presupposes some idea of the regularity of phenomena, although that idea may well be neither explicit nor universalized'.

28 The list is transmitted in two forms, by Demetrius of Phalerum cited by Stobaeus (DK1.64) and Diogenes Laertius 1.78.

29 Cf. Laks and Most 2016, VI: 114–15.

30 Scant testimonies in Radermacher 1951, 112–14 and Fowler 1997.

31 Most translators take Socrates' reply to the question that he puts on behalf of Polus at 462b (cf. n. 1 above) 'What art do you say it [rhetoric] is?' to be 'no art at all … but the thing which you say gives rise to an art in the book of yours that I was reading recently', viz. *empeiria* (e.g. Irwin 1979; Dalfen 2004; defended by Renehan 1995), but some commentators have taken the remark to mean 'something of which you claim to have made an art in your treatise' (Croiset and Bodin 1955; Dodds 1959, 223, n. ad 262b11). Even if this is right, I doubt that Polus intended a contrast between the merely empirical and the rational as the classical opposition understands it.

32 Cf. Dodds 1959: 229; Irwin 1979: 130; Jouanna 1990: 77–8; 2003: 130; Schiefsky 2005: 346–50; Cambiano 2012: 29.

33 Attributed by DK to Alcmaeon (A 11).

3 Towards a Science of Life: The Cosmological Method, Teleology, and Living Things

Klaus Corcilius

THE SIGNIFICANCE OF THE PHENOMENA OF LIFE
AND EARLY GREEK COSMOLOGISTS

The phenomena of life have special significance for us. Living things impress us in ways inanimate things couldn't. This is because livings things *do* things. They act for the sake of some purpose, a purpose which moreover seems to be their very own. They instil in us the impression that there is something they are 'up to'. This certainly seems to be the case with animals and, to a lesser degree, with plants and other growing things. Their goal-directed behaviours are presumably the reasons why living things are closer, more interesting – and sometimes also more repelling – to us than inanimate things: they have, one might say, certain *interests* they pursue. We can understand these interests and therefore interact with them in sometimes cooperative and sometimes inimical ways. This is why our attitudes towards animate things are so very different from our attitudes towards the inanimate.

There seems to be a similar prominence of the phenomena of life in the history of Greek philosophy.[1] Life and the phenomena of life captured a great part of the attention of the early so-called Presocratic natural philosophers (not to mention the even earlier mythical accounts of the origin of the world). A brief glance at the verbal index attached to Diels and Kranz's famous edition of the fragments of the Presocratics illustrates just how important the phenomena of life must have been for these thinkers. 'Soul' (*psukhe*) – a term which can have meaning ranging from 'life' or 'soul', to 'life-principle', 'cosmos', 'living thing', etc. – appears far more often than what is commonly believed to have been the single most significant term in Presocratic thought, namely 'nature' (*phusis*). Indeed, there is excellent reason to think that a significant portion of Presocratic philosophers thought of living things not merely as especially important *parts* of the physical world, but also conceived of the entire physical world as one single living thing. The very early Milesian philosophers Thales and Anaximander[2] seem to have thought so, and so do other Presocratics. Anaximenes, for instance, claims that the whole ordered universe such as we know it, the *cosmos*, is surrounded by air, which holds it together and controls it (*sunkratei*) in very much the same way our inward and likewise aery souls control us (DK13B2). This strongly suggests that Anaximenes regards the universe as a single living thing, even if he thought of it as a living thing that is very different from us. Empedocles, to cite another example, was a biological thinker in a more obvious sense. He famously depicts a "world process", which consists in an eternally recurring cycle of evolutions and extinctions of the various species of living things that populate the physical world during its different phases (DK31B17, 20, 21 26). As these examples indicate, the phenomena of life were a major, if not perhaps *the* single main, concern of many Presocratic philosophers.[3]

Aristotle, who is largely responsible for our historical knowledge of the Presocratic thinkers, says about them that they gave their explanations merely in terms of material and moving causes, i.e. in terms of what stuff things in the world are composed of and how the world as we know it came into existence; he also says that they lacked a grasp of formal causes, which we here may conveniently think of as some kind of conceptual analysis, and of final causes, i.e. of the explanation of things by the goals towards which they develop and strive. Aristotle's report seems correct; as far as the fragments that came down to us allow us to infer, the Presocratics did not have an explicit conception of teleological explanation, nor did they have anything like conceptual analysis. That, however, should not mislead us into thinking that they had no interest in the phenomena of life. Rather, Aristotle's remarks should be taken for what they are. They are statements about the absence of *explicit* conceptions of formal and final causes in Presocratic thinkers; they are not statements about the explanatory *ambition* with which these philosophers proposed their theories. On the most plausible reading, the Presocratics aimed much higher than their archaic talk of material principles and moving causes may suggest to a philosophically informed modern reader. As we have just seen, there are excellent reasons to believe that they aimed at no less than the explanation of reality as a whole and with a particular focus on the phenomena of life. And, of course, the lack of an explicit philosophical conception of formal and final causes is compatible with the pursuit of the highest philosophical ambition. What I am suggesting, then, is that the Presocratic cosmologists offered their accounts at a stage in the development of philosophical thought in ancient Greece at which some of the conceptual tools we now deem necessary for a proper understanding of life and living things had not yet been isolated and properly identified as such.[4] Thus, when the Presocratics speak about the basic stuff of the world, their understanding of 'stuff' is unlikely to have been that of lifeless matter. On the contrary, to conceive of matter as something entirely devoid of life is a feat of philosophical abstraction that involves a level of conceptual analysis that, for all we know, was unavailable at their time. On a charitable interpretation, therefore, we should take the so-called materialism of the Presocratics as attempts at satisfying the highest philosophical ambitions including rendering philosophical accounts of living things.[5] Their 'materialism', as has long been observed, is likely to have been some sort of hylozoism, where the basic constituent matter of the physical world is, in one way or the other, conceived as a bearer of life.[6]

Simplicius of Athens, a late ancient Aristotle commentator, confirms this picture. He says that the so-called material monists who posited but one material basic element of all things[7] did so already with a view to the explanation of, among other things, the phenomena of life:

> And all those who thought that the element is one, like Thales, Anaximander and Heraclitus, also every one of them looked at its efficacy and at its aptness for (biological) generation (*genesis*): Thales looked at water's capacity to generate, nourish, hold together, maintain life, and to assume shapes, Heraclitus at fire's capacity to generate animals and productive craft, Anaximenes at air's ductility and at the easiness with which it can change in both directions, towards fire and towards water, just like Anaximander did, if indeed he posited the intermediate because of its alterability.

> (Simpl. *In Phys.* 36, 8–14)

Some Presocratic thinkers, as we have seen, however, went further than that. They not only attached special importance to the phenomena of life as somehow a basic feature of the world, but developed philosophical systems that are 'biological' in a deeper sense. They made certain life-processes fundamental for understanding everything else in the universe, animate and inanimate things alike. Thus, Empedocles seems to have conceived of his cosmic cycle as an eternally recurring process of birth, life, death, and rebirth, the ultimate subject of which is an immortal and therefore divine cosmic being (DK31B17, 30). The same goes, *mutatis mutandis*, for Anaximenes, who thought of the universe as a living being that is controlled by a mind, in a way comparable to the way we are controlled by our minds. Anaximander may very well have thought similarly, even though we lack detailed knowledge of his teachings. These biological cosmologist thinkers all converge on the idea of conceiving of the universe as a single living thing, so as to, on that basis, propose 'theories of everything' that account for the entire cosmos.[8]

Are there common methodological features in the theories of these biological cosmologists? I think there are. Most importantly, they tend to approach their subject matter – physical reality as a whole – with some kind of whole/part reasoning. Anaximander, Anaximenes, and Empedocles all seem to be holists of sorts: they conceive (each in their own ways) of the physical world as a fundamentally imperishable – and therefore divine – being that contains all other living things in it as its parts, while the processes and events inside the cosmos – the generation and corruption of relatively stable structures of the parts of the cosmos, and of living structures in particular – are governed by the processes of the cosmos as a whole.[9] It seems fair to say that these early biological cosmologists approached nature through the lens of the student of living things. Three common features of their approaches stand out:

1 *Organic holism*: living things in the cosmos are parts of an overarching and fundamental cosmic living thing (interestingly, it seems that none of these thinkers employed an obviously anthropomorphic conception of life).

2 *Ultimate philosophical ambition*: as I here understand it, ultimate philosophical ambition is the project, shared by many, if not all, cosmologists, of explaining the entire universe and everything in it. These thinkers offered – each in their own way – 'theories of everything' with an unrestricted scope and the ambition of giving definitive and ultimate answers. Despite the differences in their particular doctrines, they all aimed at explanations to ultimate questions such as 'where does it all come from?', 'Where will it all go?'

3 *Methodological monism*: this is the idea that reality at large is to be investigated and explained through one single method of inquiry. Because principles[10] and explanatory methods for them are in this way the same for all things across the board, the biological cosmologists did not distinguish between domains of study: there was just one subject – reality as a whole – and one corresponding method to explain it.

In what follows I will refer to these three features as the *cosmological method*.

PLATO: CREATION AND COSMOLOGICAL TELEOLOGY

Despite the turn towards moral, social, and political issues marked by Socrates and the so-called Sophists, who exerted major influence on him, there is good reason to think that Plato stands in that same cosmological tradition. There is, to start with, a pervading concern with the soul throughout the different periods of his work. And even though the main drive for this concern seems to originate, at least in the earlier works, in ethical and religious motives,[11] Plato, in his works on natural philosophy, appears to be guided by the same methodological principles as the cosmologically minded among his predecessors. In his dialogue *Timaeus*, he offers a theory of the universe as a whole, a theory that is unrestricted in scope, organically holistic, and that aims at answering ultimate philosophical questions. Regarding the last, we may even say that the *Timaeus* pushes things to the extreme. Plato goes far beyond the ambition of the already highly ambitious Presocratic cosmologies. He not only informs us about the physical origin and future fate of the universe, as his predecessors did, but he also addresses questions such as: why is there a physical world in the first place? Why do human beings exist? What is the meaning of biological existence? Why are there the different animal species that populate the world?

Presumably owing to his ambition of answering such ultimate questions, Plato employs an incomparably more sophisticated methodological framework than his predecessors. While the latter were content with the identification of certain physical objects – elementary or any other primary physical stuff typically conceived of in a hylozoist way – with the aid of which they offered accounts of the causal history of the universe, Plato's question 'why is there a physical world in the first place?' cannot make do with such causal narratives. Plato is asking for the *point* that the existence of the universe has. With this he explicitly raises the question of the goodness of things. But this is to raise a question that is of an altogether different *kind* than the kind of questions treated by previous cosmologists, as goodness is neither a physical thing nor a physical quality. The same physical feature can serve different purposes in different contexts and at different times, and can thus be both good or bad. Thus, from a methodological point of view, asking for the goodness of things – which is to ask for the 'final cause' or the goal of things – is to pursue a project that is very different from the project of the Presocratic cosmologists.

Plato sees this very clearly, and the way he introduces this new perspective into his cosmology is, from a methodological standpoint, remarkably self-conscious. At the same time, for all his methodological innovations, Plato does not abandon the Presocratic concern with the causal and material origin of things. This creates the need to assess the *relation* between these two explanatory concerns of his cosmology. The result is a new methodological framework, which allows Plato to distinguish *types* of causes (*aitiôn genê*, 46e3) and to determine the relation between them within a unitary *system of causes*. This is the framework of 'reason/Intelligence (*nous*)' and 'Necessity (*anankê*)'. As types of causes, Intelligence accounts for things having the design that they happen to have, because it is best that way (intelligence being the sort of entity that does whatever is best[12]), while Necessity accounts for the material constituents and the causal history of things. Plato conceives of the relation between these two types of causes as strictly *hierarchical*: while the true cause of things is the goodness and purposefulness of their design, Necessity has the auxiliary role of providing the physically necessary conditions for the realisation of the good end (*Ti.* 46c–e[13]):

> Now in all but a brief part of the discourse [i.e. the discourse about
> the creation of the world in the *Timaeus*] I have just completed
> I have presented what has been crafted by Intellect (*nous*). But I need
> to match this account by providing a comparable one concerning
> the things that have come about by Necessity (*anankê*). For this
> ordered world (*kosmos*) is of a mixed birth: it is the offspring of a
> union of Necessity and Intellect. Intellect prevailed over Necessity
> by persuading it to direct most of the things that come to be toward

what is best, and the result of this subjugation of Necessity to wise
persuasion was the initial formation of this universe.

(Pl. *Ti.* 47e–48a, trans. Zeyl)

The world as we know it – the ordered cosmos with its regularities,
ordered processes, and motions – is of a 'mixed birth', where Intellect
prevails over mechanical Necessity. Intelligence wisely 'persuaded'
Necessity and thereby subjugated it to its own purpose. With this,
Plato's reflection about causes reaches a new level of abstraction.
Yet, at the same time he continues with the project of the Presocratic
cosmologists: he remains an organic holist who pursues the highest
philosophical ambition by way of a methodological monism, albeit, as
we have just seen, with a crucially reformed bifurcated methodology.
His account of the cosmos, while operating at different levels of causal
explanation, remains a single *logos* (*Ti.* 29d1, 92c4–7, cp. 27a4, c4).
Therefore, I think it is best to speak of Plato as having integrated his
novel teleological method into what fundamentally remains the same
cosmological project as that of his predecessors. One can, of course,
also put it in the reverse order and say that Plato's new causal framework integrates, or, perhaps better still, *co-opts* the old cosmological
method of his predecessors in a new and hitherto unknown method
of teleological explanation. This would certainly capture Plato's views
about the hierarchy among the different types of causes. But, however
that may be, on either description, the basic methodological architecture that underlies his cosmology is an integrated systematic framework that combines both kinds of causes to apply it across the board
to the cosmos as a whole and everything in it. And this makes Plato a
methodological monist who stands in the same tradition as his cosmological predecessors.

With his methodological innovation, Plato prefigures the distinction between teleology and mechanistic explanation that would
become so important in later philosophy. And similar things can be
said with respect to the place that Plato assigns to biological phenomena within his new methodological framework, namely the place
where the two kinds of causes *intersect*. The phenomena of life are
neither entirely due to mechanical necessity nor to intelligence: they
are a mix of the two.[14]

In comparison with previous cosmologies, two features of Plato's
conception of living things stand out: his rationalistic understanding of

life and the cosmos, and the particular mode in which he presents his cosmology. To start with the latter, Plato, unlike his predecessors, who typically sought to account for the physical world by way of immanent causes, offers a story of the *creation* of the world by a rational agent who acts from outside the world.[15] Plato, to be sure, does not explain to us why there is something (a universe) rather than nothing. He tells a story of how the universe came to be a *cosmos*, i.e. an ordered and well-structured whole, through the creative action of a divine and radically benevolent master builder, the so-called demiurge ('craftsman'). This story, in a nutshell, states the reasons why the demiurge designed the order and regularities of the physical world such as we know them, and how he realised that order in the given raw materials (the 'receptacle', which is basically chaotically moving space-matter, *Ti.* 48e–53c). In his story, Plato orients himself at what we may call a formal schema of intentional artistic production, very much like the production of a work of craft by any other craftsperson, and which he applies on a cosmological scale. Thus, the demiurge creates the ordered world on the basis of a model or plan in his mind to then impose this plan on his raw materials. The model is nothing less than the idea of cosmological life, namely the intelligible ideal of a divine animal (*zôion*), which contains all other intelligible living things in it:

> let us lay it down that the universe resembles more closely than
> anything else that Living Thing of which all other living things
> are parts, both individually and by kinds. For that Living Thing
> comprehends within itself all intelligible living things, just as our
> world is made up of us and all the other visible creatures. Since
> the god wanted nothing more than to make the world like the
> best of the
> intelligible things, complete in every way, he made it a single
> visible living thing, which contains within itself all the living things
> whose nature it is to share its kind.
>
> (Pl. *Ti.* 30c–31c, trans. Zeyl)

While the cosmological method of his predecessors took biological life for granted in one way or another, Plato offers an *explanation* as to why the visible cosmic animal – our physical world – possesses a principle of biological life, a soul (*psukhê*), in the first place. This brings me back to the first point, Plato's rationalistic understanding of biological life and living things. Plato's starting point is the unqualified goodness of intelligence (*nous*). Given this starting point and the demiurge's will to make things the best they could possibly be, the demiurge wants to make his creation as intelligent as possible. However, owing to the recalcitrant nature of the raw materials he has to work with (chaotically moving space-matter, as we have seen), an intelligent cosmos cannot be created just like that. To make the world a possible bearer of intelligence requires a soul, since, as Plato argues, it is not possible for any material being to be a bearer of intelligence without having life. In other words, the creation of soul, understood as the principle of biological life, was a necessary condition for what the demiurge really aims at, which is the production of an intelligent physical body:

> Now it wasn't permitted (nor is it now) that one who is supremely good should do anything but what is best. Accordingly, the god reasoned and concluded that in the realm of things naturally visible no unintelligent thing could as a whole be better than anything which does possess intelligence as a whole, and he further concluded that it is impossible for anything to come to possess intelligence apart from soul. Guided by this reasoning, he put intelligence in soul, and soul in body, and so he constructed the universe. He wanted to produce a piece of work that would be as excellent and supreme as its nature would allow. This, then, in keeping with our likely account, is how we must say divine providence brought our world into being as a truly living thing, endowed with soul and intelligence.
>
> (Pl. *Ti.* 30a–c, trans. Zeyl)

The ensuing creation story consists in a full account of how the divine creator endows the physical world with intelligence and rational structure *by* creating the soul of the world and by imposing it on the world's body, i.e. how the demiurge transforms his raw material, the unordered space-matter receptacle, into the cosmos, an ordered structure with regular motions and law-like processes.

Why is it not possible to build an intelligent physical body without soul? Notice that on Plato's conception the soul is not just a principle of life, as was common in Greek thought at his time, but the origin of all ordered movement. That means that, for him, constructing the soul of the world and imposing it on chaotic space-matter was the only way in which ordered movement, law-like behaviour, and, with this, intelligibility could be brought into physical existence.

The same pattern recurs in his story of the creation of mortal animals and human beings within the cosmos: a divine mind – this time not the demiurge himself but the 'lesser gods' of Greek mythological tradition, who the demiurge has commanded to imitate his creation (so as to avoid being responsible for the evils of mortal existence, *Ti.* 41a–42e) – impose intelligible structure on the recalcitrant materials from the outside, in order to render it capable of receiving intelligence. And, again, the instrument by which these lesser creators achieve their result is soul (*psukhê*).[16]

A further important (and as far as I can see also somewhat underestimated) feature of Plato's account of biological life in the *Timaeus* is that, in it, living things are not merely material parts of the cosmos; rather, animals and humans are also parts of the *teleological* order of things. They take part in the world's overall purpose of making the world an intelligent place (as much as possible, given the recalcitrant nature of the raw materials). The overall goal that guides the demiurge and his divine assistants, even in their production of biological life, is the implementation of rationality in an otherwise utterly non-intelligent space-matter. This is important because, on Plato's conception, intelligence, even though its goal, is external to, and entirely separable from, biological life. This is the case not only for our biological existences as incarnated souls, but also for the biological aspects of our very souls: the *Timaeus* emphasises that, while there is eternal life for the rational parts of our souls – our true intellectual selves – there can be no such life for our materially extended bodies (*Ti.* 41c ff., especially 43a) nor for the biological parts of our souls that regulate our bodily processes (*Ti.* 42d6–e4). So, in Plato's cosmology, the microcosmic order of things exactly mirrors its macroscopic counterpart: the soul is a necessary means for the implementation of intelligence in the physical world. Absent of such bodily implementation (or, if you prefer, 'incarnation'), intellect and rationality would be entirely independent from the body and the non-intelligent parts of the soul. Recall, the demiurge has created the soul *only because* it is otherwise impossible for any extended body to 'possess intelligence apart from soul' (*Ti.* 30b3). Thus, for Plato, the goal of biological life within the cosmos lies outside the physical world: the value of appetite (*epithumia*) and spirited desire (*thumos*), the two non-intelligent parts of the soul that regulate our biological desires and emotions, is merely instrumental. Their job is to preserve the intelligent part of the soul in an (at least initially) harmful environment. They are nothing but necessary conditions for the implementation of intelligence in living things and not desirable goals in their own right. This is crucial for Plato's conception of biological life: his teleology of living things in the cosmos is *externalist*[17] in the sense that the existence of biological phenomena is instrumental and subservient to an intelligent goal that lies outside of them, even if these phenomena are a vital part of the process of the implementation and maintenance of intelligence in the world.

Here, one may ask about lower forms of non-rational life. In which sense are animals and plants connected to the rational goal of the cosmos? Plato's answer is striking. The biological existence of plants (which for Plato are animal-like creatures in that they have sensation and feelings of pleasure and pain) and the lives of brute animals turn out to be the outcome of the moral failures of previous generations of human beings. In the cycle of transmigration of souls, which in the *Timaeus* is a constitutive part of the ordering of the cosmos, the misbehaviour of male humans leads to their reincarnation first as females and then as animals, into particular species befitting their particular failings. For instance, simpleminded humans who during their lives on earth did not take care to study the movements of the stars with due mathematical rigour are reborn as birds. In this way, Plato accounts for the existence of females and brute animals by way of the continuous moral deterioration of an original generation of male humans (*Ti.* 90e–92c). Of course, in all this the final goal for each soul is to eventually return to one's original disincarnated rational nature. Nevertheless, the driving force behind the creation of non-human biological species (and female humans!) is the moral deterioration of the first generations of original human beings. Thus, even non-rational animals exist for the sake of rationality.

To conclude this section. Plato and the early cosmologists are all fundamentally inspired by the phenomena of life. Plato's creationist cosmology represents an important refinement of the previous cosmological theories in that it (i) explicitly develops a teleological conception of life, and (ii) seeks to combine this conception with the cosmological project of the predecessors. The result is a hybrid teleological–causal history account that integrates the intelligent design of a divine and external creator with 'mechanistic' necessity within a system of cooperative causes. Still, whatever the differences between the old cosmologists and Plato – with or without teleology and creation – there is agreement in the basic approach. They all seek 'theories of everything' through a monistic method, and they agree, fundamentally, that the universe is some sort of unitary organic whole, of which the animals are parts. Although Plato's teleology differentiates him from his predecessors (and to some extent anticipates Aristotle's science of life), it remains cosmic in character, as it seeks to explain, in a total and wholesale fashion, the physical world as existing for the sake of a single outside goal, namely intelligence. From that standpoint, Plato is entirely consistent to propose a creationist, agent-centred, and externalist teleology. For only such a cosmological teleology can aspire to satisfy the ambition of explaining why there is a cosmos in the first place and why it is best thus. Plato's teleology is bounded by his cosmological ambition.

ARISTOTLE: REDUCED AMBITION, SEPARATION OF SCIENCES, AND NATURAL TELEOLOGY

So far, we have argued that the phenomena of life were crucial for Plato and the other biological cosmologists, as they served as their model for understanding the cosmos as a whole. Does this contradict our received knowledge of the histories of biology, which usually cite Aristotle as the founder, and sometimes even as the inventor, of biology?[18] It does not. When our textbooks speak of Aristotle as the founder of biology, they speak of biology as a *science*. And, typically, they add what they take the scientific character of his biological investigations to consist in. Two features are particularly important in this regard. First, that Aristotle, unlike his predecessors, based his account of living things on a systematic collection of biological data (zoological and botanical), and, second, that he made use of more or less *rigorous* scientific methods in the explanation of these data. Our textbooks are, of course, entirely correct about this. The fact that Aristotle practised biology as a science is evident from both his systematic collection of empirical data about animals, which is unprecedented,[19] and his demonstrative ambition in explaining these data, which is likewise unprecedented.[20] These features of Aristotle's biology and the way they shape his biological works have been extensively studied in the still growing literature on Aristotle's zoology and its relation to his works on scientific methodology,[21] and I will not add to it here.

What I would like to do in this chapter is to bring to attention a feature of Aristotle's thinking about living things that is no less important and, if I am correct, also philosophically more foundational for his scientific approach to living things. This is his novel *metaphysical* conception of living things as it results from his deliberate revision of the cosmological method of Plato and his Presocratic predecessors. This revision, as I will argue now, and the distinct view of living things that resulted from it, made biology as a science possible.

Rejection of Methodological Monism and the Per Se Perspective

Metaphysically, Aristotle's basic take on reality results from a radical breach with Plato's methodological monism. Methodological monism, as we have seen, takes it that there are highest principles that are both common to all things and capable of explaining reality ('being') as a whole. Against this, Aristotle insists that there are several distinct domains of reality – so-called genera – each of which is constituted by a particular kind of substance with their own, and correspondingly independent, essences and principles. Different genera cannot be reduced to one another, nor are they unified by a common superordinate genus (*Metaph.* 5.28.1024b9–16).[22] Being, in particular, is not the substance of anything (*An. post.*. 2.7.92b12–18) nor is it a genus (*An. post.* 1.7; *Metaph.* 11.2).[23] Each scientific domain has its own specific principles, and there exists no superordinate scientific genus of which these domains are parts.[24] It follows that if we, as scientists, wish to track the nature of things, we have to study reality in a compartmentalised way. Take, for instance, a zoologist who wishes to study the nature of cattle. She will fail if she takes the perspective of people who wish to eat cattle; to understand cattle scientifically is to study cattle in their own right ('as such' *per se*, *kath' hauto* in the Greek), and not as they are to beef-eaters. Scientists are supposed to study things as they are in their own right, while leaving out everything that is incidental to them (*kata sumbêbekos*),[25] as, for instance, the fact that cattle are tasty to beef-eaters. And the same goes for the other accidental features of cattle, as, e.g. the fact that there are intelligent beings in the cosmos. But Aristotle's conception of science is even stricter than that. The scientist should not even study all the features that hold of her domain *per se*: she should concentrate only on those *per se* features that hold of her domain *D insofar as* it is *D*. Take again the science of cattle. The elementary physical stuff that constitutes cattle bodies, for example, is not to be investigated by the science of cattle, because these facts, even if they are non-incidentally true of cattle, are not true of cattle insofar as they are cattle ('*qua*' cattle), but *insofar* as they are physical bodies.

Such features, therefore, pertain to a different and much more general science than the science of cattle, namely general physics. Aristotle's conception of the domain specificity of sciences is rather strict: science ought to study things as they are *per se*, explaining them with reference to their own specific principles, and *insofar* as they are what they are. This means no less than that each scientific domain will have its own specific method.[26]

Rejection of Organic Holism and Agent-Centred Teleology

Organic holism is, as we have seen above, the view that the universe as a whole is one single organism, of which the other organisms inside the cosmos are parts. But the idea that everything in the cosmos is a proper part of a single global substance violates the idea, fundamental to Aristotle's conception of science, that the different genera that populate the world have separate essences, and that the definitions of each of their essences are starting points for the scientific explanation of their other (i.e. non-essential) necessary and universal features ('explanatory essentialism' in what follows). Also, Aristotle is firmly committed to the view that the *infimae species* of things each have their own essences, and that it is the *infimae species* of any domain that the corresponding sciences are fundamentally concerned with. The science of animals, for instance, is fundamentally concerned with the *infimae species* of animals.[27] There is no straightforward sense in which different animal species, let alone all genera of living things, can be parts of one cosmic trans-generic super-organism: in Aristotle, there is no nature, soul, or life, of the world as a whole.[28] The rejection of organic holism is most conspicuous in his teleology of living things. Whereas Plato's cosmos and the things in it share an external goal – intelligence in the *Timaeus* – that is implemented with the aid of a single world soul, Aristotle has each living thing in the cosmos in possession of its own goals that are internal to them: their own souls. There is also no place in his science for an implementation of goals by external agents. The fact that living things have their own intrinsic goals is a primitive fact about natural things, not something that would require an explanation.[29] Similarly, on Aristotle's conception of teleology, goal-directed processes do not always require mental representations of the goal-state they are 'aiming' at. Teleology and intentionality can come apart. And in animate nature this is what they usually do – apart from animal and human action, which do involve mental representations of their goals. 'Nature does not deliberate' is the slogan with which Aristotle expresses this fundamental claim of his natural teleology (*Ph.* 2.8.198b20–21).[30]

Rejection of Ultimate Philosophical Ambition

Aristotle's rejection of methodological monism, organic holism, and agent-centred teleology results in a renouncement of the ultimate philosophical ambitions of his cosmological predecessors. The domain-specificity of sciences and the absence of a cosmic and teleologically superordinate organism make it virtually impossible to address the old questions typical of the cosmological method: 'where does it all come from?', 'where will it go?', 'why is there a cosmos in the first place?' For Aristotle, the existence of the universe is a static object of study. He does not explain why the world and the species that populate it came into existence, because he doesn't believe that there was any point in time when this happened. Famously, he believes the universe and the species it harbours to be eternal. Aristotle's scientific method also prevents him from asking ultimate teleological *Timaeus*-style questions such as 'why do the species we know exist?' and 'what is the point of the design of the different species?', because his rejection of organic holism and his belief in the eternity of natural species leave no room to address such questions. Instead of asking such ultimate questions, Aristotle prefers to ask *penultimate* questions such as 'why do the species that we know do exist, given the particular being (essence) they happen to have, exhibit the kinds of other universal and necessary features we observe them to have?' These are the questions of his explanatory essentialism. And although we may feel Aristotle's renouncement of the ultimate explanatory ambition of his cosmological predecessors frustrates our deepest metaphysical desires, asking such penultimate questions comes with the great advantage of allowing us to answer them by way of falsifiable and criteria-based answers, which by virtue of these features are recognisably scientific.[31]

We may say, then, that the main point of his novel metaphysical conception of living things results from Aristotle's emancipation of living things from the bounds of cosmology. For this led to a corresponding teleological upgrade of biological life forms to *ends in themselves*. This does not, of course, amount to a specifically moral sense of internal finality but to a distinctive biological one: in Aristotle's science of life the bodily constitution, processes, activities, habits, and further features that are characteristic of living things are to be accounted for as existing for the sake of nothing but the organisms' own formal natures (which for him is to say that they exist for the sake of their essential life-functions, i.e. their souls or what it is for them to be alive, *De an.* 2.4.415b12–21). The processes and motions that constitute, say, the life of a rabbit all ultimately exist for the sake of the realisation of the rabbit's own essential form, the rabbit soul, while the rabbit's body serves as the instrument by means of which the rabbit realises its own essential form by putting its body to work in accordance with its essential life functions.[32] In this way, all species of living things have their own goals specific to them, and the scientist of life can, and ought to, refer to these goals to account for the other non-essential universal and necessary features that pertain to members of that species *qua* such.[33] The metaphysical upgrade of living things to ends in themselves lies at the heart of Aristotle's novel conception of scientific biological explanation, and it is part and parcel of that conception that there are no further, teleologically superordinate goals over and above the specific essences.[34] There is, then, no teleological reason why the essential forms of living things are the goal of their body parts, growth, actions, and processes. Aristotle even goes so far as to ban from natural philosophy the investigation of goals that are not essentially the goods of the natural things under investigation:

> Hence since nature is for the sake of something, we must know this cause also. We must explain the why in all the senses of the term, namely ... and because it is better thus, *not without qualification* (*haplôs*), *but with relation to the being of each thing* (*pros tên hekastou ousian*).
>
> (Arist. *Ph.* 2.7.198b3–9, emphasis added)[35]

The natural scientist ought to study only such final causes that are specific to the being of each single natural substance under investigation. This rules out not just trans-generic goals, but all other goals the goodness of which is not specific to the natural object under investigation.[36] To render accounts of the features of living things solely on the basis that they are members of their species is fundamental for Aristotle's methodological idea of *natural teleology*. If I am correct, natural teleology is made possible by his philosophical decision to regard living things as ends in themselves – which enables him to investigate living things in their own right (or on their own terms).

Aristotle's idea of regarding living things as ends in themselves, and his attempt to give them a scientific treatment in their own right, separate from the rest of nature, as groundbreaking as it was, wasn't an immediate success. It seems that the scientific study of living things *more Aristotelico* did not really make it outside of his school, the Lyceum.[37] The dominant philosophical systems that were to conquer the intellectual world a generation after Aristotle, Epicureanism and Stoicism, certainly had no such concern with the scientific explanation of living things, and it would take many centuries before Aristotle's idea of biological explanation came to be appreciated again. But, however that may be, if the above is on the right track, then, without Aristotle's theoretical liberation of living things from the bounds of cosmology and their metaphysical upgrade to ends in themselves, biology as a science would not have been possible.

NOTES

I would like to thank Liba Taub for her help and patience. Thanks also go to Yue Lu.

1   In what follows I will try to give a brief sketch of a certain development in Greek philosophy as it could have eventually led to Aristotle's conception of the science of life. I am aware that many points I will be making are a matter of controversy in the literature. However, owing to the limited space, I will refrain from more critical discussions. Occasionally, I will refer the reader to scholarly literature.

2   If we are to believe passages such as DK11A3 (cf. the discussion in Kirk, Raven, and Schofield, 1957, 95–8); see also DK12B1–3, together with DK12A10.

3   See Kahn 1960.

4   This is also the main point of Aristotle's criticisms in his celebrated critique of the Presocratics in *Metaph.* 1.3–5 and in *De an.* 1.2–5: it is not that he thinks that the Presocratics didn't try to account for the phenomena of life; he thinks that they did so with insufficient conceptual means.

5   This highest explanatory ambition of the Presocratic thinkers is, I think, also implied by Aristotle's remark that they aimed at no less than wisdom (*sophia*). Since he has discussed wisdom previously in the *Metaphysics* as the highest and most universal knowledge of first causes and principles, Aristotle certainly does not deny that his predecessors proposed their theories with the highest explanatory ambitions; he only denies that they followed their ambition with a sufficiently elaborate set of conceptual tools.

6   Indeed, being a 'materialist' of this Presocratic kind often goes together with the belief that the world is governed by some kind of divine principle (see, e.g. Sedley 2007, 2, 5; see also Kahn 1960). The label 'materialism' should not mislead us into thinking that the theories of these early thinkers had anything to do with modern materialism, which is committed to the idea that there is an ontological and an epistemological priority of inanimate over animate nature. See below, note 7.

7   Which is why they were labelled 'material monists' by later scholars; similarly, in those early thinkers who adopted mechanical or chemical models in the explanation of the world-processes at large, nothing is implied as to whether the cosmos is a lifeless thing or not.

8 The idea of a reductive account of the phenomena of life, i.e. an account of the phenomena of life according to which life is not a fundamental but a derived feature of the world, seems to originate with Democritus. Again, I would like to refer the reader to David Sedley's discussion in Sedley 2007, 1.

9 *Mutatis mutandis* for each of these philosophers, of course. For Anaximander, see DK12B1–3, A10, 11, 14, 17; for Anaximenes DK13B2, A 11.

10 Importantly for our understanding of the history of philosophy, the ancient philosophers understand 'principle' typically, not as some kind of law, but as a first *item* in a series of causes (or grounds or events). I cannot discuss this crucial distinction here. In what follows I will use the notion of 'principle' in this ancient, item-centred way.

11 This is not to say that the conception of the soul in Plato's so-called early or Socratic dialogues is incompatible with the biological–cosmological conception of the soul in his later dialogues. See, e.g. Socrates' pronouncement about the animating role of the soul in the *Phaedo* (105c): 'What is it that, when present in a body, makes it living? – A soul.' Plato here follows what pretty much all Greek philosophers agreed upon (save the sceptics, of course), namely that there are souls (the only candidate for an exception is the peripatetic philosopher Dicaearchus, but see Caston 1997, 343). They could agree on this because they all agreed that there are living things in nature, and they all shared an understanding of the soul as the cause by which animated things are alive. They fundamentally disagreed, though, about what the soul is supposed to be.

12 Pl. *Phd.* 97c–99d.

13 See also Pl. *Phd.* 99a–c, where we find a clear antecedent of this same hierarchy of types of causes.

14 Since the whole cosmos is a single living thing (Plato is an organic holist, after all), this holds for Plato's creation story as a whole. This is also what he says in the passage just quoted in the main text (47e5–48a2): 'For this ordered world (*kosmos*) is of a mixed birth', i.e. a mix of Necessity and Intelligence.

15 For more extensive discussions of Plato's creationism in the *Timaeus*, see Sedley 2007, 93–132. See also Lennox 1985 and Johansen 2004, 69–116 for Plato's teleology.

16 In his *Timaeus*, Plato, among other things, aims at presenting a cosmological account of the soul as the principle of life and order in both the cosmos and in human beings that is compatible with the moral psychology of his earlier writings. According to the *Timaeus*, the soul is an intrinsically self-moving entity, neither material nor rational, but somehow in between intellect and matter. As a result, the soul is also *morally* ambiguous. If it masters the irrational motions and impulses of the body, then the human will live a just life, and if not, not (*Ti.* 42a–d, 87c–90d).

17 This is not a feature exclusive to the *Timaeus*; see also *Phd.* 98b, *Leg.* X 10.903b–d. James Lennox aptly labelled it Plato's 'unnatural teleology', see Lennox 1985.

18 For example, Störig 1965; Grene and Dupew 2004; Leroi 2015; Meyer 2015.

19 Aristotle's *Historia animalium*, a book packed with all sorts of observations about animals, makes this abundantly clear. Aristotle's idea in this book is to provide an exhaustive list (*Hist. an.* 1.6.491a7–14) of general information about animals insofar as they are animals, and more particularly, information about

their (i) bodily parts, (ii) actions and activities, (iii) ways of life, and (iv) character dispositions (*Hist. an.* 1.1.487a11–488b27). He also refers to this book as the 'observed facts' about animals (*ta phainomena*). Aristotle offers explanations for these facts in a separate set of treatises, in which he often explicitly refers back to the *Historia animalium*. These are the so-called etiological writings that state the causes (the 'on account of which') for the phenomena (the 'that' of a science). For a recent concise overview of Aristotle's natural science, see Althoff 2018. For Aristotle's predecessors and earlier collections of facts about animals, see Harig and Kollesch 1982.

20 If his method of demonstrative proof seems to put him somewhat at odds with modern practice in biology, which appears much less interested in scientific demonstration, it certainly certifies his scientific ambition. Aristotle's method aims at the explanation of the observed biological facts as facts about living things with reference to the soul as their essence. The study of the essence of things is for that reason a prerequisite for Aristotelian zoological study (*Part. An.* 1.1642a24–31).

21 See the writings of Kullmann 1974; Gotthelf 1976; Lennox 1980; Pellegrin 1982; and many others since.

22 For an extended discussion of Aristotle's breach with Plato's methods, see Kullmann 1974, 163–203. Aristotle also admits sciences that are concerned with quasi-domains. These are domains of scientific inquiry which are not about a given underlying class of substances, but are nevertheless treated as such. The example is mathematical sciences (*Ph.* 2.2.193b22–194a12; *Metaph.* 13.3.1078a21–31).

23 A thesis Aristotle argues for in *Metaph.* 3.3.998b22–27, and 11.1.1059b31–34.

24 *An. post.* 1.9.75b37–76a25, *De an.* 1.1.402a21–22, *Metaph.* 1070b16–17. *An. post.* 1.32 offers proofs for the impossibility of common principles for all sciences.

25 *An. post.* 1.4.73b11–12; 1.6.75a18–27; Bonitz, *Index Aristotelicus.* 714a20–35.

26 We will see below in note 36 how trans-generic statements are possible within the Aristotelian model of science.

27 *Eschata eidê*; *Part. an.* 1.4644a23–25. Facts about particular things, owing to their transitory nature, are not possible objects of science for Aristotle (*An. post.* 1.8.75b21–30, 1.31). The fact that Aristotelian sciences proceed by generic domains (*genê*) and not by species is due to methodological economy (to avoid unnecessary repetitions, *Part. an.* 1.4.644a34–b15) and has nothing to do with organic holism. On the contrary, this method presupposes the genus-specificity of sciences, as such economic measures only work on the basis of, and within, scientific genera.

28 See Bodnar 2005. This is consistent with saying that the certain *regions* of the cosmos such as the outer heavens are 'ensouled' (*Cael.* 2.13.285a29–30), and have life (in *Cael.* 1.9.279a20–22; see Johansen 2009, especially 25). I should like to note here that Aristotle's various scientific projects and the separation of sciences they presuppose are also consistent with the idea of there being a metaphysical explanatory project which is dedicated to the understanding globally of the order of the universe as a whole. This project is part of Aristotle's *Metaphysics*, not, however, part of his natural science.

29 See note 32.

30 On global teleology in Aristotle, see note 36.

31 Of course, the price for the reduced explanatory ambition is to accept a number of, as it were, metaphysical stop signs. There are the primitive assumptions of his science such as that living things have their own specific natures that dispose them to behave in certain ways, and that their processes and behaviours take place for the sake of their natures. On the Platonic conception, by contrast, we do get an explanation for these claims. These are the reasons that lead the demiurge to design the cosmos the way he designs it. Aristotle's defence of the thesis that goal-directedness in natural things is primitive in *Physics* 2.8 is difficult, as it is based on distinctions he has made in the foregoing chapters. And there is also considerable controversy about how to best interpret the chapter. I won't go into it here.

32 Which is why the living body is regarded as the tool or instrument of the rabbit's (or any other living thing's) formal nature or soul (*organon*, *De an.* 2.1.412b1–6; 4.415b19–20). As life functions tend to be complex, so is the instrumental body (*Part. an.* 1.5.645b15–20).

33 *De an.* 1.1.402a7–10; *Part. an.* 1.1.639a18–19; 641a21–26; I 3, 643a27–31; cf. *MA* 1.698a1–4; *Part. an.* 1.5.645b1–2. Aristotle calls these non-essential, yet universal and necessary features of a scientific genus that are to be accounted for by way of the definition of its essence – somewhat misleadingly – *per se* accidents (*kath' hauto sumbebêkota*, see *An. post.* 1.4.73a37–b4; 73b18–24; 1.1.75b1–2; 1.10.76b6–11; 1.22.83b17–24; 2.13.96b15; *Metaph.* 5.30.1025a30–32). He thinks that rendering successful essence-based explanations of the *per se* accidents of a certain domain of science is a test for the correctness of one's definition of the essence (*De an.* 1.1.402a7–10; 403a23–403b2).

34 In *De an.* 2.4.415a26–b6, Aristotle asks why living things maintain themselves and procreate, a question which he famously answers with reference to the eternal striving of all living things for the immortal and the divine. This, however, does not seem to be a biological question in the above sense, given that no biological species helps *realising* the goal of divinity.

35 See Ross' commentary *ad locum* and *Ph.* 199b15–18 (*ti telos*).

36 Which is not to say that Aristotle does not discuss global teleological features of natural things across genera. However, it is important to see that global teleological features of the cosmos as a whole, its order and arrangement, etc., are, in the causal order of things, *posterior* to the goal-directed activities of particular natural substances. Global teleology and the trans-generic order of the world as a whole are themes of Aristotle's metaphysics, not of his physics. In his *Metaphysics*, Aristotle can take a trans-generic, and therefore analogical, perspective on things (*kat' analogian*, *Metaph.* 12.4.1070a31–b35; *An. post.* 1.10.76a37–39). To look at the world from that global perspective is to abstract away from the otherness of the different scientific genera, in order to contemplate the commonalities that they exhibit on the highest possible level of abstraction. An example is Aristotle's statement in *De an.* 2.4 (415a23–415b7) that all living things strive to take part in the eternal and the divine by procreation. From the perspective of the study of the individual species of living things, the goal will be radically different in each case (other things have other principles), but since they all strive

to perpetuate their (in each case radically different) natures, by analogy, there is a – highly abstract – way in which it is correct to say that they all strive for perpetuation. However, the truth of such commonalities is in a way posterior to the truth of the genus-specific statements of the particular sciences (see Henry 2013, 257–8), and certainly part of an explanatory project which is distinct from natural science.

37 See Lennox 1994.

4   Aristotle on the Matter for Birth, Life, and the Elements

David Ebrey

INTRODUCTION

One of Aristotle's major contributions to natural science was his development of an idea that he called *hulê'*, which we translate into English as 'matter'. The notion of matter seems quite ordinary to us today, but Aristotle's idea was new at the time. The word *hulê'* originally meant forest, brushwood, or cut wood and, aside from a single occurrence in Plato's *Philebus* (54c), Aristotle is the first (extant) author to use the term in a general account of things in the natural world. Our notion of matter is a descendant of his, but we should be careful not to assume that he thought of it the way we do today.

One way to understand how Aristotle thinks about matter is to look closely at his *Physics (On Nature)* 1 and 2, where he describes matter at a high level of generality. This can help us understand his reasons for identifying matter as one of the principles and causes needed to do natural science. However, it does not provide much insight into what concrete role matter is supposed to play in our understanding of the natural world. Moreover, his account in the *Physics* leaves several important questions open, which can be answered by looking closely at how he uses matter in his scientific explanations. Aristotle's scientific corpus is large and in places melds seamlessly with what we would consider philosophical works. While we typically distinguish science from philosophy, Aristotle himself considered his scientific works to be part of natural philosophy.[1] Natural philosophy comprises slightly over nine hundred pages in the *Complete Works of Aristotle: the Revised Oxford Translation*. Of this, more than four hundred pages are detailed biology. Aristotle was the first systematic biologist and his biology contains his most impressive scientific work.[2] But, for Aristotle, it is important to understand the entirety of the natural world, from the elements to the cosmos as a whole. His scientific concepts are meant to apply generally to all natural things. For this reason, among others, it is illuminating to consider different places where Aristotle discusses matter. In what follows I first consider menstrual fluid as the matter of animal reproduction in the *Generation of Animals*, then the more puzzling case of the body of a living thing as its matter in the *De anima* (On the Soul), and finally the notoriously obscure matter for the transformation of the elements in *Generation and Corruption*.[3] I focus on two thorny questions about matter that arise in these works.

One question is how to reconcile two apparently incompatible ways that Aristotle discusses matter. Sometimes he treats matter as relative to some particular type of change. Thus, in the *Parts of Animals* he says that blood is matter of the body since it nourishes it (651a12–15, 668a1–4) and in *Generation and Corruption* he refers to the 'matter of size', which is the matter involved in growth (320b22–25, 321a6–7).[4] Menstrual fluid as the matter for animal generation is an example of this sort of matter that is relative to a change. According to this way of treating matter, there are different types of matter for different types of change. However, at other times Aristotle says that substances (paradigmatically, living things like trees, dogs, and spiders) are composed of form and matter, not a bundle of forms and a bundle of matters. This latter way of thinking about matter does not seem relative to a particular change in the way that the former is. Does Aristotle have a coherent notion of matter that fits with these two ways he identifies it?

The other question is how to understand the matter involved in the transmutation of the elements. Aristotle thinks that fire, earth, air, and water are the simplest bodies and that they can transform into one another. He is clear that there is a matter for the transformation of these elements, but his discussion of this is obscure. There is a medieval tradition that takes this matter to be actually nothing, but a pure potentiality to become anything. This matter is typically taken to remain through every change, not only the transformation of the elements. This traditional view, often referred to as 'prime matter', came under attack in the middle of the twentieth century, and was the subject of an intense debate.[5] Part of what gave the debate its particular fervor is that it was connected with the question of whether or not Aristotle thinks that matter must remain through every change.

In what follows, I argue that we can reconcile the two apparently incompatible ways that Aristotle describes matter, and in doing so develop a new account of the matter of the elements. There is a single, coherent notion of matter found in all three treatises, and at the same time, important differences that result from (1) the different sorts of changes under consideration, and (2) whether Aristotle is considering the matter for a specific change, or the matter for all of a substance's characteristic changes.[6] Aristotle's single coherent notion is this: matter changes insofar as it is matter.[7] It changes not in the active sense of changing something else, but in the passive sense of being itself changed. In saying that matter does this 'insofar as it is matter', Aristotle is saying that it does this because it is matter, not because of some other feature that it happens to have. Thus, the matter in a change is the thing that is properly suited to undergo that change. Just as an efficient cause, insofar as it is an efficient cause, changes something else, so matter, insofar as it is matter, is changed.

If we want to understand why something is matter in a given change, we cannot answer this generically; we need to look at the change in question. In the case of making a statue, the sculptor needs something that can retain fine levels of detail and hold its shape. Water would not work, but bronze does. Note that there are no generic efficient causes; instead, there are sculptors, doctors, and – in Aristotle's view – male *sperma* in the case of animal reproduction. Similarly, there is no generic matter; instead, there are bronze, bodies, and in Aristotle's view, menstrual fluid. Menstrual fluid, according to Aristotle, is what is properly suited to become a newborn animal. When acted on by the *sperma*, it becomes the appropriate type of animal insofar as it is menstrual fluid, not because of some other feature it happens to have. In the *De anima*, the body is what is properly suited to undergo the various changes characteristic of a given living creature. So, for example, a robin's wings allow it to engage in a characteristic activity, flying. Many of the features that Aristotle ascribes to the matter of the elements in *Generation and Corruption* do not result from general commitments he has about all matter, as is generally assumed, but rather from the specific type of change that he is considering. Aristotle's views of the elements and how they change into one another entail that the sort of thing suited to become air is the same as the sort suited to become earth, water, or fire; this is why it turns out that there is the same matter for all four elements.

GENERATION OF ANIMALS

The *Generation of Animals* is one of Aristotle's explanatory scientific treatises, that is, it seeks to determine the answers to 'why?' questions on a given subject matter. Broadly speaking, Aristotle's *History of*

Animals sets out empirical facts about animals in such a way as to make salient what explanatory relations could obtain between these facts.[8] By contrast, treatises such as the *Generation of Animals*, *Parts of Animals*, and *Movement of Animals* seek to determine the explanations for empirical facts. In particular, the *Generation of Animals* seeks to explain such things as why animals and some plants reproduce sexually and why animals resemble their parents.

Aristotle argues in the *Generation of Animals* that menstrual fluid is the matter in animal reproduction. In reproduction the menstrual fluid is the patient (in the sense of what is passive) and the male's *sperma* is the agent (what is active). On a traditional understanding of matter in Aristotle, it is crucial that it remain through a change. This causes a prima facie problem, since the menstrual fluid does not remain through the generation of an animal.[9] There is no menstrual fluid in the newborn animal. The solution, I suggest, is that while Aristotle sometimes describes matter as remaining, that is not essential to his notion of matter. Just as the agent of a change may remain through the change, but this is not what makes something the agent, so the matter may remain through the change, but this is not what makes it the matter. Although this is controversial, I would argue that it fits naturally with Aristotle's account of matter in *Physics* I and II and *Generation and Corruption* I.[10] Aristotle says in *Physics* 1.7 and 1.9 that things come to be from matter not by virtue of concurrence (*mê kata sumbebêkos*) (190b23–30, 192a31–32). Just as a doctor heals because she is a doctor, not because she happens to be a lyre player, so things come to be from matter because it is matter, not because it concurs with something else. Aristotle says in *Generation and Corruption* 1.7 that matter insofar as it is matter is passive (324b18). Matter should be understood in terms of this role in change, being the patient that undergoes the change. Thus, the menstrual fluid, as matter, is the sort of thing that is properly suited to become an animal. Not just anything can become an animal. Just as you cannot build a house out of just anything, or make an axe out of just anything, so also – in fact, to a much greater degree – you cannot make an animal out of just anything. An animal of a given species comes from the appropriate kind of menstrual fluid acted on by the appropriate kind of *sperma*. Since it is the patient of the change, the change happens within the menstrual fluid.[11] As long as we take matter to be what is suitable for undergoing a change, it does not pose a problem that the menstrual fluid does not remain. There is nothing suitable for becoming an animal at the end of the change, and so the matter does not remain.

If an interpreter is strongly committed to matter remaining through change, he or she might suppose that Aristotle must not really think that the matter is the menstrual fluid, precisely because it does not remain. But that comes at a large cost. What is powerful about Aristotle's account is that it identifies precisely the thing that is suitable for undergoing the change, and that is the menstrual fluid. That is what has the potentiality to become a fully formed organism (if properly acted upon by the *sperma*), not something else. The search for something that remains draws us away from the thing with the potential to undergo the change. Aristotle thinks that matter is a principle and a cause because it is needed to explain why changes happen; thus, it is important that we identify it as the thing with the relevant explanatory role: the menstrual fluid. Of course, merely identifying it as the menstrual fluid is not enough. If one left it there, Aristotle's view might seem open to the early modern criticism of Aristotelianism that it identifies the cause of sleep as 'dormative virtue' without explaining how wine, for example, accomplishes this effect. But Aristotle does discuss in detail in the *Generation of Animals* how menstrual fluid and *sperma*, together, bring about the formation of an animal (see esp. *Gen. an.* 1.18–23, 4.1–3). Identifying menstrual fluid as matter does not end the explanation; it identifies what plays a certain explanatory role, which then should be investigated in further detail. On Aristotle's account, menstrual fluid and *sperma* are concocted in the parents' bodies in such a way that, among other things, they have changes in their heat and coolness. These are used as tools in the production of the offspring.[12]

Matter's passivity does not mean that it is dormant or featureless. Aristotle thinks the patient in a change plays a crucial role in explaining how and why a given change happens in the way that it does. This is why Aristotle thinks we must identify the matter in a change if we want to understand the change. Sometimes interpreters talk of menstrual fluid and similar highly developed matter as 'informed' matter, suggesting that the matter's development is to be understood in terms of the contribution of form rather than that of matter.[13] But it is a mistake to think that form and matter are opposed to each other in this way. It is precisely because the menstrual fluid has these highly developed features that it is qualified to be matter: only it is suitable for becoming an animal, and in fact only the right sort of menstrual fluid for a given kind of animal. Since the menstrual fluid has a definition, it has a form, but this form is not something distinct and added to matter. On the contrary, without its form the menstrual fluid would not be suitable to undergo the relevant change, and so would not be matter. The menstrual fluid is in no way dormant or featureless, and if it became so, it could no longer be the matter for this change. Aristotelian matter is never a generic or featureless stuff; it is always something suitable to undergo some specific change or changes.

The menstrual fluid is matter for a substantial change, whereas blood, according to Aristotle in the *Parts of Animals*, is the matter for nourishment and growth.[14] Nonetheless, it works in fundamentally the same way, which is to be expected since nourishment and growth are, on Aristotle's account, types of coming-to-be (*Gen. corr.* 1.5) and menstrual fluid is a concocted form of blood (*Gen. an.* 1.19). When blood nourishes bone, there is no reason to think that the blood remains. Nonetheless, blood is, precisely speaking, the matter because it is the thing suitable to become the parts of the body. The parts of the body are sustained by blood insofar as it is blood, just as the animal comes to be from the menstrual fluid insofar as it is menstrual fluid.

THE BODY OF AN ORGANISM AS MATTER IN THE *DE ANIMA*

Next, let us consider the body as the matter of a living organism, which is introduced in *De anima* (On the Soul) 2.1. The soul, for Aristotle, is the principle of life, and so it plays an important role not only in his work devoted to the soul, but also in works that we would consider biological: the *Generation of Animals* and the works known as the *Parva Naturalia*, which discuss phenomena that are 'common to body and soul'. Aristotle thinks that living things are composed of body and soul. The body does not have some single change that it is clearly suited to undergo, unlike the menstrual fluid. Given this, many scholars have suggested that the body is identified as matter because it is what the living thing is composed of.[15] This relies on a very different criterion for something to count as matter, one not directly connected to change. I'll argue here, instead, that the body is matter because it is suitable for undergoing the various changes (*kinêseis*) that are characteristic of the living thing. An organism's body is what undergoes its natural changes, and so it is its matter.

Near the beginning of *De anima* 2.1, Aristotle declares his view, that the soul is substance as form and the body substance as matter, and the thing composed of each is also a substance (412a15–21). He then says that the soul is 'the first actuality of a natural body that has life potentially' (412a27–28).[16] Thus, the matter, namely the body, is something that has life potentially. In the next chapter, 2.2, Aristotle says that life is 'said in many ways'; reason, perception, locomotion and rest, and change (*kinesis*) related to nourishment, growth, and decay are all forms of life (413a22–25). Thus, we would expect the body to be matter that has the potential for these activities. And this turns out to be basically correct.[17]

The body and soul together compose the living thing; they are, respectively, what has the potentiality for life and its first actuality. We will examine this notion of potentiality and actuality shortly. First, we need to consider the division of labour, according to which some features of the organism are due to the soul and others to the body. What features of an organism is each responsible for? Aristotle's view is that a soul, insofar as it is a soul, does not change.[18] Instead, the changes happen in the body, insofar as it is a body. After distinguishing the soul's coincidental changes from the body's non-coincidental changes (406a16–20), Aristotle says that 'it is evident that it [the soul] changes the body' (406a30), and that the soul is thereby coincidentally changed (406a30–b3). This does not merely apply to locomotion. Living things could not digest without the soul, but the soul does not change when we digest something; the body does, in virtue of the soul. The body is what is receptive of health; health and such things reside in the body, which is disposed to receive health (414a4–14). An animal's body changes incidentally when it is blown over by a wind, but it changes insofar as it is a body when it is changed by the soul. Of course, the organism undergoes change when the body does, but it does so insofar as the body changes. There is a complicated question of whether the very same types of activities that are attributed to the whole organism should also be attributed to the body.[19] But, regardless of how we decide this, a living thing is changed in virtue of its body changing; its body is the thing suitable for changing. Whenever a living thing undergoes a change, it does so insofar as it is a body, i.e. matter. This overall picture fits with Aristotle's claim in 2.1 that the type of body that has a soul is 'organic' (412a28–b1). As Stephen Menn has argued, to call the body organic (*organikon*) is to say that it is a tool (*organon*) of the soul, the instrument by which the soul produces its characteristic activities.[20] Tools change when a craftsperson is active. Aristotle's view is that, in fact, the craft itself does not change. In a parallel way, the soul does not change insofar as it is a soul, whereas the body does.

The next step in understanding Aristotle's account of the body is to understand his claim that the body is a potential being (*dunamei on*, 413a2) and the soul an actuality (*entelecheia, energeia*).[21] Aristotle distinguishes between two types of potentiality in the *De anima* 2.1 and 2.5. His standard example is that a person who does not know something, say mathematics, has a first potentiality for mathematics. A rock, by contrast, does not have this potentiality. Once someone learns mathematics, she removes a privation, her ignorance, and now possesses a first actuality. This first actuality can at the same time be described as a second potentiality. This person has this first actuality/second potentiality even if she is asleep; if she actively thinks about some mathematics, e.g. the Pythagorean theorem, this exercise of the second potentiality is the second actuality. Aristotle says that the soul is a first actuality, which would make the body's potentiality a first potentiality.[22] The activity of living is the second actuality, the exercise of the soul.

How do we fit together these two ideas about the soul's relation to the body: (1) the soul is what produces changes and the body is what is changed, and (2) the soul is first actuality and the body has the corresponding first potentiality? While we can reconcile the two descriptions of the soul by saying that it does not change (*kinein*) but rather simply becomes active (*energeia*), that does not explain why the very same thing, the body, has these two roles, being what is changed and what has the potentiality that corresponds to the soul's actuality. Aristotle thinks that in other cases these roles do not go together: when a carpenter exercises her ability, a change happens in the wood, not in the carpenter herself, even though she is what has the first potentiality for being a carpenter. To explain why these two roles come together in the body, consider, as a parallel case, the ability to dance. This ability is a first actuality. In order to develop this ability, one needs a first potentiality that includes the capacity to move one's limbs. The ability to dance uses this capacity, thereby producing changes in one's own body – not in someone else's. The soul, for Aristotle, is like the ability to dance. An organism's soul is able to use the organism's own capacities in specific ways.[23] The body is the part of the organism that has these capacities and so it is changed when they are exercised. The body's capacities can only be exercised by the organism that has them. Thus, the body has these two roles, both what is changed and what has the first potentiality, because its potentiality is for this sort of self-reflexive change where an organism changes itself. When my potential for being a carpenter is fully realised, I can produce changes in wood, whereas when my arm's potential for moving is fully realised, I can produce changes in my arm. That is the sort of potential my arm, and in general, my body has. The body is the matter of this specific sort of self-motion.[24]

It is important not to overextend the analogy between the soul, on the one hand, and crafts and abilities, on the other. In particular, many people have the first potentiality to dance without having the ability to do so. But, according to Aristotle, the body is a potential being that cannot exist without the actuality, i.e. the soul. The body comes to be with the soul, and when we die or a limb is cut off, this is a body or limb in name only, not actually one.[25] If you think of matter primarily in terms of what remains through a substantial change, this raises a puzzle, which J. L. Ackrill develops in a classic article: the body does not exist before or after the soul, and so it seems that the matter does not remain longer than the form.[26] But again, if we think of matter as what is suitable to undergo change, rather than as what remains through a change, no puzzle arises. When a hand is cut off, what is left is not suitable for grasping; it cannot change in the ways characteristic of a hand. And when an animal dies, its body is not suitable for living in the way characteristic of an animal. It is because of the soul that the body is able to change in the way that it does, and so without the soul it no longer has the potentiality to change, and hence is a body in name only.

On Aristotle's account, the body can only be understood in terms of the activities it engages in, as determined by the soul; the soul needs the body to perform these activities. Aristotle brings out this close interrelation between body and soul at the end of *De anima* 2.2, when he argues against views that allow any soul to be in any body. This would include Plato's account of reincarnation in the *Phaedo*, *Phaedrus*, *Republic*, and *Timaeus*, where humans can reincarnate into animals. Here is how Aristotle puts his view:

> For it [the soul] is not a body, but is something belonging to a body; and because of this it is present in a body, and in a body of this

sort – not as our predecessors supposed when they fitted the soul
into the body without additionally specifying in which body or in
which sort, even though it appears that whatever happens to show
up does not receive whatever it happens upon. It happens rather
in this way, in conformity with reason: the actuality of each thing
comes about naturally in what has it in potentiality, that is, in its
appropriate matter.

(Arist. *De an.* 2.2.414a20–27)

There is an appropriate type of matter for each type of soul, and this
is the body for that soul. What makes it appropriate is that it has the
potentiality that corresponds to a given type of soul. Thus, the body
has the potentiality of sight, or of hunting down rabbits, or whatever is
appropriate for the type of living being it is. A wolf's soul could not be
in a sheep's body. What makes a wolf's body appropriate is precisely that
it can undergo the changes characteristic of wolves. If it sounds like the
body and soul are almost two sides of the same coin, that is a welcome
conclusion for Aristotle. He thinks that once we see that soul relates to
body as form to matter, we do not need to enquire into the unity of body
and soul (412b6–9). Together they form a tightly unified substance.[27]

When Aristotle says that the body is matter, he is saying that it
is the right sort of thing to undergo a whole range of changes, those
characteristic of the organism in question.[28] When an animal goes from
hungry to full, or from here to there, or from tired to awake, it is the
body, insofar as it is a body, that undergoes this change. This case is
unlike menstrual fluid, which is properly suited to just one change.
Nonetheless, the basic account of matter is the same in the *De anima*
and in the *Generation of Animals*. Matter, in general, is what is properly suited to undergo change. Matter changes insofar as it is matter.
Different sorts of things undergo different sorts of changes, so there are
different kinds of matter. The body is matter because the soul produces
in it a wide range of changes, which together constitute the life of the
organism. The body can be identified as *the* matter of an organism
because an organism is defined in terms of its way of life, and the body
is the matter for this activity.

THE MATTER FOR ELEMENTAL TRANSFORMATION

Last, let us consider the matter involved in the transformation of the
elements into one another. Aristotle agrees with Empedocles that there

are four elements (at least within the sublunary sphere): earth, air, fire, and water. He discusses them in a number of places in the corpus, in most detail in *De caelo* (On the Heavens) 3 and 4, *Meteorology* 4, and *Generation and Corruption* 2. *Generation and Corruption* 2 is his most extensive discussion of their transformation, so we will focus on it here. Aristotle clearly is committed to there being matter in this transformation, but it is controversial how to understand it. The traditional view is that he is committed to something called 'prime matter', which is pure potentiality, not actually anything, and which remains through the transformation of the elements.[29] This is generally treated as something that remains through all changes, not simply elemental transformation, and which has the potentiality to become anything. It is thought of as 'pure' matter, as opposed to informed matter, which is thought of as matter combined with some form. It is easy to see how this notion of matter could naturally lead one to think of matter as featureless stuff.

Let me briefly lay out my alternative before providing evidence for it. Aristotle thinks that there are several broad types of change; one type, substantial change, involves a substance coming-to-be, and another type, alteration, involves a change between affections that are strict contraries (not mere contradictories). In Aristotle's natural works, he considers the elements substances (e.g. *Physics* 2.1.192b8–13 and *De caelo* 3.1298a29–b1), and so, as we would expect, he says that the transformation of one element into another is a type of substantial change (*Gen. corr.* 1.4.319b14–21).[30] I argue that, nonetheless, elemental transformation works the way that alterations work. Although the elements do not themselves have contraries (as would be needed for an alteration), they are each essentially characterised by two strict contraries from among the pairs: hot/cold and wet/dry. Because of this, a change between the elements works the same way as an alteration, and so the sort of matter involved in the transformation of the elements is the sort needed for an alteration. Aristotle argues that in an alteration there is a single matter that is able to take on both the contraries, the one at the beginning and the one at the end of the change. When changing from hot to cold or from wet to dry, there is the same sort of matter at the end as there is at the beginning, because the sort of thing suitable for becoming hot is exactly the same as the sort suitable for becoming cold. Since elemental transformations simply involve changing whether an element is hot or cold or whether it is wet or dry, all of the elements will have the same matter for their elemental transformations. But we

should not think that this matter is a pure potentiality to become anything; instead, it is simply a potential to become hot or cold, wet or dry.
And we should not think that this sort of matter is involved in every
change; instead, this matter is precisely suited to elemental transformation and so only involved in it and related changes.

Let us turn to the evidence for this interpretation, filling it out in
the process. Aristotle's fullest description of this matter is in a very difficult passage in *Generation and Corruption* 2.1:

> Our own theory is that whereas there is a sort of matter of the
> perceptible things, this is not separable but is always with a
> contrariety, from which the things called 'elements' come to
> be. A more precise account of them has been given elsewhere.[31]
> However, since according to the present approach too [in addition
> to that of the *Timaeus*, which he has just been discussing] the
> primary bodies are from the matter, we must give an account of
> these too, regarding as a principle and first the matter that on
> the one hand is inseparable but on the other hand underlies the
> contraries (for neither is the hot matter for the cold nor the latter
> for the hot, but the underlying thing is matter for both); so first that
> which is potentially perceptible body is principle, and secondly the
> contrarieties (I mean, for example, heat and cold), and then thirdly
> fire and water and the like. For these change into one another,
> and it is not as Empedocles and others say (for there would be no
> alteration); but the contrarieties do not change.
>
> (Arist. *Gen. corr.* 2.1.329a24–b3)[32]

Aristotle is clear at the beginning that there is a matter from which the
elements come-to-be. (He calls them 'the things called "elements"' in
order not to endorse that they really are elements. Calling them 'elements' suggests they are the simplest things, but it turns out that they are
composed of matter and contrarieties.)[33] What is this matter for the generation of the elements? Aristotle says that it 'underlies the contraries'
and that it is 'perceptible body in potentiality'. In the next chapter he
identifies the contraries as the essential features that differentiate each
element from the others, making each the element that it is. An element
is differentiated by possessing contraries from among the pairs hot/cold
and wet/dry: fire is hot and dry, air is hot and wet, water is cold and wet,
earth is cold and dry. Aristotle is saying that the matter for the elements
underlies the contraries, which turn out to be hot/cold and wet/dry.

In the passage, Aristotle prioritises and contrasts the matter with the contrarieties: 'so first that which is potentially perceptible body [i.e. matter] is principle, and secondly the contrarieties' (329a32–34). This is connected to the previous clause, where he says that the matter underlies the contraries and that it is a principle and first. This speaks against the suggestion that Montgomery Furth and Mary Louise Gill have developed that a contrary from one pair (e.g. hot or cold) can serve as the matter for a transformation between the other contraries (e.g. from wet to dry).[34] Aristotle here contrasts matter with the contraries and prioritises it over them; thus, matter cannot be the same as one of them.[35] Moreover, the Furth–Gill interpretation runs into a problem with something Aristotle reminds us of at the end of the passage: that the contrarieties do not change. This recalls Aristotle's first argument in *Physics* 1.6 for needing an underlying thing (189a20–27). Contraries are not the sort of thing to undergo change; we need a third thing to change, which he identifies in *Physics* 1.7 as the matter, with a reference back to this 1.6 argument (190b23–33).[36] Just as the soul, insofar as it is a soul, does not undergo change, so too contraries, insofar as they are contraries, do not change. To put it somewhat differently, the contraries themselves do not have a potential to undergo change, and that is precisely what is required of matter. Furth and Gill's suggestion is driven by the thought that matter must remain through the change. But even if we accept this, Aristotle requires matter to do something else: it must be suitable for undergoing a given change. And neither hot nor cold is suitable for becoming wet or dry. Again, the focus on finding something that remains has drawn interpreters away from identifying matter as something with the appropriate potentiality. Furth and Gill are explicitly motivated by trying to avoid positing prime matter. My account offers another way to do that.

One of Aristotle's central claims is that this matter that underlies the contraries is the same in different elements. In the passage quoted above, he says that the underlying thing is the matter for *both* of the contraries. We see a similar thought in *Gen. corr.* 2.7:[37]

> The sort of thing I mean is that water can come to be from fire, and fire from this, since there is something in common, the underlying thing.
>
> (Arist. *Gen. corr.* 2.7.334a23–25)

Aristotle says that there is an underlying thing in common between fire and water. It might seem that this is supposed to follow from the fact that water can come from fire. This sort of reading might lead you to think that matter always remains through every change, which, in turn, would mean that some matter must remain in the case of animal generation. But note that in the above passage Aristotle is explaining not merely why water can come from fire, but also why fire can come from water. His explanation for this reciprocal relationship is that they have an underlying thing in common. By contrast, while menstrual fluid can transform into an animal, an animal cannot transform into menstrual fluid.[38] The fact that elements have common matter is what explains their ability to reciprocally transform, which cannot happen in animal generation. Hence, this passage gives us no reason to expect a common matter in other types of generation.[39]

Fire and water have a matter in common because of the specifics of how the elements transform into one another. The elements are transformed by changing which contraries they have from among the pairs hot/cold and wet/dry. The matter for the elements is the thing that underlies these primary contraries. Normally, for Aristotle a change between (strict) contraries is a form of alteration. So it is worth considering Aristotle's account of what underlies in cases of alteration, which he discusses in *On Generation and Corruption* 1.6:

> What is more, it is impossible for there to be alteration, or segregation and aggregation, unless there is something which acts and something which is affected. For, those who posit several elements make them come to be by their acting upon and being affected by one another, and equally those who make them come to be from a single element cannot avoid speaking of action. And Diogenes is right to say that if it were not the case that everything is from a single thing, there would not be any acting upon or being affected by one another, e.g. what is hot being cooled, and vice versa – for heat and cold do not change into each other. What changes is clearly the underlying thing; so objects between which there is action and passion necessarily have a single underlying nature. But it is not true to say that everything is of this kind, but only those things which affect one another.
>
> (Arist. *Gen. corr.* 1.6.322b9–21)

Alteration requires acting and being affected. And when one thing acts on another, the other acts back on it. Aristotle thinks that whenever a thing is affected it becomes like the thing acting on it. He uses as his example heat and cold, which, as we have seen, turn out to be differentiae of the elements. A cold thing becomes hotter when a hot thing acts on it, and the hot thing in turn becomes colder. Aristotle says that there must be the same underlying nature shared between hot and cold things in order for them to be able to affect one another. Intuitively, this makes sense. The sort of thing that is hot is the same as the sort of thing that is cold, and this is why hot and cold things can be affected by one another. In general, changes between strict contraries are changes between things that share an underlying nature.[40] Normally, such a change is simply a case of alteration. But in the special case of the elements, it is a substantial change between things with the same underlying nature, since the elements are substances differentiated by strict contraries.[41]

We can now return and provide a fuller answer to why there is not a common nature in the case of the generation of animals. The basic reason is that animals are not differentiated by contraries; thus, the matter for the creation of an animal is not the matter for a contrary. But why not think there is a common nature in all cases, rather than only in those between contraries? This is because the right sort of thing to become hot is something that has the same nature as the things that *are* hot. But the right sort of thing to become a rabbit is not something that has the same nature as the things that are rabbits. Rabbits only come from something suitable for becoming a rabbit, and making this is a complicated biological process. You cannot just take a rabbit, turn it into something else, and then directly make another rabbit out of that. By contrast, you can take something that is hot, chill it, and then make it hot again. This is why Aristotle says in the first passage quoted in this section, from *Gen. corr.* 2.1, that the matter 'underlies the contraries', without in any way restricting it to being a matter for *becoming something new*.[42]

Why should we think of the elements as having a single matter, rather than two matters, given that the ability to become hot or cold seems independent of the ability to become wet or dry? By the same token, one might worry that we should not think of the elements themselves as having a unified nature, given that they are defined in terms of being hot or cold as well as wet or dry.[43] The answer, I suggest, is that Aristotle thinks of these pairs of contraries as two aspects that together form a whole. Aristotle argues in *Gen. corr.* 2.2 that these two pairs are the fundamental features that make something tangible.

Something cannot be wet or dry on its own; it must be paired with hot or cold. Once we see hot/cold and wet/dry as the two basic dimensions of being tangible, we can see why Aristotle would think the nature of each element is unified – each is tangible in a fundamentally different way. The matter of the elements is unified, in turn, as the potentiality for being tangible. This is why Aristotle refers to the matter of the elements, in the *Gen. corr.* 2.1 passage quoted above, as 'the matter of perceptible bodies'. This is not an accidental formulation – it is the matter of perceptible bodies *qua* perceptible bodies. The most fundamental form of being perceptible is being tangible (*Gen. corr.* 2.2, *De an.* 2.2), so the matter of perceptible bodies is the matter that is able to take on any of the basic ways in which something can be tangible.

We have seen why Aristotle thinks that all four elements have the same matter. This means, at a minimum, that there is the same type of matter at the beginning of an elemental transformation as there is at the end. Does it also mean that the same token matter remains through the change? In other words, is the matter at the beginning numerically identical with that at the end? Aristotle does not seem to say anything one way or another that would directly commit him to its being the same token matter.[44] In general, he does not seem very concerned with such individuation questions in *Generation and Corruption*, although commentators are often extremely interested in this. To the extent that Aristotle thinks that only actual substances can be described as 'a this' (*tode ti*) and to the extent that what we individuate are this's, he should not think that the matter is the sort of thing that would remain. More importantly, even if he does think that it remains, this would not be because it is essential to matter that it remain, but rather because of some specific feature of the change in question.[45] There is nothing about his basic notion of matter that requires the matter for the elements to remain.

There is one important way in which the matter for the elements is different from other types of matter. Whereas the menstrual fluid and the body have independent, actual features insofar as they are matter, the matter of the elements does not seem to have any independent, actual features of its own. The menstrual fluid has certain actual features that partially ground its potential for reproduction (e.g. a certain temperature) and the eagle's body has certain actual features that partially ground its potential to fly (e.g. large wings). By contrast, Aristotle does not suggest that the matter of the elements has any actual features, and there are good reasons for him not to attribute any to it. Aristotle thinks that each element has actual features and from this we can tell that it has potential features. Anything that is hot and wet is able to be hot and wet and so also able to be cold and dry. Hot/cold and wet/dry are the most basic features of being a body, and so no other actual features could be metaphysically prior to them. If the potential to be hot/cold and wet/dry were explained by some prior, actual feature, this feature would, in turn, be prior to hot, cold, wet, and dry. But that contradicts them being the most basic features, so the potential to be hot/cold or wet/dry must not be grounded in some prior, actual feature. It is a brute potential that the elements have. We can refer to each element insofar as it has this potential to be tangible body. When we do so, we refer to it as matter.[46] This is parallel to the way that a living thing undergoes changes insofar as it is a body, i.e. matter. But, unlike a body, the matter of the elements has a pure potentiality and so to this extent there is something right about the traditional notion of prime matter. Unlike other types of matter, the matter of the elements has a potentiality that is not grounded in any actuality. But, unlike prime matter, the matter of the elements cannot become anything whatsoever, only tangible body. And unlike prime matter, it is not crucial that it remain through change.

While interpreters do not typically explain why they actively try to avoid the prime matter interpretation, we can see why they would. It seems to involve a sort of metaphysically extravagant, magical thinking: the idea that there is something that is actually nothing, but potentially everything, which remains through every change. The interpretation I've offered is not metaphysically extravagant in this way. One might think that every ability is grounded – at least in part – in some metaphysically prior, actual feature, the way that glass's ability to break is grounded in the actual molecular structure of glass. But it is not clear that every ability is grounded in this way. My suggestion is that Aristotle thinks that the elements' potential to be a perceptible body is not due to some prior, actual feature of the elements. Contemporary physics suggests that the ability to be hot/cold and wet/dry is at least partially due to more basic molecular features. But it is not clear that in contemporary physics every potentiality must be grounded in prior actual features. For example, is there some actual feature of electrons that gives them the potential to move from one atom to another? Or is this a brute potentiality that electrons have, not grounded in some prior actual feature? If we supposed that this is a brute fact about them, that would not make this ability spooky or metaphysically extravagant.

Similarly, the matter of the elements, according to Aristotle, has a brute potentiality, an ability to be any of the four basic types of tangible body, and this is not grounded in some more basic feature that they have. There is nothing spooky about this.[47]

CONCLUSION

Aristotle thinks that a fundamental feature of the natural world is that the things in it change. Thus, if we want to understand things in the natural world, we need to understand their changes. In order to understand a change, we need to grasp what is suitable to undergo this change. To grasp something in this way is to consider it as matter. Given that different things are suitable for different types of changes, there will be different types of matter, and the features of these types of matter will differ depending on the change in question. An animal's menstrual fluid is very different from its body, which is very different from fire and water insofar as they can become cold or dry. Nonetheless, Aristotle's notion of matter is fundamentally the same across a variety of scientific contexts: it is a thing insofar as it is able to undergo a given change. Examining Aristotle's scientific works helps us understand how he thinks of different sorts of matter, that is, how he thinks about the things suitable for undergoing different natural changes.

NOTES

I'd like to thank Andreas Anagnostopoulos, Emily Fletcher, Chris Frey, Monte Johnson, Sean Kelsey, Mary Krizan, Anna Schriefl, and Liba Taub, for their helpful comments on drafts, as well as the participants at the 2016 Oxford Workshop on Matter.

1 Only the *De anima* (On the Soul) is controversial. Shields 2016, for example, has recently argued that some parts of the work should be considered first philosophy (i.e. metaphysics) rather than natural philosophy. The parts I discuss here are uncontroversially natural philosophy.

2 For an introduction to interesting issues in Aristotle's biology, I suggest Gotthelf 2012a.

3 This chapter focuses on Aristotle's natural philosophy, occasionally referring to his *Metaphysics* but without relying on this work. It is often difficult to determine the dialectical structure of the *Metaphysics*, and there are questions about how to understand it as a science distinct from natural philosophy. My approach here is to provide an account of matter in the natural works, taken on their own; we can then ask how this relates to Aristotle's account of matter in the *Metaphysics*.

I think we should keep open the possibility that Aristotle operates with a broader notion of matter in parts of the *Metaphysics* than he does in his natural works.

4 In *Generation and Corruption*, Aristotle says that 'what is most strictly matter is the substratum receptive of generation and corruption; but, in a way, so is that of other changes, since all substrata are receptive of contrarieties of one sort or another' (320a2–5, Williams trans.). Cf., *Metaph.* 7.1.1042a32–1042b3, and 11.2.1069b9–20. Just as Aristotle is frequently interested in power (*dunamis*) not merely in the 'most strict' (*malista kuriôs*) sense (cf. *Metaph.* 8.1), so also he is frequently interested in matter not merely in the most strict sense. Aristotle discusses the matter of place (which is what allows the stars to move) in *Metaph.* 7.1.1042a32–1042b6, 7.4.1044b6–8; 8.8.1050b20–24, 11.2.1069b24–26.

5 The first article was King 1956. The debate was at its most intense in the 1970s. For recent discussions, see Krizan 2013 (with useful bibliography) and Henry 2015, 2019.

6 Ultimately, I think this notion is deployed throughout Aristotle's natural philosophical works, but here I limit my claims to these three treatises. It would be interesting if there are exceptions, given the broad coherence of his notion across his natural philosophy.

7 I argue that this is the notion of matter in *Physics* 1 in Ebrey 2007 and Ebrey unpublished.

8 The classic defence of this view is Lennox 1987.

9 For a classic statement of this problem, see Charlton 1970, 76–7.

10 I argue for this at length in Ebrey 2007 and Ebrey unpublished Henry (2015, 2019) also closely considers *Physics* 1 and *Generation and Corruption* 1 and argues that matter need not remain through change.

11 This is argued for in Gelber 2010. See *Physics* 3.3 for the general view that changes happen within the patient.

12 For a complementary account, which discusses the role of these motions at much more length, see Gelber 2010, especially section 6.

13 For a classic statement, see Peck 1942, xii–xiii.

14 For a discussion of blood as matter in the *Parts of Animals*, see Ebrey 2015.

15 E.g. Charlton 1970 (esp. 73); Ackrill 1972/3; Shields 2016 (esp. xvii–xxviii).

16 All *De anima* translations from Shields 2016.

17 The exception is reason (*nous*). See note 28.

18 This is emphasised in *De anima* 1.3–I.5; see especially 406a2, 408b30–31, 411a24–26. For a general discussion of the importance of this for Aristotle's conception of the soul, see Menn 2002.

19 Those who think that strictly the organism engages in its characteristic activities, but not the body, include Barnes 1971/2, 103 and Menn 2002, 100–1. Before discussing the textual support for this, suppose it is correct. If so, then (as Menn says) these activities would happen in virtue of changes within the body (except in cases of pure contemplation). The parallel with the craftsman is instructive. When a builder builds a house her hammer changes, and not coincidentally. At the same time, the builder builds the house, not her tools. This is because the builder is the unchanging efficient cause of the change (cf., 416a34–b3). The builder's body changes because of her soul; thereby, the whole builder changes. When we attribute a change to an entire organism, we are crediting its soul, as

form and efficient cause, as well as its body, as matter. The main passage cited for thinking the whole organism engages in its activities, not the body, is in *De an.* 1.4 (408b11–16). Note that Aristotle does not mention the body here at all; he simply says that it is better to say that the human pities or learns or thinks than that the soul does. For a thoughtful discussion of what we can conclude from this passage, see Lorenz 2007, 215–19.

20 Menn 2002, 108–12.

21 It is very tricky to translate these terms. *Dunamis* is sometimes translated 'capacity', sometimes 'ability', sometimes 'potentiality'. I have chosen the traditional 'potentiality' here because it seems to bridge cases that we would call a capacity, those we would call an ability, and those that seem broader than a single ability. The downside is that this term seems more abstract and theoretical, whereas the word itself is ordinary Greek. I take Aristotle to use *entelecheia* and *energeia* interchangeably in the *De anima* 2.1 and 2.5 (e.g. 412a26–27), although they may have slightly different emphases. Sometimes they refer to activities or changes, at other times to things that are not changing. I have translated them as 'actuality', although this downplays their connection to change. See Beere 2009, 3–5, 169–219 for a clear discussion of these issues and a proposal for how Aristotle understands the single notion of being *energeia* in *Metaphysics* Theta.

22 *Pace* Whiting 1992, 88–9, who takes the body to be a potentiality for the second actuality, which would make the body a first actuality.

23 In my view, the soul relates to the body in this self-reflexive way because organisms are natural things, and these have their principle of movement and rest inside of themselves (*Physics* 2.1.192b20–23), whereas artificial things, such as the products of carpentry, do not.

24 For a related idea, very briefly expressed, see Frede 1992, 104. Lorenz 2007, esp. 211–19, develops the idea that in sense perception the soul undergoes the change from first to second actuality while the sense organ undergoes an ordinary change, altering the organ.

25 E.g. *Gen. corr* 1.5.321b29–32; *Mete.* 4.12.390a10–12; *De an.* 2.1.412b19–26; *Part. an.* 1.1.640b34–641a34; *Gen. an.* 2.1.734b24–27. For a general discussion of this 'homonymy principle' and its relevance to Aristotle's notion of a body, see Frey 2007, especially section 2.

26 Ackrill 1972/3.

27 Frey 2015a, esp. 19, argues for a stronger form of unity, which is compatible with the one suggested here.

28 There is one exceptions to this, or perhaps two. First, Aristotle thinks that there is no bodily organ for the exercise of reason, although he seems to think that every exercise of reason involves an exercise of imagination, which does have a bodily organ. Second, it is controversial whether the body changes when we perceive. Burnyeat 1992 provocatively claims that there is no physiological change when we perceive. For a recent survey and proposed resolution, see Caston 2005, and for another account, Lorenz 2007. The current scholarly consensus, which I share, is that there is some sort of physiological change in the sense organ, although the exact nature of this is disputed.

29 The classic statement is Zeller 1897, 347–8.

30 Famously, in *Metaphysics* 6.16 (1040b5–10), Aristotle denies that the elements are genuine substances. But elsewhere in the *Metaphysics*, he says that they are substances (*Metaph.* 4.8.1017b10–14, 6.2.1028b8–13, 7.1.1042a6–12). More importantly, I see no evidence for such doubt in Aristotle's natural philosophy (*pace* Gill 2009). He routinely puts them in his lists of substances, and treats them as such. Moreover, change between elements is one of his two examples of substantial change in a chapter on this topic, *Gen. corr.* 1.4 (319b14–21). In my view, Aristotle uses a higher standard for being a substance in *Metaphysics* 6.16 than he requires in his natural philosophy. This said, my account can be accepted even if (like Gill 2009) one does not accept that the elements are genuine substances in Aristotle's natural works.

31 It is controversial what 'from which' refers back to in the first sentence, and what 'them' and 'elsewhere' refer to in the second sentence. For my purposes this does not matter. For a discussion of the issues, and alternative accounts, see Williams 1982, 154–6; Gill 1989, 244–5; Broadie 2004, 140–2.

32 My translation of this passage draws primarily from Broadie 2004, 140, as well as Williams 1982 *ad loc.* and Gill 1989, 244. Other translations of the *Gen. corr.* are from Williams 1982, lightly modified.

33 Crowley 2008 argues that we should not translate the phrase 'so-called elements'. I agree as a matter of translation, but think that nonetheless Aristotle's considered view is that strictly they are not elements. Cf., *Timaeus* 48b–c, where Timaeus similarly denies that the things called elements really are such. I take Aristotle in this passage to use 'contrary' and 'contrariety' interchangeably.

34 Furth 1988, 221–7; Gill 1989, ch. 2 and appendix. Krizan 2013 distinguishes between a matter that the element is composed of, and a distinct matter that remains through the change. The latter, which she calls the 'material constituent', functions the way that matter does for Furth and Gill. She offers no direct evidence that Aristotle thinks that there are these two sorts of matter. The account I offer here resolves Krizan's puzzles without positing these two different types of matter.

35 Gill 1989, 245, suggests that Aristotle means that in a given change, one contrary (e.g. hot) will be matter, which is the prior principle, and contraries from the other spectrum (e.g. wet and dry) will be the 'contraries' that are the second principles. Certainly, the natural reading of the passage is that the matter is distinct from any contraries, and that it underlies them. Aristotle never says that he is restricting his claims to only one pair of contraries. Moreover, he identifies matter simply as 'perceptible body in potentiality'. What counts as 'perceptible body in potentiality' should not change depending on whether a change happens in the hot–cold spectrum or the wet–dry spectrum; thus, the matter should be the same in both cases. Below I discuss why Aristotle calls this matter 'perceptible body in potentiality'.

36 Gill 1989 says, 'If for Aristotle the hot and the cold were not the sorts of entity that could serve as the matter for something, his statement is bizarre' (245). To the contrary, his point in *Physics* 1.6 (repeated in 1.7) is precisely that contraries, in general, cannot undergo change, which is why we need matter.

37 See also *Gen. corr.* 2.5.332a17–18, where the term 'matter' is used. Aristotle moves back and forth between claims about matter and claims about the underlying

thing in *Generation and Corruption*, just as he does in *Physics* 1. Sometimes he uses 'underlying thing' as a broader term that encompasses more than just matter.

38 Of course, adult female animals sometimes produce menstrual fluid, but such animals are not transformed as a whole in this process.

39 Williams 1982's appendix on prime matter defends the traditional prime matter view by arguing against its opponents. His best evidence is the passages I have cited above where Aristotle notes that we have the same matter, or underlying thing, for contraries. But that does not give us evidence for thinking that this matter is all things potentially, or that it is involved in non-elemental changes. Moreover, I argue below that there is no reason to think that this matter for elemental transformations remains through this change, as opposed to there being a new matter of the same type at the end of the change.

40 This also fits very naturally with Aristotle's account in *Gen. corr.* 1.7, according to which all agents and patients share a genus; this gives them a common nature that allows them to affect one another.

41 Note also that this account allows for a natural reading of Aristotle's claim in *Gen. corr.* 2.4 (331b4) that it is possible to transform from one element to the diametrically opposed element – the one that it shares no contraries with. Aristotle says that this transformation takes longer because it simultaneously changes both contraries. Furth, Gill, Krizan, and those with similar views are forced to argue that the process happens by first changing one of the contraries and then the other. But that is not what Aristotle says, and such interpreters have to try to explain why we should think of this as one difficult change, rather than two ordinary changes. On my account, each element has matter that allows it to become hot–cold and wet–dry. Given this, something could change both of these simultaneously, turning into the diametrically opposed element, but (Aristotle is claiming) that would be harder, because it is harder to change two things at once, rather than one.

42 While Broadie 2004 does not identify the matter for the elements in the way that I do, in several ways her account is similar to the one presented here. One important difference is that she argues that each element only has a matter for becoming the other elements, which she thinks in no way underlies the form of the element (see esp. 146–50).

43 Krizan 2013 usefully pushes the question of how the elements are unified in the way needed for them to be substances. She addresses the problem by arguing that one of the pair hot/cold or wet/dry serves the form of an element, and the other as the matter. While this solves the problem of not having two forms (e.g. both cold and wet), it does not seem to be sufficient to unify matter and form. In general, Aristotle's solution to this is to view matter as potentially what form is actually (cf. *De an.* 2.1, *Metaph.* 7.6), and it is not clear how Krizan's account accomplishes this.

44 There is a tricky question of whether *Gen. corr.* 1.4.319b8–18 requires that matter not remain through a substantial change. Broadie 2004 argues that this passage requires that it not remain. If she were right, then there would have to be a new matter at the end of the change of the same kind as the one there beforehand. However, I do not think that the passage requires this. In it Aristotle distinguishes between a change in the underlying thing and one in the affections. Broadie claims

that since the change is in the underlying thing, not an affection, we must think that the entire underlying thing is 'exchanged' (Broadie 2004, 124). But why not think that it is possible that part of the underlying thing stays the same while another part changes? Why must it be exchanged as a whole? In particular, how should we understand it if a substance's differentia changes? That is what happens in the case of the transformation of the elements, e.g. hot is replaced with cold. Given that changing a differentia leads to a substantial change, it seems that such a change should count as the underlying thing changing, not an affection. Thus, this passage is compatible with thinking that part of the underlying thing remains, namely the matter, while another part is 'exchanged', namely the differentia.

45 In *Generation and Corruption* 1.4, Aristotle seems to allow that numerically the same affection could remain through a generation, so that when water comes to be from air, the very same transparency could remain from the water to the air (319b21–24). If this is his view, perhaps he would also be happy to think that the very same matter could remain through the change, but then this would not be a special feature of matter.

46 In general, I have argued in this chapter that matter undergoes change insofar as it is matter. Here I am making a slightly different claim: that something (in this case the elements) is matter insofar as it undergoes a change. The point is that matter is what (properly speaking) undergoes any given change, just as the efficient cause is what (properly speaking) produces any given change. The elements can undergo a transformation into one another and Aristotle thinks there must be something in virtue of which they are able to do so. Given this, the elements must be able to be considered as matter, since they can undergo change and it is precisely in virtue of being matter that something can do this.

47 Vetter 2015 defends a stronger claim in contemporary metaphysics, that potentiality is a 'primitive or basic notion' that is not reduced to anything else (see, e.g., the introduction, 2–3). I am only claiming that it is reasonable to think of the most basic potentialities as not reducible to anything else.

5   From Craft to Nature: The Emergence of Natural Teleology

Thomas Kjeller Johansen

A teleological explanation is an explanation in terms of an end or a purpose. So saying that 'X came about for the sake of Y' is a teleological account of X. It is a striking feature of ancient Greek philosophy that many thinkers accepted that the world should be explained in this way. However, before Aristotle, teleological explanations of the cosmos were generally based on the idea that it had been created by a divine intelligence. If an intelligent power made the world, then it makes sense that it did so with a purpose in mind, so grasping this purpose will help us understand the world. This is the pattern of teleological explanation that we find in the Presocratics and in Plato. However, with Aristotle teleology underwent a change: instead of thinking that the ends were explanatory because a mind had sought to bring them about, Aristotle took the ends to operate in natural beings independently of the efforts of any creative intelligence. Indeed, he thought that his predecessors had failed to understand what was distinctive of nature, namely, that its ends work from the inside of natural beings themselves.

In this chapter I consider how Aristotle negotiates this shift from 'unnatural' to 'natural' teleology.[1] It has sometimes been suggested that Aristotle ceased to consider 'unnatural' teleology proper teleology at all,[2] or that he saw the differences as so important that only a relatively weak or insignificant analogy remained between craft and natural teleology.[3] I want to argue against such views. Aristotle inherited from Plato's cosmology a particular model of craft, which is key to understanding his natural teleology.[4] And it is only by understanding this inheritance that we can assess the extent to which Aristotle's natural teleology represents a genuine innovation.

THREE EARLY TELEOLOGISTS

Before Aristotle, teleological explanations were generally offered in the context of intelligent causes. As David Sedley has shown,[5] such teleological explanation is more widespread in the Presocratics than has been commonly thought. Let me give three brief examples. Anaxagoras said that reason (*nous*) organised and governed the cosmos. Plato and Aristotle criticised him for failing to show how reason worked for the sake of the good,[6] and for relying instead on material processes, centrifugal motions, and the like, to explain the world order. However, a failure to provide proper teleological accounts does not mean not attempting to give a teleological account. Indeed, Aristotle accepts that Anaxagoras was trying to provide a teleological account.[7] Moreover, behind Aristotle's criticism lies a distinctive and demanding conception of teleological explanation: it should not just be shown that the good occurs as a result of a certain process, or that the process generally brings about this good outcome, nor again should it merely be shown that the good causes the outcome through this process; it should also be shown how the good *as good* directs the process. It is therefore not enough for a teleological account to say that *nous* causes a good result: we need also to understand in what way the result was good such that *nous* chose to bring it about.[8]

There is some evidence that Anaxagoras did indicate how the material processes work for the best. *Nous*, he tells us, works by first separating out the various elements in the original mixture of all elements. Here the planets were formed as rocks hurled out towards the extremities of the world. This world-order also serves as a background for the creation of plants and animals. So, according to Sedley, '*Nous* is a farmer. Its creation of worlds is its way of setting up environments which enable seeds to germinate with plant and animal life the outcome.'[9] Anaxagoras may have relied on the agricultural model to suggest that *nous* operates teleologically by the processes familiar to most of us from working the land: tilling, weeding, watering, and so on, are clearly all processes informed by the good of plant growth. We would then understand the processes of nature as teleologically directed towards the variety of lifeforms we see around us. This brings us back to the importance of craft as a model of teleological causation. Farming is a craft, one which, more than some other crafts, works by facilitating processes that nature already initiates; nonetheless, its procedures are clearly regulated by the farmer's idea of the good.

After Anaxagoras, Empedocles explained the cosmos in terms of two forces, Love and Strife. They were responsible respectively for the coming together and separation of the four basic elements. At different times Love or Strife dominated. Several fine works are ascribed to Love. Since Love caused them it is reasonable to think that they are fine because Love wanted them to be so.[10] We see in the case of the eye how Love or Aphrodite fashioned the eye like a lantern illuminating man's surroundings at night allowing him to see (fragments 84, 86). It is plausible to see Love in such contexts as operating like a craftsman seeking to produce the best possible product. Fragment 24 makes the point explicit, comparing the cause of living beings to a painter:

> As when painters decorate offerings,
> men well trained by wisdom in their craft,
> who when they grasp colourful chemicals with their hands,
> mixing them in combination, some more, some less,
> from them provide forms like to all things,
> creating trees, men, women,
> beasts, fowls, water-nourished fish,
> and long-lived gods foremost in honours.
>
> (Empedocles fr. 24, trans. D. Graham)

The emphasis is on the variety and adaptation of living creatures ('water-nourished', 'long-lived'). The parallel is with the well-trained craftsman who knows what he is doing, and is able to produce a variety of colours of beauty and value, such as offerings to the gods, while the craftsman of nature mixes the elements to produce beings that are 'foremost in honour'. Clearly in both cases the value of the outcome directs the production.

Finally, the less obvious instance of Parmenides' cosmology.[11] In the first part of his poem, the so-called way of truth, a goddess describes being as changeless and unitary. Nonetheless, in the second part, the 'way of opinion', she accounts for the cosmos as subject to plurality and change. Clearly the way of opinion is cognitively inferior to that of the truth, though it may still have some credibility. In his cosmology Parmenides in fragment 12, lines 3–4 refers to a goddess (daimôn) in the middle of the cosmic rings, 'who governs (kubernai) all things: for everywhere she rules over hateful birth and mixture'. The language suggests an organising god. Again in fragment 13 the goddess is said to have 'devised' Erôs.[12] It would be the cosmic goddess's intellectual efforts, then, which are the cause of the cosmic order. Parmenides' word for this order is *diakosmos* (fragment 8.60), which implies a *proper* arrangement. So here too, it seems, we find a teleological cosmology premised on a deity who deliberates about how to make the best world.

PLATO

The sampling of three Presocratics has shown that teleological accounts were on offer prior to Plato and Aristotle and that they were cast in terms of an ordering intelligence, even craftsmanship. However, while the Presocratics used notions related to craft to explain the cosmos, they did not articulate what kind of cause a craftsman is or why it is appropriate to invoke crafts when explaining the cosmos. In the absence of any explicit theory of what it is to be a cause, this is hardly surprising. It falls instead to Plato to offer the first such theory, most clearly in his *Timaeus*.

The cosmology of the *Timaeus* is based on the premise that the cosmos was caused by a divine craftsman (*dēmiourgos*).[13] The craftsman is referred to as what is responsible for the cosmos. A distinction, however, is observed between what is responsible (*aitios*) and his cause or reason (*aitia*) for creating the cosmos.[14] The cause is god's wish to make everything as like himself as possible, which Timaeus rephrases as his wish for all things to be as good as possible, a paraphrase that follows naturally from his claim that god is all good. This cause combines two elements: a wish, which one might understand as a rational desire or desire of reason, with an object clause that specifies what the desire is for. It is the good-as-desired-by-an-intelligence, then, that works as the cause (*aitia*) of the cosmos. Later Timaeus will refer to this cause as the intelligent cause (46d8).

It is no surprise that god as a craftsman should want to make the world as good as possible. As Socrates argued in *Republic* 1 (341c–342e), the craftsman, as such, works for the best of his subject. The craftsman, then, is the kind of cause which makes things for the good.[15] Like other craftsmen, the demiurge works with materials, which he shapes to make as fine as possible. Also characteristically, the craftsman does not work to make just a part of his product fine, but strives to make all of it an ordered whole.[16]

In these respects, Plato's cosmic craftsman does not seem to differ significantly from Anaxagoras' *nous*, or Parmenides' cosmic goddess: they too were the cause of a *diakosmos*, a well-ordered whole. However, there are two other features of Plato's craftsman, which have no precedent in Presocratic philosophy, and which fundamentally shape his, and, as we shall see, Aristotle's, conception of cosmology. The first of these is that a proper craftsman looks to a model, which is an eternal character or form.[17] Thus Timaeus argues (29a) that the cosmic craftsman clearly must have looked to an eternal rather than a perceptible paradigm. Given the imperfections of the perceptible, only an eternal paradigm will make the product as good as possible. It is highly likely that Plato's notion of forms was inspired by Parmenides' description of being as eternal, changeless, and one, as we saw, but there was no clear suggestion in Parmenides that such being served as a model for whoever made the cosmos. Plato, then, is basing his notion of a craft on a distinctive and novel theory of reality, whereby there are eternal forms which craftsmen look to as the model.

The demiurge's wish to make the world as good as possible is its cause, and his strategy for making it so is likening it to the forms. However, the world is a product not just of divine intentions, but also of 'Necessity', which reason persuaded to work for good ends (47e–48a). 'Necessity' represents the processes and attributes that arise necessarily from the constitution of the simple bodies and their compounds. Timaeus refers to this necessity as the 'wandering cause' (48a7) since these processes and attributes are untrammelled by the goals or direction of reason. Still, the processes may be *used* by reason for such ends, and if so they acquire the status of 'contributory cause' (*sunaition*). The account of vision illustrates the point. Vision involves fire issuing from the eyes, meeting with daylight, forming thereby a 'visual ray', along which qualities of the sense-objects are transmitted through the body to the soul. These material processes are employed by vision, but they are not the reason why we have eyes:

> All these are among the contributory causes which god uses as
> servants in shaping things in the best way possible. But they are
> thought of by most people not as contributory causes but as causes
> of everything, achieving their effects by heat and cold, solidification
> and liquefaction, and the like. Yet they are completely incapable
> of having reason or intelligence; for the only existing thing which
> properly possesses intelligence we must call soul, and soul is
> invisible, whereas fire, water, earth and air have all come into being
> as all visible bodies. So the lover of intelligence and knowledge is
> bound to investigate, first, causes of a rational nature, and, second,

those causes that occur when things that are moved by some things of necessity move other things. Our procedure must be the same. We must deal with causes of both sorts, distinguishing those that with intelligence are craftsmen of what is beautiful and good from those which when deprived of wisdom on each occasion bring about a random disordered result.

What makes this passage crucial in the history of teleological thought is the notion of a contributory cause. One way of bringing this innovation into focus is to compare Socrates' treatment of causes and their necessary conditions in the *Phaedo* (98b–99c). Here Socrates insisted on the distinction between a proper cause (*aitia*), which would show why a certain feature was good, and that without which the cause would not be a cause. Socrates' example was the account of his sitting in prison. The cause was his thought that it was better for him to stay and face his punishment than to run away; the necessary conditions of his doing so were the workings of his legs, bones, sinews, etc. One might construe the notion of a necessary condition in two ways. One is as a mere necessary condition. In this sense there are innumerable necessary conditions of Socrates' sitting in prison which are not specifically conditions of this outcome rather than many others, e.g. the law of gravity or the presence of oxygen. But there are also conditions that are more directly linked to the *explanandum*. One might perhaps think that legs, bones, and sinews were picked out by Socrates because of their relevance to sitting. But Socrates points out that these same limbs would have been on their way to Megara had it not been for his wish to stay. This comment includes the limbs amongst those mechanisms, like heating or cooling, being added or taken away, that fail as causes because they could equally well bring about opposite results.[18] There seems therefore to be no particular explanatory link for Socrates between the necessary conditions and the proper cause: they seem rather to be mere necessary conditions.

Socrates said in the *Phaedo* that he had to abandon his search for real causes. When Plato returns to the creation of the cosmos in the *Timaeus*, the situation has changed. The key factor in this change is the introduction of the craftsmanship model. In the *Phaedo* there was no indication that the *nous* Socrates hoped for was going to work specifically as a *craftsman*; the notion of 'steering' (*diakubernan*) or ordering the cosmos was vague enough to allow for any directive action. Nor, relatedly, was there any indication how certain necessary conditions could be understood as instrumental in specifically bringing about certain good outcomes. We may indeed take Plato's and Aristotle's complaint that Anaxagoras failed to use his *nous*, referring instead just to blind material processes, as a reflection on the explanatory disconnect between a cause working for a good and the processes supposed to produce this good. This is exactly the sort of connection that is established by showing how certain processes are *instrumental* in producing the good. Necessary processes now become integrated into an overall causal story dictated by the good they serve. Craft provides such an integrated causal account. The craftsperson starts from a conception of the product they want to fashion and then reasons about the specific processes, materials, and tools that will help them bring it about. With the craft model comes, then, a form of explanation whereby causes are ordered as either directive ends or instrumental causes specifically contributing to such ends.[19] This model mends the shortcoming that Socrates saw in Anaxagoras.

Viewing material processes as contributing causes in this sense opens up another notion of necessity, what we might call 'conditional' or, with Aristotle, 'hypothetical necessity'. The thought is that certain features are necessary *if* there is going to be a certain end. One might initially hesitate to attribute to Plato this notion of hypothetical necessity. There is after all a difference between invoking necessary processes that serve an end, and considering those processes as necessary *because* they serve the end. Only the second counts as hypothetical necessity. There are several places, however, where Timaeus uses the notion of 'necessary for an end'. So at 41c the demiurge bids the assistant gods to create 'every kind of living creature which it must have *if it is* to be sufficiently complete'. Again he says of the human souls that they are embodied 'by necessity' (42a), which again must refer to the necessity of god's plan for the cosmos. The processes of vision involved irrational necessity, but they are also necessary for the end of vision: 'For I reckon that sight has become the cause of the greatest benefit to us in that not a word of all that is being said now about the universe would ever have been said *if we had not seen* stars and sun and heaven' (47a). In a similar vein, Timaeus presents pleasure and pain as a necessary consequence of the soul's embodiment (69c–d), but then also says that feeding the appetitive soul is 'necessary, *if mortals were to exist* at all' (70e5). There are, then, bodily processes that may be necessary in their own right, but are also necessary if certain divine ends are to be.[20]

It is not just the *Timaeus* that draws this nexus between contributory causes and conditional necessity. In the *Statesman* the Eleatic Visitor explains the notion of a contributory cause in terms of hypothetical necessity:

> Visitor: 'Well then, let's look at two sorts of expertise that are in relation to all the things that people do.' Young Socrates: 'Which are they?' V: 'One which is a contributory cause of production, one which is itself a cause.' YS: 'How so?' V: 'Those which do not make the thing itself, but which provide tools for those that do – tools which, if they were not present, what has been assigned to each expertise would never be accomplished.'
>
> (Pl. *Plt.* 281d–e, trans. C. Rowe)

Again the contributing cause is not a mere necessary condition. It is that of a tool required for a specific job. As Socrates says at *Cratylus* 389b–c, there is a tool that is naturally suited to each kind of function, e.g. a shuttle that is suited to each kind of weaving, and each tool must be made to suit each function. So we should understand contributing causes as necessary for the realisation of a *specific* end. A craftsperson after all chooses the instruments and materials required for a specific job; the weaver will worry about the appropriateness of his shuttle, the blacksmith about the hardness of her drill; it is not their brief to put in place the law of gravity, the light of day, the hardness of wood, or the softness of wax, or any of the umpteen general conditions that are equally necessary for their activity and many others. So if the processes invoked as contributory causes are those that serve specifically as instruments for the craftsperson, we should expect them to include not all necessary conditions, but just those that are specific to the job in hand. Of course, if you are a *cosmic* craftsman these tasks are many, but the point remains.

While previous philosophers too had seen the world as the well-ordered product of a designing intelligence and craftsman, Plato refigured the notion of craftsmanship involved in two crucial ways: (1) the production aimed to imitate an eternal form and the product was good to the extent that it was like this form, and (2) the materials and processes used in the production were understood as contributing causes specifically geared to bringing about this good and as hypothetically necessary for it. While these two features were for Plato aspects of craftsmanship, we shall see that they will be reworked as key aspects also of Aristotle's *natural* teleology.

ARISTOTLE

The Priority of Form

It is no accident that Aristotle's natural philosophy frequently refers to craft. He is writing in an Academic context, in which *the* model of teleological causation is that of craft, understood Platonically, as we have seen. He also in important ways followed it as his model for natural teleology.

In *Physics* 2, Aristotle argues that nature is said in the sense of both matter and form. He uses the analogy with craft to characterise the relationship between matter and form in natural beings. Natural beings are like artefacts in that the form is prior to the matter. For just as we say that a chunk of wood is not a bed unless it has the form of a bed, so we do not say that some matter has the nature of bone or flesh until it has the form of bone or flesh.[21] On this point he relies on a basically Platonic conception of form. The form is the object of definition, expressing the essence of this kind of thing, and the material thing qualifies as being this kind of thing only insofar as it possesses the form.

Like Plato, Aristotle understands the craftsman as thinking about this changeless, universal form. It is this form that is defined by the craft. The definition (*logos*) gives the craftsman the basic information required to bring about the product.[22] So the doctor understands what health is, its essence or form. Having this form in her mind, she is then able to realise the form in the matter. The artefact comes to be like the form the craftsman had in mind. Aristotle takes the form to be the same in all particular artefacts of a kind, as artefacts of this kind. True, all houses need not be the same – they will differ in shape, orientation, materials, colour, and so on – but they will all share certain basic features, a structure, that defines what it is to be house. The craftsman as such is viewed as the conveyer of this invariable and universal form.

In *Metaphysics* 7.7 Aristotle is concerned to show that all kinds of coming-into-being presuppose a form that is already present. There are some tricky cases of so-called spontaneous generation, say maggots suddenly appearing in food, or abnormal progeny, e.g. mules born of horses. But generally we observe that a living being is generated by a mature member of the same kind: 'man generates man' is Aristotle's motto. In artistic production, in contrast, the craftsman is not of the same kind: a man makes a house, not another man. However, the form of the house, as we saw, is already realised in the craftsman's soul in virtue of his craft. It is this form that is conveyed by the craftsman to the building materials. *Qua builder*, then, but not *qua* human, man does generate something of his own kind.

The point relates to the central difference between craft and nature: in nature the moving or efficient cause is internal to the product, in craft it is external.[23] In nature we see the same kind of thing developing into actuality by its own agency: a child grows into an adult by itself. The environment merely facilitates the natural tendency of the child to grow up. The form is already present in the matter sufficiently to propel the child to adulthood, if nothing interferes. The matter of artefacts does not generally have such tendencies: their form needs to be imposed from the outside by a craftsperson. Still, even on this point of a fundamental contrast, Aristotle does not abandon the craft analogy. For there is a special case of craft which illustrates the way nature works from within, namely, a doctor healing himself. Here too the moving cause of health is internal to the patient. To be sure, in this special case the doctor only happens to be the same as the patient – doctors mostly cure other people than themselves – while in nature agent and patient, what undergoes the change, are essentially the same. Still, the way the moving cause is present in the patient is sufficiently similar for the craft case to be illuminating.

The prior presence of form in the craftsman helps Aristotle explain natural generation in further ways. So it allows him to show what comes into being and what does not. Neither the form nor the matter is generated, he argues, only the particular composite. Consider the production of a bronze sphere. The matter, the bronze, the craftsman finds in nature, but the form too pre-exists the particular bronze sphere. For this is the universal form of sphere, and no craftsman makes what it is to be a sphere. What the craftsman does, having availed himself of the bronze and having understood what a sphere is, is to implement this form in this matter, to make this particular bronze sphere. Similarly, in nature something that already has the form of man, the universal form of human being, informs some matter. The father transmits the human form to the matter, which Aristotle explains in the *Generation of Animals* is the contribution of the female. Out of these two, this particular human being is generated.

The conception of form that allows Aristotle to establish this parity between craft and nature is again the Platonic one of a changeless, invariable form expressed in a definition. True, Aristotle also takes a swipe in *Metaph.* 7.7 at Plato for his claim that the forms are separate from the particulars they help bring about. However, this is a point worth making for Aristotle, exactly because the analogy between craft and nature has shown that the form pre-exists any particular composite created from the form. If the form pre-exists any of the particulars it helps bring about, could it not, then, also exist separately from *all* of these particulars? The answer for Aristotle, against Plato, is a 'no'. What Plato misses is the proper conception of the efficient cause: the efficient cause is a particular entity, explaining why a particular change happens on a particular occasion. If the form is to act as an efficient cause, it needs to exist as a feature of a particular. Again, 'man generates man' in the sense that a particular instance of the form generates another instance of the same form. If the form existed separately from all particulars, it could never act in this way.

Final Causation in Craft and Nature

We have seen Aristotle use the craft analogy to establish the priority of form over matter in two ways: it takes priority over the matter in the definition of what the thing is and it takes priority temporally in the generation of the thing. We shall now see how he exploits the craft analogy also to present a notion of form as function, a notion which in turn allows him to shed further light on the priority in definition of form over matter.

Of Aristotle's four causes we have already encountered three: the formal, the material, and the moving cause. However, teleology is above all about the fourth, the final cause, the end, 'that for the sake of which'. Natural beings are determined by their formal cause, as we saw. But if we ask what their form is, the most proper answer is generally their end. This end, in turn, Aristotle takes to be their proper function, that is, their ability to act or be acted on in certain ways. So what a certain living being is, for example, is primarily understood by its distinctive abilities to act and suffer in various ways. The functional understanding of the form is typical of natural beings, and contrasts, for example, with the way mathematical objects are defined. But it is not unique to them: artefacts too are defined by their function, a house by its providing shelter, a saw by cutting, or an axe by chopping. Again Aristotle uses this fact about artefacts to explain the role of function in natural beings. So in *De anima* 2.1 he argues that the soul is the form and actuality of the living body, and illustrates this view by analogy with an artefact. He says that the soul is the essence of a living body, just as the being of an axe is its ability to cut. This functional understanding of the soul allows Aristotle to understand the body as what has the ability to engage in these functions. So an eye, say, without the ability to see would be an eye in name only ('homonymously' is Aristotle's word, 412b21), just as an axe without the ability to cut is no real axe.

It is far from obvious what complex natural beings are for. Artefacts, in contrast, are typically designed with a simple function in mind. The craft analogies invite us to think in the same way about natural beings. So asking what a snail is, for example, the craft analogy shifts our attention away from a vast range of facts about it – what it is made of, what sort of shape or colour it has, its uses in cooking or medicine, etc. – to what the snail does, e.g. moving and perceiving in very specific ways. The craft analogy helps us focus on identifying the proper function of a natural being as our starting point for understanding other facts about it – how it is composed, how it is generated, grows up, feeds, and so on.

More particularly, the craft analogy helps us identify the proper function by directing us to a hierarchy of functions. For the crafts are organised hierarchically, some crafts helping realise the ends of others. So, in the example of the *Statesman*, the art of carting is subservient to the art of weaving, or in the *Euthydemus* (290b–c), the art of fishing serves the art of cooking, in both cases because the latter art knows how to use the products of the former. In *Nicomachean Ethics* 1.1–2 Aristotle argues on the analogy of the crafts, that human beings too pursue some ends as means to further ends which lead to a single end as the highest good. Approaching natural functions in this way directs us to a few structuring or architectonic functions as the most important, with other functions sub-serving them in various ways and at various removes. So the functions of living beings are hierarchically ordered: in animals, for example, nutrition serves perception, while in humans both are subservient to reason. The biological works show that there will typically not be a single function characterising one kind of living being. Animals typically display a range of irreducible differentiae, e.g. a dog is both viviparous, blooded, and four-footed. But many functions may still be seen as serving a few such characteristic functions.

Hypothetical Necessity

We have seen that Aristotle uses the craft analogy to express how the final cause works so as to structure the development, parts, and activities of natural beings. In *Ph.* 2.8 he argues for the primacy of final causation against certain opponents who took natural beings as necessarily arising from the hot and the cold and such material elements. Aristotle's reference to these opponents closely mirrors Plato's in the *Timaeus* 46c–e: those thinkers who take everything to arise by necessity, e.g. through the heating and cooling of bodies. Through the example of rainfall, which works exactly in terms of heating and cooling (198b16–21), Aristotle argues that proponents of necessity cannot explain the regularity with which good outcomes happen in nature. To explain that we need to assume that natural processes happen *for the sake* of the good.[24]

Having established that nature works as final cause,[25] Aristotle in *Ph.* 2.9 wants to show how properly to understand necessity in those cases where final causation operates. Examples from craft show that the opponents' notion of necessity is inadequate in dealing with phenomena that are teleologically explained. Take the case of a wall. If the opponents were to explain a wall the way they explain natural beings, they would have to do so by reference to the natures of each of the constitutive materials: stone sits at the bottom of the wall because of its weight, the somewhat lighter earth settles further up, and the lightest wooden planks rise to the top. However, as Aristotle points out, the wall has come about for the sake of shelter, and while it is true that it could not come about without stone, earth, and wood, or materials with such properties, the reason why the materials are there is to serve the function of a wall, protecting property and people. The opponents talk as if the materials necessitate a wall, but the materials are there in the first place only because of the final cause. The materials are there only because there is going to be a wall, so it is the wall that necessitates the presence of the materials rather than the other way around. It is this conditional dependence of the matter on the final cause that Aristotle refers to as hypothetical necessity. His term 'necessity *from* hypothesis' brings out the direction of dependence: 'if E(end), then necessarily M(matter)'. Contrast the materialist's 'if M then necessarily E'.

Aristotle generalises from the example of the wall to other cases of final causation and offers the further illustration of the saw (200a7–13). In the argument of 2.9 there is no attempt to justify the applicability of hypothetical necessity to nature in particular. Examples from craft, a wall, a saw, a house, carry the entire weight of the argument. This does not in itself weaken the argument, since Aristotle's aim is to show that where there is final causation, we need to understand the sort of necessity that attaches to the materials primarily as hypothetical rather than the necessitation by matter relied on by the opponents. To be clear: this is not to say that Aristotle denies necessitation by matter – fire does heat of its own accord, stones do fall down – only that where good ends are generally achieved, in craft as in nature, the necessity that explains how these ends come about is primarily hypothetical. Since we already know from the previous chapter that final causation does operate in both nature and craft, we can assume that if hypothetical necessity applies to craft insofar as craft displays final causation, then it will also apply to final causation in nature. However, if one did not accept the generalisation that final causation equally operates in craft and in nature, because one thought, for example, that craft only offered some weak analogue or metaphor for nature, then it is much harder to see how the argument of *Ph.* 2.9 could work.

In *Metaphys.* 5.5 Aristotle explicates the notion of hypothetical necessity in terms of a contributory cause, *sunaition*. His examples of a contributory cause are food (as in *Timaeus* 70e5), something without which one cannot exist, as well as other things which are necessary for the realisation of one's good. This notion of the necessary as necessary for an end contrasts (as in the *Physics*) with what is necessary in the sense of what is compulsory, since it has to do with what is necessary given a certain end, living or the good, as it may be.[26] The notion of a contributory cause is then a way of explicating the conception of hypothetical necessity.

We have already observed the Platonic template for the term *sunaition*. In the *Timaeus* the term applied specifically to necessary processes insofar as they were persuaded to contribute to the intelligent *aitia*. We also noted how Plato viewed such processes as necessary *if* a certain good end was to be. This link between contributory cause and conditional necessity was a particular feature of the craft model by which he explained the cosmos. Aristotle appears to have applied the model to nature, without fundamental changes, to explain how form hypothetically necessitates matter.

One might well wonder why, if Plato already offered teleological explanations in terms of functional ends and hypothetical necessity, Aristotle criticises Plato for having failed to use the final cause.[27] This is a complex issue, but it is worth pointing out that Plato often presents ends as good or beautiful, not because of their function, but because of their mathematical structure. So, for example, in the *Timaeus* he explains the beauty of the primary bodies in terms of their geometrical properties (54a).[28] If we recall that Aristotle contrasts mathematical objects with natural ones exactly on the point that their form is not functional – mathematical objects do not initiate or undergo change – we may understand why Aristotle does not think that Plato is generally clear about the proper use of final causes in nature, even if he sometimes, as we have seen, does give proper weight to the functional aspect of ends.[29] The problem may be exacerbated by Plato's understanding of the highest form, the Form of the Good, as the One: if the highest good of all things for Plato is a mathematical entity, as Aristotle seems to think, then it will not be a function of the sort that through hypothetical necessity can explain purposeful *change* in the natural world.

Two Differences between Craft and Natural Teleology: How Important Are They?

I have focused on points where Aristotle's teleology was influenced by Plato's conception of craft. I shall now look at three differences which have persuaded some scholars that Aristotle could only have intended a weak analogy between the teleologies of craft and nature.

First of all, one might think that artificial teleology importantly differs from natural teleology in that it involves *consciousness* of the end. So David Charles has argued that it is a major unclarity in Aristotle's account of nature in *Ph.* 2.8–9 that it does not distinguish clearly between what Charles calls the 'agency' and the 'nature' model of final causation.[30] The difference is that the agents are sensitive to changing circumstances and so are able to adapt their behaviour to achieve the goal in other ways. It may be that a conscious agent can track changes relevant to the goodness of an end, whereas a non-conscious agent will be locked into a pattern of behaviour that is blind to environmental variation. This point might apply equally to any intermediary ends.

Aristotle is indeed explicit at *Ph.* 195a26 that it does not matter if the good is the good itself or the apparent good when we say that that for the sake of which is the good and the end of the other things. So it seems he does not think that the sensitivity aspect of conscious agency is important to articulating what a final cause basically is. And this may have been a mistake, if we are concerned about assimilating conscious agency in general to natural teleology. However, in the specific case of conscious agency that is craft, Aristotle's assimilation can be justified, at least given his Platonic view of craft. As Sarah Broadie has argued, behind Aristotle's analogy between craft and nature is a tendency to de-psychologise craft.[31] We have seen that craft aims to realise a universal, changeless form. No variation in terms of the basic conception of what constitutes a good house is therefore to be expected. Craft differs markedly from other kinds of practical wisdom in this respect since there is no similar general conception of what constitutes, say, a generous action, the way there is a general account of health or a house. But this point extends also to a difference in the way craftspeople and other practical agents think about the way to realise their aim. Aristotle says that craft does not deliberate.[32] I take his point to be that while craftspeople may in various circumstances deliberate about how to apply their craft, the methods of production are laid down by the craft and are not themselves deliberated about. So a baker will not normally deliberate about how to make bread, though she may deliberate about how much longer to let the dough rise if it is a particularly cold day, and so on. As one might say, part of the point of knowing the craft is that you do not normally have to think out such basics: the better you are at your metier, the less you have to think about it. Whereas the practically wise (the *phronimos*) is somebody who stands out by their grasp of the particulars of the ethical situation and their ability to reason correctly about how to bring about the good given these particular circumstances, the craftsperson is distinguished simply by their ability to reproduce the universal form.[33] Deliberation is not characteristic of the exercise of craft as such.

In *Physics* 2.8 (199a9–19) Aristotle stresses the ordered sequence of steps in natural generation by analogy with the crafts. If a house, he says, had come about by nature, it would have come about in the same way as it does by craft. Since natural beings generally come about in the same way, Aristotle must be presupposing that craft is no more subject to individual variation, and he must be presupposing this as a generally recognisable feature of craft. In nature as in craft, the same form is produced by the same regular steps. And it is because craft like nature always proceeds in such ordered stages towards the same kind of end that Aristotle can conceive of craft as *completing* the natural process as a further step in the same series.

Second, Aristotle says that ends are realised last in the processes of which they are the final cause. But in conscious agency the end causes the action as an object of desire which precedes the action. But if so, it seems that ends in conscious action cannot provide proper teleological explanation. Now again this kind of objection, whatever validity it may have in relation to other kinds of agency, fails in the case of craft. Aristotle's analogy between craft and nature is not one about individual craftspeople and natural beings, but between craft and nature, and the end of craft most certainly is the finished product, not the finished product as represented to some craftsperson or other.

Third, Aristotle draws a distinction between two kinds of final cause: the objective and the beneficiary. The classic example is medicine, whose objective is health and beneficiary the patient.[34] Now generally in craft it may seem that the good in the sense of the beneficiary is external to the thing in which the objective is realised. Flautists benefit from flutes, residents from houses, riders from bridles. The beneficiary of natural processes in contrast seems primarily to be the natural being itself.[35] Oak trees benefit from the growth of leaves and roots and so on. We may therefore think that the craft analogy goes against the proper conception of good ends as internal to natural beings. However, as the example of medicine shows, sometimes in craft the beneficiary, the patient, is also that in whom the objective, health, is realised. We might say that the sameness of beneficiary and objective is a contingent feature in craft but a necessary one in nature.[36]

Also on this point Plato prepared the way. Recall Timaeus' explanation of the eyes. The cause (*aitia*) of the eyes reflected god's plan for the cosmos, helping us to become more rational by observing the heavens. Yet the purpose of the eyes is also internal to us: *we* use our eyes in observing the heavens and correcting *our own* reason. So the objective of the eyes is realised in us as their beneficiaries. Generally, though our bodies have an external provenance in god, and serve to fulfil his cosmic plan, they are not the mere instruments of some external user, but integral features of us as human beings, which we use to achieve our own ends. Even if our eyes had not been given us by god, we could still have used them to become better human beings, and so have realised their purpose. To accept this counterfactual is already to begin to see the world through Aristotle's eyes.

NOTES

1 I borrow here the terms from Lennox 1985. The term 'unnatural' is used from Aristotle's viewpoint. There should be no implication that his predecessors saw their explanations as other than natural. See, for example, Plato's *Leg.* 10 (889b–d)

for the view that it is intelligent soul that moves the cosmos that primarily counts as nature.

2 See Johnson 2005, 127: 'Plato's prioritization of art over nature, and his specification of the cause for the sake of which with reference to the whole universe, and not with reference to its individuals or natural kinds, means that he did not employ the notion of the for the sake of which as a cause – i.e. in a causal explanation.'

3 See Cooper 1982, 198, n. 2: 'one must reject the suggestion that is sometimes made that this analogy [sc. between art and nature] is central and fundamental to Aristotelian natural teleology'.

4 I am in full agreement with Sedley 2010 *that* Plato's theory of cosmic craftsmanship fundamentally shaped Aristotle's teleology, though my argument here differs in terms of how.

5 Sedley 2009.

6 Pl. *Phd.* 97d–98d; Arist., *Metaph.* 985a18–21.

7 Arist. *Metaph.* 984b19–20.

8 Not all teleological explanations need share this feature: teleological accounts have sometimes been understood historically or etiologically; see Wright 1973, 154–68. On such a theory, we need not assume that the good of the organism directed the development of the feature, though it is true to say today that the organism has the feature because it is good for it (helps it survive).

9 Sedley 2007, 23.

10 Of course, one should not assume that Love works for the good: *erôs* can notoriously be destructive. However, Empedocles' epithet 'blameless' (*philotêtos amempheos*, frag. 35, l. 13) suggests a kinder power.

11 It does not escape Sedley 2007, 8.

12 Parmenides uses the word *mêtisato*. According to Detienne and Vernant 1974, *mêtis* involves 'la délibération en vue d'un bien'.

13 See Johansen 2016.

14 'Now, let us state the reason (*aitia*) why becoming and this universe were framed by him who framed it. He was good, and what is good never has any particle of envy in it whatsoever; and being without envy he wished all things to be as like himself as possible. This indeed is the most proper principle of becoming and the cosmos and as it comes from wise men one would be absolutely right to accept it.' Translations of the *Timaeus* from Lee 2008. On the distinction between *aitios* and *aitia*, see Frede 1987.

15 Why having shown that the cause (*aitios*) is a craftsman, does Timaeus then have to ask a further question about what his reason (*aitia*) was? Because not all craftsmen act as proper craftsmen: a doctor may kill or cure, depending on the goodness of his character. Timaeus answers therefore: god was all good and only wanted the good, so he chose to work for the proper end of craft.

16 See 'if we compare whole for whole' (*Ti.* 30b); cf. *Leg.* 10.900c–905d.

17 See Pl. *Resp.* 10. Even if Timaeus at first suggests that he may have a choice; see Johansen 2015 for an attempt to explain why.

18 See Sedley 1998b, 122–3.

19 To see how calling mechanisms *sunaitia* is no small concession to their contribution to a causal explanation, see *Plt.* 281c–d, where the Eleatic Visitor argues that,

while weaving is the cause (*aitia*) of woolly clothing, those arts which produce the instruments of weaving all have a claim to being the *sunaitia*.

20 See also 68e–69a where Timaeus says that the divine cause cannot be understood or grasped without the necessary cause.

21 Arist. *Ph.* 193b7–12.

22 Arist. *Metaph.* 9.2.

23 Cf. *Gen. an.* 2.1.735a2–5.

24 See Judson 2005 for a persuasive reconstruction of the argument.

25 How the argument works, particularly whether it involves a cosmic or even anthropocentric teleology, is a matter of debate; for opposed views, see, e.g. Judson 2005; Sedley 2010.

26 Cf. *Part. an.* 1.1.642a9–13.

27 'In the same way those who say the One or Being is the good, say that is the cause of substance, but not that the substance either is or comes to be for the sake of this. Therefore it turns out that in a sense they both say and do not say the good is a cause; for they do not call it a cause *qua* good but only accidentally' (*Metaph.* 1.7.988b6–15, after revised Oxford translation).

28 See, however, *Timaeus* 87c for a good example of Timaeus linking geometrical properties with functional ones: the body requires a certain proportionality to functional well.

29 For an argument along these lines, see Johansen 2010.

30 Charles 1991. See, however, Charles 2012 for a revised interpretation.

31 Broadie 1987. She takes this to be a problem for Aristotle's use of craft, as if Aristotle's insistence on the art–nature analogy ends up distorting his view of craft. I take this view of craft rather to be a Platonic heritage which Aristotle agrees with and exploits to deliver his view of natural teleology.

32 *Ph.* 2.8.199b26–27. In favour of this reading, see Broadie 1987; against see Sedley 2010.

33 See Arist. *Nic. Eth.* 7.5.

34 See, e.g. Arist. *Ph.* 194a27–b8; Pl. *Resp.* 10.601d–e, *Euthyd.* 291c–d.

35 A passage in Arist. *Pol.* 1256b10–22 suggests that other living beings exist for the sake of man. How much weight to give to such evidence from outside the more authoritative context of the *Physics* is debated; see Sedley 1991 vs. Judson 2005. Generally, the question of anthropomorphic teleology is beyond the scope of this chapter.

36 This would parallel the contingent identity of the efficient cause with the patient in the crafts in cases like the doctor healing himself, noted above, and the essential identity of the two in natural beings.

6 Creationism in Antiquity

David Sedley

SCIENCE AND THEOLOGY

Natural teleology, associated above all with Aristotle, and dealt with in a separate chapter of this volume,[1] seeks to establish and elucidate the explanatory role of purposive structures and processes in the natural world, especially biological. Acorns exist for the sake of producing oak trees, eyelids for protecting the eyes. Natural teleology may or may not go on from there to seek the explanatory role of larger cosmic features, such as the shape and position of the earth. Much less does it need to ask – although it is not debarred from asking – the even bigger question, of how those structures and purposes came to be present in the first place. Thus it comes with no unavoidable theological implications.

That bigger question is, by contrast, the main concern of creationism,[2] the theological doctrine which, from the ubiquity of apparently purposive structures in the natural world, infers the existence of a divine creator, one whose own conscious, intelligent, and benevolent purposes have been embodied in those natural structures. Creationists need not differ from natural teleologists as to how the world and its occupants function. For example, they do not necessarily see in it the continuing presence of divine control. What they must add in order to deserve the title 'creationists' is a divine 'creator' – or, in Greek, more usually a 'craftsman' (*dēmiourgos*, anglicised as 'demiurge') – who consciously designed and built these cosmic and biological structures, typically extending from the sun's annual and daily orbits, via climates and environments, all the way down to the structures and life-cycles of the simplest organisms. However, much as in the Judaeo-Christian tradition, most of the Greek creationists paid especial attention to the divine crafting of human beings, widely regarded as the main intended products and beneficiaries of their creative act.

One might, on the basis of this contrast with natural teleology, expect creationism to be banished from any respectable book on the history of science. However, the fact is that a large part of the progress made in Greco-Roman science was achieved within a creationist framework. Take away the theology, and much of the science will go with it.

A striking example of this is Galen. The foremost medical authority of the ancient world (second century CE; see Chapter 2), in his monumental treatise *On the Usefulness of Parts*, Galen used his formidable knowledge of anatomy to demonstrate in minute detail the peerless genius of the divine creator.[3] One well-known example will suffice here: the precise number and formation of the bones in the human hand are, according to Galen's investigations, functionally perfect, without the slightest redundancy or improvability. On the basis of innumerable similar observations, Galen is able to conclude that human anatomy as a whole is unmistakably the product of a superior intelligence.

THE ATOMIST ALTERNATIVE

Galen was perfectly familiar with the rival theory of the Epicurean atomists, originating with Epicurus at the end of the fourth century BCE, but traceable back to Democritus, in the late fifth to early fourth century. The Epicureans objected to creationism on a variety of theological grounds. These were largely concerned with questioning why an already entirely happy divinity would set about creating a world, and, moreover, a world posing such glaring disadvantages for the human race, despite that race's being allegedly the prime beneficiary. But, alongside these negative arguments, the Epicureans set up their own alternative explanatory model of how seemingly purposive structures can arise by pure accident. This was based on the extraordinary power of infinity: an infinite stock of atoms randomly interacting over infinite space and time was bound at some point to form, quite accidentally, a world like ours. And in such a world, they argued, a fertile young earth was likely to generate numerous living beings, some of which could, again by pure accident, prove capable of surviving and reproducing their kind, while the remainder perished.

This partial anticipation of Darwinian natural selection has won admiration for the Epicureans, as well as for the fifth-century BCE philosopher-poet Empedocles, who had first spun the idea that present-day species are the fortuitously viable survivors of past extinctions. The fact remains that without any idea of gradual adaptation, they came nowhere near to accounting for the kind of anatomical fine detail that Galen was able to cite as testimony to divine craftsmanship. Hence in later antiquity, unlike today, it was creationism that occupied the intellectual high ground and was best supported by state-of-the-art research, especially in biology and astronomy. The Epicureans' materialistic alternative struggled to compete, while Aristotelianism, which had offered the compromise of natural teleology without a creator god,[4] was increasingly finding itself absorbed into Platonism.

SOCRATES

Galen provides an ideal viewpoint from which to look back on the history of creationism in ancient thought. Soon after his time, with the advent of Neoplatonism, philosophers' interest in divine craftsmanship was to be gradually eclipsed by a fundamentally metaphysical account of the world's causal origin as lying in procession from and return to a highest explanatory principle. But Galen himself is very much in tune with creationism's classical origins. Above all, he was an avid and admiring reader of Plato's *Timaeus*, the pivotal text of the present chapter, on which he wrote a now largely lost commentary, and to which we will turn shortly.

But before that, Galen has a surprise for us. The predecessor for whom he has the highest respect in such matters is not Plato but Socrates (*On the Doctrines of Hippocrates and Plato* 9.7.9–16). Socrates, he explains, as correctly represented by Xenophon's portrayal of him (especially *Memorabilia* 1.1, 1.4, 4.3),[5] did not waste time on speculative questions such as whether the world had a beginning, or how many worlds there are, but concentrated on attainable goods, a priority which Galen sees as the ultimate focus of his own medical work too. Socrates (469–399 BCE) is celebrated as the philosopher who turned philosophy from the study of the cosmos to questions about how to live one's life, but his seminal contribution to creationism has gone largely unrecognised. Without endorsing any cosmological theory, Socrates is portrayed by Xenophon as arguing for the existence of benevolent creator gods by direct appeal to the systematic design visible in our bodies and our environment. These are far too regular, he maintains, to be the outcome of mere accident.

That is not to say that there had been no teleological tendencies in earlier philosophers. The idea that organisms are the product of divine craft was already by Socrates' day well documented in the poetry of Empedocles, somewhat paradoxically, given that he also saw a role for natural selection. This idea of divine craftsmanship in fact had its ultimate roots in the early and revered poet Hesiod (ca. 700 BCE), who in his *Works and Days* had referred to a series of races, culminating in the human race, as products of divine creation, and in particular had described in some detail how the first woman, Pandora, was cunningly fashioned by the craftsman god Hephaestus, aided by an entire support team of other gods and goddesses. Nevertheless, in Socrates' hands divine craftsmanship came to be theorised to a considerably higher level than in those of any predecessor, in ways which would impact directly upon the teleology of Plato and, ultimately, of Aristotle too. What Socrates was, on Xenophon's evidence, the first to introduce was not divine creation as such, but the key idea that creation is a special benefaction bestowed by god on humankind.

For all its influence on later science, Socratic creationism is at root a religious rather than a scientific thesis. According to Socrates, the whole world, including lower animal species, has manifestly been created for human benefit. If the gods have done all this for us, we enjoy a unique relationship with them, one which we should express in religious devotion. This was in its day an importantly original intellectual stance. Indeed, it represents the dawn of religiously motivated creationism, a thesis that was thereafter to hold almost uncontested sway for well over two millennia, until Darwin's publication of *On the Origin of Species* in 1859.

In Socrates' eyes, the gods are not only our benefactors, but also the divine artisans who created our world and its contents, ourselves included. That the gods should do all this for us is not a matter of our mere good fortune. Gods are essentially good and beneficent, and we, as their primary beneficiaries, are linked to them by a unique bond. Study of the workings of nature is justified only to the extent that it confirms and deepens our understanding of the gods' goodness to us. True piety lies, not in uncovering the hidden structures of nature, but in appreciating the intentions and outcomes of divine creation, and thus reinforcing the special relationship that links humans to god.

This religious agenda undoubtedly helps explain why Socrates became the virtual inventor of the Argument from Design. 'Argument from Design' is a generic title for that family of arguments which seek to prove the existence of god, or more specifically of a provident god, by cataloguing the evidence for design in the world. Typically, these arguments seek to demonstrate the existence of divine craftsmanship by appealing to the most prestigious or intricate creative craft practised by man, and showing that gods' creative powers must be such as to dwarf their human counterparts.

As reported by Xenophon, Socrates' own version of the Argument from Design appealed to the expertise of representational artists, and especially sculptors. If you admire above all others an artist like Polyclitus, who can make such exquisite human figures of bronze, how much more must you revere whoever it was who made living, breathing human figures like us! And there must indeed be such a maker, Socrates adds, because the structures and attributes of human beings are far too consistently beneficial ones to have been the outcome of mere accident. Socrates' argument here centres on a detailed compilation of evidence for the beneficial purposes served by the construction of animal bodies. He cites, among many examples, the five senses, the provision of eyelids and lashes to protect the eye from damage, and the user-friendly arrangement of the teeth, with the front ones suitable for cutting food, the rear ones for grinding it. These were to become classic examples of teleology in the subsequent tradition, closely echoed by Aristotle in his physical and biological writings. Moreover, Socrates continues, the many benefactions with which human beings alone have been privileged, such as language, upright posture, and non-seasonal sex, not to mention the provision of numerous other species for us to ride, eat, etc., show that humankind alone is the ultimate beneficiary of divine creation.

PLATO AS CREATIONIST

Socrates, in Xenophon's portrayal, conducted such an appeal to the evidence of design without himself getting the least bit engaged in physical speculation about the underlying components or mechanisms. This abstention from physical theory was endorsed only by a minority of his philosophical heirs. Plato in his *Phaedo* (96a–99c) sought to circumvent it by reinterpreting its real meaning. It represented, according to his interpretation, not any disapproval of physics as such, but Socrates' recognition that he himself lacked the ability to pursue it in a properly teleological manner, a confession which he tempered with the express hope that he might learn this elusive teleological physics from others better equipped for it than himself. In his late dialogue, the *Timaeus*, Plato fulfilled this aspiration on Socrates' behalf, portraying the latter as an appreciative auditor of Timaeus' speech, in which just the right kind of teleological physics is finally worked out in detail. It should not escape notice that the gods of the *Timaeus* – a supreme deity, and beneath him a committee of secondary gods creating organic life – bear the strong imprint of Socrates' creationist theology as outlined in Xenophon's *Memorabilia* 1.4, with its ultimate roots in Hesiod's Pandora myth.

The *Timaeus* was Plato's most widely discussed and influential dialogue. Its readers were from the start divided between those who took Plato to be describing a literally datable act of divine world-creation, and those who took his creation narrative to be merely illustrative, comparable to a geometry lesson based on line-by-line construction of figures which never in fact came into existence in that way.

On the more 'literal', as well as more creationist, of the two readings, Timaeus asks whether the world had a beginning in time or has always existed, chooses the former option, and then reconstructs the likely motivation of its creator and the process by which he planned and built it. On the alternative reading, the creation story is a fiction devised to convey the world's dependence from infinite time past on a divine cause. One reason why in antiquity many of Plato's followers (though no one else, it seems) adopted this latter, 'sempiternalist' reading, was that Timaeus indisputably goes on to assert that the world will never end. The temporal asymmetry of a world with a beginning but with no end was widely felt, among Plato's critics and followers alike, to be conceptually intolerable. Another was that, according to Plato's creation narrative, time came into being only with the creation of the great celestial clock, and this would – self-contradictorily, it is alleged – place part of the creation process in a time before time![6] In reply, it has been pointed out, Timaeus warns that his creation narrative will unavoidably contain inconsistencies and inaccuracies, but that these simply reflect the limitations of human cognitive powers, and are therefore *not* a ground for dissatisfaction with it (29c–d; cf. 34b–35a).

Timaeus also conveys strong philosophical reasons for the temporal asymmetry, based partly on another of Plato's inheritances from Socrates, a very close consideration of the concept of craftsmanship. In positing that the world had a beginning, rather than having existed for infinite time past, he does not treat this as if it were part of a merely mythical narrative, but argues for it on metaphysical grounds (27d–28c): the world belongs to the realm of becoming, not that of being, and therefore must itself have 'become' in the sense of coming to exist. It is only after establishing this that he permits himself to ask about the craftsman who must now be assumed to have brought it into existence.

For example, like any good craftsman he must have focused his thought on the ideal Form of what he was trying to achieve, then embodied this as best he could in the available matter. This recalls a famous passage in *Republic* Book 10 describing a carpenter making a table as looking to the Form of Table, and applies the same principle even to the great divine craftsman. Thus the familiar craft model is from the start intimately bound up with the idea that the world, as a supreme product of craftsmanship, had a temporal beginning.

But don't artefacts also have a finite duration, and in time inevitably disintegrate? Here Plato can be seen relying on an old Socratic paradox, that any craft is a capacity for opposites. The doctor, best at saving life, is also the best at taking it; the builder, best at constructing a house, is also best at demolishing it; and so on. The same applies to the world-builder: durability being a desirable property of any artefact, this supreme craftsman must have made the world maximally durable, in fact so durable that to dismantle it again would require a craftsman as good as he is. (Think of tying a knot so tight that no one weaker than you can untie it.) But he is himself the only candidate for that role. And, being perfectly good, he has no possible motive to destroy his creation. Hence, although the world is inherently just as subject to destruction as it originally was to generation, it will *de facto* never be destroyed. The temporal asymmetry which caused Plato's readers such concern thus turns out to follow from principles of craftsmanship by which even a divine craftsman is bound.

COSMOGONIC REASONING

If, as it seems, the creation of the world was a real dated event, what does Plato offer as the motivation? Here too the creator's goodness is invoked: being supremely good, he will have wanted everything to be as good as it could be, and above all as *orderly* as possible. From this single premise, that the world had to be made maximally orderly, all the creator's major decisions about its structure are then worked out by Timaeus on *a priori* principles, with almost no appeal to empirical evidence.

A few of these structural findings were empirically untestable in any case. For instance, how many worlds did the creator make out of the available matter? 'One' is Timaeus' answer, arrived at, and unavoidably so, by entirely abstract reasoning. The further conclusion that the world is intelligent, and therefore a living being with a soul, may be put in the same category: for example, without being intelligent it would not be the *best* possible creation. But other cosmological findings might easily have been supported by familiar empirical evidence. For example, what shape did he make the world? Timaeus' answer, 'spherical', could have been backed by astronomical data, which seemed to show the rotation of its outer layer, where the fixed stars are, to be that of a perfect sphere. Instead Timaeus relies on a mixture of theoretical and pragmatic criteria for reconstructing the creator's decision: the sphere is the most beautiful of all shapes; the world has no need for asymmetry because the lack of an external environment makes unnecessary such asymmetric appendages as arms, legs and sense-organs; and so on. Similarly the question of what the world's main components are yields the answer that there are four, indeed none other than the traditional quartet of earth, water, air, and fire;[7] but the grounds given for this answer make no mention of the evident fact that the world *is* stratified into these four layers, and instead rely on an *a priori* and largely mathematical argument (30b–32c). A final example is the Demiurge's structuring of the heaven with two criss-crossing circles, those of the 'Same' and the 'Different' (roughly, the celestial equator and the ecliptic), divided according to harmonic ratios. Although Timaeus' account of this does take the celestial phenomena into consideration, it is primarily guided by the need to analyse the heavenly sphere as the world's intelligent soul, patterned after the structure of thought itself as a certain amalgam of sameness, difference, and being.

The underlying epistemology here seems to be as follows. On the one hand, reasoning about the nature of the universe has as its subject matter contingent truths, and to that extent can never aspire to the certainty characteristic of pure mathematics: its goal is not unshakeable certainty but maximum 'likelihood' (*eikos*, 29b–d). On the other hand, well-conducted cosmological thought is a very decent *approximation* to pure intellectual reasoning: it is not a fundamentally empirical exercise, but is, to a greater extent, the rediscovery of chains of teleological reasoning which must once, during the world's creation, have been actually conducted by the ideally good intellect that created it.

EXPLAINING IMPERFECTIONS

One factor that Plato recognises as complicating his creationist enterprise is that the creation process must frequently have involved compromises. A well-known example is the fragility of the human head

(75a–d). A choice facing the gods whom the creator charged with making human beings (more on them below) was between giving us greater durability and greater intelligence. Living matter could never fully combine these desiderata, and the gods' decision to favour the latter over the former was undoubtedly the wiser choice.

A widespread interpretation of such compromises as this takes Plato to identify *matter* as the cause of the world's imperfections. Importantly, creation is not *ex nihilo*, which virtually all Greek thinkers considered impossible. Hence the creator relied on a pre-existing supply of matter, on which he set out to impose the best possible order. And this matter, the interpretation goes, to some extent resisted his attempts, thus making the world less than perfect. Is this a plausible reading of the *Timaeus*?

Material stuffs are characterised by mechanical rather than end-related movements – for instance, water left to its own devices flows, fire rises, in both cases without regard to any good end served. These stuffs Timaeus tellingly calls by the names 'necessity' and 'the wandering cause' (46c). Their very presence in the world may seem sufficient to guarantee that good ends will sometimes be thwarted. But that does not straightforwardly follow. The mechanical and often chaotic behaviour of material stuffs captures what they were like *before* the order was imposed (53b). In our ordered world, they have, according to Timaeus' metaphor, come under the 'persuasion' of the world's governing *nous*: 'intelligence' or 'mind'. If that persuasion has been fully successful, matter has been organised into exactly the disposition and behaviour that the creator wanted. Would Plato really want to suggest that something as lowly and devoid of intelligence as brute matter has succeeded in resisting the will of the best being in the universe, god? Nothing in the text compels us to suppose so.

How then does matter's persuasion by intelligence work? The post-Platonic term 'matter' – what Aristotle calls *hulē* – is no better than an approximation to what Timaeus calls the 'receptacle' (*hupodochē*) of becoming. In itself this is conceived as a featureless and entirely pliable entity that underlies, and thereby provides the location of, qualitative change. As far as we can tell, this receptacle never lacks some quality or other. More specifically, prior to the world's creation, it unstably bore the 'traces' of the four primary bodies. This quartet of earth, water, air, and fire is represented at the intelligible level by four corresponding Forms, and the 'traces' were, correspondingly, chance resemblances to these four paradigms that appeared and disappeared in the receptacle.

To impose order on the chaos, the creator's task was to replace these chaotic element-traces with mathematically ideal particles designed to correspond as closely as possible to those four eternal paradigms. Each of the four was assigned as the shape of its particles one of the five geometrically perfect solids. To see how this was done, consider the case of fire. We may take it that the Form of fire is, or embodies, the essential *function* of fire, which is, in brief, to *cut* or *divide*: as flame, it does this by the dissolution of whatever it burns; as light, by dividing the visual ray. This capacity to cut was maximised by the creator by constructing fire's particles as tetrahedra, that is, regular four-faced pyramids. By contrast, earth, with its comparative stability, was composed of cubic particles.

The key point here for present purposes is that the decision to construct the world out of these four primary stuffs, and to shape their particles as illustrated above, was the creator's own supremely intelligent way of imposing order on the previously disordered receptacle. Being entirely pliable, in no way could the receptacle have resisted his will. And if in today's world any imperfections arise from the necessitating properties of fire, earth, etc., that does not mean that matter is successfully defying god's will, because those properties were the very ones that he himself chose and imposed, as being, all things considered, the best ones. Fire does continue to manifest mechanical 'necessity' in its own intrinsic behaviour, but that necessity has been harnessed ('persuaded') to serve the good ends determined by intelligence. For example, much of the world's fire constitutes the bodies of the stars, every one of them a god; and as light it provides vision, one of the greatest of divine benefactions, enabling humans to observe the regular celestial periodicities and thus advance in mathematics, and ultimately in philosophy (46a–47c). So far as one can tell from Plato's text, divine intelligence has, to precisely the extent that it wanted, succeeded in persuading fire to cooperate in achieving its ends. If for its own reasons it does not choose to persuade all of the fire to cooperate (as indicated at 48a), there is no suggestion that this is contrary to the divine will, as if intelligence had been successfully resisted by necessity. If ordinary caustic fire, despite being potentially uncooperative and destructive, remains too, there is no reason to doubt that the creator judged it on balance to be better thus.

In short, the fact that the world was generated from pre-existing matter, rather than from nothing, need not have constrained the creator's success. The only constraint, even implicitly, was that he could not choose the *amount* of matter, since there was a finite supply of it and he deemed it prudent to use this all up rather than leave anything outside the world that might later pose a threat to it (32c–33b). And there is no indication in Plato's text that this led to any otherwise avoidable deficiencies. It is more in accordance with Platonic thought to say that the world's imperfections, of which the skull's fragility is emblematic, amount to the kinds of compromise that inevitably occur whenever a paradigmatic Form is embodied in matter. Just as no material table can match the perfection of the Form of Table, so too no material world could share the perfection of the Form *it* is modelled on.

ANAXAGORAS' ANTHROPOGONY

The creation of human beings is the culminating phase of Plato's cosmogony, following in this respect a well-established Presocratic tradition. Thereafter, it was generally accepted, human agency would take over as the main guiding cause, so that cosmogony would be succeeded by cultural history.

Why then, according to Platonic creationism, were human beings created? Answering this requires a preamble about Plato's predecessors. For Socrates, we have seen, humans were created as the ultimate beneficiaries of the entire cosmogony. A generation before him, the great natural philosopher Anaxagoras had already offered his own account of the world and its inhabitants as the product of a governing *nous* – 'mind' or 'intelligence'. Socrates, according to Plato (*Phd.* 97b–99c), was disappointed by what he read about this in Anaxagoras, but we should pause to see, on the basis of his surviving fragments,[8] what stage in the prehistory of creationist thought Anaxagoras may have represented, and whether it bears in any way on the creation of humankind in particular.

Originally, according to Anaxagoras, matter was entirely mixed, and hence a bland, inert, and undifferentiated stuff. The reason why it is not still that way is that there was a second entity, *nous*, which chose to act upon this stuff, stirring it into a vortex, the rotation of which then mechanically separated it out into the layers characteristic of a world. That is to say, the heavy, dark stuff travelled to the bottom or centre, forming the earth, while the light, bright, and fiery stuff travelled to the periphery, forming the stars. In between, the other two cosmic masses, water and air, similarly formed distinct strata. The separation of the mixture is still not complete and never will be, but that the separative process still continues is illustrated by the fact that some heavy items have become caught up in the fiery stuff rotating in the heaven, as the fall of meteorites attests. Given this, Anaxagoras inferred that the same phenomenon on a larger scale accounted for the sun, which he identified as a huge red-hot stone or ingot, as large as the Peloponnese, marooned up in the ether, far from the zone it might be expected to occupy.

The basis of this rotatory movement and its consequences is a dualism of mind and matter. What I here loosely call matter is in his own diction a mixture of the world's physical ingredients, which, thanks to the cosmogonic rotation, is no longer a bland, undifferentiated blend, but whose components on the other hand can never become fully separated out. And that is how matter differs from mind. Matter is always mixed, there being, as Anaxagoras puts it, 'a portion of everything in every-thing'. The sole exception to this principle of universal mixture is mind, which he says is, on the contrary, unmixed, and which in fact owes its extraordinary power over matter precisely to this fact of being unmixed. What then is the Anaxagorean mind? Is it the familiar kind of mind that is possessed by any and every thinking being, ourselves included? Or is it a superhuman mind, capable of creating a world – in other words, what most thinkers would in this context call a divine creator? It is both.

Mind is something we are all familiar with because we each have a portion of it in us, making it directly open to inspection – or perhaps, more accurately, to introspection. It is thus from familiarity with our own minds that we appreciate two things in particular about mind as such. One is that mind has a unique capacity to initiate and steer the motion of matter, the matter in question in our own case being our bodies. The other is that when mind moves matter, it can foresee the consequences of those changes, and can therefore plan for them.

Given, then, that our world is maintained by motion, that of the heavens in particular, and that *something* must have initiated this motion and foreseen all along what its result would be, namely an ordered world, what could that thing be but mind? The latter point, that the cosmogonic mind must have foreseen the outcome of the rotation it brought about, can be inferred from Anaxagoras' fragment B4a:

> These things being so, one must believe that there are many things
> of all kinds in all the things that are being aggregated, and seeds of
> all things, which have all kinds of forms and colours and savours.
> And that human beings were compounded, and all the other
> animals that have soul. And that the human beings, for their part,
> have cities that they have populated and farms that they have
> constructed, just as where we are. And that they have both sun and

moon and so on, just as where we are. And that their earth bears many things of all kinds, of which they harvest the best and bring them to their dwelling to use. So much then for my statement about the separation – that it would not happen only where we are, but elsewhere too.

Although mind is not explicitly mentioned in these lines, there is little doubt that what are being described are the beneficial outcomes of mind's 'separations' of matter, not only in our world, but in other parts of the universe too. As indicated in the last sentence, there is no reason why our own region of the universe should have been uniquely privileged, so we should expect that what mind has planned and executed in order to create our world, it has repeated elsewhere to create other worlds. In our world there are, as Anaxagoras points out here, innumerable kinds of seeds from which plants and animals have grown, and which continue to provide crops for farmers to cultivate and harvest, aided by the sun and the moon. (The moon was believed to provide signs for the benefit of farmers.) Anaxagoras infers that the other worlds have been so structured as to provide the same benefits.

What is most striking is that the other worlds are inferred each to have their own sun and moon. Recall that for Anaxagoras the sun is a red-hot stone, anomalously trapped in the ether; it can be added that the moon is, similarly, a massive fragment of earth, again isolated in the ether, and drawing light from the sun's glow. When Anaxagoras makes clear his expectation that each of the other worlds should also have precisely one sun and one moon, as ours does, it is a natural implication that in our own world too the displacement of these two huge bodies is not taken by him to be merely accidental. Rather, he is assuming that mind plans and creates worlds, our own included, specifically with a view to the needs of human societies, and that providing the necessary conditions for agriculture, among which a sun and a moon are prominent, is one part of that task.

Hence in Anaxagoras' cosmogonic theory there is good reason to conclude that our world was planned, designed, and created by mind to provide the right conditions for the emergence of life, and more specifically, for the benefit of its human inhabitants, enabled to farm and thus survive. Whether this was done by mind as a beneficent act is less clear, because human beings themselves are the world's principal vehicles of mind, and if they are created *by* mind that might just as well be for its own benefit as for theirs. Nevertheless, in at least a limited sense, Anaxagoras' account of creation can surely be called anthropocentric.

ANAXAGOREAN MIND

Both Plato and Aristotle were later to complain that Anaxagoras, despite trumpeting the powers of mind, in practice made no use of its intelligent powers in accounting for good features of the world. But they did not read carefully enough. When we scrutinise his dense and difficult text with sufficient care, as I have just tried to do for fragment 4a, it becomes increasingly clear that the cosmogonic mind that he postulates is a providential creator of worlds, systematically aiming for and achieving overall beneficial outcomes.

Now consider Anaxagoras' fragment B12, a kind of eulogy of mind:

(a) The other things share a portion of each, but mind is something infinite and autonomous, and is mixed with no thing, but it alone is by itself. For if it were not by itself, but were mixed with something else, it would share in all things, if it were mixed with any of them – for in each a portion of each is present, as I have said earlier – and the things in the mixture would prevent it from controlling any thing in such a way as it does in being alone by itself. (b) For it is both the finest and purest of all things, and it possesses all understanding about each, and has the greatest strength. And the things that have soul, both the larger and the smaller, are all of them controlled by mind. (c) And the entire rotation was controlled by mind, so as to make it rotate in the first place. And at first it began to rotate in a small way; now it is rotating more; and it will rotate still more. And the things which are being mixed, separated and segregated, mind understood all of them. And both what they were going to be like and what they used to be like, both the things that are not now and the things that are now, and what they will be like, mind arranged them all, and also this rotation which is now being undergone by the stars, sun, moon, air and aether that are being separated off. And it was the rotation itself that made them be separated off. And the dense is being separated from the rare, the hot from the cold, the bright from the dark, and the dry from the wet. (d) There are many portions of many things. But nothing is totally separated or segregated, one from another, except mind. All mind is alike, both the larger and the smaller, while no other thing is like anything else. But the things that it has got most of in it, those are what each single thing most evidently is and was.

Notice that in this text the subject, 'mind', refers equally and without explicit distinction to animal minds, as in the second half of (b), and to the mind that created the world, as in (c). In (d) Anaxagoras says, 'All mind is alike, both the larger and the smaller.' There is no reason not to take 'larger' and 'smaller' here literally. My mind or yours could never create a world, and it is reasonable to assume that the mind that made our world had to be a much larger one than either of them. But in every respect other than size, we are here assured by Anaxagoras, all minds – our individual minds, the cosmogonic mind, and presumably also the minds of dogs, bats, and bees – are homogeneous. The world-creating mind may think bigger and more complex thoughts than our minds do, and move bigger masses of matter, but it nevertheless thinks, and acts, in what is fundamentally the same way.

Then is the world-creating mind a creator god? Possible grounds for saying so are that it functions as a superhuman intelligent agent, which in an ancient Greek context is the main qualification for being a god, even if for completeness its immortality would have to be mentioned as well; and also that Anaxagoras' fragment B12, whose fulsome praise of mind's wonderful powers we have just read, reads much like a hymn.

But there are more and stronger grounds for doubting that it is a god. For instance, Anaxagoras appears very careful to avoid applying the actual language of divinity to it. This silence about its divinity, even in *the* focal passage about mind, is unlikely to be a mere accident of textual survival and loss. We can usefully compare a parallel case of terminological abstinence on his part. In fragment B17 he insists that the Greek verbs meaning 'come to be' and 'perish' are strictly incorrect, a metaphysically misleading way of talking about what are in reality combinations and separations of stuffs which themselves endure. True to his word, he systematically respects this principle throughout his preserved fragments, never once using the offending verbs, but replacing them with talk of ongoing combination and separation. His scrupulous avoidance of the language of divinity gives the impression of being similarly motivated. Whether or not he dared to say it explicitly, he did not believe that talk of 'god' or 'the divine' captures the truth about the cosmos and its origins, and he censored his own language accordingly. He could, instead, have permitted himself some conventional use of religious language, if only in order to protect himself from the charge of impiety, an offence for which he was in the end exiled from Athens.

Seen in this light, the resemblance of the cosmogonic mind's powers to those of a traditional god, and the quasi-hymn composed to emphasise this resemblance, need not be hinting that the cosmogonic mind is actually divine. They may be intended to achieve the opposite result, namely to *replace* traditional divinities with a purely natural power. Recall his thesis of the homogeneity of mind. It favours the idea that the cosmic mind is not superhuman, since qualitatively it is the very same power as is present, albeit in smaller portions, in each of us. Anaxagoras can legitimately be understood as *reducing* 'god' to a familiar power, mind, just as he reduced coming to be and perishing to mixture and separation. Such a reduction of god to mind was echoed by his near-contemporary the tragedian Euripides, in his characteristically daring line 'Zeus, be he natural necessity or the mind (*nous*) of mortals' (*Troades* 886). It is no surprise that Euripides too is reported to have faced trial for impiety.

But perhaps the most important consideration is the following. When Anaxagoras picked out mind as being at once the bearer of knowledge and the initiator of motion, far from being in any way a theological stance this was one half of an original and historically significant metaphysical thesis, the dualism of mind and matter. Previous philosophers had typically tended towards a kind of monism, treating matter as if it were itself inherently endowed with vital properties. This made the existence of animate beings like us unproblematic, but at the price of threatening to make everything else animate as well, even rocks and corpses. Thales (early sixth century BCE), conventionally considered the first philosopher, was remembered for saying 'All things are full of gods,' and that at least one kind of stone, the magnet, must have a soul, since it has the power to move iron. Anaxagoras evidently sought, in response, a metaphysics capable of separating the animate from the inanimate, and found it in a second principle, mind, which he saw as irreducibly different from matter, and present in some bodies while absent from others. Such a dualism, considered in its own right, had no need for the concept of god, and by his scrupulous avoidance of theological language, Anaxagoras was surely recognising as much. Even the portion of mind which was large and powerful enough to plan and shape the matter of a whole world was nevertheless just that, mind.

This brings us to a historical paradox. On the one hand, Anaxagoras turns out to have been the first creationist, that is, the first to postulate a purposive agent which created the world as a craftsman creates an artefact. Moreover, there is some sense in which the ultimate intended beneficiary of the creation was humankind. On the other hand, Anaxagoras' creative agent was no god, but a familiar ontological component of the physical world, the power which we call mind and witness constantly acting on our own bodies. Creationism, it turns out, in this way first entered the Western canon as a scientific and non-theological, possibly even anti-theological, theory of origins. Theological creationism, as we have encountered it in Socrates and Plato, was a later development.

ANTHROPOGONY IN THE *TIMAEUS*

We may now return to Plato's *Timaeus*, and specifically to the question of why his divine creator should have included humankind in his world-plan. Contrary to the anthropocentric tendency of Anaxagoras and Socrates, according to Plato the world was created not for the sake of humankind, but with a quite different end in view: to maximise the orderliness of matter. Why then need it even include human beings? Plato's answer is clear, but is arrived at by the following circuitous chain of inferences.

In order to be the best possible product, the world had to be intelligent. To be intelligent, it had to be a living being. Therefore the Form on which its craftsman modelled it had to be the Form of Living Being, or Animal. Since this generic Form contains all the species of animal, the world's likeness to its model would be maximised only if it too contained members of all these species, whereas so far it contained only one species, the fiery star gods who were an integral part of the newly created fiery upper zone. Analogously to the divine residents of the fiery zone, all the animals who were natural residents of the other three zones – air, land, and water – had now to be added, including men (meaning male human beings). The world itself already had a soul, but now all the newly created animals needed their own souls too, which the creator made, giving them the same structure as he had to the world-soul, albeit of inferior quality. These souls were immortal and recyclable, and would in each incarnation need to occupy and animate an animal whose degree of elevation or debasement matched their own. To the lesser gods that he had created the demiurge delegated the task of creating mortal bodies suitable to house these souls. The initial archetype that the lesser gods created was man. Later, when souls originally suitable for animating men had degenerated morally, they would be demoted to the role of animating lower beings, albeit with the chance of later redemption.

Thus the reason for the creation of man was to initiate a process that, when complete, would populate the world with all animal kinds, in the interests of an admittedly somewhat abstruse ideal of cosmic completeness. It would be misleading, however, to infer that men were no more essential to the process of world-creation than worms

or pigs were. Plato inherited Socrates' conviction that man is a divinely privileged species, but adapted it to his additional Pythagorean-
derived belief that the soul survives death and transmigrates between
species. Degraded souls move down the natural scale, first from men to
women, and then on down into quadrupeds, and, lower still in a quite
literal sense of 'lower', into legless creatures like snakes, and, below
even them, into fish. But promotion is possible too, and the very highest
reward for virtue may even take a soul above human incarnation, into a
state of blissful disembodiment.

It is against this background that we must understand Plato's
theory of the origin of species. What the gods initially devised and
created, according to him, was just a single species, man: the male
human being was their archetype. It was in order to provide bodies
suitable to house souls that had lost their moral fibre that the gods
went on to create women, and as souls accumulated further vices, ever
lower and lower species would be added, until the animal kingdom was
complete. But none of these involved a genuinely new programme of
species design. Rather, the original male human body was progressively
adapted. For example, following the introduction of women, with the
progressive further degeneration of souls the originally upright body
had to be bent downwards towards the ground, the arms converted into
legs, and the approximately spherical head elongated in such a way as
to squash flat and thus render inert the naturally circular motions of
reason. In constructing this system of punishment and redemption,
Plato became the very first thinker to conceive the idea that one species
has transmuted into others by adaptation, and that in consequence
all animal species, humans included, are biologically interrelated.
However, the transmutation he had in mind was the very antithesis of
Darwinism. Not evolution but, we might rather say, devolution. Not
the descent of man, but a descent *from* man to lower species.

These metamorphoses are made by Plato to sound more like
fable or myth than science, but it is striking how, in the course of his
semi-mythical exposition, he can on occasion deliver an unexpectedly
reasonable scientific application of his devolutionary theory. Consider
toenails. In a Darwinian age, toenails are evidently vestigial claws,
no longer serving their original defensive or locomotive function, and
therefore excellent evidence that humans were not directly created
but evolved from other species. If you were designing humankind *ab
initio*, you would never bother with the toenails. To Plato, with his
theory of devolution, toenails are, on the contrary, a manifestation of
divine providence. The gods who originally created man, he maintains,

intended him all along as an archetype, ready to undergo conversion into lower species. And that was why, according to Plato, their archetype included toenails, waiting to be developed into full-scale claws or hooves when needed at a later stage in biological history.

Those who find this mode of explanation hard to treat seriously might be more impressed by its power to explain the male nipple. By following Plato's devolutionary principles, we can work out that the nipple, although without the least functionality in the original male human beings, was deliberately included in the archetype in order to be developed into a vital nutritional tool, as soon as the next stage, the formation of women, arrived.

I earlier considered, and answered negatively, the question of whether matter is the source of bad in the world as conceived by Plato. We now have a more plausible candidate. The existence of moral badness, and a great many of the harms people suffer as a result of it, can be accounted for by the moral degeneration of souls. Yet that degeneration serves what is ultimately a greater good, the world's completeness; for without it there would be no souls suitable for animating the numerous lower life-forms, and the world would remain an incomplete copy of its eternal model. Plato's version of divine creation thus becomes arguably the first to maintain that individual moral badness, although undesirable in itself, is a necessary part of a greater cosmic good.

DIVINE ENGINEERING

Let us return, finally, to the Argument from Design, which infers the existence of one or more benevolent divine creators from the evidence of their benefactions. Plato knew this argument (*Laws* 10.886a2–4), but avoided using it, considering it potentially impious even to call into question the existence of a good deity (*Timaeus* 29a). Xenophon's Socrates was its first champion, and from him it passed to the Stoics, self-declared 'Socratics' who from around 300 BCE took over as the leading flagbearers of creationism.

Socrates had chosen statues as his point of comparison: god's achievement in creating living, self-moving beings outclasses the genius of the best human sculptor, who can make no more than static dummies. The Hellenistic age, in which Stoicism rose to become the dominant philosophy, was also an age of astonishing engineering advances. A mechanical sphere that reproduced all the major astronomical cycles[9] was built by Archimedes, whose archetype was followed by other models, including one that survives today as the 'Antikythera mechanism' and another said to have been constructed by the Stoic philosopher-mathematician Posidonius. These advances enabled the Stoics to update Socrates' Argument from Design, replacing sculptures with astronomical spheres (Cic. *On the Nature of the Gods* 2.88). Anyone, they argued, even the most uncivilised of barbarians, would instantly recognise one of these spheres as the product of intelligence. Yet the world itself is the great original mechanism of which these spheres are mere replicas. Who then can doubt that the world too is the product of a designer, indeed of a designer whose brilliance outclasses that of the great Archimedes himself?

NOTES

1 Chapter 5 by Thomas Kjeller Johansen.
2 The history of creationist thought in antiquity has not traditionally been a recognised topic of study. However, the ground covered in this chapter is more fully explored in Sedley 2007. The only other monograph on (approximately) the same theme is Theiler 1924.
3 Hankinson 1989.
4 See also Chapter 3 by Corcilius and Chapter 5 by Johansen in this volume.
5 On these chapters of Xenophon, see esp. Powers 2009.
6 This remains to the present day a widely asserted ground for preferring the sempiternalist interpretation. See, e.g. Baltes 1996.
7 See Chapter 4 by Ebrey in this volume.
8 The remains of Anaxagoras' writings are edited by Curd 2007, albeit with a some-what different interpretation from the one that follows.
9 See Chapter 10 by Taub in this volume, and Jones 2017

7   What's a Plant?

Laurence M. V. Totelin

INTRODUCTION

Ask yourself: what is a plant? You will probably answer that it is an organism able to photosynthesise chlorophyll.[1] Depending on your level of knowledge in biology, your answer will be more or less elaborate. Now, ask a young child what a plant is, and their answer is likely to be very different. Their definition may centre on the notion of plant rootedness: a plant is something that is rooted to the ground and cannot move as a result.

The Greeks and Romans could not observe photosynthesis; their definition was of necessity different from our modern scientific definition. Rootedness and lack of movement were important tenets in ancient definitions of plants, but these characteristics were neither necessary nor sufficient to define vegetal life. The main issue for ancient philosophers was whether plants are sentient or not; and if they are, from what type of sensation do they benefit?

In this chapter, we focus on ancient definitions, implicit or explicit, of plants. We start with a concrete example, that of coral. In antiquity, coral – a marine invertebrate in modern biology – was often classified among the plants, but was said to feel in some way. We then turn to Aristotle's definition of plants, which was pivotal in ancient thought on the topic. Next, we examine the philosophical discussions that preceded and followed Aristotle's writings on the topic, focusing on the notion of plant sensation (or lack thereof). We also discuss non-philosophical texts in which plants are endowed with sensations and even feelings. Finally, we consider ancient debates on the status of the embryo: does it live the life of a plant? Is it a plant? Or is it something between a plant and an animal?

A PLANT NAMED CORAL

Ovid's *Metamorphoses* recounts numerous stories of fabulous transformations. Among them is the tale of how the severed head of the

Gorgon Medusa had the power of turning seaweed into plants with hard boughs.[2] The hero Perseus, after slaying Medusa, deposited her head on a bed of vegetation:

> He [Perseus] washes his hands, victorious, in drawn sea water
> And lest the hard sand damages the serpent-bearing head,
> He softens the ground with leaves and sprouts born under the sea;
> He spreads them, and on these he places the head of the daughter
>   of Phorcys, Medusa.
> The sprouts, fresh, filled with moisture and living pith,
> Snatch the monster's power and, at its touch, they harden
> And acquire a new firmness in boughs and foliage.
> The sea Nymphs attempt the marvellous deed
> On more seaweeds and, as it affects them in the same way, they
>   rejoice.
> And they sow the seeds from these, scattering them through
>   the waves.
> Now, coral still retains that nature:
> It becomes hard at the touch of the air:
> A pliant twig (*vimen*) in the sea, above it, it turns to stone (*saxum*).[3]

For our purpose, the significant part of this passage is the classification of coral as a plant: it is a pliant twig under the sea – the word *vimen* is a botanical term – but above the water, it turns to stone. Ovid employed botanical vocabulary throughout the passage; there is no doubt he was talking about vegetation, until we reach the final word: stone (*saxum*). In terms of modern biology, coral is neither a plant nor a stone: it is a marine invertebrate. But in antiquity, and until the eighteenth century, there was some discussion as to the classification of this particular living being.[4] Theophrastus, the successor of Aristotle at the head of Lyceum and author of two important botanical treatises (*Enquiry into Plants* and *Causes of Plant Phaenomena*), described coral in his tract on stones, but employed botanical terms: 'Coral, for it is like a stone, is red in colour, and is rounded like a root. It grows in the sea. And by its nature, the Indian reed is not very different.'[5] In his *Enquiry into Plants*, Theophrastus did not allude to this resemblance of coral to the Indian reed.[6] On the other hand, he did refer to some plants growing in the Gulf of Heroes that are 'like stone in appearance'.[7]

Following the example of Theophrastus, the authors of various ancient lapidaries, the specialised treatises devoted to stones and their properties, defined coral as a stone that was first a plant. The Orphic Lapidary, for instance, records the following verses:

> For it first grows as a green grass, but not on the ground,
> Which, as we all know, gives solid food to plants, but in the sea,
> The sterile sea, where are born the seaweeds and the light mosses.[8]

The poet then went on to recount the story of the origin of coral. Pliny too described coral among the minerals, in Book 32 of his *Natural History*, but specified that it was first a bush (*frutex*), green in colour, with white berries (*bacae*).[9] Elsewhere, however, Pliny reported a fragment of Juba of Mauretania, the learned king, about two sea plants that turn hard upon being plucked: the hair of Isis and the eyelid of the Graces. The latter, Juba informs us, can 'feel/perceive' (*sentire*) when it is plucked.[10] The pharmacologist Dioscorides, for his part, classified coral more squarely among the plants, and gave an interesting synonym for it: *lithodendron*, literally 'the stone tree'.[11] Finally, the late antique philosopher Nemesius (end of the fourth century CE) gave the name 'zoophyte' (*zōophuton*) to organisms that occupy a position between plants and animals, specifying that

> He [the creator] created the bivalves and the coral like sensitive trees. He rooted them in the sea like plants and put shells around them like wood, and made them stationary like plants; but he endowed them with the sense of touch, the sense common to all animals, so that they are associated with plants by having roots and being stationary, with animals by the sense of touch.[12]

In this definition, coral is rooted like a plant but possesses the sense of touch like animals. This definition is typically Aristotelian, and builds upon the notion of continuous change within nature, often referred to as *scala naturae*, the chain of nature (see below). However, Aristotle himself did not coin the word 'zoophyte', which only occurs from the second century CE onwards.

There were, then, several different classifications of coral in antiquity. For some it was like a plant; for others, it was a plant that hardened in contact with the air; or a plant that truly changed into stone when exposed to air; or a living being occupying a space between a plant and an animal. The myth of the origin of coral certainly conferred an animal aspect to the ancient classification of coral: it grew under the influence of Medusa's blood, wherefrom it took its red colour. We have also noted that, in some ancient accounts, coral or coral-like organisms were believed to feel or to be endowed with some sense-perception. The example of coral certainly makes one wonder what constituted a plant in antiquity. We now turn to that question, starting with Aristotle's definition of a plant, which is the most comprehensive ancient definition – and the most discussed in antiquity.

ARISTOTLE'S DEFINITION

Aristotle dealt at length with the definition of a plant in his treatises on animals, as it was crucial for him to pinpoint the difference between a plant and an animal. There were several aspects to his definition. First, a plant is not endowed with locomotion; it cannot change its position in space, as it is rooted.[13] This statement, however, is not equivalent to arguing that a plant cannot move, for plants grow and decay, two phenomena that Aristotle classified as movements.[14] Besides, some animals – in particular testacea – are not capable of locomotion. Lack of locomotion, in itself, is not sufficient to define a plant. What distinguished a plant from an animal in the philosopher's mind was the possession of sensation. As succinctly expressed in *On the Soul*: 'plants only possess the nutritive faculty, while others [living beings] have the sentient faculty'.[15] Aristotle's nutritive part of the soul (*threptikon*), which he sometimes called the vegetative part of the soul (*phutikon*), is responsible for growth, decay, nutrition, and generation.[16] As a result of their possessing only the nutritive part of the soul, plants have as their final cause, as their main aim, the production of seed, which will allow a new generation of plants to take their place.[17]

As humans are animals – animals endowed with the rational part of the soul (*logismon*) – they must by necessity possess the nutritive/vegetative part of the soul. Aristotle clearly stated this fact in the *Nicomachean Ethics*:

> The excellence of this [vegetative part of the soul] therefore appears to be common to all [animate beings], and not only to humans. For it seems that this part or faculty [of the soul] is most active during sleep, but you cannot distinguish a good from a bad man when they are asleep.[18]

The vegetative/nutritive part of the soul is most active during sleep, but it also plays a crucial role during the embryonic state of an animal's life:

> If it is necessary for the animal to possess sensation, and if it becomes an animal when sensation occurs, one must consider that the initial condition is not sleep but similar to sleep, and that it is of a type similar to that of plants. For it is agreed that during this time animals live the life of a plant.[19]

Aristotle added that some embryos only possess the vegetative part of the soul potentially, but not yet in actuality:

> With regards to the nutritive soul, it is clear that one must acknowledge that seeds and foetations that are not separated possess it potentially but not in actuality, until, as happens in the separated foetations, they obtain their nourishment and exert the function of the nutritive soul. For at first it seems that all these [living beings] live the life of a plant.[20]

What are 'separated' and 'unseparated' foetations? A good example of an 'unseparated foetation' is the young of a viviparous animal, which cannot survive outside the womb of its mother. That animal relies entirely on its mother's uterus for nourishment, and hence only possesses the potential for the nutritive soul, and can be said to 'live the life of a plant'. Indeed, it relies on its mother in the same way as a plant relies on the earth for its growth.[21] In this context, the umbilical cord plays the same role as roots in plants.[22] A good example of a 'separated foetation' is a fertilised hen's egg, which contains all the nourishment necessary for development into a chick. In many ways, a plant seed is like an egg; indeed, earlier, Aristotle had quoted, and expressed agreement with, a verse from the philosopher-poet Empedocles: 'so the great trees lay eggs; the olives first'.[23] Although Aristotle did not state this explicitly, it is clear that, in the passage quoted above, he did not consider the plant seed entirely analogous to an animal egg: a plant seed requires the earth (or an earth substitute) to germinate. Only then will it be able to draw its own nourishment and possess the nutritive soul in actuality rather than potentially.

Another interesting question Aristotle raised in relation to plants was whether they possessed the nutritive part of the soul in all their parts. It is a well-established fact that plants can grow from slips, that is, from parts cut away from a mother plant. If the nutritive part of the soul is responsible for generation, and if a slip can grow into a plant, then the slip must contain the nutritive part of the soul:

> It is clear that plants, when they are divided, continue to live, and similarly for some insects among the animals, as if [the segments] possessed their own soul, similar in kind, but not in number.[24]

Aristotle, however, acknowledged that it is not always easy to determine whether an organism is sentient or not. As a solution to that issue, he developed the idea that nature progresses continuously – without breaks – from the inanimate to the animate. He explained this notion, which later became known as the *scala naturae*, the great chain of being, in several places. For instance, in Book 7 of the *Enquiry into Animals*, Aristotle expressed this principle in general terms and then gave some examples of boundary beings between plants and animals:

> Thus, nature changes little by little from the inanimate [things] to the animals, so that, on account of the continuity, the boundary between them escapes our notice, and we do not know to which of the two categories the middle belongs. For after the inanimate kind of things, first there is that of the plants. And among these, one differs from the other in seeming to participate more in life; but on the whole this kind appears almost animate in comparison with the other bodies, while in comparison with the animals, it seems inanimate. The change from these [sc. the plants] to the animals is continuous, as has already been stated. For some beings in the sea might make one doubt whether they are animal or plant. For they grow attached, and when detached many of them perish. For instance, the pinnas [bivalves] grow attached, and the razor-clams, when pulled up, cannot live. And in general, the entire kind of the testaceans resembles plants in comparison with the animals that move. And concerning sensation, some of them give no sign of it whatsoever, while others faintly ... But the sponge resembles plants in all respects.[25]

Thus, according to Aristotle, the sponge is in all respects similar to plants; that is, it has no sense-perception. Yet the philosopher classifies the sponge among animals.[26]

There was a further complication to the issue of plants' lack of sensation. Aristotle recognised that plants, although not capable of sensation, can be affected by sensibles:

> And for this reason, plants are not endowed with sense-perception, even though they possess one part of the soul and are somehow affected by tangible things: for they can be cold or warm. The reason for this is that they possess neither the mean nor the principle such as to receive the form of sensible things, but they are affected by [these forms] in union with their matter.[27]

This is a complex passage, but Aristotle seems to indicate that plants are affected – a passive state of being – by sensibles *qua* sensibles, not by the notion of these sensibles.[28] Plants cannot desire things, they do not possess the appetitive faculty of the soul (*orektikon*), as according to Aristotle, desire and appetite require sensation.[29]

Aristotle's definition of a plant was pivotal. All philosophers after him had to engage, in one way or another, with it. Theophrastus, interestingly, chose almost to ignore these discussions, referring only once to the nutritive part of the soul in his botanical works, and never once discussing the notion of continuous change in nature, whereby plants are at the bottom of a chain.[30] Theophrastus was also critical of overreliance on the use of analogies between plants and animals to understand plants. For instance, he discussed the validity of the comparison between plant seed and embryo (which he did not divide into 'separated' and 'unseparated'), and suggested that perhaps one ought to consider plant fruits and seeds to be parts (*merē*, one of the central concepts of Theophrastean botany) of a plant 'even though we [do not consider] embryos [to be part] of animals'.[31] In many ways, then, the philosopher who wrote most about plants in antiquity was highly unusual. Instead of pondering on the definition of plants, he observed and described them in great detail – or at least this is the case in the Theophrastean writings that have come down to us. It is perhaps when philosophers were concerned with nature as a whole, and generation in particular, that they acutely felt the need to define plants. The main issue was whether plants were endowed or not with sense-perception. That question had been asked by the earliest Greek philosophers, the Presocratics, and remained a central question throughout antiquity and beyond. I now turn to this topic and offer some pointers for the study of plant sensation in antiquity.

ONCE MORE, WITH FEELING

As we have seen, Aristotle conceded that plants could be affected by sensibles, but he was adamant that they did not have desire or appetite. He had most probably developed that notion in response to Plato's assertion, in the *Timaeus*, that plants possess a type of soul, that which is elsewhere called the appetitive or desiring faculty (*epithumētikē*):

> And what we are now discussing [sc. plants] partake of the third type
> of soul, the one located between the midriff and the navel, which
> has no part in opinion or reason or mind, but only in perceptions of
> pleasure and pain that accompany them.[32]

In the next sentence, which is extremely difficult to interpret, and which has raised debates in antiquity and beyond, Plato stated that this part of the soul is always passive (*paschon*).[33]

Some Presocratic philosophers appear to have gone even further than Plato in attributing some sensation to plants. There are, however, serious issues in attempting to determine what the Presocratics exactly argued as we do not have fragments of their writings on this topic but rather second-party, usually biased, testimonies. For instance, Nicolaus of Damascus, who was a first-century CE Aristotelian, wrote that:

> Now, Anaxagoras and Empedocles assert that plants have desire and
> sensation, pain and pleasure, and Anaxagoras <naively> asserts that
> they are animals and that they feel joy and sadness – and he cites
> as proof the shedding of their leaves in due season ... Anaxagoras,
> Empedocles and Democritus maintained that plants possess reason and
> understanding. But we must refrain from this abominable nonsense.[34]

Add to this the issue that Nicolaus' text is not preserved in its original Greek, and it becomes impossible to know what faculties Anaxagoras, Democritus, or Empedocles attributed to plants.

Active after Aristotle, the Stoics in general, and Chrysippus in particular, denied all sensation and desire to plants, and apparently went as far as denying them the status of living beings. Again, these statements are preserved in doxographic writings and can at times be very difficult to interpret. Here is, for instance, how the Christian Clement of Alexandria summarised the thought of the Stoics in this matter: 'The Stoics do not call the vegetative faculty "soul" ... According to the Stoics a plant is neither ensouled nor an animal [or alive]. For an animal is an ensouled being.'[35] Thus, according to this testimony, the Stoics did not deny a vegetative faculty to plants, but they did not consider this faculty to be a type, part, or faculty of the soul. As a result, Stoics did not call plants 'animals'. Galen, the prolific physician-philosopher, who was often critical of the Stoics, also tells us that they talked about the 'nature' of (phusis) plants rather than their 'soul' in a passage where he located the seat of the vegetative soul in the liver:

> For the liver is the origin of the kind of power that also exists in plants. For now, let us call it a 'power', although we shall later demonstrate more precisely that the liver is the origin of many powers, and it would be best to talk of 'essence of the soul' rather than 'power' contained in each of the three [main] internal organs: in the brain, the rational [substance]; in the heart, the spirited [substance]; and in the liver, the desiring [substance], or as the Aristotelians call it, the nutritive, vegetative or generative. They take the name in each case [from an activity]: vegetative from growth; nutritive from nourishment, and generative from generation. But Plato calls it 'desiring' from the multitude of desires. The Stoics, however, do not call the governing [principle] in plants 'soul' at all, but rather 'nature'.[36]

This passage is typical of Galen's philosophical eclecticism: there he clearly equated Plato's desiring soul with Aristotle's nutritive/vegetative soul, and located the seat of that soul in the liver, as Plato had done with the desiring soul. Elsewhere, the physician expressed allegiance with the Stoic notion of plants' nature:

> But we are persuaded that the greatest virtue of language is clarity, and we know that nothing compromises it more than unfamiliar terms. For that reason, according to the common usage, we say that animals are governed by their soul as well as by their nature, whereas plants are governed by their nature alone, and that their growth and nutrition are the effects of nature and not the soul.[37]

Galen also subscribed to the Aristotelian idea of continuous change in nature, arguing that the lowest animals only possess touch:

> Therefore, nature appears, as it were, to have certain steps, the first being that in which it has moved a short distance from the plants, producing an animal that has only one sense, touch; the second, that in which it adds taste; the third, that in which it adds smell; then in the fourth step, it adds hearing; and in the fifth, vision.[38]

In this passage, then, where Galen gave a clear hierarchy of the senses, he appeared to deny plants any sensation. However, in another treatise, *On my own Opinions*, which he intended for a different, more select, readership than 'mere physicians', he discussed the Platonic notion whereby plants are endowed with a certain form of sense-perception. Galen argued that plants are only able to perceive what is appropriate and inappropriate for them, thus allowing them to attract what they require for growth and to repel what is harmful to them, which in turn makes them useful as drugs. Galen noted that the Platonic theory could be misunderstood:

> For this reason, there is a (possible) misunderstanding in the argument although Plato clearly stated that there is a different sort of perception in plants, (a misunderstanding) if his audience understood him to mean that there is in plants a cognitive faculty of what is appropriate or inappropriate. For plants have the capacity to distinguish between these things alone, and it is brought about by affections of pleasure and pain or affections similar or akin to them, while the vegetable soul shares in no other kinds of sensory diagnostic. It cannot distinguish things by how their qualities appear to sight, sound, smell, taste or touch, but only by whether they can nurture it or not.[39]

In short, plants do not possess sense-perception, but a basic form of perception that manifests itself in affections of the soul that are similar to pleasure and pain.[40]

There is no space here to discuss the definitions of plants contained in the numerous, and lengthy, treatises of the Neoplatonic philosophers. However, we will say some words about this topic at the end of the chapter, when considering whether the embryo is a plant or not.[41] While philosophers endlessly debated on the sensations of plants – or lack thereof – other ancient authors simply assumed their existence. Witness the well-known story of the hatred between the vine and the cabbage, reported, for instance, by Theophrastus:

> Some plants do not destroy [other plants] but rather overpower them by the properties of their saps and smells: for instance, the cabbage and the laurel with the vine. For, they say, the vine can perceive smells and draw them up. This is why, when a vine shoot finds itself near these plants, it turns away and looks away, as if their smell was abhorrent. And Androcydes used this as a proof that a remedy made

from cabbage against wine would get rid of drunkenness. For, he argued, the vine, being alive, flees its smell.[42]

If Theophrastus was representing Androcydes' thoughts accurately, then his vine was endowed with the sense of smell (and not simply affected by smells) and could actively react to smells.[43] The hatred of the vine for the cabbage was the best-known ancient example of plant antipathy. There were many others: antipathies between the sweet bay and the vine; the olive and the oak; the oak and the walnut; the cabbage and the cyclamen; the cabbage and origano; the radish and the vine.[44] Cases of friendships, by comparison, were much rarer, although that between rue and the fig tree was noted by several authors.[45] Now, in ancient philosophy, the concepts of antipathy and sympathy do not necessarily imply sense-perception, but this is not how they were popularly interpreted.

Roman agronomists and Pliny often imbued plants with feelings, more particularly in the context of plant generation. For instance, the fourth-century agronomist Palladius thus described the way in which the laurel reacts when a cherry scion is grafted into it: 'the cherry is grafted [literally: inserted into] to the laurel, who is constrained to bear; the face of the virgin [laurel] colours with an adoptive modesty'.[46] It is not possible to graft a cherry to a laurel, but Palladius may be discussing *Prunus laurocerasus* L., the cherry laurel, which as its name indicates bears resemblance to the cherry, in particular in its fruits.[47] Palladius' description is highly anthropomorphic and filled with sexual allusions. The laurel, a virgin, is raped by the cherry and forced to carry adoptive children. As a result of this assault, the laurel feels shame: the Latin word *pudor* comes last in verse 144, thus putting it in emphasis.

While Palladius' cherry suffered rape, other plants experienced all the desires and pleasure of love. Here is how Pliny described the vine's desire for the poplar that supports its growth:

> In the Campanian country, [the vines] marry the poplars, and embracing their brides and climbing with wanton arms in a knotty way through their branches, they reach their tops, at such a height, that a hired vintager asks by contract for a funeral pile and a grave [before climbing].[48]

It was usual to refer to this process as a marriage – we would call it a coupling – in Latin. The earliest Latin prose text preserved, Cato's *On Agriculture*, advised to 'see that the trees are well wedded' (*maritae sint*).[49]

Filial love too, albeit of a rather incestuous nature, is described in Latin agronomical literature. Columella, in his poetic book on horticulture, thus depicted the mutual desire the lettuce and earth experience for each other in the spring:

> While it [the lettuce] desires to unite with its desiring mother,
> And this softest mother lies beneath the yielding field,
> Ready to generate; now is the generative season for the world;
> Now love hastens to sexual union; now the spirit of the world
> Is made mad by Venus' goads, and driven by desire,
> It burns to give birth and to fill everything with its offspring.[50]

In the Greek and Roman worlds, the earth was considered to be a female goddess, a fertile mother. Interestingly, Columella chose lettuce to illustrate the power of spring: lettuce was considered to be a powerful an-aphrodisiac, a sleep aid, in antiquity.[51]

As a final example of plants experiencing feelings, let us examine the famous ancient story of the love between the 'female' and the 'male' date-palms.[52] Pliny the Elder and Florentinus (a third-century CE author) gave detailed accounts in anthropomorphised terms: the female palms are suffering from love sickness as women would do.[53] An allusion to that story is also found in *Leucippe and Clitophon*, the second-century CE Greek pastoral novel by Achilles Tatius.[54] The version transmitted by the historian Ammianus Marcellinus is perhaps less known:

> And the palms themselves are said to marry, and it is easy to distinguish their sex. It is also said that the female trees generate when they are covered with the seeds of the males. They tell that they take pleasure in this mutual love, and that this is clear from the fact that they lean against each other and cannot be separated even by strong winds. And if the female is not smeared by the seed of the male as usual, she suffers an abortion and loses her foetuses/fruits prematurely. And if it is not known with which tree the female is love struck, her trunk is smeared with her own perfume, and the other tree naturally takes in the sweetness of that smell. It is with such signs that originates the belief that they somehow couple together.[55]

Ammianus' palms are 'married', a union that legitimises sexual lust and childbearing. The palms in the account of Basil of Caesarea – a Church Father – are far less chaste:

Among the fruit-bearing trees, they even divide the palm trees into male and female. And you might see that which is called female lowering its spathes, as if lusting for this and longing for the male's embrace. Those who care for these plants throw on the spathes what is comparable to the seed of the male, which they call *psēn*; the [female] palms appear as if they experience pleasure, then they redress their spathes again, and the foliage of the tree regains its usual aspect.[56]

In terms of modern biology, palm trees are dioecious, that is, the male and female organs of reproduction are found on different individuals, thus necessitating the intervention of a pollinator to bring fruits to maturity. The ancients had no such theory of pollination, but they had observed in the palm trees a process that could quite easily be explained by analogy with animal behaviour. Analogy played an important role in ancient botanical thinking, as it helped explain what is difficult to perceive with the senses. Many of the 'popular' stories I have discussed here relate to plant generation because it is in some ways much more complex than animal generation. The ancients observed that the fruit/seed of plants would often develop into a new generation of tree, but in the majority of cases – the case of the palm being an exception – they could not witness the moment of union between plants. In addition, they had also observed that many plants could be propagated through slips, which requires no union between plants. Finally, they argued that some plants could grow spontaneously.[57] By comparison with such vegetable complexity, love stories involving humans appeared extremely simple.

In other respects, however, plant generation is easier to observe than animal generation. Once a seed has been sown or a slip planted, it is relatively simple to witness its growth. For that reason, botanical analogies play an important role in ancient embryological treatises, to which we now turn.

THE ROLE OF ANALOGY IN EMBRYOLOGICAL WRITINGS

Ancient embryological treatises contain – perhaps surprisingly – a lot of information on the physiology of plants.[58] The earliest fully preserved embryological treatise, the Hippocratic *On the Nature of the Child*, is no exception in this matter, as it includes an extremely long botanical excursus focusing mostly on the growth of plants.[59] The author develops a theory whereby the earth contains the juices/humours necessary for the growth of all plants. Those juices, however, are not distributed in a uniform manner geographically: in some regions, some juices will be absent, thus preventing the growth of the plants that require them. The author of *On the Nature of the Child* introduces and concludes his excursus in the following manner:

> The nourishment and growth of the child comes from whatever goes from its mother to the uterus, and whatever health or weakness the mother possesses, the child will have the same. In the same way, the things growing in the earth are nourished by the earth ... Now I shall get back to the point for the sake of which I discussed these things. For I maintain that all things that grow in the earth live from the moisture of the earth, and that whatever type of moisture a particular earth contains in itself, the plants too will have it. In the same way, the child lives from its mother in the uterus, and whatever level of health the mother displays, the child will display too. If someone wants to reflect upon what I have said about these things, from beginning to end, they will discover that human growth (*phusin*) is entirely comparable to that of things that grow in the earth.[60]

I have translated the word *phusis* in this passage as 'growth'. However, as we have already seen, the word can also be translated as 'nature', since the state of a living being is the result of its growth. For the Hippocratic author, plants and humans share a *phusis*, and it is this commonality that makes plants helpful in explaining what is mostly unperceivable to the senses: an animal or human embryo.

The notion of plant *phusis* also played an important role in Stoic embryological thinking, as in the following summary of their argument:

> He [Chrysippus] believes that the foetus in the womb is nourished by nature (*phusei*) like a plant. When it is born, its *pneuma* being cooled and hardened by the air, changes and becomes alive/animal. Hence, the soul (*psuchēn*) rightly gets its name from cooling (*psuxin*).[61]

The Stoic embryo, then, is not an animal; it only becomes so at birth. During gestation, an embryo is governed by nature (*phusei*) rather than by the soul, and is therefore like a plant. It possesses a *pneuma*, a breath, rather than a soul. That breath is hot and is cooled down and hardened at birth. In the Greek language, the nouns 'soul' (*psuchē*) and 'cooling' (*psuxin*, from the verb *psuchein*, 'to cool down') sound similar, thus explaining the etymology in the above passage: the soul is the result of a cooling down. Galen criticises the idea of a cooling down at birth in the following passage, which also employs botanical similes:

> Look at it this way: this plant is going to become an animal not by losing the power that it had from the beginning [sc. the nutritive power], but by acquiring another one. When it is fully developed and released from the uterus it must move from place to place. It could not do this if it became cold, like trees, or if it lacked organs for locomotion. Therefore, in order to be hot in the measure in which it is proper for an animal to be hot, and in order to be able to change its place, it acquired two additional sources, one the source of the organs that will preserve for it its natural heat, the other of the organs that will serve all its voluntary actions. It will use these organs later.[62]

Here the physician explicitly states that the embryo *is* a plant, not that it 'lives the life of a plant'. Slightly earlier in the treatise, Galen had indeed indicated that, unlike Hippocrates (i.e. the author of *On the Nature of the Child*), who called the foetus that moves a child, he would name it a plant: 'but at this point I need not talk about the foetation as an animal, for as a plant it obtained all its generation and formation from the seed'.[63] To Galen, the foetus only became an animal when its heart started to beat, the heart being the second main internal organ to develop. Before the first heart-beat, the embryo was governed by the liver (the first organ to develop) and the nutritive part of the soul, which is located in the liver.[64] With the first heartbeat, the embryo started to resemble the living beings such as the testacea, which are very low in the animal hierarchy. The process of transformation of the embryo from plant to animal was therefore progressive and only really ended after birth, when the highest sense – sight – was fully developed.

One could not end this chapter without a mention of the embryological treatise *To Gaurus*, attributed to Galen in the manuscript tradition, but actually by the Neoplatonic philosopher Porphyry.[65] The style of the treatise is very complex; it consists in a series of propositions followed by counterarguments, and it is at times difficult to determine what exactly Porphyry himself was arguing. Put simply, Porphyry argued that the embryo is not an animal, whether this be potentially or in actuality. Rather the embryo is nourished like a plant throughout pregnancy: it gets its nourishment from the mother through the umbilical cord as a plant would through its roots.[66] At the time of conception, the vegetative power of the father, present in the semen, joins the vegetative power of the mother in the uterus, where they blend together.[67] Porphyry's embryo only becomes an animal after birth, but this does not mean that he agrees with the Stoic notion of nature and *pneuma*, which is cooled down at birth and becomes a soul: quite the contrary, the Stoics are severely criticised in *To Gaurus*. In the process of explaining what the embryo is, Porphyry naturally had to address the issue of whether plants have sensation or not. This led him to comment on the difficult passage of Plato's *Timaeus* mentioned earlier in this chapter. For Porphyry, plants – and embryos – only experience sensations in a passive manner.[68]

Porphyry, like other Neoplatonist philosophers, argued that both a man and a woman contribute a part of their vegetative soul to the embryo. The mother contributes more than mere nourishment to the embryo; she also makes a psychological contribution. This means that, for the usual analogy between animal mother and earth to work, the Neoplatonist philosopher had to posit that the earth possessed a vegetative soul-power. Porphyry, however, was rather unusual in this respect, as he abandoned the idea that embryos are nourished by the mother like plants are nourished by the earth. Instead, the relation between his embryo and its mother is analogous to that between a scion and a rootstalk.[69] The analogy is thought-provoking, even though Porphyry's botany is rather complex and perhaps even muddled.[70]

Thus, to some philosophers the embryo lived the life of a plant, or was a plant, for parts or the entirety of pregnancy. Most debates posited a dichotomy between plant and animal. In a few late texts, however, a new possibility arose: the embryo might be a zoophyte, a boundary being between plant and animal. The first preserved text to raise that possibility is Philoponus' *Commentary on Aristotle's On the Soul*: 'for [embryos] are joined together to the mother and they are bound like a part that is subordinate to her, and they are moved in the same way of zoophytes'.[71]

John of Alexandria also toyed with the idea that the embryo is a zoophyte in his commentary on the Hippocratic *On the Nature of the Child*, but rejected it. He also rejected the more common idea that the foetus is nourished like an animal or like a plant, and raised a fourth possibility:

> We state that they [authorities] have wrongly taken it that every
> nourished being is nourished either as a plant or as a zoophyte
> or as an animal only. I, for my part, say that the nourished being,
> namely the offspring, is nourished in the same way as seeds of corn

are nourished. And if you say that the seed is nourished as a plant potentially, in the same way I say that the offspring is nourished as an animal potentially.[72]

Unfortunately, John of Alexandria did not pursue the topic any further, making it very difficult to know what he meant. It appears that to him the embryo is potentially an animal, and is nourished as such, not as an animal, a plant, or a zoophyte. To John, the analogy between an embryo and a plant seed is only that; the embryo is not a plant.

CONCLUSIONS

The ancient question 'what is a plant?' is a difficult one, one that leads us straight into ancient debates on the nature of soul, and on the boundaries of animal life. No two philosophers would have defined a plant in the same way. In this chapter, I have tried to present as many opinions as possible, but there were of course many more. However, whether they called it 'nature', 'vegetative part of the soul', or 'appetitive part of the soul', most philosophers agreed that humans had in themselves something that followed the rules of the vegetable world. This idea has still some currency in modern medical practice and ethics, when debates arise around the limits of consciousness and persistent vegetative states.

Although Theophrastus is a significant exception here, many ancient philosophers considered vegetative life to be the lowest, simplest type of life: studying plants helped understand animals, and more particularly, humans. In non-philosophical texts, however, the picture is more complex. When a mythical character metamorphosed into a plant, that plant carried in itself all the complexities of its former self, and often continued to express emotions through swaying or crying tears.[73] There, it is the origin myth that enables the reader to understand a plant's nature. It still remains that, while it was possible for a human to become a plant, once the metamorphosis had happened, there was no turning back. A plant had to remain a plant.

NOTES

The first draft of this article was written during a stay at the Fondation Hardt in Geneva. I wish to thank the Fondation for its hospitality. During my stay, I benefited immensely from discussions with Jaap Mansfeld. Many thanks also to Liba Taub for inviting me to contribute to this volume, for her constructive comments, and for her editorial work.

1 For an introduction to plants, see Walker 2012. For the ancient definition of plants, see Hardy and Totelin 2016, 64–70. Unless stated otherwise, all translations from the Greek and the Latin are mine.

2 On ancient coral, see Pottier 1887 (still very useful); Hünemörder and Pingel 1999; Magdelaine 2000.

3 Ov. *Met.* 4.740–52.

4 The French naturalist Jean-André Peysonnel was the key figure in classifying coral among animals. He did so in a manuscript presented to the Royal Society of London, an account of which is to be found in Watson 1751.

5 Theophr. *De lapidibus* 38.

6 Theophr. *Hist. pl.* 4.11.13.

7 Ibid., 4.7.2.

8 Orphica, *Lithica* 517–19.

9 Plin. *HN* 32.22.

10 Ibid., 13.142.

11 Dioscorides 5.121.

12 Nemesius, *De natura hominis* 1.3, trans. Sharples and van der Eijk 2008, 38.

13 On the Aristotelian definition of plants and their relations to other living beings, see Lloyd 1996, 67–82.

14 See, e.g. Arist. *Part. an.* 1.1.641b5–8.

15 Arist., *De an.* 2.3.414b1.

16 This part of the soul is called 'vegetative' at *Eth. Nic.* 1.13.1102a23 and 1102b29.

17 See, e.g. Arist. *Gen. an.* 1.23.731a25–26; *Hist. an.* 7.1.588b24–27

18 Arist., *Eth. Nic.* 1.13.1102b4–6.

19 Arist. *Gen. an.* 5.1.778b32–779a1. On Aristotelian embryology, see most recently Connell 2016, in particular 139–41 for the analogy between embryo and plant.

20 Arist. *Gen. an.* 2.3.736b8–12.

21 Ibid., 2.4.740a24–27.

22 Ibid., 2.4.740b8–10.

23 Ibid., 1.23.731a5 = DK31B79.

24 Arist. *De an.* 1.5.411b19–22. On generation of plants from slips, see Hardy and Totelin 2016, 134–5.

25 Arist. *Hist. an.* 7.1.588b4–21. See also Arist. *Part. an.* 4.5.681a12–15. What Aristotle meant by 'continuously' is debated by scholars: see Granger 1985.

26 On the place of the sponge in Aristotle's biology, see Lloyd 1996, 75–6.

27 Arist. *De an.* 2.12.424a32–b3.

28 See Panagiotou 1975; Andersen 1976.

29 Arist. *De an.* 2.3.414b2–6.

30 Theophr. *Caus. pl.* 1.12.5.

31 Theophr. *Hist. pl.* 1.1.3.

32 Pl. *Ti.* 77b.

33 For a good summary, and Galen's commentary on the passage, see Wilberding 2014, 252–7.

34 Nicolaus, *De plantis* 1.1.3, 10.815a17–b19, trans. Drossaart Lulofs and Poortman 1989, 126–8 = DK 31A70.

35 Clem. Al. *Strom.* 8.4.10.4 and 8. On Chrysippus and plants, see fragments collected by Dufour 2004, 157–61.

36 Galen, *De placitis Hippocratis et Platonis* 6.3.7, trans. De Lacy 2005, 375, slightly modified. For an introduction to Galen's theory of the soul, see Donini 2008.

37 Galen, *De naturalibus facultatibus* 1.1 (2.1–2 Kühn).

38 Galen, *De semine* 2.5.67 (De Lacy 1992, 194 = Kühn 4.639).

39 Galen, *De propriis placitis* 15.7, trans. Nutton 1999, 122, slightly modified.

40 See Wilberding 2014 for a fuller discussion of Galen's theory.

41 Much can be found on the topic in Wilberding 2015.

42 Theophr. *Hist. pl.* 4.16.6.

43 On Androcydes, who may have been a physician to Alexander the Great, see Jacques 2008.

44 See Pease 1927 for these stories.

45 Plin. *HN* 19.156.

46 Palladius, *De insitione* 143–4.

47 On impossible grafts in antiquity, see Pease 1933; Thibodeau 2011, 145–50.

48 Plin. *HN* 14.10.

49 Cato, *Agr.* 32.

50 Columella, *De re rustica* 10.194–9.

51 See Dioscorides 2.136.1.

52 On these stories, see Georgi 1982; Hardy and Totelin 2016, 132–3. On genders attributed to plants in antiquity, see Tortzen 1991; Negbi 1995; Foxhall 1998.

53 Plin. *HN* 13.34–5; Florentinus ap. *Geoponika* 10.4.

54 Ach. Tat. 1.17.

55 Amm. Marc. 24.3.12-13.

56 Basil of Caesarea, *Homiliae in hexaemeron* 5.7.

57 For an overview of ancient plant generation, see Hardy and Totelin 2016, 127–43.

58 For insights into ancient embryology, see the essays collected by Brisson et al. 2008.

59 On this excursus, see Lonie 1969.

60 *De natura pueri* 22, 27.

61 Chrysippus fr. 806 = Plut, *De Stoic. Repugn.* 41.1052f–1053a. On the Stoic conception of the embryo, see Gourinat 2008.

62 Galen, *De semine* 1.9.18-20 (4.546 Kühn), trans. De Lacy 1992, 97.

63 Galen, *De semine* 1.9.10 (4.543 Kühn).

64 See Boudon-Millot 2008 for an introduction to Galenic embryology.

65 See Wilberding 2011 for an introduction to the question of authorship.

66 Porph. *Ad Gaurum*, 12.4.

67 Ibid., 10.4–5.

68 Ibid., 4.8.

69 Ibid., 10.1–2.

70 See Wilberding 2015, 424–6 for fuller discussion.

71 Philoponus, *In de anima* (15.214 Hayduck 1897).

72 John of Alexandria, *Commentarii in Hippocratic librum de natura pueri* 5.23 (152 Duffy).

73 See, for instance, the stories of the metamorphoses of the Heliades and Myrrha (Ov. *Met.* 2.319–40, 10.298–502).

8   Meteorology

Monte Ransome Johnson

Greco-Roman meteorology will be described in four overlapping developments. In the archaic period, astro-meteorological calendars were written down, and one appears in Hesiod's *Works and Days*; such calendars or almanacs originated thousands of years earlier in Mesopotamia.[1] In the second development, also in the archaic period, the pioneers of prose writing began writing speculative naturalistic explanations of meteorological phenomena: Anaximander, followed by Heraclitus, Anaxagoras, and others. When Aristotle in the fourth century BCE mentions the 'inquiry that all our predecessors have been calling meteorology' (338a26), he is referring to these writers. In the third development, the first two enterprises were combined: empirical data collection about meteorological phenomena began to be married to naturalistic theoretical explanation. This innovation was prompted by Democritus and synthesised in its most influential form by Aristotle. At this point more sophisticated techniques of both short-term weather forecasting and long-term speculation about global climate change were also developed. In the fourth development, the wider implications of the naturalistic explanation of meteorological phenomena were contested. The views of 'meteorologists' had been controversial since the archaic period because they were perceived, and sometimes intended, to displace the divine prerogatives and undermine traditional religion. These controversies intensified throughout the classical and Hellenistic periods.

Aristotle established meteorology as a science. Whereas his predecessors had discussed meteorology in all-encompassing cosmological works, he conducted a systematic investigation devoted entirely to meteorological phenomena, entitled *Meteorology* (*Meteôrologikôn*).[2] Although he agreed that 'meteorology'[3] was continuous with natural inquiry, and although some of his contemporaries used the term interchangeably with 'astronomy', Aristotle carefully differentiated the subject from related ones,[4] and described its unique methodological features. He specified in his logical works how the practical-empirical and theoretical-explanatory parts of meteorological inquiry could be related to one another as sub-alternate sciences so as to produce scientific demonstrations (*apodexeis*) and causal explanations (*aitiai*). And in the *Meteorology* he offered mathematical explanations of optical meteorological phenomena such as halos and rainbows that conform to his methodological standards. Aristotle also methodically collected the meteorological views of his predecessors; meteorology comprises a significant part of doxographical literature.[5] Finally, Aristotle's meteorology was immensely influential on the subsequent development of the science, beginning in the Hellenistic era, when his views were adapted even by competing schools of Epicureans and Stoics. Later meteorology was mostly written as commentary on Aristotle's *Meteorology* well into the early modern period.[6] As an influential historian of meteorology stated: 'the system established by Aristotle remained for nearly two thousand years the standard textbook of our science'.[7]

ASTRO-METEOROLOGY AND WEATHER SIGNS

In the astro-meteorological almanac in *Works and Days*, Hesiod structures his advice on farming and sailing according to risings and settings of prominent heavenly bodies throughout the solar year, beginning with the harvest at the Pleiades' rising (in early May); ploughing is supposed to begin when the Pleiades set (in early November). In between is 'the season of toilsome summer ... men are weakest, for Sirius parches their head and knees, and their skin is dry from the heat'.[8] Hesiod here refers to the position (in mid-July) of Sirius, the brightest star in the night sky, also known as the Dog-star.[9] He recommends cutting wood around early October: 'when the strength of the sharp sun ceases from its sweaty heat, as mighty Zeus sends the autumn rain, and a mortal's skin changes with great relief – for that is when the star Sirius goes during the day only briefly above the heads of death-nurtured humans'.[10] Under Sirius, the weather is hot and dry – Hesiod almost seems to imply that the position of the star is the cause of the dryness and heat. When Sirius changes position, the heat dies down, then Zeus causes rain.

More prosaic calendars, called *parapêgmata*, were originally inscribed on stones and erected as monuments in public places as instruments for tracking cyclical phenomena by means of a movable peg; specimens dating back to the fifth century BCE survive.[11] Literary *parapêgmata* were written on paper. The following excerpts are from the *parapêgma* attributed to Geminus.[12]

> The Sun traverses *Cancer* in thirty-one days. The 1st day: According
> to Callippus Cancer begins to rise, summer solstice, and there is
> a change in the weather ... 27th: ... According to Eudoxus Sirius
> rises in the morning, and for the next fifty-five days the Etesian
> winds blow ...
>
> The Sun traverses *Leo* in thirty-one days. On the 1st
> day: According to Euctemon Sirius is visible, stifling heat follows,
> there is a change in the weather ...
>
> The Sun traverses *Scorpio* in thirty days ... On the 4th
> day: According to Democritus, the Pleides set at the same time as
> daybreak, wintery winds for the most part, and cold, there is now
> frost, it tends to be wintery, trees really begin to lose their leaves.

As in Hesiod, the rising of Sirius is associated with summer and hot, dry weather. But the accounting is more specific and detailed, and covers a greater variety of phenomena, and authorities are cited, like in a modern scientific paper.

Democritus is one of the most frequently cited authors in literary *parapêgmata*.[13] His predictions are usually accompanied by the qualifying expressions 'for the most part' (*hôs ta polla*) and 'tends to' (*philei*) (as in the above quotation), whereas the other authorities simply assert (as Hesiod did) that storms, winds, etc. do occur at the indicated time. These qualifiers indicate awareness of variation from the annual norm, and thus represent a more advanced concept of meteorology than is evident in the astro-meteorological *parapêgmata* based on fixed points in the solar year.

Pliny the Elder in general follows Hesiod in structuring recommendations for farmers according to the solar year, but he noted that 'Democritus thinks that the weather through the winter will be the same as it was on the shortest day and the three days that surround it, and he thinks so too in regard to the summer and the weather at the summer solstice.'[14] Democritus developed techniques of short-term weather forecasting, even for the weather of the next few days or hours,[15] and was reputed to have been successful.[16] Pliny reports that 'Democritus urged his brother Damasios, who was reaping his harvest on a very hot day, to stop harvesting and to gather what he had already cut and put it under cover. A few hours later his forecast was confirmed by a fierce rainstorm.'[17] Although his interest in these phenomena may have been largely theoretical, it may also have had other practical applications in addition to farming,[18] including medicine.[19]

These developments influenced later literature on weather signs. The work *On Signs*,[20] usually attributed to Theophrastus, was probably based on a work by Aristotle of the same title, which was in turn probably based on a lost work of Democritus.[21] In it certain meteorological phenomena are described as indicated by various signs (stars, sun, moon, comets, thunder, lightning, rainbows, halos, insects, birds, spiders, worms, frogs, and mammals). Within each section (in the order: rain, wind, storms, fair weather), the signs are given as in the following: 'Often (*hôs epi to polu*), an iridescent halo shining either around or through a lamp is a sign of rain from the south'; 'If it is not rainy at <the rising of> Sirius or Arktouros, there will be, for the most part (*hôs epi to polu*), rain or wind at the time of the <autumnal> equinox'.[22] The general formula is:

If there is A <sign>, then ('for the most part') there will be B <signified>.

It is notable that *On Signs* is arranged according to event signified, not according to sign, which would be more useful for weather forecasting. This indicates a more theoretical purpose for collecting data on correlated meteorological phenomena than is evident in the astro-meteorology of Hesiod and the *parapêgmata*.[23]

METEOROLOGY AND THE INQUIRY INTO NATURE

Hesiod frequently describes meteorological events as intentional acts of the gods.

Sailing is in good season ... for fifty days after the solstice, when the summer goes to its end ... You will not wreck your boat then nor will the sea drown your men – so long as Poseidon, the earth-shaker, or Zeus, king of the immortals, does not wish to destroy them; for in these gods is the fulfillment, both of good and evil alike. That is when breezes are easy to distinguish and the sea is painless: at that time entrust your swift boat confidently to the winds, drag it down to the sea and put all your cargo into it. But make haste to sail back home again as quickly as possible, and do not wait for the new wine and autumn rain and the approaching winter and the terrible blasts of Notus, which stirs up the sea, accompanying Zeus' heavy autumn rain, and makes the sea difficult.[24]

Homer too had held the gods responsible for meteorological events.[25] About a century after Hesiod, in the first prose books written in Greek, Anaximander began offering naturalistic explanations of the same meteorological phenomena. For example:

Winds occur when the finest vapors of the air are separated off and
when they are set in motion by congregation. Rain occurs from the
exhalation that issues upwards from the things beneath the sun, and
lightning whenever wind breaks out and cleaves the clouds.[26]

Anaximander held that the earth was originally covered by water; the
sun caused most of the moisture to evaporate away; the remaining
salty part is the sea. The evaporation causes winds; winds enclosed and
compressed by clouds eventually tear out, causing explosions, thunder
and lightning. The model of the sun acting on the moist surface of the
earth so as to cause a 'vapour' (atmis) or 'exhalation' (anathumiasis)
was immediately developed by Anaximenes[27] and Heraclitus as the
basis for explanation of all meteorological phenomena.[28] Heraclitus
distinguished two exhalations, relating them to a series of elemental
transmutations of fire, a view later adapted by Aristotle.[29]

By the mid-sixth century BCE Ionians were investigating every
variety of meteorological phenomena mentioned in the epics, and had
already developed competing explanations. Anaximander was also 'the
first to depict the inhabited earth on a chart'.[30] He conceived not only
of the shape of the entire earth, but also its relation to the stars, sun,
and moon, and realised that earth has antipodes. His outlook was global
and he offered his explanations in the context of a comprehensive cosmogony, zoogony, and anthropogony. The resulting 'naturalising' picture is as different from the 'theologising' one of Homer and Hesiod as
prose is different from poetry.[31] Nowhere is this difference more vivid
than with respect to meteorological phenomena.

Against the background of astro-meteorology and parapêgmata,
what stands out most in Anaximander and his successors is the concern to explain the phenomena. Against the background of Homer and
Hesiod, what stands out is the naturalistic and non-theological perspective of the explanations.[32]

There is little evidence about Anaximander's, Anaximenes', or
Heraclitus' knowledge of astro-meteorology or practical interests in
weather signs. It is only with Democritus that we have clear evidence
of interest in both the empirical-practical and explanatory-theoretical
dimensions of meteorology.[33] It is also with Democritus that the replacement of intentional actions of the gods with natural causal explanations
becomes an explicit programme.

Democritus also expanded the reach of meteorology to include both
shorter- and longer-term phenomena. We already saw that Democritus

developed techniques of short-term weather forecasting. He also specu-
lated about changes in the global environment, asserting that the earth is
warming up and drying out, causing overall sea levels to decrease.[34] Such
speculation was related to Democritus' all-embracing physical theory.
A papyrus records his view on how the sea came into existence:

> in liquids, as in the universe as a whole, like is sorted out together
> with like as a residue of putrification and it is by this process of
> congregation of like elements that the sea and other salty substances
> are formed ... Democritus says that the most astonishing and
> paradoxical works of nature come about in the same way, as there
> are not many differences among the elements composing the earth.[35]

We see a similar employment of explanatory analogy in his explanation
of wind:

> Democritus says that when there are many particles, which he
> calls atoms, in a confined empty space, the result is wind; on the
> other hand, the air is in a peaceful, still state when there are few
> particles in a large empty space. In a marketplace or street, so long
> as there are few people, one can walk without interference, but
> when a crowd converges in a confined area, there is quarrelling as
> people bump into each other. In exactly the same way, in the space
> surrounding us, when many particles have filled a small region,
> inevitably they bump into each other, push forward and get pushed
> back, become entwined and get forced together.[36]

It is characteristic of Democritus to explain large-scale phenomena
by analogy to small-scale ones. He also pioneered giving multiple
explanations of meteorological phenomena, for example, earthquakes.[37]
Such explanations were designed to remove the terror of natural phenomena caused by the belief that gods inflict them on humans as punishment.[38] Democritus claimed that astonishment at meteorological
phenomena caused belief in gods:

> Some people think that we arrived at the idea of gods from the
> remarkable things that happen in the world. Democritus ... says
> that the people of ancient times were frightened by happenings in
> the heavens such as thunder, lightning, thunderbolts, conjunctions
> of stars, and eclipses of the sun and moon, and thought that they
> were caused by the gods.[39]

Democritus offered to remove their astonishment and fear by explaining all such phenomena according to naturalistic explanations, thus obviating the perception of divine intervention.

THE BACKLASH AGAINST METEOROLOGY

In a lost play by Euripides, the trickster Sisyphus claims that a 'shrewd and clever man invented for mortals a fear of the gods' and

> placed them where they might make the greatest impression upon human beings ... where he knew that fears come to mortals ... from the vault on high, where they beheld the shafts of lightning and fearful blows of thunder and star-filled gleam of heaven ... parade-ground for the brilliant mass of the sun and source of rainfall moistening the earth below.[40]

The speech evidently represents the views not of Euripides himself, but of naturalists like Anaximander and Democritus. Popular depictions of 'meteorologists' conflated them with healers and itinerant priests who claimed possession of wisdom unavailable through traditional state religion.[41] Aristophanes' *Clouds*, performed in 423 BCE, capitalises on this conflation in a hilarious way. Strepsiades, desperate to relieve himself of debt, visits the 'Thinkery' where 'meteoro-sophists' offer to teach how to make the worse argument defeat the better; he encounters 'Socrates' suspended up high in a basket making 'accurate discoveries about meteorological phenomena'.[42] 'Socrates' is portrayed worshipping meteorological phenomena as if they were gods: 'O Lord and Master; measureless Air, who hold the earth aloft, and you, shining Empyrean, and ye Clouds, awesome goddesses of thunder and lightning.'[43] He is even portrayed denying the existence of traditional gods, 'disproving' their existence by replacing Zeus' rain and thunder with naturalistic explanations.[44]

Plato worked to deflect such views from Socrates. In his *Apology*, Socrates is portrayed refuting the accusation that he is 'a student of all the meteors and things below the earth' (18b7–8). Negative attitudes about 'meteorologists' persisted throughout antiquity.[45] Plato was sensitive to how they affected the perception of philosophy; his Socrates complains that 'they mention accusations available against all philosophers, about the meteors and things below the earth, about not believing in the gods, and about making the worse argument the stronger' (23d5–7). In the *Phaedo* Socrates claims that only in his youth did he dabble in meteorology, a passing interest he lost when disappointed by Anaxagoras' failure to explain how the phenomena are caused by an intelligent mind (*Phd.* 96a–e). Aristotle too reports that Socrates (in contrast to Democritus) turned his attention away from natural phenomena and towards political affairs (*Parts of Animals* 642a24–31; *Metaphysics* 1078b17–23).

Aristophanes falsely portrayed Socrates as a naturalistic philosopher to brilliant comedic effect, but the meteorological explanations and characters he devised are closely modelled on the kind of explanations found in the doxography of early Greek meteorology, for example in 'Socrates'' explanation of how clouds cause thunder: 'when they fill up with lots of water and are forced to drift by necessity (*di' anagkên*) sagging down with rain, then run into one another, and become sodden, they explode and crash' (376–8). Diogenes of Apollonia (ca. 425 BCE), a contemporary of Aristophanes, had made 'air' a leading cosmological principle, and apparently wrote a work dedicated to meteorology.[46] Anaxagoras and Empedocles were even more famous philosophers of this ilk, reputed for their ability to predict the weather.[47]

Plato mocks 'meteorologists' like Anaxagoras, and politicians who associate with them, like Pericles, in the *Phaedrus* (270a). In the *Timaeus*, he elaborates intelligent-design creationism, but conspicuously leaves out central meteorological topics such as thunder and lightning, treating only hail and frost extremely briefly (59de), in a 'diversion' from 'the things that always are, deriving instead a carefree pleasure from surveying likely accounts about becoming'.[48] Later, he harshly condemns 'meteorologists', describing their devolution in his comedic reincarnation scheme: 'Birds as a kind are the products of a transformation ... They descended from innocent but simpleminded men, men who were meteorologists (*meteôrologikôn*), and who in their naivety believed that the most reliable demonstrations concerning those things could be based upon visual observation.'[49] Plato's antipathy to meteorology was thus caused not only by the longstanding association of meteorology with irreligious naturalism, but more specifically by the necessary dependence of meteorology on empirical methods.

ARISTOTLE'S *METEOROLOGY*

Plato's antipathy towards empirical science in general and meteorology specifically stands in stark contrast to Aristotle. In the *Posterior*

Analytics Aristotle points out that the phenomena identified by the empirical sciences can be explained by mathematical sciences.

> It is for the empirical scientists to know the fact, and for the
> mathematical scientists to know the reason why; for the latter have
> the demonstrations of the causes (*tôn aitiôn tas apodeixis*), and often
> the mathematical scientists do not know the fact, just as those who
> study universals often do not know some of the particulars because of
> lack of observation ... Related to optics as this is related to geometry,
> there is another science, that of the Iris. Here it is for the natural
> scientists to know the fact, and for the students of optics (either of
> optics *simpliciter* or of mathematical optics) to know the reason why.[50]

'Empirical scientists', then, state facts about Iris phenomena (e.g. halo or rainbow),[51] while 'mathematical scientists' provide the explanations. This expression 'empirical scientists' is interesting because earlier in the same work Aristotle lays down stringent regulations for demonstration according to which mere observations of empirical facts would be considered insufficient for scientific knowledge. In 1.3 he holds that scientific knowledge can be expressed in the form of syllogisms which can be expressed in the following generic form:

> If (1) A <major term> of every B <middle term>, [Major Premise] and
> if (2) B of every C <minor term>, [Minor Premise] then (3) A of every
> C. [Conclusion]

Aristotle's explanatory syllogisms are more complex than the simple weather sign formula: 'If there is A, then (for the most part) there will be B.' With Aristotle's syllogisms we are dealing with not one but two conditional propositions, as well as a third proposition (the conclusion) necessitated by them; and the propositions include three terms, not just two.

In the context of demonstrations involving mixed 'empirical' and 'theoretical' sciences, the empirical sciences are placed 'under' the theoretical ones in the technical sense of explanatory sub-alternation. The conclusion, which is the proposition stating a fact observed by an empirical science, is demonstrated by means of propositions from explanatory mathematical sciences.

For example, consider Aristotle's explanation of the halo. Empirical meteorology identifies the fact that the halo always appears as a full circle around a luminous body like the sun or moon. Another science, which turns out to be a mixed mathematical-physical science called 'mathematical optics', in turn explains these facts by supplying the cause for the phenomena. The explanation of the halo phenomenon is that in the clouds 'tiny and uniform' particles (ice crystals) are suspended and act as mirrors which reflect (prisms which refract, actually) sight-stream to (light from, actually) a heavenly body at a constant angle from a viewer, so that every particle at a certain angular distance (e.g. 22°) becomes illuminated, producing the *appearance* of a complete circle around the moon or sun. Optics thus provides the reason for the phenomena observed in the empirical science of meteorology. Optics is in turn sub-alternate to geometry, which supplies the immediate principle on which explanations in meteorological optics ultimately depend. Consider the following syllogism.

> If (1) a circle is attributable to every figure with limits all equidistant from a single point; and if (2) a figure with limits all equidistant from a single point is attributable to every light reflected by tiny, uniform mirrors; then (3) a circle is attributable to every light reflected by tiny, uniform mirrors.

The major premise is a geometric definition of a circle. The syllogism gives a geometric explanation of the optical theorem stated in the conclusion. This conclusion can in turn be used as the major premise in another syllogism explaining an empirical fact.

> If (3) a circle is attributable to every light reflected by tiny, uniform mirrors; and if (4) a light reflected by tiny, uniform mirrors is attributable to every halo; then (5) a circle is attributable to every halo.

Thus the empirical fact about the halo, that it is circular, is explained on the basis of material and moving causes (reflection of sight-streams by mirrors), and a formal cause (the geometrical definition of a circle). Aristotle's explanation of the halo in *Meteorology* 3.2–3 thus conforms to his strict account of scientific demonstration in the *Posterior Analytics* (where, as we saw, geometry, optics, and Iris phenomena were instanced as a paradigm of scientific sub-alternation).[52]

As the example shows, true observations of 'empirical' meteorology are necessary but not sufficient for scientific knowledge, and can only contribute to knowledge when subordinated to theoretical and explanatory sciences. At the same time, mere theoretical statements about the causes of meteorological phenomena (such as those that survive in our doxography of Anaximander) do not constitute scientific knowledge in Aristotle's technical sense, since causal explanations must be wedded to empirical observations which produce the less well-known, posterior, and mediated conclusions. Otherwise the explanations would not be better known than, prior to, and explanatory of anything, that is, they would not have any subject matter for which they provide the demonstrations. Only the marriage of causal explanations to empirical data produces viable scientific knowledge. Democritus seems to have been the first to recognise this in practice; Aristotle, however, is to be credited with working it out in theory, indicating the logical form that meteorological arguments must take if they are to be scientific.

Aristotle recognises several kinds of causes as middle terms in scientific demonstrations, and in *Posterior Analytics* 2.11 he offers a meteorological example: 'if it thunders, when the fire is extinguished, it is necessary for it to sizzle and make a noise, and also (if things are as the Pythagoreans say) it has the aim of threatening those in Hades in order to make them afraid' (94b32–4). Thunder is noise in the clouds, and this is explained by recognising it in the class of 'fire-extinguishment'. Fire extinguishment in general causes a sizzling noise. Thunder can thus be explained as having a certain form, resulting in a 'formal' explanation.

What about the final cause explanation of thunder? The bizarre 'Pythagorean' explanation embodies the archaic theology of Hesiod. Both the formal and final explanations could easily be formulated as syllogisms, but are both explanatory? Aristotle does not, of course, actually hold that thunder is caused by Zeus for the purpose of terrorising sinners in Hades. What the example shows is that the one kind of explanation (the 'Pythagorean') can be replaced with another (the 'formal' explanation). It is not appropriate to explain every phenomenon by reference to every kind of cause, and many kinds of phenomena, such as eclipses, should not be explained by a final cause.[53] Cases of multiple explanation involving material and moving and formal and final causes occur regularly and as a rule in his biological writings, but in the *Meteorology* Aristotle does not offer *any* final cause explanations – the absence of teleology is conspicuous and noteworthy.[54] And in the *Physics*, Aristotle raises a famous *aporia* about such final cause explanations.

> There is an *aporia*. What prevents nature from acting neither for
> the sake of something nor for the better, but just as Zeus makes

rain (*huei ho Zeus*) not in order to make the crop grow, but out of necessity? For what rises up must be cooled, and what has been cooled, having become water, falls down. This having occurred, it incidentally happens that the crop grows. And similarly, if the crop is destroyed on the threshing-floor, it does not rain for the sake of this (in order to destroy the crop), but this happened incidentally.[55]

Aristotle argues that the kind of explanation given here (and elsewhere[56]) for rainfall, which refers only to material and moving causes (in describing a kind of evaporative cycle through elemental transmutation), is not sufficient in the case of biological explanations, a point he reiterates in a methodological preface to the biological works (*Parts of Animals* 1.1). For example, absolute necessity cannot explain why teeth grow sharp in the front and broad in the back, thus reliably serving a clear purpose (biting and chewing). But rainfall is different: crops may either be helped or hurt by rain if not removed from the threshing floor when a storm happens to come, as Democritus reportedly pointed out to his brother Damasios.[57] Absolute necessity is the cause of the evaporative cycle and thus of rainfall, but its effects may be beneficial or harmful, depending on application or failure of human art. In the case of teeth, the same kind of absolute necessity cannot explain the inherent usefulness of the result, and so a different kind of necessity must be at work, which Aristotle in *Physics* 2.9 calls 'hypothetical necessity', comparing it to the kind of 'necessity' employed in art. In neither case, however, can luck be the cause:

> for teeth and all other natural things either invariably or for the most part (*hôs epi to polu*) occur in a given way, but of none of the results of luck or spontaneity is this true. And we do not think that it is the outcome of luck or concomitance that there is a lot of rain in winter, but only if there is a lot of rain under the Dog-star (*hupo kuna*); nor that that there are heat-waves under the Dog-star, but only if there is a heat-wave in winter.

(Arist. *Ph.* 198b36–199a3)

In this second meteorological example in the *aporia*, Aristotle refers to the 'empirical science' of astro-meteorology which, as we saw, observes the fact that Sirius is accompanied by heatwaves. The question of how to explain such regularities is the subject of the *Meteorology*.

In the opening of *Meteorology*, Aristotle makes reference to his discussion of causes in the *Physics* when describing where meteorology fits into the overall scheme of natural science: 'We have previously spoken about the primary causes of nature, and about all natural motion ... There remains a part of our investigation that all our predecessors have been calling meteorology.'[58]

> Meteorology is concerned with those incidents that are natural, though more disorderly (*ataktoteran*) than that of the first of the elements of bodies. They take place in the region nearest to the motion of the stars. Such are the Milky Way, and comets, and the movements of meteors. It studies also all the affections we may call common to air and water, and the kinds and parts of the earth and the affections of its parts. These throw light on the causes of winds and earthquakes and all the consequences the motions of these kinds and parts involve. Some of these things we are puzzled about, while others we can touch on in a way. Further, the inquiry is concerned with the falling of thunderbolts and with whirlwinds and fire-winds, and further, the recurrent affections produced in these same bodies by concretion.

By 'more disorderly than that of the first of the elements', Aristotle is referring to the motions of the stars in the 'upper' region (including the outermost 'fixed' stars, planets, sun, and the innermost celestial body, the moon), all which he takes to be composed of a special element ('ether'), the natural motion of which is circular.[59] The categorical differentiation of the area beyond the moon as immutable, eternal, and perfect stems from Pythagoreanism, and the idea that phenomena close to the earth involve 'more disordered' things is present in Plato's distinction between accounts of 'the things that always are' and 'likely accounts about becoming' (*Timaeus* 59c–e).

In the region below the moon, Aristotle holds that things are composed of four different elements and do not move in orderly circles but rather in two 'more disorderly' ways: (1) they move rectilinearly, fire and air naturally upwards away from earth as a result of their relative lightness, and water and earth downwards, towards earth, thanks to their relative heaviness; and (2) they transmute, as with air and water in the evaporative cycle. Aristotle stressed that the entire lower region is composed of these four elements, and it is 'their incidental affections' (*ta sumbainonta pathê*) that is the subject of meteorology (339a20–1). This strict differentiation between the heavenly and meteorological spheres precludes the earlier view, held by Anaximander, Heraclitus, and others, that the exhalations from the earth 'feed' the heavenly bodies, and it allowed Aristotle to envision a completely terrestrial evaporative cycle.[60]

The elements are the *material* cause of all meteorological phenomena. The motions and changes in the terrestrial region are continuous with those in the celestial, 'which therefore steer every potentiality of it' (339a22–3); in this way the movement of the celestial element is the primary *moving* cause for all motion in both regions. Most important is the movement of the sun, which melts the uppermost terrestrial region, also called the 'tinder' region (340b10–15). In this way, heat is communicated downwards to the water and earth, giving rise to two different kinds of 'exhalation' (*anathumiasis*): one arising from the water, which is 'more vaporous' and wetter; and another from the air, which is 'more windy' and drier, like smoke. The moist (*hugra*) and dry (*xera*) exhalations never exist in pure forms but are always mixed, and we name a particular exhalation on the basis of which quality predominates (2.4.359b28–32). The moist exhalation is heavier and so naturally falls below the drier and lighter, and the result is two stratified regions we identify with the regions of air and fire. The 'tinder' region, being hot and dry, frequently bursts into flame, causing several kinds of meteorological phenomena which differ according to the position and quantity of inflammable material: 'shooting stars' (1.4), aurorae (1.5),[61] comets (1.6–7), the Milky Way (1.8). The lower regions include a great intermixture of air and water, and are also affected by the sun: as the sun approaches and recedes from earth, its heat produces dissolution and composition of materials, resulting in the generation and destruction of terrestrial things, meteorological, mineralogical, and biological. The sun causes water near the surface of the earth to be heated and thus become lighter and to rise upwards, turning into air, at which point it rises further until it cools and condenses, turning back into water, becoming heavy, and falling to earth as rain (1.9.346a). The same moist exhalation causes clouds and mist (1.9), and, under certain circumstances, dew and frost (1.10), snow and hail (1.11–12). The dry exhalation is the cause of wind (2.4), and when trapped inside the earth, earthquakes (2.8), and when trapped inside a cloud, thunder (2.9); extremely large quantities of dry exhalation cause hurricanes, typhoons, fire-winds, and thunderbolts (3.1).

Aristotle insists that the exhalations are twofold (341b8). The Ionians explained meteorological phenomena by a single exhalation undergoing a linear and unidirectional transformation. Aristotle updates the theory to fit with his doctrine of elements. Although the result might not fully cohere with the theory of elements in other works, Aristotle can be interpreted as virtuously developing an independent science of meteorology with its own appropriate principles, combining the doctrine of elements and the doctrine of exhalations in a creative and influential way.[62] The fact that in so doing he elaborates his views largely by way of criticising his predecessors shows us a lot about his scientific method in general.[63] Aristotle invokes several new kinds of information to defend his views over earlier theories. For example, he brings in the results of recent astronomical research to support his view of the structure of the cosmos and the nature of the exhalations. He also brings new empirical observations, including some of his own, to support his own theories and refute those of his predecessors.[64] He also brings in recent geographical researches to support his account of rivers and terrestrial waters (1.13) and of the size and shape of the inhabited world (2.5).

The result is an astonishingly ambitious attempt to comprehend the meteorological situation of every region of the terrestrial globe and the universal history of its climatic and geographic changes (1.14). Aristotle for the first time divided the globe into five zones by reference to the heavenly sphere, a fruitful methodology for scientific climatology.[65] The term *clima*, which means 'slope', referred originally to the inclination of the earth's axis with respect to the plane of the local horizon,[66] and later to one of the zones defined by two lines of latitude of the earth, beginning with the five zones of Aristotle. The term 'climate' has become identified with the meteorological conditions prevailing in any zone of earth over a long period of time. Aristotle used his division of the earth into zones to speculate about the global climate, including the north and south poles, and he also discussed differences in climate on the basis of longitude, speculating about the extreme east or west of the 'habitable zone'. To reason about these far-off places, he employs both 'demonstrative calculation' (*logos deiknusin*), meaning mathematical techniques, and empirical 'facts known to us from journeys by sea and land' (362b15–20).

Aristotle asserts that 'one area does not remain earth, another sea, for all time, but sea replaces what was once dry land, and where there is now sea there is at another time land'.[67] The process, he insists, occurs in accordance with an order (*taxis*) and a cycle (*periodon*). He explains why the changes escape our notice: 'because the whole natural process of the earth's growth takes place by slow degrees and over periods of time which are vast compared to the lengths of our life, and whole peoples are destroyed and perish before they can record the process from beginning to end'.[68] War, disease, and famine destroy civilisations, and break others up by forcing migrations; environmental changes cause catastrophic agricultural failures that make people move or die out. People tend to settle in places that are wet and do not perceive the gradual change of the place to marsh and then desert: 'the advance is gradual and takes a long time, so that there is no record of who the first settlers were or when they came or in what state they found the land'.[69] He goes into a fair amount of detail about Egypt and Greece.

Up to this point Aristotle seems to be adapting Democritus' account, according to which the whole earth is in a process of warming and drying up, causing lowered sea levels that will eventually result in the drying up of the whole sea (352a; cf. 356b10), a view that Aristotle contemptuously dismisses in giving his own account of the origin, saltiness, and future of the sea (2.1–3). Aristotle criticises the unidirectional picture of 'global drying': 'it is true that there is an increase in the number of places that have become dry land and were formerly submerged; but the opposite is also true, for if they look they will find many places where the sea has encroached'.[70] New empirical evidence is used to confirm the existence of both desertification and sea-level rise. Again, these processes are cyclical and 'just as there is a winter among the yearly seasons, so at fixed intervals in some great period of time there is a great winter and excess of rains. This does not always happen in the same region of the earth.'[71] This is clear evidence that the ancients comprehended the reality of global and cyclical climate change (one is tempted to translate 'great winter' as 'ice age'), and the threat it poses to human civilisations through desertification and soil erosion, rising sea levels and cataclysmic flooding.

Like Democritus, Aristotle discusses long-term climate change in addition to regular seasonal variation of weather. The dry and moist exhalations cause wind and rain respectively. The sun approaching the earth draws up the moist exhalation with its heat, and receding condenses the vapour due to cold; being cold, the vapour falls downwards as rain; this, Aristotle explains, is why there is more rain in the winter than summer, and during night than daytime (359b34–360a3). A parallel process working through the dry exhalation is the cause of winds. Variation in weather (especially rain and wind) is to be explained on the basis of which exhalation predominates, the moist or the dry, and so this is also the basis of explaining drought (360a34–b5). For example, calm weather around the rise of Orion (early July) is due to the fact that the heat of the sun has scorched up and dispersed both the moist and dry exhalations, so that it neither rains nor is windy (2.5.361b14–30). Similarly,

> the Etesian winds blow after the summer solstice and the rise of the Dog-star <i.e. Sirius>; they do not blow when the sun is at its nearest nor when it is far off. They blow in the daytime and drop at night. The reason for this is that when the sun is closer it dries the earth too quickly for the exhalation to form.[72]

Here we have the official moving and material cause explanations of the data contained in astro-meteorological *parapêgmata*, and specifically of the phenomena used as an example in *Physics* 2.8. Notice that in accordance with his solution to the *aporia* about final cause explanations, Aristotle refers only to material and moving cause explanations of rainfall and heatwaves in the *Meteorology*.

All phenomena explained by exhalations are real products of the action of the sun's heat on elemental materials, but Aristotle also identifies meteorological phenomena that are actually optical illusions, including halos (3.2–3) and rainbows (3.4–5).[73] This is one of the most innovative aspects of his meteorology.[74] The explanation of the halo, discussed above, is particularly fascinating because it is a sublunary object that appears to be perfectly circular, like the objects in the celestial realm. Such phenomena were treated in archaic thought as prerogatives of the gods, as were rain, thunder, etc. Xenophanes asserted that 'Iris' (i.e. the cause of rainbows and halos) was actually a cloud.[75] Anaxagoras is credited with first recognising 'reflection' of the sight-stream as from a mirror (what turns out to be refraction of light from a prism) to be the cause of such phenomena.[76] Aristotle continues in this tradition by classifying the phenomena, outlining the outstanding problems and alternative explanations, bringing new empirical observations and new explanatory theories to bear, and by applying geometry and optics. His explanations are the earliest ones we have to be accompanied by lettered geometric diagrams, diagrams that were utilised throughout the Renaissance and early modern science, and are still utilised (though with some important modifications) in contemporary textbooks of meteorological optics.[77]

By contrast, less successful aspects of Aristotle's meteorology show him classifying two kinds of phenomena as meteorological which today we regard differently: the first are geological, namely metals and minerals; the second are astronomical. The second kind of conflation is not very surprising, given the meaning of the word 'meteor', but it is more problematic because the alternative theories available to Aristotle seem better. Aristotle was compelled by his assumptions to posit that rectilinear shooting stars (what we now call 'meteors', using the name of the genus for this species) were not celestial but rather sublunary phenomena. Aristotle was partially right about this: although meteors originate from outer space, they only become visible when falling through the earth's atmosphere where they burn up. But in the case of comets and the Milky Way the same assumptions led Aristotle astray. The Pythagoreans and others held that comets were planets that only appear at long intervals (342b29–343a1). Aristotle dismisses these views and offers two explanations of his own, recognising two different kinds of comets.[78] The explanations may cohere with the principles of Aristotle's meteorological theory, but they involve him in many absurdities, as ancient commentators pointed out.[79] Theoretical convictions about the unchanging celestial region may also have clouded Aristotle's observations (and those of other Greeks), leading to a failure to recognise astronomical phenomena like novae and supernovae.[80] The methodological remark with which Aristotle prefaces his account of comets was thus very appropriate: 'We think that we have adequately explained things unapparent to sensation if we have referred them to what is possible' (344a5–7). This remark has had considerable resonance in the philosophy of science.[81]

HELLENISTIC METEOROLOGY

Given Aristotle's statement of caution about meteorological explanation, and living in our own age of 'climate scepticism', we might expect that ancient sceptics showcased meteorology as a subject of ever-clashing dogmatisms, filled with doubts which call for suspension of judgement. In fact, we do not find them casting any doubt on astro-meteorology or meteorology whatsoever. Even the Pyrrhonian sceptic Sextus Empiricus seems to accept astro-meteorology as a valid science, contrasting it with the pseudo-science of astrology.[82]

In accordance with Aristotle's statement that we must accept 'adequate explanations' that refer to 'what is possible', meteorology ended up one of the least dogmatic and contentious areas of Hellenistic physics, at least with respect to individual explanations (not, however, in the interpretation of the theological implications of the explanations). Consider Theophrastus' treatise *Meteorology* (or *Metarsiology*).[83] Theophrastus briefly lists multiple causes for several phenomena: of thunder seven, of lightning four, of clouds two, etc. Theophrastus seems to enumerate every *possible* explanation for a given phenomenon.[84] Some have interpreted Theophrastus' work as a collection of earlier opinions (a doxography), but Theophrastus may endorse each multiple cause, either because he identifies several species of thunder, lightning, etc., or because he acknowledges an inability to demonstrate the definite cause, so that each of the explanations remains possible, none necessary.

Although for early stoicism we have only a summary of their meteorological views, Aristotle's influence is evident.[85] The fragments of Posidonius' work on meteorology indicate that his views, which were decisive for later Stoicism, were also heavily influenced by Aristotle.[86] Seneca's *Natural Questions* frequently references Aristotle, usually in agreement. This was the longest and most detailed investigation of meteorological topics surviving antiquity after Aristotle's *Meteorology*, and was the main source for meteorology in the Latin Middle Ages.[87] Seneca's explanations of particular phenomena are consistent with the foregoing tradition in being naturalistic.[88] But his overarching goal is to support a Stoical conception of the relationship between humans and gods, and to demonstrate the importance of god in creating and maintaining the cosmos.[89] Seneca thus interweaves his meteorology with theological and moralistic digressions completely alien to Aristotle.[90] Following Posidonius and earlier Stoics, Seneca accepted the validity of divination by comets and lightning.[91] These are not just vestiges of archaic views about meteorology, but a concentrated attempt to revive a theological view of the world. Whatever its other merits, however, Seneca's work did not advance meteorological science much beyond Aristotle.[92]

But advancing meteorological science was unlikely to have been the point. Like the Pseudo-Aristotelian *On the Cosmos*,[93] which may have in part been a response to Epicurus' *Letter to Pythocles*, Seneca's *Natural Questions* is probably best interpreted as a literary 'riposte' to Lucretius' Epicureanism.[94] Lucretius' didactic epic *On the Nature of Things* represents a thoroughgoing Epicurean naturalistic account of cosmology and meteorology designed to liberate us from the fear that the gods control nature. According to Epicurus, we undertake natural inquiry only to free ourselves from fear. In a letter to a disciple, he advises:[95]

> Do not suppose that there is any purpose to knowledge of
> meteorological phenomena (*ta meteôra*), whether considered in
> conjunction with other things or in their own right, other than
> tranquility (*ataraxia*) and firm conviction, just as with everything
> else ... Everything goes smoothly and in conformity with the

phenomena as long as everything is accounted for according to the multiple method, as long as we accept, reasonably, what is said with plausibility about them. But whenever one accepts one theory and rejects another that is equally consonant with the phenomena, it is clear that he deserts all genuine science and falls into myth.

For Epicurus, giving naturalistic explanations is all that is required of meteorology, so long as they are plausible enough to displace fears about the gods.[96] Furthermore, we need not (and should not) arrive at a single definitive explanation, rather we should enumerate as many explanations as are plausible and fit with our naturalistic assumptions; 'exclusion of myth is the sole condition necessary'.[97]

For Aristotle, by contrast, meteorological inquiry is undertaken not primarily for a practical purpose but for the sake of theoretical knowledge. Just because an explanation can dispel fear does not qualify it as a good explanation; Aristotle criticises both mythic accounts and naturalistic accounts that he thinks are implausible. Responding to Democritus' multiple explanations for earthquakes, Aristotle offers his own unified account in 2.8. While Aristotle explains multiple species of phenomena, e.g. several kinds of comet, and allows that there may be multiple causal factors involved in a single explanation (e.g. material and a moving causes), he does not allow multiple independent explanations of the very same phenomenon: he offers exactly one explanation for every meteorological species that he identifies, even while acknowledging that we may only find 'adequate' explanations that refer to 'what is possible'.

Epicurus, however, berates those who insist on a single explanation: 'to supply one cause for these facts, when the phenomena suggest that there are several different explanations, is the lunatic and inappropriate behavior of those who are obsessed with a pointless astronomy and of certain others who supply vain explanations, since they do not in any way liberate the divine nature from burdensome service'.[98] So, for example, Epicurus offers multiple possible explanations of comets,[99] including the Aristotelian one (that comets are an inflammation in the upper atmosphere), and one Aristotle rejects (that they are planetary phenomena, connected with the heavenly bodies). Both are offered as plausible explanations in an extremely non-committal way. Since Epicurus does not accept that the celestial and terrestrial regions are composed of fundamentally different kinds of matter, he is not constrained by Aristotle's presuppositions. In a contrasting case, Epicurus offers multiple explanations of the halo but not the (correct) one given by Aristotle, presumably because it would conflict with his own assumptions about the nature of sensation.[100] But Epicurus accepts any and every naturalistic explanation that can be adapted to his own principles.

What he does exclude are any theological or mythological explanations. Epicurus' naturalistic meteorology stands at an opposite extreme from the theology of the early archaic period, according to which gods cause meteorological phenomena in order to benefit or harm humans. In the centuries after Anaximander, both the empirical inquiry into weather signs and the theoretical explanation of meteorological phenomena were developed, and eventually integrated by Democritus. Aristotle embraced meteorology in his own physics and put the long-developing inquiry on a basis of scientific methodology. Whatever role the divine plays in his wider cosmology and metaphysics, Aristotle's meteorological explanations are purely naturalistic, and involve no teleology whatsoever. The Epicureans had merely to extend this philosophical tradition and did not feel the need to refute alternative explanations. Thus Epicurus seems to have borrowed directly from Theophrastus' work and to some extent may be following his practice of offering multiple explanations,[101] and he could also rehabilitate some earlier explanations rejected by Aristotle, beginning, of course, with those of Democritus. Some of his explanations of meteorological phenomena are unique and pioneering,[102] but Epicurus does not harp on these dogmatically.

The main purpose of Epicurean meteorology was to use naturalistic explanations to obviate the need for traditional theology. This is exactly what Lucretius aims to do in *On the Nature of Things*, and this in turn is what Seneca tried to counteract in his *Natural Questions*. The story about the origin of meteorology as a science (though perhaps not as philosophy) ends here, but the legacy of ancient meteorology continues in the fact that we still conceive of meteorology as an integrated empirical and explanatory science, and in many ways a mathematical science, one with both theoretical and practical aspects and implications. With the recent controversies over global climate change, something ancient scientists had already acknowledged as fact, we also see that the ideological controversies connected with meteorology remain an important part of the story.

NOTES

1 See Graßhoff 2010, 2012.
2 A likely date of around 341–330 BCE can be inferred from the fact that the *Meteorology* was circulated prior to certain geographical facts which suddenly became apparent during the expedition of Alexander into Asia (see Bunbury 1883, I: 401 n. 1).

3 The abstract noun 'meteorologia' at 338a26 means 'discussion of meteors' (ta meteôra), and the title Meteôrologikôn means '<Books> of discussions of meteors'; the exact title may be due to an editor; one manuscript has just Meteôrôn: Of Meteors. The term meteôra (met-êor-ôs) is compounded from meta- (amid or among) + aer- (from aeirô, meaning to lift, raise, or be suspended); ta meteôra are literally, then, 'lofty or uplifted things'. Capelle 1912 details the gradual distinction of meteorology and atmospheric phenomena from astronomy, astrology, astrophysics, and sidereal phenomena.

4 Aristotle included many phenomena as meteorological that are now considered astronomical, such as comets, and others now considered geoscience, such as earthquakes. Aspects of meteorology eventually developed into independent specialised sciences including geography, geology, geophysics, geodesy, hydrology, oceanography, mineralogy, seismology, climatology, and atmospheric chemistry. These sciences, including meteorology, are now collectively referred to as geoscience.

5 Mansfeld 2010a, 239–41, 38–49. See also Taub 2003, 117.

6 Greek commentaries on Aristotle's Meteorology were written in the second century CE by Alexander of Aphrodisias, and in the sixth century by two pupils of Ammonius, Olympiodorus of Alexandria and John Philoponus. (The remains of Philoponus' commentary have recently been translated by Kupreeva 2011, 2012; Kupreeva's introductions contain excellent overviews of Aristotelian meteorology.) Syriac, Arabic, Persian, Hebrew, and Latin traditions eventually developed: Arabic translations and commentaries from the eighth to the fourteenth century CE (Lettinck 1999); Greek commentaries on the work resumed in tenth-century Byzantium, and by the eleventh century Aristotelian meteorology was transmitted into pre-modern Europe (Telelis 2012, 9–12). Translations of Aristotle's Meteorology and of Alexander's commentary were studied and commented on throughout the Renaissance and early modern period. See also Fritscher 2008, 536–8.

7 Hellmann 1908, 228; more recently, Mourelatos 2005, 285; Fritscher 2006, 799.

8 Hes. Op. 584–8, trans. Most 2007.

9 Holberg 2007.

10 Hes. Op. 414–19, trans. Most 2007.

11 Lehoux 2007, 12, 22.

12 Appended to his Isagoge, a first-century CE work; the parapêgma cites no author later than the third century and probably antedates the late second (Lehoux 2007, 157–8). The translation is by Lehoux 2007, 233–5.

13 Such as those of Geminus, Pliny, Ptolemy, and the Byzantine work Geoponika. See Lehoux 2007, 493.

14 Plin. HN 18.231, trans. Rackham 1950.

15 Sider 2002, 292–3, citing evidence from the Byzantine work Geoponika, which is ignored or mishandled by the standard collections of Democritus' fragments.

16 See also Plin. HN 18.273–4; a virtually identical story is told by Aristotle of Thales profiting from meteorological forecasting (Pol. 1.11.1259a6f; cf. Diog. Laert. 1.26; Cic., Div. 1.49.111.

17 Plin. HN 18.341, trans. Sider 2002, 296, adapted.

18 Sider 2002, 300–1.

19 Democritus' lost work On Things Unseasonable and Seasonable probably discussed the interplay between climate and medicine. The same topic was treated extensively in the Hippocratic treatise On Airs, Waters, and Places, in which it is argued that medicine has an important connection to meteorology: 'If

someone supposes all these things to belong to meteorology (*meteôrologa einai*) he will change his mind, learning that astronomy contributes no small part to medicine, but a very great part. For along with the seasons changes the diseases and the digestive organs' (2.21–26, trans. Jones 1923). Democritus very likely influenced the author of this text. See now Liewert 2015, 41–2, who presents a comprehensive study of the history of meteorological medicine.

20 Sider 2002, 293–7.

21 Sider and Brunschön 2007, 42. According to a gloss in the list of Democritus' writing, the work entitled *The Great Year, or Astronomy* included a *parapêgma*. The text reads *Megas eniautos ê Astronomiês parapêgma* (Diog. Laert. 9.48). Sider 2002, 298–9 convincingly argues that the term *parapêgma* was inserted as an editorial comment and was not part of the original title.

22 From sections 13 and 23 of *On Signs*, trans. Sider and Brunschön 2007; on the formula, see 34–5.

23 Sider and Brunschön 2007, 30, 37.

24 Hes. *Op.* 663–70, trans. Most 2007.

25 E.g. *Il.* 16.385–8; *Od.* 14.300–5.

26 Hippol. *Haer.* 1.6.7, trans. KRS. See also Aëtius 3.3.1–2; Sen. *QNat.* 2.18.

27 Arist. *Mete.* 365b6; Theophr. apud Simpl. *in Phys.* 24.22; Aëtius 3.3.2.

28 Clem. Al. *Strom.* 5.104.1–3; Diog. Laert. 9.9–10.

29 Kahn 1960, 99, 109, has thus argued that meteorology was a remarkably conservative line of inquiry stemming from the tradition of Anaximander. See also Taub 2003, 9–10; Mourelatos 2005, 285. See Wilson 2013, 54–60, for an interesting and more nuanced view of the influence of Heraclitus on Aristotle.

30 Agathemerus 1.1, trans. Kahn 1960, 82.

31 The concept of nature is absent from Homer and Hesiod. Aristotle distinguishes between those who frame accounts of the gods (*theologeô*, 983b29), like Hesiod (984b27–9), and those who frame accounts about nature (*phusiologeô*, 988b27), called 'naturalists' (*phusiologoi*, 986b14, 989b30, 990a3, 992b4). See Kahn 1960, 4 n. 1.

32 It is possible that Anaximander imbedded his naturalistic accounts in a larger cosmological framework in which justice plays a role; see the 'fragment' preserved by Simpl. *in Phys.* 24.17; Kahn 1960, 35–9.

33 On the empirical side are Democritus' contributions to the *parapêgmata* literature, mentioned above. On the explanatory side, he wrote a work *On Nature*, as well as works on 'causal explanations' (*aitiai*) of things in the 'heavens', of 'airs' (*aerioi*), of 'surfaces' (*epipedoi*, sc. of the earth), and of 'fire and things in fire'.

34 Arist., *Mete.* 356b; cf. 353b.

35 DK68A99a = *Hibeh Papyrus* 16.62, trans. Taylor 1999, 102–3.

36 Sen. *QNat* 5[4].1.2, trans. Hine 2010.

37 Arist., *Mete.* 365b1–6; Sen. *QNat* 6.20.1–4.

38 Democritus described the end of natural science as 'removal of astonishment or wonder' (*athaumastia*) and 'not being shocked' (*athambia*), not being disturbed (*ataraxia*), and not being upset (*anekplêktos*). See Cic., *Fin.* 5.8.23; Strabo 1.61; Stob. 3.5.74; Euseb., *Praep. evang.* 14.27.4.

39 DK68A75 = Sex. Emp., *Math.* 9.24, trans. Taylor, 140. See also Philodemus, *On Piety*, P.Herc. 1428, fr.16.2–11; Lucr. *DRN* 5.1186–94; Clem. Al., *Protr.* 68.5, *Strom.* 5.102.

40 The translation is by Kahn 1997, 247–8.

41 Marciano 2006.

42 Ar. *Nub.* 228, trans. Henderson 1998.

43 Ibid., 264–6, trans. Henderson 1998.

44 Ibid., 366–71.

45 For example, Lucian offers the following advice: 'The common way of life is the best, and you will act more wisely if you stop doing meteorology (*meteôrologein*) and examining ends and origins, and repudiate those wise syllogisms and consider that sort of thing nonsense' (*Menippus* 21, trans. Harmon 1961).

46 Diogenes of Apollonia is credited with a work on meteorology by Simplicius, *In Phys.* 151.20. Jones 1923 goes too far in saying that the Hippocratic *On Airs, Waters and Places* is 'derived' from Diogenes.

47 Anaxagoras (510–428) had famously demonstrated weather prediction abilities by wearing a raincoat to a public event on a sunny day during which the weather indeed turned to rain (see Sider 2002, 287–8). Empedocles (493–433) reportedly claimed to be able to control the weather, and Gorgias supposedly witnessed him doing so. Gorgias remarks on 'the meteorologists who, by removing one belief and replacing it with another belief, make things that are uncertain and unclear appear before the eyes of belief' (*Encomium to Helen* 13 = DK82B11).

48 Pl. *Ti.* 59d, trans. Zeyl 1997.

49 Pl. *Ti.* 91d6–e1, trans. Zeyl 1997, adapted.

50 *An. Post.* 1.13.78b34–79a13.

51 Iris was Zeus' messenger in the *Iliad*; rainbows and halos are her prerogative (e.g. 17.546–552, 23.198–211). Aristotle discusses Iris phenomena in *Mete.* 3.

52 See further Johnson 2009.

53 *Metaph.* 8.4.1044b8–12; see further Johnson 2005, 156.

54 Johnson 2005; Wilson 2013.

55 Arist. *Ph.* 2.8.198b16–23.

56 *An. post.* 2.12.96a2–7; Arist., *De insomniis* 3.457b31–538a1; *Mete.* 1.9.346b16–31; *Part. an.* 2.7.653a2–8; cf. *Metaph.* 6.2.1026b27–35; Johnson 2005, 150–6.

57 See above n. 17.

58 338a2–26, trans. Webster 1931, adapted. The following inset quotation continues to 339a5.

59 For an enlightening discussion of this distinction and the issues related to it, see Falcon 2005, 2–13.

60 Fritscher 2006, 798.

61 On Aristotle's successes in classifying ancient aurorae, see Stothers 1979.

62 Wilson 2013, 37–8.

63 Freeland 1990.

64 As has been shown with respect to comets and hail by Freeland 1990. Wilson 2013 builds on Freeland's point and shows this with respect to several other kinds of meteorological phenomena.

65 The theory of zones may have originated earlier, with Parmenides. According to Strabo, 'Posidonius says that Parmenides took the lead in dividing the earth into five zones' (Strabo 94). The authoritative Bunbury 1883 states: 'the division of the terrestrial globe into zones … [is] said to have originated with Parmenides, but … was developed in a more systematic form by Aristotle. It was the latter who first defined them in the sense in which they are understood by modern geographers' (Bunbury 1883, II: 227); and Tozer 1964 concurs: 'Aristotle is the first writer in whom we find an attempt to determine these limits on scientific principles' (179).

66 Neugebauer quoted in Taub 1993, 67–8.

67 351a22–5, trans. Lee 1952, adapted.

68 351b8–13, trans. Lee 1952.

69 351b25–7, trans. Lee 1952.

70 352a21–5, trans. Lee 1952.

71 352a28–32, trans. Lee 1952.

72 361b35–362a3, trans. Lee 1952.

73 See Boyer 1987; a magisterial history of the explanation of the rainbow. His discussion of Aristotle's contribution is on 41–65.

74 Taub 2003; Johnson 2009; Stothers 2009.

75 Aëtius 2.20.3.

76 Aëtius 3.5.11.

77 Johnson 2009.

78 See Freeland 1990; Wilson 2013.

79 E.g. Philoponus, *In Meteorologia* 97,22–98,13, 113,34–117,7 (citing Damascius).

80 Lloyd 1996, 164.

81 Hankinson 2013, 77–8.

82 Sext. Emp. *Math.* 5.1–2.

83 The work survives in Syriac and Arabic translation. For text, translation, and commentary, see Daiber 1992.

84 For example, he remarks that 'these are the causes by which lightning *can* occur' (2.17, trans. Daiber 1992, 262).

85 Diog. Laert. 7.151–4.

86 Kidd 1988, 84–5; 1992, 294–5; Fritscher 2008, 536. Alexander, *In Mete.* 3.3 explicitly says that Posidonius followed Aristotle's explanation of the halo.

87 Fritscher 2006, 798; 2008, 536.

88 Hine 2010, 8, 139.

89 Thom 2014, 1, 107–19.

90 Inwood 2005.

91 E.g. Sen. *QNat.* 2.32.

92 Graver 1999, 52–4; Hine 2010, 7–8. As Hine points out, the most important exception is his vigorous defence of the view that comets are planetary and not sublunary phenomena. Seneca's work remains crucial for its preservation of earlier views, and is fascinating from the literary and philosophical standpoint, as Taub 2003 (141–61), Inwood 2005, and Williams 2012 bring out well.

93 See Thom 2014.

94 Graver 1999, 51; Hine 2010, 5; Williams 2012, 9.

95 *Ep. Pyth.* 85–7, trans. Hankinson, 79–80, adapted. See also *RS 9*.

96 Taub 2009, 121.

97 *Ep. Pyth.* 104.

98 *Ep. Pyth,* 113, trans. Inwood.

99 *Ep. Pyth.* 111.

100 Namely, that sensations do not present illusions but reliable impressions that emanate directly from the surfaces of aggregate bodies such as clouds (see Johnson 2009).

101 Sedley 1998a, 125–6.

102 E.g. the formation of ice (*Ep. Pyth.* 109).

9   Ancient Greek Mathematics

Nathan Sidoli

This chapter is addressed to those who wish to read the primary sources of Greco-Roman mathematics, either in the original languages or in modern translations. Hence, it focuses on the kinds of mathematics that was disseminated in treatises written by scholars who were members of a relatively small literary elite. This theoretical style of mathematics was not the only kind of mathematics practised in Greco-Roman antiquity, and, indeed, the total number authors of philosophical mathematics must have been dwarfed by the number of individuals who used practical mathematics in their daily work, and who passed on such mathematical skills to their sons, disciples, and apprentices.[1] Nevertheless, the literary works produced by this self-selected group of individuals have elicited the admiration and study of mathematical scholars throughout the centuries, and have justly been regarded as one of the most important products of ancient scholarship.

The modern reader who encounters these works in their original presentation may, however, have the uncanny feeling of experiencing something that is at once both reassuringly familiar and yet strangely alien. Much of the mathematics that we learn in school derives from Greco-Roman origins, but many of the actual interests and methods of ancient mathematicians are no longer part of our approach to mathematics. In order to read the ancient sources, however, we must try to recreate their interests and to follow through with their methods. This chapter is meant to be an introduction to this process.

It begins with a discussion of the evidence itself, with emphasis on how far removed this often is from the mathematical activity we are trying to understand. It then situates the production of literary mathematical texts in a broader context of mathematical activities, including oral presentation and material practices. Finally, special topics of mathematical practice are addressed: the overall role of structure, the production of various types of argument, the function of constructions and constructivist thinking, and the execution of operations and algorithms.

SOURCES FOR THEORETICAL MATHEMATICS

Our evidence for ancient Greek mathematical activity comes, almost exclusively, from texts that were passed down through the medieval period in contexts that were often not devoted to mathematical activity and by individuals who generally did not themselves produce original mathematics. Although this is true for all of the ancient Greek theoretical sciences, the situation is perhaps more pronounced in the case of mathematics.

The manuscript sources are divided by modern scholars into direct and indirect traditions. The direct tradition consists of manuscripts of source texts, in Greek, while the indirect traditions are made up of commentaries and summaries in Greek along with translations and their commentaries, largely in Arabic and Latin (Lorch 2001). For understanding Greek mathematics, the most important indirect traditions are the Arabic translations that derive from the eighth- and ninth-century translation activity in Baghdad, and the twelfth- and thirteenth-century Latin translations, from either Greek or Arabic. From this description, it might seem that the direct tradition could be treated as the principal source, so that the indirect traditions could be neglected except in cases where the direct tradition was deficient.

The difficulty with this assumption, however, is that even in the direct tradition the mathematical texts were subjected to numerous revisions over the centuries, the details of which are now mostly lost to us. In the case of religious and literary texts, the actual words of the original author were considered sacrosanct and the ancient and medieval editors conceived of their role as the preservation of these words themselves. In the case of the exact sciences, however, the texts were often edited by scholars who were themselves expert in the fields that the texts transmitted. These scholars often took the scope of their role to include a correction of the words of the text based on their own understanding of the ideas that the words conveyed. Hence, the Greek mathematical texts must be understood as canonical in the sense that the canon was somewhat flexible and subject to repeated reinterpretation. Both the selection of texts that we are now able to read, and the specific words in which we read them, are the result of this repeated reworking and re-examination of the canon. For these reasons, in order to determine how Greek mathematics was actually practised, we are often in the position of having to reconstruct a lost context of mathematical activity on the basis of both the direct and indirect traditions. In order to get a sense for some of the vagaries of this transmission, we will consider a few illustrative cases in some detail.[2]

The work of Archimedes (ca. 280s–212) will furnish our first example (Heiberg and Stanatis 1972). We know of this corpus through a number of early modern copies of a lost Byzantine manuscript, a thirteenth-century Latin translation by William of Moerbeke (ca. 1215–86) made on the basis of this and another lost Byzantine manuscript, and a third Byzantine manuscript that was made into the famous palimpsest in the twelfth century (Clagett 1976; Netz and Noel 2007; Netz et al. 2011). Neither the Arabic nor the pre-Moerbeke Latin tradition is crucial in our assessment of Archimedes' writings. Although the Arabic tradition is important for some of the minor works,[3] it appears that *On the Sphere and Cylinder* was the only one of Archimedes' substantial treatises that was translated into Arabic. Hence, our knowledge of Archimedes is based on three, presumably independent, Greek manuscripts that were probably produced as part of the Byzantine revival of the ninth century and one or two other Greek manuscripts that were in Baghdad around this same time. In fact, compared with other major Greek mathematical sources, such as the works of Apollonius (late third century BCE) or Pappus (early fourth century CE), this is a fairly rich basis. One thing that we notice immediately, however, is that a number of treatises – including those on which Eutocius (early sixth century CE) wrote commentaries – are written in Koine, whereas other treatises are partially written in Archimedes' native Doric.[4] Since Eutocius himself, and others in his milieu, edited the works they studied, we may presume that these changes in dialect were introduced by such editorial work. We cannot now know what other changes were introduced in this process. We cannot be certain that the texts were not already edited before the late ancient period and we also do not know what changes were introduced around the ninth century in Constantinople when the three Byzantine manuscripts for which we now have any direct evidence were produced. Nevertheless, it is clear that late ancient and medieval editors felt that they were fully justified in making fairly extensive changes without comment.

The next example that we will look at is that of Apollonius (Heiberg 1891–3; Toomer 1990; Decorps-Foulquier and Federspiel 2008–10; Rashed 2008–10; Rashed and Bellosta 2010). We know the Greek version of Apollonius' *Conics* through a single Byzantine manuscript, of which all other extant manuscripts are copies (Decorps-Foulquier 1999). What we find in this manuscript, however, is not an original work by Apollonius, but an edition of the first four books of the original eight made by Eutocius, over six centuries later, as part of his project to expound classical works of advanced Hellenistic geometry. A second important Greek source for Apollonius' activity comes from another single Byzantine manuscript containing Pappus' *Collection* – a loose grouping of writings on various mathematical topics. From this text we learn about aspects of Apollonius' work for which we would not otherwise have any evidence, such as his interest in systems of large numbers, or his adherence to Euclid's organisation of geometry into those fields that can be handled with elementary constructions (straight lines and circles), with conic sections (parabolas, hyperbolas, and ellipses), and those that require more involved curves (spirals, quadratrixes, cissoids, and so forth).

For our understanding of Apollonius' mathematics, however, the Arabic tradition is as important a source as the Greek. In the ninth century, a group of scholars around the Banū Mūsā acquired a copy of the *Conics* in a version which had not been modified by Eutocius, but from which the eighth book had already gone missing. Through the mathematical work of al-Ḥasan ibn Mūsā (mid-ninth century CE), the chance discovery of a copy of the Eutocius version in Damascus, and the philological and mathematical expertise of Thābit ibn Qurra (ca. 830s–901) and others, an Arabic version of the seven remaining books was eventually completed (Toomer 1990, 621–9; Rashed 2008–10, 1.1.501–7). When we compare this version with the Greek, there are a number of differences, but it is not clear which one is closest to whatever Apollonius wrote (Rashed 2008–10, 1.1.12–25, 44–5). Indeed, we no longer posses the *Conics* that Apollonius wrote. We have the descendent of an edition made by Eutocius, in Greek, and another of that made by the scholars in the circle of the Banū Mūsā, in Arabic. The Arabic tradition has also preserved *On Cutting off a Ratio*, a text in what Pappus calls the 'field of analysis', otherwise only known from a discussion in Pappus' *Collection* 7. Hence, in order to try to evaluate Apollonius' mathematics, it is necessary to read a variety of texts, none of which he actually wrote, and some of which are not even translations or summaries of his work.

As these two examples serve to show, the significance of the manuscript tradition for interpreting the received text has to be evaluated independently in each case. Nevertheless, it is clear that the texts with which we have been working have been modified over the centuries. This is even more pronounced in the case of the texts that were more often read, such as the *Elements* or the treatises of the so-called *Little Astronomy*.[5] The Greek text of the *Elements* is preserved in two main versions: that in most of the manuscripts is called 'the edition of Theon' although there is some disagreement among the principal sources, while another, non-Theonine version, is extant in one manuscript. At the end of the ninth century, there were apparently a number of Arabic versions – two translations by al-Ḥajjāj (late eighth/early ninth century) and a translation by Isḥaq ibn Ḥunayn (830–910) that was revised by Thābit ibn Qurra – of which only Thābit's correction remains, but not without substantial incorporation of the older versions (Lo Bello 2003, xiii–xxix; De Young 2005, 176–7). All of the various Arabic texts, however, are different, in places, from the Greek, and it is not clear that the Greek versions have not also undergone some changes since the Baghdad translations were made (Knorr 1996; Rommevaux, Djebbar, and Vitrac 2001). This means that the Arabic versions should also be used to assess the original source, but this is made difficult by the numerous variants in the Arabic tradition and the fact that only parts of the text have been published (Engroff 1980; De Young 1981; Brentjes 1994).

A similarly complicated assortment of variants can be found in the sources for the group of texts known as the *Little Astronomy*, in the late ancient period, or the *Middle Books*, during the medieval period. By the late ancient period, these texts were grouped together by teachers like Pappus and described as the texts to be mastered between Euclid's *Elements* and Ptolemy's *Almagest*. Hence, these treatises, like the *Elements*, were often studied, and thus often edited. For example, there are two substantially different Greek versions of Euclid's *Optics* and *Phenomena* (Jones 1994; Knorr 1994), while there are at least three early Arabic versions of the *Spherics* by Theodosius (early second/ midfirst century BCE) (Kunitzsch and Lorch 2010) and at least two of *On the Sizes and Distances of the Sun and the Moon* by Aristarchus (early third century BCE) (Berggren and Sidoli 2007). Once again, there are differences between the Greek and Arabic traditions, such as extra propositions in the Arabic *On the Sizes and Distances* or in the Greek *Spherics*. Moreover, it is often difficult to decide, in any objective way, which variant should be ascribed to the older source.

Because the texts of Greek mathematics have been subjected to repeated editorial work, we must regard them as historically contingent objects – in some ways created by the process of transmission itself. The texts, as we find them, are the products of a literary culture, produced by literary practices and made for literary consumption. Nevertheless, the mathematics that they contain was originally produced in a context of activity, now mostly lost to us, of which the production and consumption of literary texts formed only a part.

MATHEMATICAL PRACTICES

Although almost none of the surviving documents tell us how Greek mathematicians actually taught and produced mathematics, we can make some conjectures about this based on what the sources do say, and the types of mathematics that are preserved. In the following, we will examine three primary nexuses of mathematical activity: oral practices, material practices, and literary practices. In our sources, we can perceive a gradual transition from a more oral tradition, based around public arguments made about diagrams and instruments, to a more literary tradition that involved reading and writing texts containing elaborate arguments, tables, and special symbols that would have been difficult for anyone to follow without engaging the written works as material objects.

Of the formative, primarily oral, period of Greek mathematics, we know very little. It is now generally accepted that the Greeks produced little or no deductive mathematics before the mid-fifth century BCE, when Hippocrates was active. It was also around this time that Greek mathematicians began writing down their results (Netz 2004, 243–86). Nevertheless, it is clear that the practice of mathematics at this time was still highly oral. John Philoponus (mid-sixth century CE) tells us that Hippocrates learned mathematics during his time in Athens, by associating with philosophers, while he was waiting for the resolution of his lawsuit against certain pirates who had plundered his cargo (*in Phys.* A2185a16). From Plato's writings, we have the images of Socrates teaching Meno's slave boy mathematics by discussing diagrams in a public square, and Theaetetus (early fourth century BCE) and Socrates working through a question pertaining to commensurability, which was presumably meant to be reminiscent of the way Theaetetus had studied mathematics under Theodorus (late fifth century BCE; *Meno* 82a–85b, *Tht.* 147d–148b). When we reflect on the fact that deductive mathematics arose during the period of the sophists, when Greek, and particularly Athenian, culture put a premium on the ability to persuade others of one's position in public forums, it is clear that mathematical practice also originally involved the oral presentation of arguments in public spaces.

Moreover, throughout the ancient period, the most common institutional location for mathematical activities was in schools that were predominantly devoted to teaching philosophy and rhetoric. Since there were no schools of higher mathematics, we must assume that the bulk of the higher education of mathematicians, like other intellectuals, took place in schools of philosophy, where they studied the skills of winning others to their position through oral disputation and rational argument. We still find considerable evidence for such oral practices in the elementary texts, such as Euclid's *Elements* or Theodosius' *Spherics*. The format of the propositions and the repetitive language lends itself to oral presentation and memorisation,[6] and the fact that earlier propositions are often referenced by repeating the enunciation indicates that the listener was expected to learn the propositions by memorising the enunciations.[7]

As well as drawing diagrams and making arguments about them, Greek mathematicians engaged in a range of material practices involving specialised instruments, of which we now have only indirect evidence. It has long been recognised that the constructive methods of Euclid's *Elements* are a sort of abstraction of procedures that can actually be carried out with a straightedge and collapsing compass. More recently, it has been recognised that the constructions of Theodosius' *Spherics* are also meant to be applicable to actual globes (Sidoli and Saito 2009). The construction of mechanical globes was brought to a high level by the most mechanically orientated of the ancient mathematicians, Archimedes. We are told that the consul Marcus Claudius Marcellus brought back to Rome two devices built by Archimedes for modelling the heavens (Cic. *Rep.* 1.14), and, according to Pappus, Archimedes wrote a book on *Sphere-Making* (*Collection* 8.3). Hence, as with oral practices, we find that the material practices have left their mark in the preserved texts.

In a number of places, mathematical authors explicitly describe the sorts of instruments that they used in the course of their research. Eutocius attributes to Plato, somewhat dubiously, a sort of mechanical sliding square, which could be used to find two mean proportionals between two given lines (Heiberg 1891–3, 3.56–8; Knorr 1989, 78–80). Diocles (early second century BCE), in *On Burning Mirrors*, describes how we can use a flexible ruler, made of horn, to draw an accurate parabola (Prop. 4). Nicomedes (mid-third century BCE) is said to have built a mechanical device for inserting a line of a given length between two given objects, known as a *neusis* construction (Heiberg 1891–3, 3.98–106). These and many other passages make it clear that Greek mathematicians were engaged in a range of material practices that involved the accurate reproduction of the objects that they studied.

Interest in the mathematisable properties of instruments is also evidenced from texts like Pappus' *Collection* 8, which shows how to carry out geometric constructions with a straightedge and a compass set at a fixed opening (Jackson 1980). Moreover, a number of fields of applied, or mixed, mathematics were based around the set of operations that could be carried out with specific instruments. Ancient gnomonics, the study of sundials, was based on constructions that could be carried out with a set-square and a normal compass (Vitr. *De arch.* 9.7; Ptol. *Analemma* 11–14). The methods developed for projecting the objects in the surface of a sphere on to a plane were closely related to the practices involved in drawing star maps in the plane (Ptol. *Planisphere* 14–20). Finally, the analemma methods of spherical astronomy involved the use of analogue calculations that were carried out by performing physical manipulations on a prepared plate, and in some cases a hemisphere (Ptol. *Planisphere* 9–13; Sidoli 2005).

Whereas these activities were mostly employed in research and teaching, there were also material practices that involved the production and use of literary texts. One important area of this activity involved the production of literary diagrams. Whereas we have descriptive evidence that Greek mathematicians were concerned with the visual accuracy of their drawings, the figures that we find preserved in our manuscript sources are so far from such accuracy that it seems there must have been special principles operative in the production of these literary diagrams. In the manuscript sources, we find, for example, a square representing any rectangle, a regular pentagon representing any polygon, circular arcs representing conic sections, straight lines representing curved lines, curved lines representing straight lines, and so forth.

The two most consistent features of these diagrams are the use of an unnecessarily regular object to represent a general class of objects, and a basic disregard for visual accuracy in favour of the representation of key mathematical relationships (Saito and Sidoli 2012). It seems that ancient authors developed a type of diagram that would be easy to copy and which could be used as a schematic, in conjunction with the text, to produce a more accurate diagram when the need arose. The literary diagram was an object of communication that served to mediate between the readers and the mathematical objects under investigation. As Greek mathematics became literary, the diagram secured a central place in the production of mathematical texts so that we find diagrams even in places like *Elements* 7–9, on number theory, where they often do not convey essential information and appear to be merely a literary trope.[8]

All of our preserved texts, however, come from the fully literary period, and hence we see little change in the use of diagrams in our sources. This can be contrasted with the use of tables. Whereas it would be possible to follow the mathematical details in Euclid's *Elements* in an oral presentation, in order to verify even a simple calculation in Ptolemy's *Almagest* one needs to have access to a copy of the chord table. While the proto-trigonometry of Aristarchus' *On the Sizes and Distances of the Sun and Moon* can be followed in detail with just a working knowledge of geometry and some arithmetical calculation, the chord-table trigonometry developed by Hipparchus (mid-second century BCE) and others in the late Hellenistic period was a literary practice involving the consultation and manipulation of written sources.

The literary practices of Greek mathematicians naturally extended to the production of the texts themselves. Greek mathematicians were members of a small group of individuals in Greco-Roman society who produced works of high literature and they took pains to secure this social role. It has been argued that there are parallels between both the language and the structure of Greek mathematical works and other types of literary production (Netz 1999b, ch. 4; 2009). It is also clear that Greek mathematicians, like other ancient intellectuals, engaged in various editorial and pedagogical projects to revise their works and to make them more accessible to students and less specialised readers (Cameron 1990; Mansfeld 1998).

This was true not only for the structure and overall presentation of their works, but also for the language itself. Although individual authors had their own personal style, Greek mathematicians developed a distinctive mathematical style that can be recognised in all their theoretical texts (Mugler 1959; Aujac 1984; Federspiel 1995; Acerbi 2011b). This style becomes especially conspicuous when we see it mishandled by a non-mathematician, such as in an argument by Theon of Smyrna (early second century CE) that if the parameters of Hipparchus' solar model are given, the position of the sun is determined (Hiller 1878, 157–8).

It is not clear to what extent the homogeneity of mathematical style was due to the attention of the original authors or to the care of their later editors; nevertheless, already by the middle of the Hellenistic period the production of mathematics had become a fully literary activity, closely involved with the careful study of written works. This must have formed yet another barrier to entry into the small group of individuals who produced original mathematics. While a fair number of people may have studied the mathematical sciences by attending lectures and sessions at various schools, only a small number of these could have advanced to the study of written mathematical texts, either by being wealthy enough to buy their own books or by being bright enough to be considered worthy of studying their teacher's books.

STRUCTURES

A striking feature of Greek mathematical texts is their organisation. Like other literary texts, Greek mathematical works were divided into books. The books often varied in length, which depended on the mathematical content they developed. In the case of the more elementary texts, such as the *Elements* and the treatises of the *Little Astronomy*, which would have often been used in teaching, these books began immediately with mathematical content. More advanced works, however, often began with an introduction, for example in the form of an epistle to a colleague or student, in the Hellenistic period, or, in the imperial period, more commonly a short address to a student or patron. These epistles provide introductory material meant to be useful for understanding the goal of the theory developed in the text and the tools used to develop it (Mansfeld 1998). The mathematics itself is then divided up into clear sections: an introduction, which often includes definitions or axioms, followed by various units of text. In the medieval manuscripts of most ancient mathematical texts these units are numbered as propositions; however, even in unnumbered texts, such as Ptolemy's *Planisphere*, the sections are clearly distinguished. Propositions, as a type of textual unit, are then grouped together into theories, which are only differentiated on the basis of mathematical content. For example, *Elements* 1 begins with a theory of triangles and their congruency, followed by a theory of parallelism and a theory of area, which are then used to prove the so-called Pythagorean theorem, *Elements* 1.47. The interweaving of, sometimes, obscure individual units to form an overall theory produced an element of narrative that Greek mathematicians had great skill in exploiting (Netz 2009, 66–114).

The most common types of unit are the two types of propositions that the ancients called *theorems* and *problems* – in which, starting with some set of initial objects, a *theorem* shows that some property is true of these objects, while a *problem* shows how something can be done, and then demonstrates that what has been done is satisfactory.[9] These are what we find making up the majority of theoretical treatises. There are, however, other types of units, such as *analysed propositions* (analysis/synthesis pairs), *metrical analyses, computations, tables, algorithms,* and *descriptions.* Not all of these types of texts are found in all works and some of them, such as tables, are rarely found outside the exact sciences. For example, a description is a discussion of a mathematical figure or model that explains the properties of the objects but contains little or no argument. While these are common in the exact sciences, they are rare in pure mathematics; an exception is Archimedes' *Sphere and Cylinder* 1.23.[10]

It was recognised already by Proclus (fifth century CE) that a Euclidean proposition is carefully structured (Friedlein 1873, 203; Netz 1999a; Acerbi 2011b, 1–117). He names the following parts: *enunciation* (protasis), *exposition* (ekthesis), *specification* (diorismos), *construction* (kataskeuē), *demonstration* (apodeixis), and *conclusion* (sumperasma).[11] This exact division, however, is limited to the theorems and problems of *Elements* 1. In more involved problems, such as *Elements* 3.1 – find the centre of a circle – or *Spherics* 2.15 – draw a great circle through a point tangent to a lesser circle – there are two further parts: first, there is a specification of the problem followed by a construction that solves the problem, then there is a specification of the demonstration followed by a second construction for the sake of the demonstration. Moreover, other elements can also be recognised. It has been noted that in many cases the beginning of the demonstration makes explicit reference to statements that are made possible by the exposition or the construction, in a section that modern scholars have called the *anaphor* (Federspiel 1995, 1999). Like the other parts of a proposition, the usage of the anaphora is not rigid and in some case, as *Elements* 3.1, it blends seamlessly into the demonstration.

The flexibility of these divisions must be emphasised. Outside texts that became pedagogical, such as the *Elements* or Theodosius' *Spherics*, these parts did not seem to exercise much constraint and we find Archimedes, Apollonius, and Ptolemy mixing them up or omitting them all together. Nevertheless, the realisation that Greek mathematical units are structured has led to useful insights and a number of scholars have put forward structures for various units. It has long been accepted that there are four parts in a standard problematic analysed proposition: *transformation, resolution, construction*, and *demonstration* (Hankle 1874, 137–50; Berggren and Van Brummelen 2000). More recently, the *diorism* has been added to these four, and it has been noted that in the case of theoretic analysed propositions the division is somewhat different: *construction, deduction, verification, inverse deduction* (Saito and Sidoli 2010; Sidoli and Saito 2012). In the case of Diophantus' problems, we can again recognise various parts although they are not always clearly distinguished: *enunciation, instantiation, treatment, solution*, and *test*.[12] All of these structures, however, seem to have functioned more as guidelines than as dictates for acceptable practice, and although their existence may owe much to later editorial efforts, they are still useful to us in reading and understanding Greek mathematical texts.

As well as the structures found in the arguments themselves, as discussed in the previous section, we also find structure at the level of individual verbal expressions. Greek mathematicians, of course, developed a system of technical idioms to handle their discipline.[13] As well as a nomenclature, which became fairly standardised over time, they developed formulaic expressions that allowed them to condense their texts and help their readers keep mindful of the mathematical objects themselves. Since Greek mathematics was still essentially rhetorical, the use of operations and constructions was facilitated by a highly abbreviated diction that relied on various features of the Greek language in order to function. The fact that ancient Greek is a gendered, inflected language with a definite article allowed Greek authors of all genres to condense their terminology through various types of ellipsis that would not be possible in languages like English, Latin, or Arabic. In mathematics, particularly, these expressions needed to be highly regular in order to still be intelligible. This process led to the use of formulaic expressions involving particularities of the language such as the use of prepositions and number-and-gender agreement between definite articles and nouns (Netz 1999b, 127–67). In this way, *hē hupo tōn ABΓ* (the [feminine] between the ABΓs) means *angle ABΓ*, whereas *to hupo tōn ABΓ* (the [neuter] between the ABΓs) means *rectangle AB × BΓ*. These processes allowed Greek mathematicians to make involved statements without unnecessary verbiage so as to focus attention on the objects and their relations. These expressions, however, cannot be literally translated into English. For example, Archimedes uses a sentence that would be literally translated as 'the of the on the AΘ to the on the ΘB having gained the of the AB to the ΘB is the on the AΘ to the between the ΓΘB' to convey $(AΘ^2 : ΘB^2) × (AΘ : ΘB) = AΘ^2 : (ΓΘ × ΘB)$ (Heiberg and Stanatis 1972, 3.220). It should be clear, however, that these expressions could be used to express patterns of abstract thought, even in the absence of symbolism.

ARGUMENTS

The core element of theoretical mathematics was the argument. As is well known, Greek mathematical texts often begin with definitions that state properties of various objects. In some cases, these properties can then be used to make further claims. If the objects involved in the assertion of a proposition are insufficient to actually carry through the proof, new objects are introduced through constructions – which are discussed below.

The argument itself begins with references back to the objects that are introduced and then named in the beginning, or brought in by the construction (Acerbi 2011b, 73–5). It then proceeds by making claims about instantiated objects, usually in the form of letter-names. It has often been claimed that a Greek proof is actually about a specific, instantiated object, but this neglects the manner in which these letter-names are introduced. When an object is introduced into the domain of discourse this is done with an expression such as 'let there be an object, *AB*' – so the object is *any* one of the type of objects under consideration and its letter-name is simply a way of referring to it (Federspiel 1995, 1999; Acerbi 2011b, 39–57). Hence, the letter-name is a sign, referring not to a specific object but to any member of the class of objects that the proposition concerns. This generality is maintained throughout the argument and becomes clear whenever the text refers back to what has gone before – for example, references to the construction, or a previous proposition are almost always general claims (Acerbi 2011b, 26–32).

The necessity of the argument is produced by a deductive chain of assertions that some relation, or property, holds for some object (Netz 1999b, ch. 5). Each step of this chain can be justified on the basis of either a definition or some previously established result. Often these previously established results are found earlier in the same work, but they may also be part of a broader set of theorems assumed to be known to the reader, known as the *toolbox* by modern scholars, and made up largely of propositions of the *Elements* (Saito 1997, 1998; Netz 1999b, 216–35). The standard form of synthetic argument is a chain of assertions that two objects have some relation, or that an object has a certain property, but analyses also contain deductive chains asserting that certain objects are *given*, and in various ways.

The simplest argument type is direct. After the assumed objects have been stated and any necessary constructions performed, some claims can then be asserted about these objects. In simple cases, these claims can lead directly, through a chain of implications and operations, to the conclusion. More often, however, other starting points must be introduced: either through a new appeal to the construction, introducing a new construction, appealing to a previous theorem in the same work, or in the toolbox. References to previous theorems, and to the theorems of the toolbox, are often invoked by a brief summary of the enunciation, or simply by a generalized claim of the mathematical fact.

A common form of argument is the indirect argument, in which a claim contrary to what the mathematician wishes to prove is assumed, followed by constructions and arguments leading to a contraction with the hypotheses, with established results, or with some feature of the mathematical objects in question that is taken to be inherently obvious. Although indirect arguments are very common in our sources, not all Greek mathematicians found them satisfactory: Menelaus (turn of second century CE) tells us in the introduction to his *Spherics* that he will avoid them (Krause 1936, 118; Sidoli and Kusuba 2014, 167; Rashed and Papadopoulos 2017: 697).

Another common argument type is the proof-by-cases. In some of the proofs-by-cases found in the geometrical books of the *Elements*, it is not clear whether the cases were part of the original composition or if they were added by later editors. In the number theory, however, it is certain that proof-by-cases was an integral part of the original approach. Arguments by cases were also combined with indirect argument, as in the double-indirect argument, often used by Archimedes, and some-times called the method of exhaustion. Using this argument structure, one shows that two objects are equal by showing that one is neither greater nor less than the other. Archimedes uses this form of argument in *Measurement of the Circle* 3 to show that a circle is equal to a right triangle that has one leg equal to the circle's radius and the other leg equal to the circle's circumference.

Occasionally, we find an argument in two parts, or which extends beyond a single unit of text. The most common case of this is found in simple converses. In order to prove that *A* holds if and only if *B*, Greek mathematicians would often first show that *A* implies *B* and then that *B* implies *A*, in two separate propositions, for example in *Elements* 1.5 and 6, or 1.17 and 18. Another example of this sort of extended argument was a two-stage method of showing that four magnitudes are proportional, $a : b :: c : d$, which involved first showing that the proportion holds when *a* and *b* are assumed to be commensurable, and then, in a second argument using this and a double-indirect argument, showing that the proportion also holds when *a* and *b* are incommensurable. This structure was used in Archimedes' *Equilibrium of Planes* 1.6 and 7, Theodosius' *Spherics* 3.9 and 10, and Pappus' *Collection* 5.12 and 6.7–9 (Knorr 1978; Mendell 2007).

An interesting type of argument that extends beyond a single unit is the analysis/synthesis pair, which consists of an assumed construction, a deductive argument concerning *givens*, a treatment of the limits to the possibility of solution and of the total number of solutions, a construction, and a deductive argument concerning the relations and properties of geometric objects. From a purely deductive perspective, the analysis is unnecessary, so that the reasons for providing it must have been expository. A *problematic analysis*, can provide a motivation for the initial construction steps of the synthesis and point the way towards an articulation of the limits to possibility of solution, while a *theoretic analysis* can provide insight into how the main relation of the theorem was obtained (Saito and Sidoli 2010; Sidoli and Saito 2012).

The argument was the locus of deduction and hence can be regarded as the core of theoretical mathematical activity. Although mathematicians clearly put considerable care into making arguments, they left few discussions about what constitutes a valid argument. Hence, in order to understand their philosophy of mathematics, we must read the mathematical texts themselves, paying attention to the overall structures which the individual arguments compose.

CONSTRUCTIONS

One of the most distinctive methodological features of Greek mathematics is the use of constructions. Construction, or construction-based thinking, is found not only in geometry but also in number theory, pre-modern algebra, the exact sciences, and in general investigations of what, and how, mathematical objects are given.

Constructive techniques are conspicuous in elementary geometry. Recently, much attention has been paid to the role of diagrams in Greek mathematical thought (Manders 2008; Netz 1999b, 12–67; Le Meur 2012); however, it is only through the mediating process of construction that the diagram has any deductive force (Avigad, Dean, and Mumma 2009; Sidoli and Saito 2009). Constructions are used in very nearly every proposition in order to introduce new objects whose defined properties are then used as starting points in chains of deductive inference.

Constructions played a different role in *problems* than in *theorems* and in the demonstration section of a *problem*. In the *Elements*, construction postulates are introduced to justify the construction procedures that are used in *problems*, but not necessarily those used in *theorems*. More elaborate construction procedures are set out and then justified in *problems*. The construction of a problem uses postulates, or previously established problems, to show that there is an effective algorithm for producing the sought object. The construction of a theorem, or of the demonstration of a problem, however, can call on a wider range of constructive assumptions (*Elements* 1.4, 6, 8), or even involve impossible, or counterfactual, constructions (*Elements* 1.6, 7 and 3.1). In other geometrical texts, a variety of constructive processes are used that are never explicitly postulated, such as setting a line of a given length between two given objects (a *neusis* construction), or passing a plane through a solid object – for examples, see Archimedes *Spiral Lines* 5–9, or Apollonius *Conics* 1.4–14.

In geometric texts, different verbs were used to denote various types of constructions, depending on what the geometer intended to do. Lines could be *produced* (*agō*) between two given points, circles *drawn* (*graphō*) with a given centre and passing through a given point, solid objects *cut* (*temnō*) by a passing plane, diameters in spheres *set out* (*ektithēmi*) on plane survaces, parallelograms *erected* (*sunistēmi*) on given lines, and so forth. In the enunciation of *problems*, these operations were stated in the infinitive, whereas in the construction of either type of proposition they were generally stated in the perfect imperative passive. Despite the fact that the construction is explicitly stated as complete, it is clear that it represents the most active part of mathematical practice. Moreover, the construction is often the most creative part of a mathematical argument, since it introduces new objects into the domain of discourse, which are entirely at the mathematician's discretion.

Although construction is generally associated with geometry, constructivist thinking permeated other branches of Greek mathematics as well. All of the problems in Euclid's number theory, *Elements* 7–9, show us how to *find* (*euriskō*) numbers, which are hence assumed to exist from the beginning (Mueller 1981, 60). The problems in Euclid's number theory, however, are the active components and provide the algorithms that are used in the rest of the theory. In geometric texts, as well, objects that are assumed to exist are sometimes *found* by construction – such as the centre of a circle, in Euclid's *Elements* 3.1, or of a sphere, in Theodosius' *Spherics* 1.2 – so that these problems are conceptually related to the algorithms in the number theory. Furthermore, in works of pre-modern algebra, such as the *Arithmetics* of Diophantus (ca. third century CE), a number of different constructive operations are invoked such as *find* (*euriskō*), *separate* (*diaireō*), *add* (*prostithēmi*), and *make* (*poieō*). Although these expressions assume the existence of the numbers involved, because rational numbers are expected, limits to the possibility of solution must sometimes be invoked. One of Diophantus' problems, such as *Arithmetics* 2.8 – '*Separate* a proposed square into two squares' – can later function as an algorithm used in further problems, in much the same way as a problem in the geometric texts (Tannery 1893, 90). One difference is that for Diophantus the constructive procedures are themselves joined together, making a series of conditions for the solution to the problem, such as *Arithmetics* 1.7 – '*Take away* two given numbers from the same number and *make* the remainders have a given ratio to one another' – whereas in the geometric texts only one construction is stipulated and all the conditions are expressed as modifications of the objects, such as Theodosius' *Spherics* 2.15 – 'Given a lesser circle in a sphere and some point on the surface of the sphere that is between it and the circle equal and parallel to it, *draw* through the point a great circle tangent to the given circle'

(Tannery 1893, 24; Czinczenheim 2000, 102). This difference occurs both at the grammatical level and also in terms of the procedures of solution. In geometric problems, there is only one verb, in the infinitive, and a single geometric object is constructed satisfying all of the conditions, which are stated as modifications of the nouns. In Diophantus, the conditions are stated as a series of verbs and they are satisfied individually as the problem proceeds.[14]

The notion of construction was so fundamental for Greek mathematicians that they developed a sort of conceptual framework to handle constructive processes as a theory of *givens*, formalised in Euclid's *Data* (Taisbak 2003). Given objects exist in a definite and often unique way and their properties are known and manageable (Acerbi 2011a). Given objects, or properties, are those that are found at the start of the discourse, that are constructed at the discretion of the mathematician, or that can be inferred to be given based on these. The *Data* shows us how to make inferences about given objects or properties. The late-Platonic commentator Marinus of Neapolis (late fifth century BCE) reports a number of definitions of the concept of *given*, which he attributes to various mathematicians (Menge 1896, 234–6). After discussing various ways that we can understand the notion of *given*, Marinus settles on the concepts of *known* (*gnorimon*) and *provided* (*porimon*), claiming that what is provided is that which we are able to *make* or to *construct*, for example drawing a circle or finding three expressible lines that are only commensurable in square (Menge 1896, 250, 240). This agrees with Euclid's definition of given in the *Data*. Def. 1 reads, '*Given* is said of regions, lines and angles of which we are able to provide an equal' (Menge 1896, 2). The notion of *provision* was an attempt to formalise the productive processes through which the mathematician gained mastery of the subject. Its formalisation was meant to facilitate the types of inferences that mathematicians made in geometrical analysis – starting with the *analytical assumption* that a certain configuration exists containing the sought object, one then started with objects in this configuration that were either already or assumed to be known, or could be readily constructed, and then proceeded, through a chain of inferences, to show that the sought object was also *given*.

In later readings of the *Data*, the notion of *given*, and hence of *provision*, was expanded to include computations and other sorts of deductive inferences. Later authors, such as Heron and Ptolemy, constructed *chains of givens*, where each step can be referred to a

purely geometric theorem of the *Data*, but which are in fact used to justify computational procedures, involving arithmetical operations and
tabular functions.[15] We can call these chain of inferences *metrical analyses*, since they show how to construct a sought number.[16]

In these ways, construction fulfilled a number of important
roles for Greek mathematicians. On a practical level, construction
formalised and abstracted various active procedures that were necessary
in actually doing mathematics. On a more theoretical level, it allowed
mathematicians to introduce new objects whose properties could then
be used to prove theorems or solve problems. On a fundamental level, it
provided instantiations of objects with known properties to be used in
mathematical discourse.

OPERATIONS AND PROCEDURES

Although, in a general sense, we can regard constructions as operations,
in this section we focus on those operations that can be performed on a
statement, expression, or number. While there is relatively little oper-
ational mathematics in elementary geometrical treatises, such as the
early books of the *Elements* or Theodosius' *Spherics*, as soon as we
begin to read higher geometry, number theory, pre-modern algebra, or
the exact sciences, we encounter long passages of deductive reasoning
in the form of chains of mathematical operations.

From both a theoretical and practical perspective, Greek
mathematicians privileged operations on ratios and proportions over
arithmetic operations. A theoretical justification for many of the
common ratio manipulations that were in use was provided by *Elements*
5, which is thought to have been formulated by Eudoxus. Almost all of
the theorems of the second half of this book deal with manipulations
that can be carried out on proportions. For example, the operation of *separation* (*deilōn*), justified in *Elements* 5.17, entails inferring from a proportion of the form $a : b :: c : d$ one of the form $a - b : b :: c - d : d$, where
$a > b$. The operation of *combination* (*sunthentos*), justified in *Elements*
5.18, is the converse. Although in the *Elements* these operations are
only justified for proportions, Greek mathematicians also applied them
to ratio equalities and, occasionally, equations or inequalities.[17]

This gives the impression that Greek mathematicians sharply
distinguished between proportions and equations, and there is some
truth to this. Equations were taken to be statements about different
things that were *equal in quantity*, whereas proportions were claims

that two ratios were *the same*. Nevertheless, despite this distinction, Greek mathematicians were aware that equations and proportions could be interchanged, and occasionally subjected equations to ratio manipulations, or proportions to arithmetic operations.[18] Of course, all of the ratio manipulations can be rewritten as arithmetic operations, but Greek mathematicians apparently had no interest in doing so. In fact, even in places where one might expect to find only arithmetic operations, such as in the calculation of the size of a length or an angle by Aristarchus or Archimedes, we still encounter the use of ratio manipulations.

Greek mathematicians, of course, also performed arithmetic operations; however, they did not spend much effort attempting to formalise or justify these operations. More difficult operations, such as taking roots, are not explicitly discussed in much detail in our sources before the late ancient period.[19] Arithmetic operations were performed on individual terms, whole proportions and ratio inequalities, and equations.

The three ancient and medieval algebraic operations were probably regarded as special cases of such arithmetic operations, applicable under certain specified conditions. In the introduction to his *Arithmetics*, Diophantus describes the two primary pre-modern algebraic operations that can be performed on an equation to solve for an unknown number. He says that if 'a kind (*eidē*)[20] becomes equal to the same kind but not of the same quantity, it is necessary to take away the similar from the similar on each of the sides, in order that that kind should be equal to kind' (Tannery 1893, 14). In other words, given an equation in which numbers, some number of unknowns, or higher terms are found on both sides of the equation, to subtract the common term from both sides, so as to bring it to the other side – as we would say. The second operation is 'to add a kind lacking from either of the sides, in order that an extant kind will come to be for each of the sides' (Tannery 1893, 14). That is – as we would say – to make all our terms positive. These operations may be repeated as necessary until only one of a number, some number of unknowns, or higher terms are found on each side of the equation. The third operation is not stated until it is needed at the beginning of the Arabic Book 4, which follows the Greek Book 3. The text says that, if after the other two operations have been performed we have a statement equating unknowns of higher degree, then, 'we divide the whole by a unit of the lesser in degree of the two sides, until there results for us one kind equal to a number' (Sesiano

1982, 88). In other words, we reduce the equation to the lowest degree possible. There is no attempt in the text to formally relate these operations to operations of arithmetic or to develop further operations to be carried out on equations on analogy with the other arithmetic operations. Hence, they appear to have been treated separately as an operation for eliminating lacking (negative) terms, an operation for grouping like terms on one side of the equation, and an operation for reducing certain equations of higher degree.

Series of operations were also arranged in algorithms. In *Elements* 7 there are a number of problems that involve algorithms, for example *Elements* 7.2 – find the greatest common measure of two numbers – or 7.34 – find the least common multiple of two numbers. The only actual operations involved in these problems, however, are arithmetical and they are not postulated, but simply assumed as obvious. As with all problems, following a presentation of the algorithm, there is a proof that the algorithm accomplishes its goal.

In other authors, such as Diophantus and Ptolemy, we have less formal approaches to algorithms and computational procedures that involve a series of arithmetic operations and are generally unjustified (Acerbi 2012, 183–9). These algorithms proceed by a chain of instructions, in the second person imperative, and may involve the use of parameters of calculation and entries into tables, as well as arithmetic operations. Parameters of calculation are often distinguished from the data for any particular procedure with the word 'always' (*aei*). The results of table-entries and calculations can be set aside and then brought back in at some later stage of the procedure.

There are also algorithms in which each successive operation is carried out directly on the result of the proceeding operation, which are often presented in a context of justification (Acerbi 2012, 190–9). For example, Heron, in *Measurements* 1.8, gives a general algorithm for finding the area of a triangle given its sides, which is followed not by a proof, but by a computed example (Taisbak 2014). This justificatory section ends with a short *metrical analysis* before the example, which for Heron functions as the synthetic construction of a particular number given some assumed values, and which he calls the 'synthesis'. This was Heron's general approach to *metrical analysis*: first an 'analysis', justified by steps of the *Elements* and the *Data* that if certain values are assumed as given, the sought value can be shown to also be given, followed by a 'synthesis', in which the sought value is computed from some values assumed as given.

An interesting type of *metrical analysis* is found in trigonometric texts, such as Ptolemy's *Analemma* or *Almagest*. Here we find general statements of an algorithmic procedure using the *givens* terminology, where each step can be justified by a theorem of the *Data*, but actually refers to arithmetical operations, ratio manipulations, entries into a chord table, and so forth. Ptolemy apparently thought of these arguments as justifying a computational procedure, by referring each of its steps to a theorem of the *Data*. On the other hand, he does not seem to have regarded arguments by givens and computations as an analysis/synthesis pair, since he always only gives one or the other, and he sometimes later refers to a calculation as a proof.

CONCLUSION

It is now generally recognised by historians of ancient and medieval mathematics that ancient Greek mathematics is not *our* mathematics (Høyrup 1996). Nevertheless, Greek mathematics was one of the great productions of ancient scholarship – particularly in its desire to produce arguments that established both generality and necessity, in its endeavour to formalise mathematical knowledge through structure and regularity, in its goal of producing problem-solving techniques through constructive processes under the mathematician's control. It is for these reasons that Greek mathematical texts were read and reread over many centuries by creative mathematicians such as Ibn al-Haytham (ca. 965–ca. 1040), Abū Naṣr Manṣūr ibn ʿIrāq (ca. 960–1036), Jordanus of Nemore (thirteenth century), Francesco Maurolyco (1494–1575), Pierre Fermat (1601–65), and Isaac Newton (1642–1726).

I hope that this chapter will have highlighted some of the characteristics of Greek mathematics that make it distinctive, so that we can study this material as a style of mathematics different from our own, but nonetheless, as belonging to mathematics. In this way, we can more effectively compare Greek mathematics with other ancient ways of doing mathematics, and with the medieval approaches to mathematics that built on, and broke away from, ancient Greek works.

NOTES

This chapter was written in 2015.

1 Asper 2009 provides a discussion of the differences between the theoretical and practical traditions of mathematics.

2 For the Greek manuscript tradition, see Acerbi 2010, 269–375; Vitrac n.d.; for the Arabic tradition, see Sezgin 1974–9.

3 For example, Knorr 1989, 375–816, has argued for the importance of the medieval tradition of *Measurement of the Circle*.

4 The question of Archimedes' dialect is made difficult by the fact that much of the Doric in the received text was produced by the editor, J. L. Heiberg, in response to the fact that the manuscripts contain a strange mixture of Koine and Doric; Heiberg and Stamatis 1972, II: x–xviii; Netz 2012).

5 Vitrac 2012 gives a discussion of the editorial production of the *Elements*.

6 Netz 1999b, 127–67, discusses the formulaic nature of Greek mathematical prose. Although he focuses on the cognitive roles of formulae, it is also clear that they would have facilitated memorisation and oral presentation.

7 This is also supported by the format of three of the papyri containing material from the *Elements*: *P. Oxy.* I 29 (*Elements* 2.4 and 5), *P. Oxy.* 5299 (*Elements* 1.4, 8–11, 14–25), and *P. Berol.* 17469 (*Elements* 1.8–10); see Sidoli 2015, 392–3.

8 It should be noted, however, that there are some cases where the diagrams help us understand both the proposition and the argument (Bajri, Hannah and Montelle 2015, 559–68).

9 Definitions of *theorem* and *problem* are given by Pappus and Proclus (Hultsch 1876, 30–2; Friedlein 1873, 200–1).

10 This unit is unnumbered in the manuscripts.

11 The conclusion is almost certainly a late addition in the Greek tradition of the *Elements* (Acerbi 2011b, 38–9).

12 The names given to these parts by A. Bernard and J. Christianidis are different, but the parts appear to be the same (Christianidis 2007; Bernard and Christianidis 2012). See also Christianidis and Oaks 2013, 130–4.

13 Heath 1896, clvii–clxx; 1912, clv–clxxxvi, provides useful introductions to Greek mathematical terminology, and there have been a number of studies of the language of Greek mathematics (Sidoli 2014, 29).

14 For *Arithmetics* 1.7, the two conditions are rather simple, but they are still handled sequentially. For more involved problems the conditions are solved individually. For example, in *Arithmetics* 3.1, after satisfying two of the conditions, Diophantus says 'two of the conditions (*epigmata*) are now solved (*lelumena*)' (Tannery 1893, 138).

15 The expression 'catena dei dati' is due to Acerbi 2007, 455.

16 This type of argument is called an 'analysis' by Heron throughout his *Measurements*, and by Pappus in his commentary on Ptolemy's *Almagest* 5 (Rome 1931–43, 35).

17 See, for example, Aristarchus' *On the Sizes and Distances of the Sun and Moon* 4, or Archimedes' *Sand Reckoner* (Heath 1913, 367; Heiberg and Stamatis 1972, 2.216–58).

18 See, for examples, Aristarchus' *On the Sizes and Distances of the Sun and Moon* 4, Apollonius' *Conics* 1.15, or Ptolemy's *Almagest* 1.10 (Heath 1913, 367; Heiberg 1891–3, 1.63; Heiberg 1898–1903, 1.45–6).

19 The extraction of square roots is described by a scholium to *Elements* 10, and Theon in his *Commentary to the Almagest*. Heron gives an example of taking a cube root, but does not give his method in detail (Heath 1921/81, I: 60–2).

20 In Diophantus' terminology, a *kind* is mathematically related to what we would call a term of a polynomial, although he does not appear to have conceived of a polynomial as a series of terms combined by operations.

10 Astronomy in Its Contexts

Liba Taub

Astronomy has often been called the oldest science, and some ancient Greek authors acknowledged a debt to Babylonian predecessors.[1] Many of the earliest Greek philosophers are credited with astronomical observations, predictions, explanations, and discoveries.[2] Yet, throughout much of Greco-Roman antiquity – and later – astronomy was regarded as a branch of mathematics, along with arithmetic, geometry, and harmonics. This view of astronomy – as a branch of mathematics – raises questions about what constituted astronomy, as well as its relationship to philosophy. Furthermore, many of those who pursued theoretical astronomy were also known for contributions to time-reckoning, calendar production, weather prediction (useful for navigation, agriculture, medicine, and commerce), and astrology (a particular type of astronomy);[3] some are also credited with the design and use of models and instruments, including globes and sundials. There may be a temptation to distinguish between the 'theoretical' and the 'practical' – a distinction encouraged, in part, by Aristotle – but such a bifurcation risks presenting a skewed view of astronomy in the Greco-Roman world.[4] In a number of influential ancient authors – philosophers as well as mathematicians – links between philosophy and astronomy and between the theoretical and practical were emphasised, culminating in Claudius Ptolemy's claim that astronomy is the highest form of philosophy, a theoretical endeavour with practical benefits. There are some basic questions to be considered. What is astronomy? What is it for? How does it relate to different types of knowledge, including philosophy? How does it relate to different parts of life?

DEFINING 'ASTRONOMY'

The term 'astronomy' (from the Greek *astronomia*) refers to the study of the stars, broadly understood to include what were called by the ancient Greeks the wandering stars or planets (including the sun and moon), as well as the so-called fixed stars (which keep their positions relative to one another, what we refer to as asterisms and constellations).[5] Astronomy may – but does not always – involve observation, description, explanation, and prediction.

How does astronomy relate to other forms of knowledge and expertise? In Greco-Roman antiquity (and for hundreds of years following), astronomy and philosophy concerned with nature (*physis* = nature; physics) were typically understood to be distinct realms of enquiry, the first pursued by mathematicians, the latter by philosophers concerned with nature. Astronomy was one of four kinds of mathematics said to have been identified by the Pythagoreans: arithmetic, harmonics, geometry, and astronomy.[6] Some ancient discussions describe astronomy as offering an account of the apparent motions of astronomical bodies using geometrical models,[7] in contrast to natural philosophy, which was concerned with explanation of the cosmos as a whole (and the totality of matter), including the heavenly bodies.

The Greek noun *kosmos*, meaning 'order' or 'adornment' – from which the English word 'cosmetic' is derived – is related to the verb *kosmein* (to order, arrange, adorn), and gradually developed a restricted sense, probably only by the fifth century BCE, referring to the universe as a whole. The connection between the later sense of 'universe' and the earlier meaning of 'order' or 'ornament' is significant, for even in the restricted usage of 'the universe', the idea of order and beauty persists. Furthermore, the sense of beauty was not merely an aesthetic, but also a moral description.[8]

There was no unanimity amongst those Greeks and Romans writing about the study of heavenly bodies and phenomena as to where such study sat in relation to other intellectual endeavours (and, indeed, exactly which bodies and phenomena to consider). Philosophy included the study of nature, physics, and physics and astronomy were understood to use different approaches to the study of the cosmos and celestial phenomena.[9]

Philosophers generally regarded astronomy as a branch of mathematics; Plato and Aristotle both make this clear, as do others, including much later ancient authors. For example, the sixth-century philosopher Simplicius, who in his commentary on Aristotle's *Physics* quoted from Alexander of Aphrodisias (late second to early third century CE), who he noted had quoted carefully from Geminus' (first century BCE) abridged commentary on Posidonius' (ca. 135–ca. 51 BCE) *Meteorologica*, outlines the differences between natural philosophy and astronomy. (He also states that Posidonius' work was influenced by Aristotle.) His detailed listing of the links between the sources for his account emphasises the longevity of this understanding of the distinctions between physics and astronomy.

Simplicius quotes at length from Alexander:

> It is the concern of natural science to enquire into the substance of the heavens and the heavenly bodies, their powers and the nature of their coming-to-be and passing away; by Zeus, it can reveal the truth about their size, shape and positioning. Astronomy does not attempt to pronounce on any of these questions, but reveals the ordered nature of the phenomena in the heavens, showing that the heavens are indeed an ordered cosmos.

Astronomy, by this account, 'also discusses the shapes, sizes and relative distances of the earth, the sun and the moon, as well as eclipses, the conjunctions of heavenly bodies, and qualities and quantities inherent in their paths'. Furthermore, it is explained that as astronomy 'touches on the study of the quantity, magnitude and quality of their shapes, it understandably has recourse to arithmetic and geometry in this respect'. It is acknowledged that 'the astronomer and the natural scientist will accordingly on many occasions set out to achieve the same objective in broad outline, for example, that the sun is a sizeable body, that the earth is spherical'.[10] However, their methods are different. Simplicius, as he ends his quotation, makes it clear that 'Geminus, or Posidonius as presented by Geminus' shows the influence of Aristotle in distinguishing this way between physics and astronomy.[11]

The articulation of methods for addressing scientific problems is a hallmark of the Greek approach to explaining the natural world. Plato was credited in antiquity with having set what was to become the fundamental task of astronomy. According to Simplicius, in his commentary on Aristotle's *De caelo* (*On the Heavens*), the second-century CE Peripatetic Sosigenes reported that Plato set

> the mathematicians the following problem: What circular motions, uniform and perfectly regular, are to be admitted as hypotheses so that it might be possible to save the appearances [=phenomena] presented by the planets?[12]

Simplicius describes a problem set up by the assumption – ascribed to Plato – of the regular circular motion of the stars. If regular circular motion is assumed (or hypothesised), the apparent lack of conformance to that assumption must be explained. The task of astronomy becomes the explanation of how the phenomena (especially the apparent motions of the 'wandering' stars – the planets) conform to the assumption of regular circular motion. To do this would be to 'save the phenomena'.

In his commentary on the *Physics*, Simplicius included in his quotation from Alexander the example of how Heraclides of Pontus (fourth century BCE) attempted to 'save the phenomena'. Heraclides suggested that 'the appearance of irregularity in the sun's path can be saved if the earth moves in some way, and the sun stays still in some way'. The view reported by Simplicius is that '[i]n general it is not the concern of the astronomer to know what by nature is at rest and what by nature is in motion; he must rather make assumptions about what stays at rest and what moves, and consider with what assumptions the appearances in the heavens are consistent'. However, the astronomer is not totally ignorant of natural philosophy, for 'he must get his basic principles from the natural scientist, namely that the dance of the heavenly bodies is simple, regular and ordered'. And then, working 'from these principles he will be able to show that the movement of all the heavenly bodies is circular, both those that revolve in parallel courses and those that wind along oblique circles'.[13] The geometrical formulation of the problem faced by astronomers is fundamental here: geometry was understood – for many subsequent centuries – as the language of astronomy. (Nevertheless, as Simplicius and other Greek and Roman authors on astronomy attest, other branches of mathematics, including arithmetic, were also relevant to astronomy.)

'SAVING THE PHENOMENA'

The identification of the phenomena to be accounted for by astronomy is also part of the Greek legacy. Certain phenomena were the focus of explanation (such as the so-called wandering stars or planets, and the fixed stars), while others were not treated by astronomers (for example, comets might be explained as part of meteorology, as part of physics).[14] Phenomena were known either by first-hand observation or by second-hand sharing of data.

The status of the phenomena within the Greek scientific enterprise, especially astronomy, was discussed in antiquity and continues to be by modern scholars, including philosophers of science; there is a vast literature on the subject. Realism posits that the world described by science is real and exists as described;[15] in contrast, instrumentalism regards scientific theories as useful in understanding the world and particularly in predicting phenomena, whether or not those theories truly describe the world as it is. Instrumentalism can be understood as shifting the focus of evaluation from the entities postulated to predict the phenomena towards the consideration of whether the interpretation offered adequately predicts or explains the phenomena. Instrumentalism supports the view that accounts can be developed to describe how the world works, while these accounts of the world are not (necessarily) descriptions of what really exists.[16] The meaning of 'saving the phenomena' has been the subject of continuing debate.[17]

A number of influential scholars have argued that a form of instrumentalism underpinned the ancient aim of 'saving' the phenomena. (Think here of Simplicius' comment that it is not the concern of astronomers as to which bodies are at rest.) In 1908, the French physicist, historian, and philosopher of science, Pierre Duhem (1861–1916) published an essay that has had significant influence on philosophers and historians of science, *To Save the Phenomena (ΣΟΖΕΙΝ ΤΑ ΦΑΙΝΟΜΕΝΑ: Essai sur la notion de théorie physique de Platon à Galilée)*. He did not use the term 'instrumentalist', but others have applied the word to his description of the 'method of the astronomer' (in contrast to that of the physicist). Duhem stated that 'when its geometric constructions have assigned each planet a path which conforms to its visible path, astronomy has attained its goal, because *its hypotheses have then saved the appearances* [phenomena]'.[18]

According to Simplicius, Eudoxus of Cnidos (ca. 390–ca. 340 BCE) was the first to account for the apparently irregular motions of the celestial bodies by using only uniform, circular, and regular motions in order to describe or 'save' the phenomena.[19] Very little about Eudoxus' life and work is known with any certainty, and none of his works survive, only accounts and fragments in other ancient authors. There is evidence that he founded a school at Cyzicus.

Eudoxus used nested homocentric spheres to describe the apparent motions of each of the heavenly bodies (reported by Aristotle, *Metaphysics* 12.8). Simplicius, in his commentary on Aristotle's *De caelo*, explained that, according to Eudoxus, the path of a planet describes a figure called a 'hippopede' (or horse-fetter, which looked something like a modern figure 8 on its side). Using this, Eudoxus was able to account for and 'save' various phenomena in an approximate way.[20] Many scholars, including Duhem, have assumed that Eudoxus did not believe that his geometrical model had any physical reality. This might qualify Eudoxus as an 'instrumentalist', but the paucity of our knowledge of his work makes speculative any statement regarding the intention underlying his astronomical solution. However, we do know more about Plato's ideas about astronomy, in addition to what is reported by Simplicius.

THE PLACE OF ASTRONOMY

Since antiquity, Plato's role in shaping the agenda for ancient Greek astronomy has been highlighted. For Plato, astronomy was part of broader culture. For example, in the *Republic* (Book 7), he outlines the type of education necessary for philosopher-kings. They must receive preliminary training in music and gymnastics, after which they will proceed through a course of mathematical studies that includes arithmetic, geometry, stereometry (the study of solid bodies), astronomy, and harmonics. These disciplines – including astronomy – serve as a propaedeutic to the study of dialectic, not to a career in mathematics.

Plato's views on the sort of astronomy that is appropriate to serve as a preliminary study to dialectic have been much discussed. In the *Republic*, Socrates asserts that 'if, by really taking part in astronomy, we're to make the naturally intelligent part of the soul useful instead of useless, let's study astronomy by means of problems, as we do geometry, and leave the things in the sky alone'.[21] One crucial element is the notion that astronomy is done by addressing *problems*, and that astronomy is linked to specific kinds of mathematics, that is, geometry and stereometry. The injunction to 'leave the things in the heavens alone' – by paying attention to the instruction to 'proceed by means of problems' – seems to favour what may be called an 'a priori' astronomy, that is, an astronomy that proceeds from assumptions, in a way similar to that by which geometry relies on definitions.

The interpretation of this passage has provided work not only for philosophers wishing to understand Plato's views on the proper education for philosopher-kings (and how astronomy contributes to that), but also for historians and philosophers of science attempting to understand the relations between theory and observation, between explanation and explananda. Such considerations have shaped how philosophers as well as historians of astronomy have understood what counts as astronomy, for Plato and his successors.[22]

Aristotle's views on astronomy to some extent reinforced those of Plato, especially regarding astronomy as a branch of mathematics. Both Plato and Aristotle emphasised the theoretical nature of astronomy. Neither engaged in astronomy themselves; nevertheless, their views helped shape how astronomy was defined and understood.

In the *Metaphysics* (1025b3–1026a31), Aristotle describes the organisation of rational knowledge as comprising three types: the practical (*praktikē*), the productive (*poetikē*), and the theoretical (*theoretikē*). Theoretical knowledge (*theoretikē*) is further divided into three types: mathematical, physical, and theological. In the *Physics*, Aristotle distinguishes the different subjects of physics and mathematics: nature (*physis*) is a principle of motion and change; because of this, in order to understand nature, we must understand what motion is, otherwise nature itself would be unknown (*Ph.* 200b12–14). However, because natural bodies contain surfaces, volumes, lines, and points, these are studied by mathematics (*Ph.* 193b23–25).

Aristotle raises the question as to whether astronomy is 'different from natural science [physics] or a department of it'. He notes that 'it seems absurd that the student of nature should be supposed to know the nature of the sun or moon, but not to know any of their essential attributes, particularly as the writers on nature obviously do discuss their shape and whether the earth and the world are spherical or not.' Elaborating on the differences between the aims and approaches of physics and mathematics, Aristotle states that

> the mathematician, though he too treats of these things [such as the shape of the earth and whether the earth and the universe are spherical ... he] does not treat of them as the limits of a natural body; nor does he consider the attributes indicated as the attributes of such bodies. That is why he separates them; for in thought they are separable from motion, and it makes no difference, nor does any falsity result, if they are separated.[23]

Here, and in the *Metaphysics*, Aristotle's view is that physicists treat the natural bodies and the principles of their motion, and mathematicians treat the figures of these bodies in abstraction from their matter, eliminating all sensible qualities (such as weight).[24] However, this does not result in a clean divide between physics and mathematics, for Aristotle also conceives of a set of mixed mathematical/physical sciences in which a mathematical science supplies the principles that explain the phenomena identified by an 'empirical' or 'physical' science. Examples of these sets of mathematical/physical sciences are arithmetic/harmonics, geometry/optics, stereometry/mechanics.[25]

While portions of both Plato's and Aristotle's discussions of the nature and place of astronomy as a type of knowledge emphasise its mathematical approach, a concern with the phenomena – and even the physicality of the astronomical bodies themselves – is in evidence in other accounts of astronomical work. Indeed, some of those who devised mathematical models to 'save the phenomena' also engaged with phenomena in other ways, including constructing tangible models to depict phenomena of the night sky, as well as sundials and astrometeorological calendars to aid in time-reckoning and weather prediction.

SENSIBLE MODELS

Just as astronomy is often considered to be the oldest science, so it is often regarded as the first to have developed instruments and tangible models. This may be puzzling if we understand astronomy to be fundamentally a mathematical type of knowledge, and have in mind the claim in *Republic* 7 that the value of geometry is to turn us from the perceptible towards the intelligible (the contemplation of which is the goal of philosophy).

This understanding of Plato's conception of mathematics – as ultimately contributing to philosophical aims – underlies the tradition in which he was said to have disapproved of the use by mathematicians of mechanical constructions and instruments. Plutarch (born before 50 CE, died after 120 CE) explains that both Eudoxus and Archytas (ca. 400–350 BCE), as well as their followers, used sensible and instrumental support in addressing problems not capable of proof by logical and geometrical demonstration. He reports that 'Plato was upset and maintained against them that they were destroying and ruining the value of geometry, since it had fled from the incorporeal and intelligible to the sensible, using again physical objects which required much common handicraft.'[26] By Plutarch's account, Plato disapproved of using instruments or tangible models to help solve problems.

Nevertheless, we know from ancient accounts that whilst geometrical models were devised to explain astronomical phenomena, physical objects were also being made to depict the night sky, astronomical bodies, and their motions. Much of what we know about the physical models – such as globes – is reported within contexts chronicling the achievements of philosophers. Cicero (106–43 BCE; *Rep.* 1.14), quoting Gaius Sulpicius Gallus (second century BCE), credits Thales with the invention of the celestial globe. Diogenes Laertius (2.2) (probably first half of third century CE) credits Anaximander with the construction of such a globe.[27] Furthermore, according to the principal speaker in Plato's *Timaeus* (40c–d), it is impossible to describe the motions of the celestial bodies without visible representations. F. M. Cornford thought that the sort of model referred to may have corresponded to some type of open-work armillary sphere, composed of rings (from Latin *armillae*).[28]

Timaeus describes (36b–d) the way in which the Craftsman fashioned the stuff of the soul to make the circles which include the motions of the astronomical bodies, referring to the second circle as being inside the first. Cornford argued that by describing one circle as inside the other, Timaeus appeared to be describing circles with physical dimension, not only those that would appear on the surface of a celestial globe, as those would all have the same diameter. In a three-dimensional model, one circle could be located inside, or within, the other circle. Cornford argued that Timaeus' model would have used rings, rather than a solid sphere, as the latter would have hidden the inner circles from view.[29]

But how do we reconcile the claim – placed in the mouth of Timaeus, but possibly representing Plato's own views – that visible models are required to comprehend the astronomical motions with Plato's apparent disapproval of sensible and instrumental approaches? Ian Mueller suggested that while there are apparent tensions between the role of mathematics in the *Republic* (with its emphasis on the intelligible) and the *Timaeus* (which highlights the importance of the perceptible, for example, at 47b–c), mathematics can be understood to have a mediating role between the perceptible and the intelligible.[30]

Whilst we might be tempted to suggest that only philosophers relied on tangible models to study the night sky and understand the *Timaeus*, we have a good deal of evidence that mathematicians also used instruments and models; several are credited with their design and construction. For example, followers of Eudoxus constructed instruments to demonstrate his mathematical model of planetary motion.[31] No example of an ancient armillary sphere survives, but Geminus, in his *Introduction to the Phenomena* (16.12), distinguished between 'ringed spheres' (*krikōtai sphairai*) and 'solid' ones (*stereai*), that is globes, indicating that he knew both.[32]

The Greek term for sphere-making, *sphairopoiïa*, referred to the construction of celestial globes, as well as other physical models illustrating the motions of the sun, moon, and planets.[33] None of these models of planetary motion survives, but we have numerous descriptions of such objects attributed to both mathematicians and philosophers. For example, several ancient authors mention Archimedes' models. Cicero credited him as the first to have designed a model depicting the motions of the planets, rather than a solid celestial sphere.[34] Pappus of Alexandria (ca. early fourth century CE) reported that, according to Carpus of Antioch (dates unknown; possibly first or second century CE), Archimedes wrote a work *On Sphere-Making* (*Peri sphairopoiias*).[35] But such model-making was not monopolised by mathematicians: Cicero also reported that the philosopher Posidonius had built a planetary model.[36] Significantly later, in the second century CE, both the Alexandrian astronomer Ptolemy (*Planetary Hypotheses* 1.1) and the physician Galen referred to models of planetary motion and their makers.[37]

Celestial globes depicted the fixed stars. Ptolemy provides detailed instructions for the construction of a solid celestial globe in the *Mathematical Syntaxis* (also known as the *Almagest*) 8.3. From his comments in another passage (7.1; Heiberg II: 12), it seems that his predecessor Hipparchus had made a globe, and offered detailed descriptions of the constellations to be drawn on the surface.[38] Hipparchus and Ptolemy may have used the celestial globe to facilitate various calculations, for example of star phases.[39] In seventh-century Constantinople, Leontius Mechanicus wrote a work on globes, explaining that his aim was to produce one that agreed with the description of the night sky in the Greek astronomical poem of Aratus (ca. 315 to before 240 BCE), known as the *Phainomena* (English: *Phenomena*).[40] This poem – based on a prose work of the same name by Eudoxus – was well known in antiquity.[41] Aratus provides a description of astronomical phenomena, as well as weather signs.

The title of Eudoxus' now-lost *Phainomena* suggests that while he offered a geometrical model to account for planetary motion, he was also engaged with what is visible in the sky. Various anecdotes associate him with instruments whose functions are linked to astronomical observations used for practical purposes. He is credited with the invention of a type of sundial (Vitruv. *De arch.* 9.1), and is mentioned as an authority in the astrometeorological calendars known as *parapēgmata*.[42]

THEORETICAL AND PRACTICAL ASTRONOMY

There is sometimes a tendency to distinguish between – and even contrast – theoretical mathematics (such as the geometrical modelling of planetary motions) and practical mathematics (including the construction of sundials). However, practical knowledge (including observational data) informed the theoretical, while the theoretical in turn informed the practical (including the application of mathematical knowledge for practical purposes). The distinction between theoretical and practical mathematics is between the different ends for which they are pursued. Theoretical mathematics (including theoretical astronomy) is pursued for the sake of knowledge itself, whereas practical mathematics (including practical astronomy) is undertaken for some practical end (such as sundial design, to aid in time-reckoning). The appellation 'practical' relates to the ends and applications of knowledge, not to the method or instrumentation employed. What we know of the work of a number of mathematicians – either through their own surviving writings or through ancient reports – indicates that they engaged in both theoretical and practical astronomy. Furthermore, the interests and needs of consumers and patrons of astronomical work varied. For example, within Roman imperial culture the production of astrological horoscopes, as well as the production of a calendar (by Sosigenes, on behalf of Julius Caesar), occupied the time and effort of some expert astronomers.[43]

Because Greek science has so often been understood as part of the philosophical enterprise, there has been an understandable tendency on the part of historians to focus on texts, emphasising theoretical concerns. Yet – as we have already seen – some of the written evidence credits individual mathematicians and philosophers with practical astronomical work, including sundial design. Turning to evidence of ancient objects associated with astronomy, while some things do survive (for example, a fragment, presumably of a celestial globe, now in the Neues Museum in Berlin), these are not always well understood. In some cases we have only descriptions, but not the actual object. And, as is the case with the written evidence, some of the physical evidence is literally fragmentary, including the now-famous Antikythera Mechanism.[44]

What do we know about the instruments associated with astronomical practice? Ptolemy provides detailed descriptions of a number of them in the *Mathematical Syntaxis*, including an armillary sphere and a parallactic instrument, designed for observations intended for specialist astronomical work. Furthermore, he indicates that some people were engaged in instrument-production.[45] From several authors (including Geminus), we understand that ringed (or armillary) spheres were apparently used as demonstration and teaching models.[46] Such instruments and models do not survive from antiquity; however, there are some pictorial representations (for example, in mosaics).[47]

Surviving artefacts as well as written testimony provide evidence of practical uses of astronomy, including telling the time of day and year (useful for many applications, including agriculture, medicine, commerce, and astrology), and also for indicating or predicting weather. The 'practical' uses of astronomy are the ends and applications of knowledge (for example, for agriculture and navigation); such practical uses are not necessarily related to instrumentation or methods, but examples of instruments with practical benefits (including sundials) do survive.

The practical application of astronomical observations and knowledge was not only the province of specialists. For example, the poet Hesiod was credited with practical astronomical knowledge, through his inclusion of a sort of 'farmers' almanac' in the *Works and Days*. He also gave advice about the best time to take to the sea: an often quoted passage (663–5) indicates that familiarity with astronomical events (in this case the 'turning' of the sun) was important in determining seasons of the year.[48] Well over a thousand years after Hesiod, a Latin author, Vegetius, in his *Epitome of Military Matters* (written after 383 but before 450 CE), also addressed the ancient poet's question about which times it is safe to sail, advising (at 4.39) that travel at sea be undertaken after the rising of the Pleiades until the rising of Arcturus, because the force of the winds is lessened in summer. That knowledge of astronomical signs was not purely the province of specialist astronomers is also emphasised by Vegetius (4.40), who explains that 'the days of new moons too are filled with storms and are very much to be feared by navigators, as is understood not only by scientific study but the experience of common people'.[49] Furthermore, Vegetius goes so far as to caution that, even though fixed dates for the rising and setting of stars (which may be linked to storms) are given by some authors, there are limits to the use of astronomical observations for navigation, because the human condition prevents full knowledge of heavenly causes. Ptolemy had earlier also acknowledged such limits, explaining that astronomy (and indeed navigation itself, like medicine) is a stochastic art, which can only aim at success, not promising a certain result.[50]

Nevertheless, we have abundant evidence of various techniques to determine and indicate the time of year. Some of this evidence – like the fragments of the Antikythera Mechanism – has only been known since the early twentieth century, including the fragments of stone inscriptions found at Miletus that were identified as examples of the astrometeorological texts known as *parapēgmata*. The physical form of *parapēgmata* suited their use: the stone fragments (dated to the late second and early first century BCE) have peg-holes, representing days in the year; a peg was placed in the appropriate hole to mark the day. *Parapēgmata* were used to correlate astronomical events (such as star phases) and seasonal weather. In the *parapēgmata*, statements about phenomena are often of the form 'according to X', where X names a well-known authority, such as Eudoxus, as well as groups of people, including 'the Egyptians'.[51] The ability to locate the peg in the inscription (or the date in the written calendar) obviated the need to look at the sky to determine the stellar phases and the time of year.[52] *Parapēgmata* allow those who are literate but not expert in astronomical observation to make use of astronomical information for weather prediction. The surviving fragments are relatively large, suggesting that they were originally on public display, and their size indicates substantial investment in recording and publicising astronomical information, suggesting that this information was thought to have public benefit.

While there are few extant *parapēgmata*, more than five hundred stone sundials that were intended to be in a fixed position survive from antiquity.[53] A relatively large number have the equinoctial and solsticial lines labelled, indicating that they were used to mark the time of year and season, as well as the time of day. Such stone dials may have served several functions, as a calendar as well as a time-finding instrument, and filling a decorative as well as practical role. Like the *parapēgmata*, they relied on considerable investment, as well as requisite skills, for their manufacture. While D. R. Dicks suggested that the *gnomon* (shadow caster) is probably the oldest known 'scientific' instrument, with regards to sundials we should understand the term 'scientific' not as indicating that the instrument was typically used for the study of natural phenomena but, rather, as referring to a technology that relied for its working on natural (in this case, astronomical) phenomena.[54] The application was practical, even while the design of the instrument may have been based on some theoretical knowledge.

Both philosophers and astronomers are associated with sun-dial invention and design. Diogenes Laertius (1.23) credited Thales with knowledge of the solstices, used to indicate times of the year. He reported (citing Favorinus, ca. 85–155 CE) that Anaximander of Miletus was the first to 'discover' the *gnomon*, that he set one up in Lacedaemon to mark the solstices and equinoxes, and also constructed hour-indicators.[55] The Roman architectural writer Vitruvius (first century BCE; *De arch.* 9.8) provides a detailed discussion of sundials, describing at least a dozen different types. In many cases the design is attributed to a particular individual, including several famous astronomers, such as Aristarchus; Vitruvius (*De arch.* 9.1) reports that both Eudoxus and Apollonius were credited with the invention of a sundial known as the *arachne*.[56] While specialist knowledge was not needed to use sundials, their design depended on mathematical skill to determine the lines to be drawn in order to function as time-finding instruments.[57] Both Vitruvius and Heron of Alexandria (fl. 62 CE) described the use of the *analemma* to find geometrically on a plane those arcs and angles that determine a point on the celestial sphere. Vitruvius was concerned with the construction of sundials, while Heron was interested in the determination of distance between two geographical locations. Ptolemy, with his interests in time-reckoning, astronomy, and geography, also wrote a work on the *analemma*.[58]

The word 'horoscopy' refers to 'watching the hours', and in his astrological work, the *Tetrabiblos*, Ptolemy (3.2) refers to various horoscopic instruments, including solar instruments that made use of a gnomon (which he warns can shift) as well as waterclocks, which may also incur irregularities. The term 'horoscopic' may refer to other types of instruments as well, and various artefacts relating to the practice of astrology survive, including 'horoscopic' boards used to illustrate planetary alignments in astrological contexts.[59]

ASTRONOMY AND PHILOSOPHY: THE ASTRONOMER AS PHILOSOPHER

Little is known about the life of Claudius Ptolemy, the Alexandrian mathematician and author of works including the *Mathematical Syntaxis*, the *Tetrabiblos*, the *Geography*, and the *Harmonics*, as well as number of lesser known works, including the *Planetary Hypotheses*.

The *Suda*, a tenth-century historical lexicon, describes Ptolemy as an Alexandrian philosopher.[60] This description of Ptolemy as a philosopher may be surprising; after all, his reputation relies primarily on his work as a mathematician and astronomer. Yet, in the very opening lines of his great astronomical work, Ptolemy flags his interest in philosophy; in fact, he claims to be doing what he argues is the highest form of philosophy: mathematics. He was concerned about the relationship of the theoretical to the practical, and with the great benefit to be gained by pursuing astronomy.[61]

He begins the *Mathematical Syntaxis* as follows:

> The true philosophers, Syrus, were, I think, quite right to
> distinguish the theoretical part of philosophy from the practical. For
> even if practical philosophy, before it *is* practical, turns out to be
> theoretical, nevertheless one can see that there is a great difference
> between the two: in the first place, it is possible for many people
> to possess some of the moral virtues even without being taught,
> whereas it is impossible to achieve theoretical understanding of the
> universe without instruction; furthermore, one derives most benefit
> in the first case from continuous practice in actual affairs, but in the
> other from making progress in the theory.[62]

He goes on to discuss Aristotle's distinction of theoretical philosophy into three principal categories: physics, mathematics, and theology (that is, metaphysics). Ptolemy claims that both physics and theology rely on guesswork, rather than knowledge.[63] Unlike Aristotle, who gave primacy to metaphysics, Ptolemy emphasised the epistemological status of mathematics.

Furthermore, for Ptolemy, the practice of astronomy has an ethical dimension. Crucially, for him, the improvement of humans is possible because of the physical structure of the cosmos, which reinforces and enables influences (and analogies) between the celestial and the earthly, between the divine and the human. By studying these relations – literally embodied in the physical world that we perceive visually in the sky above us and aurally through musical sounds – and by describing them mathematically, we can achieve some measure of the cosmic divinity.[64] That astronomical bodies have special significance for human souls is an idea that Ptolemy articulated in the *Syntaxis*. Like Plato and Aristotle, prominently amongst others, Ptolemy regarded the astronomical bodies as divine. He argued that their study is an ethical endeavour, because by studying and emulating their motions astronomy enables us to become as similar to the divine as is humanly possible.

Ptolemy concludes his first chapter by proclaiming the value of studying and teaching astronomy, pointing to the underlying ethical motivation, which will also result in practical benefits:

> With regard to virtuous conduct in practical actions and character, this science [astronomy], above all things, could make men see clearly; from the constancy, order, symmetry and calm which are associated with the divine, it makes its followers lovers of this divine beauty, accustoming them and reforming their natures, as it were, to a similar spiritual state.[65]

On his account, astronomy is beneficial to a greater extent than any other kind of theoretical philosophy or science (here, especially, read 'physics') because of its epistemic value. Astronomy, as a branch of mathematics, produces knowledge, rather than conjecture, and in this way is distinguished from both physics and theology.

Astronomy is also distinguished by the object of its study: it examines objects that are eternal and unchanging. Ptolemy subscribes to Aristotle's view that the region of the *ouranos* above the moon is ungenerated, unchanging, and indestructible; only the region below the moon is subject to generation, destruction, and change. The astronomical bodies are divine, and characterised by virtuous qualities: constancy, symmetry, order, and calm. By studying these, astronomers are able to model their behaviour on divine bodies that are intelligible and can be known and understood. Those who pursue astronomy are able to reform their nature to a spiritual state similar to that of the heavenly bodies.

Ptolemy was not the first of the Greeks to suggest that knowledge of the heavenly bodies could contribute to a better life; this is a very practical benefit of astronomy. Hesiod, towards the end of the *Works and Days*, makes it clear that knowledge of the astronomically based calendar will be crucially important for leading a good life and avoiding difficulty. Centuries later, Plato offered an account of the world in which humans can bring their souls into harmony with the cosmic order through perception of the divine heavenly bodies.[66] Furthermore, for Plato mathematics enables humans to connect with the divine. Mueller has summarised Plato's position, noting that he provided 'a comprehensive picture of the cosmos divided into a higher divine, intelligible world and a lower human, sensible world'. He further explains that Plato 'saw the task of the individual, on which his well-being, his divinization, depends as a matter of somehow attaching himself to that higher world'. Mathematics – in the broad sense encompassed by the philosopher-kings' mathematical curriculum – provides the crucial link between these two worlds. In the *Republic*, the way in which the higher world is expressed through the mathematical organisation of the lower world is highlighted, while in the *Timaeus*, Plato emphasises the role of mathematics in 'directing the attention of the potentially divine individual away from the lower world to the higher world and its apex, the form of the good'.[67] He highlights the moral benefit that can be achieved through the study of mathematics.

The study and teaching of mathematics, and astronomy in particular, is the most ethically beneficial philosophical activity, in Ptolemy's view. As in Plato's *Timaeus* (47c–e, 90c–d), the study of the harmonious motions of the celestial bodies brings about a similar harmony within the astronomer's soul. In this way, the astronomer achieves an ethical transformation, in which the parts of his soul are brought into a harmonious arrangement. The study of mathematics, including astronomy, achieves two aims: producing theoretical knowledge and providing human beings with the means to activate ethical improvement. By studying and teaching mathematics, specifically astronomy, Ptolemy argued that he was pursuing the highest and best type of philosophy.

In Ptolemy's great work on astronomy, mathematics, especially astronomy, is presented as having merged with philosophy, allowing the mathematician/astronomer to act as a philosopher. Ptolemy himself claimed to be a philosopher, and regarded his own astronomical work as an example of the best type of philosophy, simultaneously theoretical and ethical. In his view, astronomy is not merely theoretical, but practical in the most important sense, enabling and facilitating the good life. Here we see a convergence of the philosophical, the theoretical, and practical aspects of astronomy, implying – indeed, emphasising – that there is ultimately no tension between them.

NOTES

I thank Monte Ransome Johnson, Nick Jardine, Seb Falk, and Arthur Harris for their comments on an earlier version of this chapter.

1 According to the fifth-century BCE historian Herodotus (2.109.3), the Greeks learned about the celestial sphere and the *gnomon* – the shadow caster used to

find the time of day – from the Babylonians. Aristotle refers to Egyptian and Babylonian accounts of astronomical observations at *De caelo* 292a7–9, from which he states some information used by the Greeks is derived. For more on Greek and Roman perceptions of Babylonian astronomy, see Jones 2016, 502–3; for a modern perspective on the relationship between Babylonian and Greco-Roman astronomy, see Jones 2018, passim. See Chapter 13 by Zhmud, in this volume, on the history of astronomy in antiquity.

2 Thales of Miletus (fl. 586 BCE) – traditionally regarded as the first of the ancient Greek philosophers – was credited by Herodotus (1.74.1–3) as having successfully predicted a solar eclipse. On modern assessments of the prediction, see Jones 2018, 396, who notes that early predictive methods were not sufficiently sophisticated to enable the forecast of an eclipse at a particular locality; see also Mosshammer 1981. Plato (*Tht.* 174a) and Aristotle (*Pol.* 1.1259a5–19) also gave accounts of Thales' astronomical interests.

3 Claudius Ptolemy (second century CE), in the opening to the *Tetrabiblos* (1.1), explains that there are two kinds of astronomy; the second of these (the subject of that book) is what we refer to as 'astrology'.

4 See Cuomo 2019, arguing against 'two cultures' of theoretical vs. practical mathematics. See also Asper 2009, maintaining a 'two cultures' view. These 'two cultures' were challenged earlier by Tybjerg 2003, 2005.

5 Jones 2018, 374, notes the difficulty of exactly defining the scope of astronomy in the Greco-Roman world.

6 Proclus *In Eucl.* 35–36 (Friedlein). At 38 Proclus (412–85 CE) remarks on Geminus' (first century BCE) rather different division of mathematics. These 'sister' studies of mathematics became known as the quadrivium during the medieval period; the division of labour between mathematicians and philosophers was demarcated in formalised ways, for example, within the organisation of university education.

7 Ptolemy's *Mathematical Syntaxis* (also known as the *Almagest*) is the most important exemplar of the application of geometry; in Book 1.9 he begins his geometrical discussion.

8 See, for example, Pl. *Ti.* 40a. See Vlastos 1975, 3–4; Taub 1993, 138–9; Carone 2005.

9 The term *kosmos* is used differently by different ancient authors. In his commentary on Aristotle's *Physics*, Simplicius (291.27) uses the term to refer only to the heavens. Johnson 2019 has argued that the concept of *kosmos* featured more prominently in Pythagorean, Atomistic (Democritean and Epicurean), Platonic, and Stoic physics than in Aristotle's physics. However, Aristotle considers the explanation of the natural motion in the heavens to be part of physics; see, for example, *De caelo* Book 1 and 2.

10 Simpl. *in Phys.* 291, 22–292, 5, trans. Fleet 1997, 47.

11 Simpl. *in Phys.* 292, 30–32, trans. Fleet, 48.

12 Simpl. *in Cael.* 292b10 (488.21–24 Heiberg), trans. in Duhem 1969, 5. For a discussion of some issues in the text, see Vlastos 1975, 59–60, 110–12. Regarding the source(s) of the attribution of the problem to Plato, see Mittelstraß 1963; Knorr 1990; Zhmud 1998, 2005, 2006, 86–7. See also Kalligas 2016, esp. 183–6, on the formulation presented by Theon of Smyrna (fl. ca. 115–40 CE) in *On Mathematical Issues Useful for the Reading of Plato*.

13 Simpl. *in Phys.* 292, 20–29, trans. Fleet 1997, 48.

14 For the ancient Greeks, meteorology dealt with those things that are high up (*ta meteōra*); see Taub 2003. Johnson, Chapter 8 in this volume, discusses ancient differentiations between astronomical and meteorological phenomena.

15 The twentieth-century American philosopher Wilfrid Sellars (1975, 289) aimed 'to formulate a scientifically oriented, naturalistic realism which would "save the appearances" '; Mourelatos (2013) used his approach to interpret Parmenides' work.

16 The questioning of what we see as not being really real fits with Plato's views. Vlastos 1975, 111–12 (note M) comments on how, for Plato, a rational account may 'save' seemingly contradictory phenomena.

17 For an entrance into the discussion, see Lloyd 1991b, 1987b, 293–319. On Aristotle's views related to phenomena, see Owen 1961/86; Feyerabend 1985, 224; Nussbaum 1986; Long 2006. 'Saving the phenomena' continues to be discussed by modern philosophers; for example, see Bogen and Woodward 1988; Teller 2010.

18 Duhem 1969, 6, his emphasis.

19 Simpl. *in Cael.* 293a4 (492.31–493.5 Heiberg).

20 Simpl. *in Cael.* (293a4–11) (496.29–497.4 Heiberg). Not all phenomena could be explained by his model, such as the changing brightness of planets. Although the ancient descriptions of Eudoxus' astronomy are brief, several nineteenth- and twentieth-century scholars reconstructed the geometry thought to underlie his solution. The scholarly literature on Eudoxus is extensive; for a start, see Tannery 1876, 1883; Neugebauer 1953; Mendell 1998; Yavetz 1998. Knorr 1990 has argued against the suggestion that Eudoxus was responding to a problem set by Plato.

21 Plato *Resp.* 530b–c, trans. Grube, rev. Reeve (ed. Cooper 1997), 1146.

22 As an introduction, see Mourelatos 1980; Mueller 1980; Vlastos 1980. On some early modern astronomers, see Jardine 1979.

23 Arist. *Ph.* 193b26-35, trans. Hardie and Gaye (ed. Barnes 1984), I: 331.

24 Arist. *Metaph.* 1061a28–b2.

25 See Johnson 2015.

26 Plut. *Marcellus* 14.5–6, trans. Huffman 2005, 366.

27 On extant ancient celestial globes, see Dekker 2013, ch. 2; Evans 1999, 238–41.

28 Cornford 1975, 74–5.

29 Cornford 1975, 75–6. He describes the armillary sphere in some detail, suggesting that the outermost ring was intended to correspond to the equator of the sphere of the fixed stars. Cornford reinforced his reading of this passage as referring to a demonstrational armillary sphere by his inclusion of an image of an eighteenth-century armillary in the frontispiece to his book; see also 76, n. 2.

30 Mueller 2005, 115 regards the apparent tension as being related to the emphasis of each work, rather than doctrine.

31 Sedley 1976, esp. 27–8, 31–4, 37–9.

32 On Geminus, see Evans and Berggren 2006. A later commentator on Plato, Theon of Smyrna (second century CE), discussing the cosmic vision of the spindle and whorls at the end of the *Republic* 10 (616b–617b), mentions that he had made a sphere, based on the explanation there; Theon of Smyrna, *Mathematical Knowledge Useful for Reading Plato* (Hiller 1878, 146). See also Theon (trans. Dupuis 1892), 239; Evans 2003, 125–6, 129; Jones 2015, 86–7, 101.

33 According to Proclus (*In Eucl.* 41), Geminus and unnamed others regarded sphere-making as part of mechanics, itself a branch of mathematics. See also Hamm 2016.

34 Cic. *De rep.* 1.14; sadly, the entire work does not survive, and part of the description is lost. See also Cic. *Tusc.* 1.25, *Nat. D.* 2.35; Ovid, *Fasti* 6.277–80.

35 Pappus 8:2–3 (3.1026 Hultsch; trans. ver Eecke 1933, 813–14). Archimedes' book is no longer extant, and may not have been by Pappus' time. On Carpus, see Heath 1921/81, II: 428.

36 Cic. *Nat. D.* 2.34.

37 Ptol. *Planetary Hypothesis* 1.1 (Heiberg 1907, 70); Galen, *On the Usefulness of Parts of the Body* 14.5 (2.295 Helmreich edn). Jones 2015, esp. 84–7.

38 See also Toomer 1984, 327, n. 48.

39 See Evans 1999, 241.

40 See Savage-Smith 1985, 12–15; Turner 1994, 62.

41 Taub 2010; Gee 2013.

42 See Lehoux 2007 for details of the Geminus *parapēgma* (226–39) and Ptolemy's *Phaseis* (261–309), both of which cite Eudoxus.

43 On calendars, see Feeney 2008; Hannah 2009, ch. 3, 2013; Jones 2017, ch. 4; on astrological horoscopes, see Heilen and Greenbaum 2016.

44 For the fragment (Antikensammlung, Berlin, identification number SK 1050 a), see www.smb-digital.de/eMuseumPlus?service=ExternalInterface&module=colle ction&objectId=697976&viewType=detailView; see also Evans 2016, 148–9. On the Antikythera Mechanism, see now Jones 2017. See also Price 1974.

45 Ptol. *Syn. Math.* 5.1, 5.12; *Planetary Hypothesis* 1.1 (Heiberg 1907, 70). See also Price 1957.

46 Geminus 16.10–12; Ptol. *Syn. Math.* 8.3.

47 For example, the depiction of the muse of astronomy, Urania, in the third-century (ca. 240 CE) mosaic from a Roman villa in Vichten, Luxembourg, now in the Musée National d'Histoire et d'Art, Luxembourg; see www.mnha.lu/fr/ Archeologie.

48 While the use of astronomical observation for navigation in the Greco-Roman world has often been assumed, and a number of authors (including Homer) mention in passing the importance of stars for seafaring, we have very few details of actual practice. Ptolemy (*Geography* 1.7) quotes Marinos on celestial navigation, criticising his data and raising questions regarding the astronomical observations. In any case, what Marinos describes seems to be about pointing in the right direction: 'Those who set sail from Arabia to Azania direct their sail towards the south and the star Canopus'. Trans. Berggren and Jones 2000, 66.

49 Trans. Milner 1996, 147.

50 Ptol. *Tetrabiblos* 1.2; on stochastic *technai*, see Lloyd 1987b, 162; Taub 1997, 86.

51 Hannah 2001; Taub 2003; Lehoux 2007. In addition to the inscribed stone versions of *parapēgmata*, literary forms were also produced; for example, Claudius Ptolemy was responsible for a literary form of *parapēgma*, *The Phases of the Fixed Stars*. See Johnson, Chapter 8 in this volume, which also discusses *parapēgmata*.

52 Lehoux 2004, 239; Graßhoff 2017.

53 A survey of all known Greek and Roman sundials has been undertaken, alongside detailed analyses and the creation of three-dimensional models and a database of ancient sundials; see Graßhoff et al. 2016 for the database. See also Gibbs 1976; Hannah 2009; Talbert 2017.

54 Dicks 1970, 166. However, see also Ptol. *Syn. Math.* 1.6 (Heiberg I: 20) on the way in which gnomons (and also the centres of armillary spheres) can be understood as operating as if they are at the centre of the earth.

55 Diog. Laert. 2.1.

56 In the *Planisphere,* Ptolemy describes how a plane diagram of the celestial sphere can be produced using methods mathematically related to what is now referred to as stereographic projection; in this work, Ptolemy refers to a 'spider', in the context of horary instruments (14). A Greek version of the work no longer survives; for an Arabic version and translation, see Sidoli and Berggren 2007, esp. 101, 126–7, where the form and function of the 'spider' are considered.

57 See Fritsch, Rinner, and Graßhoff 2013.

58 Vitr. *De arch.* 9.7; Heron, *Dioptra* 35; see also Evans 1998, 132–41; Sidoli 2005. Ptolemy's *Analemma* is preserved in a Latin translation produced by William of Moerbeke (died ca. 1286); only a portion of the Greek text survives. See Neugebauer 1975, II: 839–56.

59 Such as the so-called Tabula Bianchini, now held in the Musée du Louvre; see Heilen and Greenbaum 2016, 130.

60 The *Suda* (Adler π 3033) reports that Claudius Ptolemy lived during the time of King Marcus, presumably the emperor Marcus Aurelius (161–80 CE).

61 See also Feke 2012; Wietzke 2017.

62 Ptol. *Syn. Math.* 1.1 (Heiberg I: 4), trans. Toomer 1984, 35.

63 Ptol. *Syn. Math.* 1.1 (Heiberg I: 6).

64 Taub 1993, particularly chs. 2, 4, 5. See also Feke 2009, particularly the 'Conclusion', 221–8, and Feke 2018, 204.

65 Ptol. *Syn. Math.* 1.1 (Heiberg I: 7), trans. Toomer 1984, 36–7.

66 Pl. *Ti.* 47a–e; cf. Taub 1993, 147–50.

67 Mueller 2005, 117.

11 Ancient Greek Mechanics and the Mechanical Hypothesis

Sylvia Berryman

There is a real danger, in approaching the topic of the history of mechanics in antiquity, of becoming entangled in modern terminology. E. J. Dijksterhuis, in his 1961 classic study *The Mechanization of the World Picture*, approached the ancient antecedents to his topic by looking at the history of atomist thought; it could be equally misleading to suppose that the history of mechanics in antiquity coincides with the development of mathematical laws to describe the motion of heavy bodies. If we look instead at the history of the body of technology that the ancient Greeks called 'mechanics' – *ta mêchanika* or *hê mêchanikê technê* – and the theories evolved to explain their workings, we would be tracing a different story. The latter is the topic of this chapter.

My purpose is not to provide a complete survey of inventions or devices, but to consider the intellectual impact of mechanics on ancient Greek thinking about the world. The idea of a 'mechanical world picture' was a central motif in the emergence of the New Science of the seventeenth century. We know that the recovery of ancient Greek mechanical texts, especially those of Archimedes and Hero of Alexandria, were important inspirations for this motif.[1] A question naturally arises: if these ancient Greek texts inspired such a response in the early modern period, did the ancient Greek philosophers not consider the implications of their mechanics as a model for explaining the natural world?

Histories of science traditionally claimed that ancient Greek intellectuals devalued mechanics because it was regarded as trickery, or as working 'against nature' and thus not subject to systematic investigation. These explanations have now been discredited.[2] It also appears that some ancient Greek philosophers did consider the possibility of a mechanical universe, and even conjectured that human beings might work like wind-up devices. But others offered more weighty objections to such a mechanistic picture of the natural world. There are traces in late antiquity of a fascinating controversy about the explanatory limits of mechanics, a controversy that shows how seriously some figures embraced its explanatory power.

A BRIEF HISTORY OF THE DISCIPLINE OF
MECHANICS IN ANCIENT GREECE

'Mechanics' seems only to have come into use as a category in the mid-fourth century BCE. The ancient Greek term *mêchanê* refers merely to a device of some kind: it is used in many non-technical senses, and has a broad field of reference. Despite Plato's abundant references to the arts and crafts of his day, he makes no mention of *mêchanikê technê*, and only once uses a related term, *mêchanopoios*, of a maker of military devices.[3] Plutarch (first century CE) and Diogenes Laertius (third century CE) both credit the development of a field called 'mechanics' to Archytas, a Pythagorean and associate of Plato's: Archytas is said to have systematised mechanics using mathematical principles. In Aristotle's *Posterior Analytics*, mechanics is listed alongside optics, harmonics, and astronomy as one of the sciences subordinate to mathematical principles;[4] it is also mentioned with optics and harmonics in the *Metaphysics*.[5] Unfortunately, however, there is little to tell us what the term *mêchanikê* refers to in these texts.

One of the more comprehensive accounts of the scope of the discipline, that by Pappus of Alexandria (fourth century CE), lists several branches of the field, which he says date back to 'the ancients'. These are devices to lift great weights with a lesser force; catapults to hurl stone and iron armaments; irrigation instruments for raising water more easily from a depth; imitations of living beings by pneumatic devices, or by cords and ropes, or by floating bodies, or by time-pieces worked by water; and 'spheres', three-dimensional models of the heavens. Proclus (fifth century CE) gives what is on some points a strikingly similar catalogue, with parallels in phrasing and structure, indicating that both were drawing on a common source. Proclus situates mechanics within a broader notion of natural philosophy: he includes a general category of equilibrium and 'centres of weight',[6] and a final category encompassing the entire art of moving matter. Such a varied list suggests that the field of mechanics was something of a conglomeration, and that the connections between its various branches were only loosely conceived. Philoponus (sixth century CE) comes closest to offering a general characterisation of mechanics as a discipline, when he describes it as focusing on two questions: how to lift a given weight or to raise water.[7]

The fact that Aristotle in the *Posterior Analytics* lists mechanics among the disciplines that are intermediate between physics and mathematics[8] indicates that mechanics first came to be regarded as a discipline because there was thought to be some mathematical basis for the operation of various devices. Unfortunately, he refers to a different branch of mathematics each time – geometry and stereometry – and does not explain the connection. The use of devices in weight-lifting seems to go back to the building of temples, which required hauling massive blocks of stone. Large numbers of labourers were employed, but overseers seem to have recognised the value of levers and pulleys in increasing the amount of weight that any given person could lift. At some point it was recognised that a lever twice as long could lift twice the weight, and that similar ratios could be achieved with the pulley or windlass. The balance was used in trade: Plato recognised that a weight twice as far out on a balance arm could balance an equal weight at half the distance from the fulcrum.[9]

There are reports that, around 399 BCE, Dionysius of Syracuse began investing in the development of ballistic technology, which led to improvements in catapult building.[10] Catapults were used in sieges for battering down city walls: small improvements in firing range would have considerable military consequences, so there were huge incentives to experiment and find the optimal range. By at least the third century BCE, mathematical formulae were used for calculating the dimensions of catapults. Smaller prototypes would be developed with optimal fire power and then scaled up, using formulae to keep the critical dimensions in the same proportion. Cube roots were needed for these calculations. Since Archytas was the first to find a way to calculate cube roots, it may be for this reason that he was reported to be the first to 'systematise' mechanics, i.e. to establish the mathematical basis for the field of ballistics.[11]

The earliest surviving treatise, the Aristotelian *Mechanica*, is primarily concerned with a group of devices centred around the balance and the lever, including pulley, wheel, wedge, windlass, rudder, and forceps – though not the screw – and with the mathematical principles thought to underlie them. While this text was sometimes ascribed to Aristotle, most scholars now agree that it was mostly likely written in the early third century BCE, by a member of Aristotle's school. Strato of Lampsacus, who became the third head of Aristotle's school, from 287–268 BCE, is a likely candidate. Aristotle makes limited use of mechanical theory elsewhere in his work, and seems to reject some of its central claims. Most tellingly, the treatise distinguishes natural and non-natural motion in a way that is in conflict with Aristotle's doctrine.[12]

The *Mechanica* is important not only because it details a number of devices – primarily those used to lift weights – but also because it posits a theory uniting them and accounting for their operation. The author views circular motion as critical to the special power of these devices: they are described as 'lifting a greater weight with a lesser force'. Although a reference to the sophistic claim to 'make the worse argument seem the better' has often been noted, the author does not seem to regard the devices as deceptive or magical. Rather, he tries to give an analysis of the special properties of circular motion to account for this ability.

Included in the collection is a temple ornament worked by hidden intersecting wheels, probably toothed. As worshippers turn a wheel on entering the temple, an ornamental bird is seen to rotate.[13] Display devices, often statues of human or animal figures with some kind of simple animation, are classified – judging from Pappus' catalogue – as a distinct branch of mechanics. Ctesibius, an inventor who lived in Alexandria in the early third century BCE, invented large-size parade float versions for royal processions. An entire genre of theatrical display pieces developed during the Hellenistic period. Some worked by intersecting toothed wheels turning one another; others used running water or steam to create what were called 'pneumatic' effects. Ctesibius invented elaborate water-driven public clocks, and a water organ that used water pressure, pump, and valves to selectively force air through different sized pipes, producing sounds.

A traditional Greek serving instrument, the *klepsydra* or 'water thief', was known at least since the fifth century, and was considered one of the simplest pneumatic devices. A glass bulb with a narrow neck and holes in the bottom, the *klepsydra* enabled a *sommelier* to serve wine neatly by blocking the neck, creating an air-lock to prevent the wine from flowing out. A genre of ingenious 'surprise vessels' exploited similar techniques. More elaborate display pieces were developed with whistles, valves, steam pressure, and self-starting siphons. A story tells of Ctesibius inventing pistons in the course of trying to hang heavy mirrors in his father's barber shop. He recognised the power of the rush of trapped air that could be suddenly released, and apparently tried to harness this for catapult technology.[14]

Philo of Byzantium (late third or second century BCE) wrote an elaborate compendium of the pneumatic devices of his day, as well as a book on ballistics. These are the only two books of the nine-book compendium of mechanics that have survived, at least in part. Philo included books on harbour making and siege defence, as well as the traditional devices associated with the lever.[15] In his discussion of catapult technology, we see indications that a connection was drawn between the 'spring of the air,' i.e. the force of trapped air artificially compressed, and the tension or *eutonia* of the sinews that were used in spring-catapults. It is probably no coincidence that the idea that matter itself has a tension that can be used to transmit effects across distance came to play an important role in natural philosophy during the third century.[16]

Archimedes (d. 212 BCE), who was regarded in antiquity as a practitioner of mechanics as well as mathematics, worked with weight-lifting technology, ballistic devices, irrigation instruments, floating bodies, and sphere making. It can be difficult to separate myth from reality in stories of devices ascribed to him, since his reputation rivalled that of the mythical inventor Daedalus.[17] The water-screw named after him may have been adopted from Egypt, where it was used for raising water between levels; he may have been the first to include this device in the same group as the balance and lever and offer a mathematical description of its operation. Reconstructing a story of him inventing a planetary device that showed eclipses requires making assumptions about the astronomical theory he may have used to model the motions of the 'wandering stars', i.e. sun, moon, and the five planets known to the ancients. While optimistic reconstructions propose that Archimedes could predict eclipses, a more cautious assessment is that he used a three-dimensional model to display how eclipses were caused by the blocking of light.[18]

Archimedes was apparently interested in developing unifying mathematical theories to explain the operation of devices, not only in ingenious constructions. He wrote a number of treatises that are lost, concerning problems of balance and equilibrium.[19] His most intriguing text, the *Method*, speculates about a way to find areas of irregular shapes by taking slices and setting them equal to a regular shape on an imaginary two-dimensional balance. This text, which was transmitted only in a damaged copy, is now being reconstructed thanks to the recovery of more text on a palimpsest.[20] Plutarch (first century CE) reports that Archimedes was reluctant to engage with the impure art of practical mechanics,[21] but this may reflect as much on Plutarch's own agenda as on Archimedes'.

The Hellenistic period was evidently a time of great advances in mechanical technology, particularly with the patronage of the arts and sciences at the Ptolemaic court in Alexandria. Unfortunately, our records from this period are particularly scanty. We learn much from Vitruvius (first century BCE), whose treatise on building techniques is an important witness to the state of ancient Greek technology at the time of the ascendancy of the Romans. He includes traditional weight-lifting devices and elaborate time-pieces, and also musical instruments and a hodometer. Hero of Alexandria (first century CE) provides more detail on Hellenistic mechanics. He was himself an inventor and theorist of mechanics. His compendium of theatrical devices shows the popularity of animated displays used as part of narrative theatrical presentations: painted 'lightning bolts' falling from the sky, accompanied by thunder; a statue of Hephaestus in his workshop, with his hammer-arm moving up and down. Hero includes a genre that he takes personal credit for, the mobile automaton. A device on wheels was working by a falling weight on a rope wound about the axle. The weight is slowed by the flow of millet from an upper to a lower chamber, so that the *impresario* could open the trap-door and leave before the device began moving, apparently of its own accord.

Hero's compendium of pneumatic devices includes a long theoretical introduction. Although the explanations it offers for pneumatic effects have been retrojected to third-century authors, I believe that it is a compilation of all available explanations – some of them mutually incompatible – including one that may have been invented by Hero himself.[22] He suggests that the ability to force additional air into an airtight container shows that there are void gaps between tightly packed particles, and also that particles deform when they are artificially squeezed more closely together, rebounding violently when released. The 'spring of the air', discovered by Ctesibius, required modifying traditional particle theory, which had posited rigid atoms. The hypothesis of deforming particles rules out any thesis equating the account with traditional atomism; the mutual incoherence of different accounts speaks against tracing the treatise to a single philosopher, rather than regarding it as a compilation.

Hero also explored the theory of weight-lifting technology in his *Mechanica*, a text that survived only in Arabic translation. He considered the possibilities for connecting the theory explaining the motion of these devices with the free fall of bodies. He quantified powers by thinking of them as comparable to the weight required to counteract them: this technique imaginatively applies methods of mechanics to the investigation of causes that were otherwise difficult to conceptualise or measure.[23]

Pappus of Alexandria, a mathematician working in the fourth century CE, surveyed the history of mechanics from the perspective of late antiquity.[24] Pappus emphasises the mathematical aspects of mechanics, not the ingenuity of devices invented. He notes that there were three classic mechanical problems: to raise a given weight with a given power, to duplicate the cube, and to find whether a wheel with a given number of teeth will mesh with another with a fixed number of teeth. The third problem is an issue for mechanical devices based on toothed wheels. The duplication of the cube – i.e. the calculation of cube roots – was also one of the three classic problems of ancient Greek mathematics. It is important for catapult building, as mentioned earlier; various ways to solve the problem using instruments were offered. The first classic problem is a calculation problem, based on the idea that various devices – windlasses or pulleys as well as levers – could be used to increase the amount of weight lifted by a given 'power'. Just as a lever twice as long could lift twice the weight, a chain of intersecting gears with the right proportions could, in principle, be used to enable someone to raise *any* given weight. This kind of problem involves idealisation: ignoring practical limits on the extent to which 'mechanical advantage' can be increased indefinitely.

A device called the *barulkos* or 'weight-lifter' consists of a gear train displaying the method of solution: it appears in Hero of Alexandria's *Mechanica*, and may have been the kind of device used by Archimedes in a famous feat, towing a ship single-handedly. Evidently, the point of this device was not to reduce the need for maritime manpower. Rather, it should be regarded as a demonstration of the potential of theoretical mechanics.[25] To see the significance of this, and the controversy it provoked, we need to consider more closely some of the theoretical claims made for mechanics in antiquity, and the reactions they provoked.

HOW MANY PHILOSOPHERS DOES IT TAKE TO HAUL A SHIP?

Mechanics as a discipline was not unique in applying mathematics to natural philosophy. Aristotle lists mechanics as one of the four fields – along with geometrical optics, harmonic theory, and astronomy – that stand between some branch of mathematics and natural philosophy. In his physics, Aristotle also theorised that proportional ratios held between various parameters involved in motion: that a projectile would move at half the speed through a medium twice as dense, or that an equal power would move half the weight twice the distance in an equal time.[26] However, at the time it was not possible to make precise measurements of parameters like the speed of moving bodies or the density of a medium. Establishing quantitative covariations would have been much easier in the case of devices, since it would be possible to measure and manipulate the relevant parameters.

We see this emphasis on precise and covarying proportions in the surviving mechanical texts. The Aristotelian *Mechanica* elaborated on the proportionalities involved in moving weights. It notes that a lever allows someone who has only a limited amount of power to move proportionally more weight, because the power would be applied at the end of a longer lever throughout a longer time interval as the lever arm traverses a greater arc. This goes contrary to any suggestion that devices were seen as magical or supernatural. Mathematical formulae were also used in ballistics, as noted above: their range could be increased by enlarging the devices while keeping the proportions between the parts constant.

Nonetheless, some mechanics had doubts about the degree to which the proportions of mechanical devices could be extended indefinitely. Philo notes some practical problems with the technique of scaling up catapults; Vitruvius reports on a fiasco that occurred when the devices built were too cumbersome and became bogged down in mud.[27] These limitations were apparently perceived by some mechanics not as mere engineering problems, but rather as limitations to the applicability of the theory. For Philo, these issues showed that a theoretical claim – one generated by applying a mathematical formula – needs to be checked against experience. He does not reject the use of such formulae, but voices doubts about the generality of some of the claims made for them.[28]

The application of mathematics to problems in mechanics is also evident in the notion that the causes of motion can be added together. We see in the Aristotelian *Mechanica* the idea of adding together two motions, even if they go in different directions. We can represent quantities of motion by arrows of proportional lengths, diverging at the appropriate angle. The combined result will move along a diagonal of the parallelogram drawn on the original two arrows.[29] The same technique was later used to represent forces of different strength and direction. This is an important innovation: when Aristotle considered combining 'powers', he regarded the stronger one as *overcoming* the weaker, not of the two being added together.[30] Treating the elusive notion of forces or powers as measurable quantities that could be used in calculations was central to the development of the new mathematical physics of the early modern period.

Philo of Byzantium certainly mentions some contexts in which mechanics of his day were attempting to consider how to combine the causes of motion. He objects to this procedure as unsound. Two tugs pulling a boat do not make it go twice as fast; trying to increase the power of a catapult by doubling the springs can lead to the catapult arm breaking. He expresses the practical mechanic's doubts over the idealising ambitions of the advocates of a mathematical and theory-driven approach to mechanics.[31]

Philo was not alone in questioning the indefinite projection of the proportions found in mechanics. A fascinating text from the sixth century CE questions Archimedes' boast that he could move the earth. Archimedes was taken not merely to assert his ability to move a great weight – to haul a ship – but also to be making more general claims that threaten Aristotelian natural philosophy and its account of form. The Aristotelian Neoplatonist Simplicius' reaction to Archimedes' claims may indicate that, in late antiquity, some figures advocated a philosophically ambitious view of the capabilities of mechanics.

To understand Simplicius' reaction, we need to consider Aristotle's statement of the 'ship-hauler' problem. Aristotle had noted that, while it takes ten men to haul a ship a given distance, this does not mean that one man can haul the same ship a tenth of the distance. The ancient Greeks did not use a concept comparable to the modern notion of friction, i.e. an independent factor to be factored in along with the causes of motion. Rather, Aristotle posited that – whatever proportions hold between various parameters – there is a lower limit to the application of those ratios. This idea of lower limits became connected to the theory that form played an ineliminable explanatory role in the natural world and that material-efficient causal explanations could play only a limited role by themselves.

In *Physics* 7, Aristotle connects a problem about hauling a ship to other questions about properties that stand in quantitative relationships:

> for it does not follow that, if a given motive power causes a certain amount of motion, half that power will cause motion either of any particular amount or in any length of time: otherwise one man might move a ship, since both the motive power of the ship-haulers and the distance that they all cause the ship to traverse are divisible into as many parts as there are men. Hence Zeno's reasoning is false when he argues that there is no part of the millet that does not make a sound ...
>
> if that which causes alteration or increase causes a certain amount of increase or alteration in a certain amount of time, it does not necessarily follow that it will do half in half the time or in half the time half: it may happen that there will be no alteration or increase at all, the case being the same as with the weight.[32]

The reason why one man can't haul a ship was not explained by a specific impediment like the modern notion of friction: rather, the problem is understood as a version of the *sorites* problem, the so-called paradox of the heap. Zeno had argued that a single grain of falling millet necessarily makes a sound: that sound would be proportional to the sound made by a falling bushel of millet, in the ratio that the grain stands to the bushel. Aristotle denies this. While Aristotle recognised proportionalities between distance, time, and power moving a projectile, he also thought that there are limits to these covariations.

It may be no coincidence that, a century later, Archimedes chose the problem of hauling a ship: plausibly, he saw himself as defying Aristotle with his demonstration.[33] The point of Archimedes' second most famous saying – 'give me somewhere to stand and I will move the earth' – is likely a hyperbolic assertion that he could calculate a mechanical solution to the problem of moving a weight of any size. He claims, that is, that the proportional ratios at work in mechanical devices can be extended indefinitely, calculating – theoretically, of course – the scale of a device big enough to move the earth. In the context of Aristotle's denial that one man could haul a ship, Archimedes might be making more than an empirical point about the capacity of levers and pulleys. He *might* have been making a much more general challenge to Aristotle's view about the relationship of parts to the whole.

And he was so taken. Simplicius' response to Archimedes' boast indicates the generality and breadth he takes it to have:

Aristotle refutes it [sc. Zeno's argument] by claiming that it is not the case that every power is capable of moving every magnitude, not even in any amount of time whatever ... For instance, if one [person as part] of a hundred moved a hundredth of a ship along with the others, themselves moving their respective hundredths, it is not the case that accordingly one ship-hauler by himself will move a hundredth of the ship which has been detached, even if it seemed that 'so great a portion' of the weight was being moved by each portion of the power when it was together as a whole.

[Aristotle] gave the cause of this, [namely,] that when a whole exists the parts do not exist 'in the whole' actually but rather potentially ... But when the power has been partitioned, he says, the proportion is not preserved, though it is preserved when it is combined.

But it is obvious that neither the one ... millet seed ... will make a sound, nor will the one ship-hauler move the whole ship the least distance whatever in the greatest time whatever. On the other hand, it is worth seeking the cause why, though the proportion is preserved in the case of half, perchance, of the power and the weight, *it does not proceed forever* ... Archimedes, having constructed, [using] this proportion of the mover, the thing being moved, and the distance, the weighing instrument called the *kharistion*, made that [famous] boast, '[Give me] somewhere to stand, and I will move the earth', *as though the proportion proceeded forever.*

One must state, then, what indeed was also stated concisely earlier, that it is not the case that every power is naturally constituted to move every weight either the least distance whatever or in the greatest time whatever, nor again is every magnitude naturally constituted to make a sound, but there is some limit, both of the least power which when detached is no longer able to move even any weight whatever any distance whatever, and also of the greatest weight being moved.[34]

Simplicius, then, expands the range of the claim made by Aristotle from the hauling of a ship to a whole range of problems about the relationship of part to whole. Simplicius positions Aristotle as though he were explicitly rejecting the premises of one of the central problems of mechanics: to move a given weight with a given power. That problem assumes that the ratios involved in mechanical advantage can be extended indefinitely. Simplicius twice uses a technical expression, 'the proportion proceeds forever'.[35] This expression seems to refer to the notion that relative proportions can be extended indefinitely:[36] it stands in contrast to the idea that there are lower limits to these proportions, i.e. the doctrine that came to be called *minima naturalia*.[37]

Aristotle was not attacking mechanics, or doubting the capacity of devices to move greater weights. Rather, the reference to the *sorites* problem about the millet seed indicates that he was rejecting the compositionality of the properties of a whole from the properties of the parts. Clearly the historical background to this change of emphasis needs unpacking. We need to be cognisant of the differences in the state of mechanical theory between the three historical periods connected by this passage: Aristotle's fourth-century natural philosophy; Archimedes' mathematised mechanical feats of the third century BCE, following perhaps the most fertile century in ancient Greek science; and Simplicius' understanding, in the sixth century CE, of the threat posed to Aristotelian natural philosophy by the claims of mechanics.

It was central to Aristotelian natural philosophy that qualitative transformation was an ineliminable feature of the natural world, i.e. that it was not merely a rearrangement of some lower-level matter, as some materialists thought. This was not an isolated article of faith, but central to the idea that some individuals have 'natures' which direct their changes and transformations. Some wholes are more than the sums of their parts. Artefacts like tables might merely be a given quantity of wood arranged in a given shape, but organisms could not be similarly accounted for. Instead, they had natures that were not reducible to the sum of the material components. Even organic tissues like blood were thought to have their own unique and ineliminable properties: they were homogeneous in composition, not decomposable into components. The components, when fused into a new whole, have their original properties only potentially: the properties of a whole could not be inferred by summing those of the components.[38]

This issue resurfaced in a later debate as to whether some higher order properties could be regarded as the *product* of the material components. The issue was raised about psychological properties and their relationship to bodily mixtures, but the debate also had an airing at a much simpler level concerning chemical properties.[39] Brian Copenhaver has argued that Galen's category of properties that are not explicable in terms of their material components is the origin of the idea that some properties are 'occult'.[40]

Medicine recognised a need to explain why certain drugs were able to produce properties that were not evident in the drug itself: some cool liquids caused us to become heated, or moist gels might have a drying effect. This suggested that the properties of mixtures were not simply a sum of the properties of their parts, and that some *powers* of mixtures could only be assessed by considering their effects, not inferred from their manifest properties.[41] The Neoplatonists held that higher level properties were not *produced* by the material, but that the material merely provided the suitable conditions for the properties to 'supervene', i.e. to enter into the material world anew from – it seems – the Platonic realm.[42] Whatever the contribution of Platonic metaphysics, empirical reasons were offered for this 'mere suitability' thesis.

Philoponus, a Neoplatonist Aristotelian, offers some empirical reasons for rejecting the view that qualities are produced by the matter. He describes the case of heating honey, and notes that a gradual change in a material property of the honey – its heat – can suddenly produce a considerable change in its colour, liquidity, and taste. This discontinuity, he suggests, is enough evidence that the matter is merely the suitable base on which qualities supervene, and that the qualities are not a mere product of the properties of the material base.[43] This doctrine of suitability for supervening qualities was linked to the idea that there are *minima naturalia*, lower limits for the appearance of certain qualities.[44] The relationship between matter and supervening quality was not straightforwardly linear, on this view: proportional covariations only hold within certain limits.

The controversy about chemical transformation may seem a long way from the problem of hauling a ship. But Simplicius' reaction to Archimedes shows that the idea that 'proportions proceed forever' was taken as a rejection of the form–matter relationship at the heart of Aristotelian natural philosophy.[45] We find a somewhat cryptic reference to this idea in Plotinus, the great theorist of the Neoplatonic synthesis in the third century CE. Plotinus objects that those who rely on 'leverage' to account for the cosmos are discounting qualitative alteration.[46] Philoponus also argues that accounts of the natural world based on the appeal to lever-technology miss the fact that the body needs to be suitable to receive soul: a soul can't re-enter a body once the suitability is lost.[47]

These remarks, in isolation, may not seem to signify much. But what does it mean to explain everything by appealing to 'leverage' – *to mochluein* – unless this is a metonym for mechanics as a whole? If we gather together the scattered evidence, it seems that quite a few figures in late antiquity were intrigued by the potential of mechanical theory to offer a new picture of the workings of the natural world.

THE MECHANICAL HYPOTHESIS IN LATE ANTIQUITY

Philosophers had drawn analogies to devices since Presocratic times. It is tempting to refer to these as 'mechanical': historians have claimed that there were 'mechanical conceptions' as far back as Homer. Because of the variety of modern meanings of the term 'mechanical' and the need for historical work to focus on 'actor's categories, it can be helpful to restrict the claim that some thinker has a 'mechanical' conception of the natural world to cases where the thinker is drawing on a theory of how things work in the field of mechanics, and applying it to the natural world. There is no evidence of this in Homer.[48]

Natural philosophy from Aristotle's day onward was dominated by a controversy over whether we need to think that some things have natures that give an internal direction to their development: acorns do not merely happen to turn into oak trees. Rather, that is the natural end of their growth, and occurs because they have an internal form. Many philosophers who accept the need for form and for teleological explanation also use analogies to artefacts in explanation. The interesting thesis inspired by the development of mechanics is that natural things might work *entirely* like artefacts: that there is no need to posit internal forms, since we can account for their functioning purely by the arrangements of the material parts, just as we do with working artefacts.

It is important to this kind of mechanical hypothesis that the natural world is thought to *work* like a mechanical device. For example, there is a reference to *machina mundi* in the Epicurean philosopher Lucretius (first century BCE): he might seem to be calling the world a machine. However, the text only talks about the world being a complex arrangement.[49] By contrast, a text in the Aristotelian corpus, dated to the end of the first century CE, offers a much more explicit claim that the cosmos might function like a machine:

> It is more noble, more becoming ... [that] his power, penetrating the whole of the cosmos, moves the sun and moon and turns the whole of the heavens ... the most divine thing of all is to produce all kinds of result easily by means of a single motion, just like the operators

of machines, who produce many varied activities by means of the machine's single release-mechanism. In the same way too the men who run puppet-shows, by pulling a single string, make the creature's neck move, and his hand and shoulder and eye ... So also the divine being, with a single movement of the nearest element distributes his power to the next part and then to the more remote parts until it permeates the whole.[50]

Other texts from late antiquity echo this idea that a divine creator of the cosmos would be seen to be more powerful if it was not engaged in the ongoing operation of the cosmos, but rather constructed it like the wind-up devices on public display that run by themselves.[51] This comparison suggests that there is no ongoing intelligent direction of the cosmos, and that efficient-causal processes alone govern the sequences of events. Most often the idea is mentioned by its detractors, so we possess few details. Nonetheless, it is clear that some figures in late antiquity contemplated a 'mechanical world picture'.

Theatrical devices like Hero's automata were operated by weights attached to ropes, causing other mechanisms to move. We don't have much evidence of how widely available these were: Philoponus tells us they were on display at weddings.[52] It seems to be these wind-up devices that inspired the idea that the natural world might also function 'automatically', i.e. by efficient-causal processes without ongoing intelligent direction. They may not have operated for as long, or in such complex ways, as modern clockwork, but the suggestion was enough.[53] What wind-up devices seem to supply – in the absence of the idea that determinate and global causal laws govern all natural processes – is the idea that complex causal sequences could produce a determinate result, and moreover that a single causal trigger could produce multiple and complex outputs that are different in kind from the triggering cause.[54] It seems to be the *sequencing* of complex causal processes from a single triggering cause that spurred the analogy.[55] Wind-up devices illustrated the possibility that apparently intentional results could be produced by efficient-causal processes, given the construction of the device. As in the early modern period, the 'mechanical hypothesis' need not eliminate appeal to divine artificer, but merely showed how efficient-causal processes could bring about results that appear to be those of intentional design.

Mechanical analogies were offered, not only for the functioning of the cosmos as a whole, but also for the functioning of organisms. While

Hippocratic doctors used analogies to pneumatic devices to a limited extent, use of mechanical analogies in medicine evidently flourished in the Hellenistic period.[56] Tertullian reports that Strato of Lampsacus saw Ctesibius' water-organ as a model for the operations of the soul through the nervous system.[57] Galen vociferously rejects the appeal by some doctors to techniques from pneumatics to account for the fluid dynamics of the body. His rejection depends on the claim that they can't explain the idiosyncratic powers that give each organ of the body its peculiar ability to attract, repel, and assimilate appropriate fluids.

Like Simplicius and Plotinus, Galen sees the mechanical analogy as threatening the basis of hylomorphism, the idea that organisms are form–matter compounds and cannot be understood without recognising the role of form in explaining their functions. He credits some doctors with appealing to mechanical wind-up devices to account for the complex sequences of changes in organic growth. He rejects this possibility on the grounds that it puts too much faith in the precision of material processes and their ability to reproduce complex sequences of changes accurately.[58]

Unfortunately, evidence of the 'mechanical hypothesis' in antiquity is generally recorded by its detractors, who seldom give much detail on how it was formulated, or by whom. The surviving text that is most informative is a thought-experiment by Gregory of Nyssa. While he is also concerned to reject this hypothesis, he first formulates it clearly:

> We see many such things contrived by the makers of machines,
> in which they arrange matter skillfully to imitate nature. Their
> contrivances do not show similarity to nature in appearance alone,
> but also sometimes in motion, and in representation of a kind of
> voice, when the mechanism reverberates in its sounding part. In
> such cases indeed the phenomenon does not lead us to suppose that
> an intelligent power brings about in each machine the appearance,
> form, sound, or motion. If we should say that the same also happens
> in the case of this mechanical instrument of our nature, we might
> say that no intelligent essence is infused in us according to the
> peculiarity of our nature, but some kinetic power resides in the
> nature of the elements in us. Such activity would be a result.[59]

As well as articulations of a mechanical hypothesis, we also find responses indicating that natural philosophers saw the need to critique this hypothesis. Proclus devotes an entire treatise to the refutation of the proposal by a mechanic named Theodorus, who apparently proposed a thoroughgoing mechanical picture of the world. Unfortunately, Proclus' focus is on the problem of causal determinism suggested by this model and its implications for divine providence, so we receive little detail about how it works.[60] One reason given for the rejection of this analogy concerned its inability to account for human thought: the suggestion is made that, because we are able to conceive and build devices, we can't be devices ourselves.[61] Other reasons given are more basic to the foundations of natural philosophy. Philosophical defenders of teleological causation in late antiquity suppose that organisms need an internal nature or qualitative powers directing their functioning, because of the complexity of functioning forms that need to be replicated in organisms.[62]

The world is not a machine: why might it be important that this analogy was considered in antiquity? The analogy was important in the early modern period because it suggested a research programme that proved very productive at a certain stage in the development of the sciences. Because mechanical devices are considered to be the sum of their parts, and to be subject to mathematical proportions, the 'mechanical world picture' suggested a certain style of investigation.[63] The application of techniques from studying the 'power' of mechanical devices to other contexts suggested techniques for quantifying forces.

In antiquity, the shortcomings of the mechanical hypothesis looked greater than its strengths, at least to those whose views are recorded. There were some legitimate reasons for rejecting it. It is a great loss that we know so little about this earlier appearance of a motif that proved so fruitful a millennium later. In the early modern world, the 'machine analogy' seems to have preceded the articulation of a programme for a mathematical physics. It may be that, in antiquity, the reverse was true: that Archimedes envisioned the power of applying mechanical thought to natural philosophy in advance of popular uptake of a machine analogy.

But perhaps, after all, he was only moving a ship. It may only be in a context where the possibility of a mechanical universe was being openly considered that Archimedes' boast would have suggested such vaunted philosophical ambitions to Simplicius. Unfortunately, the evidence is lost: we scarcely know what Archimedes might have done with a place to stand.

NOTES

1 Rose and Drake 1971.
2 Cuomo 2000; Schiefsky 2007; Berryman 2009.
3 Pl. *Grg.* 512B5.
4 Arist. *An. post.* 1.13, 78b37; cf. 1.9, 76a24.
5 Arist. *Metaph.* 13.3, 1078a16.
6 Cf. Simpl. *In Cael.* 543, 30.
7 Philoponus, *In Categoriae.* 119.7
8 Arist. *An. post.* 1.9.76a24; 1.13, 78b37
9 Pl. *Protag.* 356B.
10 Marsden 1969; Cuomo 2007; Rihll 2007.
11 Huffman 2005.
12 For arguments that Aristotle engaged more thoroughly with mechanics, see Hussey 1991; De Groot 2014; cf. Berryman 2009, 2014.
13 The association of this device with temple practices in Egypt is an additional reason why this text is thought to be more likely Strato's than Aristotle's.
14 Vitruvius, *De arch.* 9.8.2-3; Athenaeus, *Deipn.* 4.174; Philo, *Bel.* 78.8; Marsden 1971, 184.
15 Philo, *Bel.* 59.12.
16 Vegetti 1993; Berryman 2009.
17 Jaeger 2008.
18 Neugebauer 1975, II, 664–9; Evans 1998, 20, 213; Keyser 1998, 246; Bowen 2002.
19 Drachmann 1963, 114–33.
20 Netz and Noel 2007.
21 Plut. *Marcellus* 14.5–6.
22 Berryman 2009.
23 Drachmann 1963; Schiefsky 2008.
24 Cuomo 2000.
25 Drachmann 1958; Simms 1995; Jaeger 2008, 101–22.
26 Arist. *Ph.* 4.8.215b1–11; 7.5.249a1–3.
27 Gros 2006.
28 Philo, *Bel.* 50; Lloyd 1973, 99; Rihll 2007, 153.
29 Sambursky 1962, 62–70; Hussey 1991; Berryman 2009.
30 Berryman 2009; cf. Hussey 1991.
31 Berryman 2009.
32 Arist. *Ph.* 7.5, 250a15–21, 250b4–9, trans. Hardie and Gaye. Cf. *Ph.* 8.3.253b17–19.
33 Drachmann 1958; Simms 1995.
34 Simpl. *In Phys.* 7.1108.28–1110.17, trans. Hagen 1994 (slightly modified). I have used 'power' to translate *dunamis*.
35 Simpl. *In Phys.* 1109.25; 1110.4–5.
36 Nicomachus, *Introductio Arithmetica* 1.19.2.4; 1.19.14.1.
37 De Haas 1997; Murdoch 2001. Murdoch notes that Arist. *Ph.* 1.4.187b35–188a1 is the origin of the doctrine.
38 Arist. *Gen. corr.* 1.10.327b23–33. On the perceived importance of this to Neoplatonist natural philosophy, see De Haas 1999.
39 Sorabji 2002; Berryman 2005.

40 Copenhaver 1998, 459.
41 Galen, *De temperamentis* 3.684–92.
42 Sambursky 1962, 106–10; Todd 1972; Berryman 2005.
43 The term has a slightly different meaning in the ancient context than in recent philosophy: see Berryman 2005. Sambursky 1962, 43, highlights this passage.
44 Sambursky 1962, 106–10; Todd 1972; De Haas 1997, 1999; Murdoch 2001; Berryman 2005.
45 Themistius also presents the ship-hauler problem as a question of part–whole relationships: Themistius, *In Ph.* 207.10–208.11.
46 Plotinus, *Enneades* 3.8.2, 5.9.6
47 Philoponus, *In de An* 107.26–109, 6, esp. 108.5–11; Sambursky 1962, 109; Berryman 2005.
48 Berryman 2003.
49 Lucretius *DRN* 5.96; Berryman 2003. The Aristotelian *de Mundo* may be the earliest surviving instance of a mechanical analogy for the cosmos: Mansfeld argues that it 'can hardly be dated earlier than the late first century BCE': Mansfeld 1992, 400; cf. also Thom 2014.
50 Arist. *Mund.* 398b7–22, trans. Furley 1955.
51 Sextus Empiricus, *Math.*9.111–5; Lactantius, *Div. inst.* 2.5.13; Synesius, *Aegyptii sive de providentia* 1.9.36.
52 Philoponus, *In de generatione animalium* 77.16.
53 *Pace* Mayr 1986, who stresses the importance of clockwork in the emergence of the mechanical worldview.
54 Berryman 2007.
55 Henry 2005; Berryman 2007, 2010.
56 Von Staden 1996.
57 Tertullian, *De anima* 14.
58 Galen, *Nat. Fac.*; *Foet. Form.* 4.688–9; Berryman 2002b.
59 Gregory of Nyssa, *De anima et resurr.* 46.33.11, trans. Roth 1993.
60 Proclus, *De prov.* The device used as analogue seems to be a theatrical display, not a clock as Steel 2007 suggests.
61 Gregory of Nyssa, *De anima et resurr.* 46.37.33; Proclus, *De prov.* 12.65.
62 For more on this theme, see Berryman 2007.
63 See, e.g. Des Chene 2001; Gabbey 2001.

12 Measuring Musical Beauty: Instruments, Reason, and Perception in Ancient Harmonics

Massimo Raffa

Where does musical beauty come from? Can it be comprehended into rules or formulae? Since music was ubiquitous in the life of the ancient Greeks, it is no surprise that they posed these questions, thus triggering one of the most fascinating debates in their intellectual history.

INTRODUCTION: MUSICAL LISTENING IN ANCIENT GREECE

Ancient Greek music was essentially monodic, which means that it consisted mostly in a single melodic line. Instrumental accompaniment did exist, of course, but was kept at an ancillary level lest the clarity of the text be compromised. Solo singers and choruses were usually accompanied on pipes (*aulōidia*) or chordophones (*kitharōidia*), or both. Although large orchestras were an increasingly common sight under Hellenistic sovereigns, a plurality of performers did not involve anything similar to either modern polyphony (i.e. two or more simultaneous parts melodically and rhythmically independent from one another) or harmony (i.e. the simultaneous combination of notes into chords which are generally meant to sustain a melody). Instead, melodies were performed in unison or octaves and the instrumental accompaniment of songs basically consisted in doubling the melody (preferably an octave above, as the sources seem to suggest), at most adding slight variations to the melodic line (a procedure called *heterophony*).

From our post-dodecaphonic perspective, such music may appear unsophisticated, if not primitive: none of its features is even remotely comparable to the intricacies of modern compositions. Yet, whatever the technicalities in its making, musical expression always has a complexity to it. Listeners react to even the humblest melody at different levels, some of which seem no more than automatic responses – such as tapping fingers along or accompanying the rhythm with bodily movements – while others reach deeper, into the sphere of emotions. Besides, when we find ourselves waving a hand in the air so as to follow the 'melodic line', this indicates that we have been projecting the melody on to a sort of space – whereas there is in fact no 'musical space' outside the listener's mind. Again, when listening to a melody for the first time, we may recognise some of its patterns and anticipate where it might be heading. This postulates that, as our melody unfolds, we are able to compare it with the parts of the same melody we have already heard and stored in our short-term memory, as well as many other melodies which are present to our long-term recollection: a very complex procedure, but one that everyone – except for the completely tone-deaf – carries out almost inadvertently. This mixture of physical, psychological, and cultural elements is the basis for any further assessment of musical beauty.

To the ancient Greeks, musical listening must have been a sort of 'one-dimensional' experience, no 'depth' being provided by any counterpoint or accompaniment with chords. The author of the pseudo-Aristotelian *Problems of Harmony* significantly claims that a melody, *qua* a succession of differently pitched notes, possesses character (*êthos*), while a consonance – i.e. two consonant notes heard simultaneously – does not.[1] Accordingly, musical composition (*melopoiïa*) basically amounted to creating a path which moved through a series of diachronic steps from one note to another; and it is precisely on the nature, size, and mutual relationship of these steps that most of the reflection on musical beauty focused. The branch of knowledge that grew out of this investigation was called 'harmonics' (*harmonikē*) and was regarded as part of the broader field of *mousikē*, which also included rhythmics (*rhythmikē*), metrics (*metrikē*), organology (*organikē*), composition (*poiētikē*), and performance (*hypokritikē*). Despite its assonance with analogous words in modern languages, Greek *harmonikē* had nothing to do with the construction and concatenation of chords; it was rather aimed at ascertaining which intervals could or could not be arranged to form scales and melodies, and for what reasons. This required, quite obviously, that intervals be measured in some way and grouped into categories according to some criteria which we will be briefly discussing in due course. At the risk of oversimplifying, one might describe the attitude of the ancient Greeks towards musical beauty as oscillating between two extremes. One is the idea that if music strikes us as beautiful, this must be because it shares its features with something more important, such as the structure of the universe, the human soul, or both; in this view, what makes music beautiful is to be looked for *outside* music itself, such as in proportions or numbers. At the opposite extreme lies the claim that the criterion of beauty is *intrinsic* to the constituents of music, i.e. pitched sounds, and the ways in which they are organised.

THE BASIC INTERVALS AND THE 'RATIONAL' ASSUMPTION

In the earliest stages of ancient Greek musical practice, scales did not encompass an octave, nor did they include a fixed number of notes. Melodies were arranged starting from a much narrower range, spanning over what we now call a fourth – in modern parlance, for instance, the descending interval A^1–E^1 (the numbers in apex mean that the two notes belong to the same octave). This span was originally called *syllabā* ('what is grasped', probably by a lyre-player's hand), without any reference to the number of notes included. The range of an octave was reached at a later stage, apparently by adding a second interval at the top of the first one: for instance, a fifth E^2–A^1 on top of the fourth A^1–E^1 would produce the octave E^2–E^1. The added fifth was referred to as *di'oxeiân* ('through the high [strings?]') and the resulting octave as *harmonia* or even *systēma*[2] ('something that has been put together'). This jargon, which in all likelihood originated from practical musicians, is first found in a fragment of Philolaus of Croton, a Pythagorean roughly contemporary with Socrates,[3] and was probably old-fashioned even at his time, dating back perhaps to sixth century BCE or earlier. By the fifth century BCE, therefore, the basic intervals were the octave, the fourth, and the fifth (E^2–A^1 or B^1–E^1). They happened to be the first intervals in the so-called harmonic series (i.e. the series of sounds whose frequencies are integral multiples of the frequency of a given note) and were plainly distinguishable from one another owing to their relatively large size. Any further development of Greek music theory, up to the much more elaborate stages of late antiquity, would be based on these three intervals, each of which from the very beginnings was regarded as 'consonant' (*symphōnoi*, i.e. pleasant when its constituent notes were heard simultaneously).

Philolaus' vocabulary is interesting in many respects. He calls the octave *diploon* ('double'), the fifth *hēmiolion* ('in the ratio of 3/2'), the fourth *epitriton* ('in the ratio of 4/3'); the term *epogdoon* ('in the ratio of 9/8') indicates the difference between the fifth and the fourth – an interval later authors refer to as *tonos* ('tone'). All these names reflect the quantitative aspects involved in the production of the corresponding intervals. For an octave to be obtained, for instance, on a couple of pipes of equal section – like those of the panpipe, the so-called *sŷrinx* – the one producing the lower note needs to be twice as long as the other; for a fifth, one and a half times longer; for a fourth, four thirds longer. Some later traditions credit Pythagoras with the 'discovery' of these proportions, others cite Hippasus of Metapontum (an early fifth-century Pythagorean) or Lasus of Hermione (sixth century, not a Pythagorean); however, the 'experiments' attributed to them – with bronze discs of different thickness, vases, pieces of metal or wood of different dimensions, or cups filled with liquid at different levels – are not to be thought of in any modern sense. They were meant less to *discover* anything new or to *prove* a theory than to *confirm*, to *show*, and somehow to *legitimate* what must have been empirically known to practical musicians, instrument-makers, and thinkers since very ancient times.

Thinking of musical intervals as ratios implied conceiving of a single interval not as an item per se, but as a relation between two magnitudes. As a consequence, operating with intervals – as in adding or taking away – amounted to operating with the ratios that express them. *Adding* an interval to another corresponded to *multiplying* their ratios and, likewise, *taking away* to *dividing* them by one another. If a fourth was added to a fifth to form an octave, for instance, the corresponding representation procedure in term of ratios was not $4/3 + 3/2$ but $4/3 \times 3/2 = 2/1$; and if a fourth was taken away from a fifth to obtain a tone, the arithmetical procedure was $3/2 : 4/3 = 9/8$. Accordingly, adding two intervals of the same size amounted to elevating their ratio to the second power and so on: the ditone was expressed by the ratio $81/64 = (9/8)^2$, the tritone by $(9/8)^3$, etc. Philolaus also mentions an interval smaller than the epogdoic, the *diesis* ('something that has been thrust through something else'), which was the difference between a fourth and a ditone. Its ratio was therefore $4/3 : (9/8)^2 = 256/243$ and could be calculated without any instrument. (These were, in fact, the intervals used by Plato's Demiurge in constructing the World Soul.[4])

THE SMALLER INTERVALS AND THE 'LINEAR' ASSUMPTION

Philolaus, however, does not seem to always think in terms of ratios. The Greek word for 'ratio' is *logos* (masculine), but all the adjectives he uses (*hēmiolion, epitriton*, etc.) are neuter and imply the noun *diastēma* ('distance'). In principle, the notion of 'distance' involves thinking of notes as items placed on a spatial continuum, in the same way as there are points on a straight line or finger-holes on a pipe; an interval will be, therefore, a *segment*, and the notes its *extremes*. An important corollary of this assumption is that any interval, *qua* length, is susceptible of division into two or more equal parts, which in most cases is impossible with the 'rational' theory. In this way, the notion not only of 'semitone', but also that of 'quarter tone' and, in principle, of even smaller intervals becomes possible. From the 'rational' standpoint, instead, halving a tone requires extracting the square root of the ratio 9/8, which does not exist (of course in the realm of integers), since 8 is no square number. This is true of all the intervals that share the form $(n+1)/n$, the so-called epimorics (*logoi epimorioi*) or superparticulars, since no two successive integers are both square numbers. It seems that the two assumptions coexisted in Philolaus' thought, for he reportedly conceived of two intervals by no means expressible through ratios: the *schisma*, i.e. a half *comma* (the *comma* being the difference between a tone and a double *diesis*), and the *diaschisma*, i.e. a half *diesis*.[5] One may speculate that he found the linear assumption more useful than the other one for handling the extremely small intervals below the *diesis*.

Philolaus' and other fifth-century thinkers' interest in such intervals can hardly be a coincidence. During the classical period (fifth to fourth century BCE), Greek musical language became more elaborate, as a result of both the intrinsic evolution of its technical means and the rise of the more spectacular performances favoured by theatrical audiences in Athens as well as other democratic *poleis*. Musical scales tended to assume a more standardised form; the main intervals were now named after the number of notes they contained (*dia pente* instead of *di'oxeiân* and *dia tessarōn* instead of *syllabā*), while the name for the octave, *dia pasôn* ('through all the notes'), still carried the idea of unity and cohesion that was also implicit in the ancient names *harmonia* and *systēma*.[6] However, the octave, the fifth, the fourth, and the tone were but the skeleton of the different scales; their flesh, as it were, was the intervals which filled each of the two fourths which made up the scales. And while the 'skeleton' had never been a matter of dispute, below the fourth when it came to intervals smaller than the fourth began a realm of great variety. The different sizes of the intervals formed by inserting two notes between the fourth's boundaries produced different tetrachordal patterns and, accordingly, different genera,[7] which since the fourth century BCE on began to be roughly grouped into the three main categories of diatonic, chromatic, and enharmonic. Because they were smaller than the smallest concord (the fourth), these intervals were non-consonant by nature; they were also less easily distinguishable from one another for the non-specialists, sometimes – as in the case of the bottom intervals in the enharmonic genus, the so-called *pyknon* – almost to the point of imperceptibility. Moreover, unlike the larger intervals, their quantitative features did not leap to the ear in such a way as to allow an observer to immediately connect a certain relation between two magnitudes to a given interval. It is no surprise, therefore, that a vast debate arose in the late fifth and fourth century BCE on the tools with which to investigate so slippery a matter.

COPING WITH REAL MUSIC: RATIONALISM AND EMPIRICISM

About a generation after Philolaus flourished, another outstanding Pythagorean of *Magna Graecia*, Archytas of Tarentum, appeared.[8] To our knowledge, he was the first who tried to express the structure of the different tetrachords by means of ratios. Our sources credit him with having proposed the following series:[9]

Diatonic	9/8 x 8/7 x 28/27	= 4/3
Chromatic	32/27 x 243/224 x 28/27	= 4/3
Enharmonic	5/4 x 36/35 x 28/27	= 4/3

These are the most ancient divisions known to us of genera other than the simple diatonic; indeed, they might be the most ancient divisions of all, since there is no explicit evidence that Philolaus actually theorised an epogdoic–epogdoic–*diesis* sequence. Archytas reveals himself as a true Pythagorean as he clearly sticks to the multiplicative assumption, thus setting the tone for any successive attempt of the same sort: from now on, dividing a tetrachord would mean finding three ratios the product of which equalled 4/3. A glance at his ratios shows he pursues an ideal of mathematical coherence, if not 'beauty'. He uses almost exclusively superparticulars, a particular category of ratios to which the Pythagoreans, for more than one reason, attached a special value.

First, this was the form of all the ratios expressing the fundamental concords[10] and the first non-consonant one (the tone); second, because they amounted to an integer plus a simple fractional part of the same integer, they were more easily detectable than others at first sight (at least for the major ratios: grasping a 2/3 or 4/3 relationship between two lengths is one thing, a 128/127 one is another); finally, ancient Greek language allowed them to be indicated by one-word expressions such as *hēmiolios*, *epitritos*, *epitetartos* (5/4), etc., while non-superparticulars required lengthy periphrases (e.g. *ta oktō pros ta tria* for the 8/3 ratio).[11] One might suppose, therefore, that Archytas thought superparticulars particularly elegant or at least convenient; to express the ditone of the enharmonic, for instance, he chose the approximate 5/4 over the non-superparticular $81/64$ (= $9/8^2$). However, the fact that he also used non-superparticular ratios – see the two upper intervals of the chromatic genus – shows that he may not have deemed 'superparticularity' *strictly* essential to the beauty or acceptability of *any* interval and was prepared to sacrifice part of the formal elegance of his divisions in order to comply with a different kind of assumption, namely the influence of the instrumental tunings and techniques of his time.[12] His theory can be seen, therefore, as an attempt to balance the interest in heard music and the abstraction from perception. It is this sort of compromise that Plato may have criticised, in a famous passage of the *Republic*, for being content with 'seeking numbers in the audible concords' instead of 'ascending to the problems' and 'asking which numbers are concordant and which are not, and why it is so'.[13] It is hardly a coincidence that Plato ignored his friend Archytas' divisions in his account of the World Soul in the *Timaeus*.

Archytas was not the only one to cope with the challenges posed by heard music. Among those concerned with very small intervals one should also mention the theorists or practical musicians – or both: we need not distinguish here – usually referred to as *hoi harmonikoi*, 'the harmonicists'. The appellative, which is found in Plato's and Aristoxenus' writings, is less the definition of a proper 'school' than a comprehensive indication for the non-Pythagorean predecessors of

Aristoxenus. Their method appears entirely empirical: although none of their work has survived, we can infer from a passage of Plato[14] that they used strings to seek the smallest possible interval. We need not assume that they invented any new instrument for the sole sake of acoustical experimentation; they are more likely to have used existing musical instruments with a new purpose. It stands to reason that they would work on two or more strings, first tuning them in unison and then gradually altering the tension of one of them in order to get a note higher or lower enough to be regarded as different from the other one; or, alternatively, that they would tune a couple of strings at a given interval and use a third one to try to divide it into two smaller intervals.[15] This is consistent with another criticism brought against them by Aristoxenus,[16] that they would focus on the sole enharmonic (not by chance, the genus which included the smallest possible intervals) and ignored the others. Whatever their procedures, the outcomes were bound to depend on the individuals' ability to distinguish between two or more almost equally pitched notes – a flaw Plato would sarcastically harp on, portraying them while 'talking of something they call "densifications" (*pyknōmata*) and laying their ears alongside, as if trying to catch a voice from next door' and quarrelling over what they thought they had heard.[17]

Plato's judgement may have been clouded by his aversion to experimental sciences; Aristoxenus, on the other hand, may have been biased by his natural hostility towards nearly any other music theorist of his time. We, however, should take the activity of the *harmonikoi* more seriously. To begin with, they were probably the first to use instruments to investigate the structure of musical scales and to discover something *new* instead of *confirming* what mathematical speculation had already indicated as correct, as the Pythagoreans did. Moreover, if their search for the least perceptible gap between two pitches was aimed at describing any other interval as a multiple of this unit, they might have tried to work out a system for indicating effectively the size of every possible interval – a task that Greek musical notation, as far as we know, never managed to fully achieve. The diagrams with which they are said by Aristoxenus to have illustrated their theories are probably the first attempt to graphically describe something so immaterial as the form of a musical scale. There is no evidence whatsoever of how these diagrams may have looked, but from a brief remark by Aristoxenus on them being 'compressed' or 'densified',[18] one may infer that they displayed some sort of signs – perhaps dots or lines – drawn very close to one another in order to represent the tiniest intervals.

BEYOND THE NUMBERS: 'DYNAMIC' CONCEPTIONS OF MELODY

Whether conceived of as ratios or lengths, musical intervals had been so far treated as something *static*, of which the sizes were measured per se, regardless of the melodic context in which they occurred. The nature of a fifth, for instance, was thought to lie either in the ratio of 3/2 or in a distance of two and a half tones, no matter what position it may have occupied in a particular scale or at what stage of a particular melody it may have occurred; which evidently failed to account for the fact that two intervals of the same magnitude were not perceived as identical to one another if they occurred between different couples of notes in the scale. If we consider the so-called Greater Perfect System (GPS), i.e. the standard two-octave scale to which music theorists refer from Aristoxenus' time onward, the fifth between the *nētē hyperbolaiōn* and the *paranētē diezeugmenōn* would hardly be perceived as the same interval occurring between the *lichanos mesōn* and the *parypatē hypatōn*. On the threshold of the Hellenistic period, however, the debate about music was dramatically enlivened by Aristoxenus of Tarentum, a disciple of Aristotle with a Pythagorean background (not by chance was he a fellow citizen of Archytas'), who introduced the notion of *kinēsis tês phōnês*, 'the movement of the voice'. His claim that harmonics is only concerned with the voice that moves (or, better, is perceived by the listener as moving) from a stable and recognisable pitch to another – the so-called intervallic voice (*phōnē diastēmatikē*) – is preliminary to his study of the role played by each note in the context of its own scale and the melody to which it belongs (he refers to this attribute of notes as *dynamis*, 'power'). Aristoxenus sees musical intervals as something *dynamic*, i.e. the steps through which a melody 'goes' where it is meant to go according to its *physis* ('nature') and *êthos* ('character'). The extant part of Book 3 of his *Harmonic Elements* is shaped as a series of axioms and propositions that recall, to a certain extent, Euclid's *Elements*[19] and aim at describing which steps a melody can or cannot take after reaching a particular note, as well as which arrangements of notes are more melodic (i.e. acceptable in the making of a melody), which ones are less melodic, and which unmelodic at all. On the one hand, Aristoxenus intends to establish harmonics as a science of its own, grounded in Aristotelian epistemology and no longer subordinate to mathematics or geometry. On the other hand, insofar as his theory bears on the composition of heard melodies – perhaps indeed, in the part now lost, on the issue of modulations, which had become crucial to musical aesthetics at that time[20] – it provides useful tools not only for 'pure' theorists, but for practical musicians as well.

In this framework, not much room is left for the issue of measurement. Aristoxenus clearly espouses the linear assumption, as shown by his regular usage of the enharmonic *diesis* (i.e. a quarter tone, the smallest possible interval, which is the same as Philolaus' *diaschisma*) and other difficult intervals such as 7/12 of a tone (i.e. the enharmonic *diesis* plus 1/3 of a tone). However, although he is often portrayed as a fierce opponent of the Pythagoreans, he never claims their doctrines false; he simply waves them aside as 'most extraneous' – *allotriōtatoi* – to the goals of harmonics,[21] nor does he recommend any experimental procedure for pinpointing intervals. The ability to grasp intervals correctly is *presupposed* by his approach: it is something one must have already mastered through habit and practice *before* tackling the study of harmonics. He deems the classification of magnitudes per se considerably less important than the understanding of how intervals function in context; indeed, some difficulties and apparent inconsistencies in the 'theorems' of Book 3 can be arguably overcome by postulating that he sometimes uses the names of intervals quite loosely, for instance calling *ditonos* the upper interval of any tetrachord in which the two lower intervals altogether amount to less than a half of the entire fourth (i.e. they form what is called a *pyknon*, 'something dense'), even if its magnitude does not happen to equal an exact ditone.[22] Music is beautiful, in Aristoxenus' view, not because it can be described through numbers or shares some features with numbers, but to the extent to which it fulfils its own *physis* by 'moving' and unfolding through time, note after note.

There was in fact a potentially pernicious weakness in the Pythagorean approach. Insofar as it failed to demonstrate *why* musical beauty should depend on non-musical factors, such as a particular category of ratios or other numerological features, it ultimately relied on an unsubstantiated assumption. The theoretical reasons for preferring superparticulars over other ratios were fragile in many ways, for some superparticulars did not express concords (e.g. 5/4, which was a sort of ditone, see above), while, conversely, some concords were not expressed by superparticulars, as shown by the emblematic case of the eleventh, i.e. the interval composed by a fourth plus an octave, as in

A^1–D^3. Although perfectly consonant to the ear, it corresponded to the non-superparticular ratio of 8/3 (= 4/3 x 2/1).[23] For this reason, we are told, some Pythagoreans had gone so far as to deny the eleventh the status of a concord,[24] which implies that at some stage their preference for superparticulars had grown into the rule whereby all concords *had* to be expressed by superparticulars. Another case in which arithmetical speculation prevailed over perception is the Pythagorean algorithm for establishing a hierarchy among concords. They, we are told, took away the number 1 from both the numerator and the denominator of each ratio, then added the differences to one another, thus obtaining numbers, which they called 'dissimilarities' (*ta anomoia*): the lesser the dissimilarity, the more consonant the interval, e.g. 1 for the octave (2/1 → 1+0=1), 3 for the fifth (3/2 → 2+1=3), and 5 for the fourth (4/3 → 3+2=5). Such a calculation, which reportedly dates back to early Pythagoreanism, perhaps to Philolaus,[25] appears quite arbitrary and has no relation to any experimental procedure.[26]

It is issues of this sort that another disciple of Aristotle and a contemporary of Aristoxenus, Theophrastus of Eresus, may have intended to expose in his treatise *On Music*. We are in no position to reconstruct the whole work; however, in a portion preserved by Porphyry,[27] which deals with the nature of music, he claims that if notes were nothing but quantity, everything involving quantity should be a note, which is absurd. Music must have some trait specific to it, which makes it what it is and nothing else. This peculiarity (*idiotēs*) of pitch is therefore a quality (*poiotēs*) rather than a quantity (*posotēs*); it cannot be identified with either numbers, speeds, measures whatsoever, or even 'distances'. Although Theophrastus' extant discourse dwells much more on the negative part than the positive, one gathers that the specificity of music lies in the way in which notes reach the ear. The movement of higher notes is sharper and tends to catch the listener's attention immediately, while lower notes fill the space around, as it were, more equally. Accordingly, pleasantness arises from the blending of these qualities and not from any relation between numbers.[28] The movement productive of melody (*kinēma melōidētikon*) originates when the soul discharges itself from evil emotions – an idea evidently akin to the Aristotelian conception of *katharsis*. It is unclear how exactly Theophrastus thought that the soul managed to convey its inner activity into the outward movement proper to music, i.e. pitch variation; answering such a question would have been tantamount to comprehending how the soul 'knows' where notes 'are'. About four centuries later, Claudius Ptolemy would portray the soul as capable of pinpointing on the windpipe, as though on a natural *aulos* or a hidden monochord (see below), the right spots from which to utter this or that particular note; this was possible, in his view, because the soul could calculate and *measure* the different distances of these spots from the end of the windpipe – i.e. the air external to the body.[29] Ptolemy's explanation obviously presupposes a quantitative approach; as far as Theophrastus is concerned, we have no idea if or how he had tried to solve the problem, but we can be fairly sure that his solution did not involve any measurement.

THE QUARREL OVER INTERVALS: REASON VS. PERCEPTION

Theophrastus' position remained an isolated one (except perhaps for that of Panaetius the Younger, see below); we would not even know about it were it not for Porphyry's quotation. Aristoxenus, on the other hand, had plenty of followers: later sources often mention *hoi Aristoxeneioi*. As we have seen, being antagonistic to Pythagoreanism was not his main purpose, for his goals were of a different nature.[30] Yet, several sources from later centuries represent the debate on music in the Hellenistic period as the battlefield between Pythagoreans and Aristoxenians. Ptolemaïs from Cyrene (third/first century BCE?), in her handbook entitled *The Pythagorean Elements of Music*, draws a distinction whereby the Pythagoreans deemed reason capable of understanding harmonics without any support from perception, except for some 'initial sparks' (*zōpyra*: the image might refer to the evidence of fundamental concords, see above); while, in cases of disagreement, they sided with reason and blamed the inadequacy of perception – a description that perfectly matches the Pythagoreans' treatment of the eleventh (see above). On the contrary, 'some of the musicians who follow Aristoxenus', although their theory relied on some kind of reasoning, proceeded from an 'instrumental attitude' (*organikē hexis*) and chose to be guided mainly by perception and to refer to reason only when necessary.[31] A very similar view is shared by a first-century CE theorist called Didymus in the treatise *On the Difference between the Aristoxenians and the Pythagoreans*.[32]

The third-century BCE pseudo-Euclidean treatise *Division of the Canon* (*Sectio canonis* in Latin), which recapitulated the bulk of Pythagorean harmonics into a series of theorems,[33] may have contributed to establishing this dichotomy. The word *kanōn* indicates the monochord, an instrument basically consisting of a single string stretched over a ruler running parallel to it and a movable bridge (*hypagōgeus*) for modifying its effective vibrating length. Later Pythagorean sources attribute its usage and possible invention to Pythagoras; however, there is no mention of it before the fourth century BCE and the whole development of Pythagorean harmonic until the *Sectio* can be accounted for without postulating that it was used.[34] Even in the *Division* itself, its role is less *heuristic* than *demonstrative*, for it was meant not to add new theorems, which could not have been discovered otherwise, to the corpus of existing knowledge, but to simply allow the researcher to present the results he had achieved through arithmetical procedures to the eyes and ears of his audience, in order to *show that* they were true, not to *validate them* experimentally. Quite paradoxically, the monochord could have perfectly served the heuristic purposes of the *harmonikoi* (see above), insofar as the extremely tiny intervals they sought could have been obtained on a single string by sliding the movable bridge infinitesimally; indeed, moving the bridge after plucking the string, while it was still vibrating, could have enabled them to pinpoint the very moment, if any, in which one note became another. The fact that, as far as we know, the *harmonikoi* never used this instrument can be accounted for, I believe, by suggesting that they were practical musicians by trade, while the monochord was essentially a 'scientific' tool.[35]

The author of the *Sectio* had made it clear, *inter alia*, that six tones of 9/8 in a row did not equal an octave,[36] and that it was impossible to halve a *pyknon*,[37] thus challenging the very foundations of the *harmonikoi*'s and Aristoxenus' theory. For the first time, the irreconcilability between the multiplicative and the additive approaches, which already existed in principle (see above), had been made explicit and organised into a form that was clearly meant to give the status of an axiomatic science to the sole 'canonic' harmonics. After the appearance of the *Sectio*, music theorists started polarising around either assumption. A debate arose as to whether or not the word *diastēma* should be used as a perfect synonym of *logos* – a matter that had not worried either Philolaus or Plato.[38] A full account of this quarrel would exceed the purposes of this outline: suffice it to recall Eratosthenes, who, on the one hand. was adamant in keeping the two notions separate,[39] while, on the other hand, if we are to believe Ptolemy's disappointingly dry testimony, produced divisions of his own in order to render Aristoxenus' tetrachords in 'rational' terms.[40]

However, irreconcilability in theory is one thing, incommunicability in practice is another. One should not smell Aristoxenian orthodoxy every time the word 'semitone' pops up in musical contexts. After all, those practical musicians and music teachers may have found it handier to speak of semitones and quarter tones even if they knew that such intervals were mathematically impossible, just in the same way as nowadays evcryone speaks of 'sunrise' even knowing that, in principle, the sun does not 'rise'. We cannot tell if there were such things as 'Aristoxenian handbooks' for singers and instrumentalists, for no work of this sort has survived; however, as suggested by some hints found in more theoretical writings, the basics of Aristoxenian theory lent themselves to being spoon-fed to music students, through vivid images from everyday life, much more easily than any inquiry into ratios. Thus, the unequal-toned sounds (*psophoi anisotonoi synecheîs*), whose transitions to different pitches were unclear to the ear, were compared to the colours of the rainbow;[41] the intervallic movement of the voice (see above) was illustrated with the example of a log – i.e. the continuous voice – broken by the wind into pieces – i.e. the different notes;[42] finally, the internal intervals of a tetrachord were represented spatially, for instance as the distances between the columns of a temple or a porch,[43] and their different sizes were exemplified with the larger or narrower steps one could take within a given space, e.g. a room.[44]

At some point the need for a solution of this dichotomy must have dawned on theorists too. Panaetius the Younger, a mathematician whose chronology is uncertain but whose thought, insofar as it acknowledges the importance of the monochord, seems to presuppose the *Sectio*,[45] provides us with an original point of view. What we hear, he claims in a treatise entitled *On Ratios and Intervals in Geometry and Music*, is neither quantities nor strings' lengths; therefore, saying that a note is twice as long or big as another would be pointless (in this particular respect he seems to draw on Theophrastus, see above). The usefulness of the monochord lies, therefore, not in its revealing anything about the nature of intervals, but in its helping our sense perception, which is naturally weak, to connect what we hear to some visible relationship between the strings' lengths, for sight is more accurate than hearing. On the other hand, speaking of 'semitones' would be, in principle, nonsensical too, for a semitone is perceived per se and not *qua* 'a half of a tone', just in the same way as a mule (*hēmionos*, from *hēmi-*, 'half' and *onos*, 'ass') is perceived *qua* an animal of its own and not as 'a half of an ass', and a 'semi-vowel' is not obtained by 'halving' a vowel. The only way to make sense of both the multiplicative and the additive vocabularies of musical intervals is, therefore, to be aware that they are metaphorical by nature: they are used, as Panaetius puts it, 'abusively' (*katachrēstikôs*).[46]

A NEW BALANCE

Panaetius' notion of the inadequacy of sense perception may have paved the way for Claudius Ptolemy (first–second century CE), who carried out the most important effort known to us to theorise a new balance between reason and perception. Because of the weakness of senses, Ptolemy claims in the opening chapters of his *Harmonics*, we can perceive only by approximation, whereas precision (*to akribes*) belongs to reason. Two important corollaries follow as far as music is concerned: (1) hearing is never wrong: it can be, at worst, unrefined, especially when it comes to small intervals; (2) the outcomes of reason cannot contradict what is heard (in accordance with the principle of *sōizein ta phainomena*, 'saving the phenomena'); if they do, this means that their assumptions are faulty.[47] Perception is thus given the task of *verifying* the hypotheses of reason. This explains Ptolemy's unprecedented heed to the making and accuracy of acoustical instruments. He takes the trouble to demonstrate geometrically why the lengths marked on the monochord's ruler are exactly the same as the corresponding ones on the string;[48] indeed, the monochord itself, inasmuch as it allows listeners to focus on a single note at a time, is inadequate to his agenda. In order to show that six tones do not equal an octave (see above), Ptolemy, unlike the author of the *Sectio*, uses an eight-stringed *kanōn*,[49] so that the listener can compare the pitch of the sixth tone with that of the octave without having to move the bridge. He goes so far as to devise a special four-stringed *kanōn* – called *helikōn* – to make all the fundamental concords audible and to use a fifteen-stringed one to demonstrate the structure of a whole two-octave system.[50] (See Figure 12.1.)

However, despite his repeatedly claimed independence from the alleged excesses of both the Pythagoreans and the Aristoxenians, Ptolemy appears closer to the former. When he mocks the Pythagoreans for rejecting the eleventh (see above), he is not content with simply appealing to the Aristoxenian argument that adding an octave to an interval does not relevantly affect the listener's perception of the interval itself; instead, he cannot help adding a sort of arithmetical

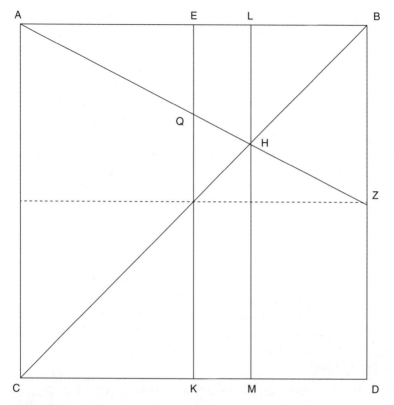

Figure 12.1   The *helikōn* (Ptol. *Harm.* 46.2–47.17 Düring).

AZ and CB are bridges; AC, KE and ML are equally pitched strings. Assuming that they are tuned on *A*, the notes are as follows: AC=*A*; BZ=ZD=*A*¹; EQ=*A*²; KQ=E; LH=*D*¹; MH=*D*.

proof, comparing the addition of an octave to an interval to the addition of the number 10 to another number, on the grounds that in neither case is the nature of the interval or the number altered (2+10=12 retains the nature of number 2, 5+10=15 of number 5, and so on).[51] Even in confuting the doctrine of the 'dissimilarities' (see above), he supports the perceptual argument with a mathematical one: such calculation is pointless, he says, because it gives different results for the same ratio, depending on the terms in which the ratio itself is expressed (if one, for instance, expresses the ratio of the octave in its simplest form, i.e. 2/1, the dissimilarities will equal 1; but if the same ratio is in the form 6/3, the dissimilarities will be 7).[52]

Likewise, his tetrachordal divisions reveal his zeal for mathematical beauty (*to eulogon*, as he calls it). We have seen that, at least since Archytas, dividing a tetrachord had meant finding three ratios, *mostly* superparticulars, the product of which equalled the ratio of a fourth (4/3). Ptolemy makes a point of using *only* superparticulars and, in order to do so, embarks on a mathematical *tour de force* the core idea of which is to divide the fourth into two superparticulars, thus obtaining two intervals that are near-equal to each other, and then to divide again either of these superparticulars into two other superparticulars, thus obtaining a genre with *pyknon* (see above), if the second division affected the lesser ratio, and a genre without *pyknon* if it affected the greater:[53]

Genera with *pyknon*	enharmonic	5/4 x 24/23 x 46/45	= 4/3
	soft chromatic	6/5 x 15/14 x 28/27	= 4/3
	tense chromatic	7/6 x 12/11 x 22/21	= 4/3
Genera without *pyknon*	soft diatonic	8/7 x 10/9 x 21/20	= 4/3
	tense diatonic	10/9 x 9/8 x 16/15	= 4/3
	ditonic diatonic	9/8 x 9/8 x 256/243	= 4/3
	even diatonic	10/9 X 11/10 x 12/11	= 4/3

These series of ratios are the products of pure calculation; yet, in Ptolemy's view, perception will necessarily approve them because they do not contradict perceptual data but refine them, in the same way as one acknowledges a compass-drawn circle as more precise than a freehand-drawn one when looking at the two synoptically.[54]

REASON KNOWS BEST: NEOPLATONISM AND EARLY CHRISTIANITY

With the advent of Neoplatonism, the assessment of music gains particular relevance within the broader discussion of how sense organs communicate with the soul. According to Porphyry of Tyre (second–third century CE), perceptual data are 'purified' from matter (*hylē*) and reduced to pure forms (*eidē*), which are finally presented to the soul in order to be comprehended by the intellect (*noûs*). On the other hand, the soul is able to scrutinise these forms because it already contains them independently of perception. Reason, Porphyry says, is like a king who, although sitting in his palace, knows what his scout – i.e.

perception – is going to report to him *before* and *better* than the scout himself.[55] Porphyry's balance is thus shifted in favour of reason.

The musical writings of the later centuries do not bring any substantial novelty. Music was on its way to being included in the quadrivium along with arithmetic, geometry, and astronomy, and its beauty was valued insofar as it reflected cosmic harmony. Not even Christian intellectuals were immune to the fascination of this idea. I should like to close this chapter by recalling a wonderful piece of prose from Clement of Alexandria's (second–third century CE) *Exhortation to the Heathen*. The *logos* of God is pictured like a 'New Song' (*âisma kainon*) that creates a new world by *tuning* it into a new musical scale. The vocabulary shows that Clement has in mind a real tuning process: the Song 'softens (*emalaxen*) the wrath of fire with air, as if mixing Dorian with Lydian', thus harmonising 'the extreme notes of the universe melodiously'; as a result, harmony 'stretches from the middle (notes) to the boundaries and from the extremities to the middle again' and permeates 'the whole of this universe'.[56] Clement presented the New Song as the one that would obliterate Orpheus and all the 'garbage' of the pagan musical past. Had he had the chance, though, to actually listen to this purportedly 'new' attunement of his, he would have probably found it disturbingly similar to the *systēmata* of Aristoxenus, Ptolemy, and the league of other pagan *musikoi*.

NOTES

1 Arist. [*Problems*] 19.27.
2 On this usage of σύστημα, see Raffa 2014.
3 Philolaus. fr. 6A Huffman 1993 *ap*. Nicom. *Ench*. 9; Stob. *Ecl*. 1.21.7d; see also Porph. *In Ptol. Harm*. 119.19–120.3 Raffa = 96.29–97.8 Düring.
4 Pl. *Ti*. 35a.
5 Philolaus, fr. 6B Huffman 1993 *ap*. Boethius, *De mus*. 3.8, p. 278.11 Friedlein. The ratio of the *comma* should be 9/8: $(256/243)^2 = 9/8 \times 59,049/65,536 = 531,441/524,288$, a ratio whose square root cannot be extracted. The same is true of 256/243, the ratio of the *diesis*.
6 For an ancient attempt to explain the name *dia pasôn*, see Arist. [*Problems*] 19.32.
7 The different types (genera) of tetrachords differ from one another according to the position of the two internal notes, for the extremes always encompass a fourth. Generally speaking, in the diatonic genera the second note from the top is closer to the first, which leaves more 'space' for the two remaining intervals of the tetrachord. In the chromatic genera the second note is lower, and therefore the second and third interval of the tetrachord are more 'compressed', as it were; even more so in the enharmonic genera.
8 On Archytas' chronology, see Huffman 2005, 5–6.

9　Archyt. test. A16 Huffman 2005. See Barker 2007, 292–302; Hagel 2010, 171–82. Whether his decision is to be connected to his alleged discovery of the impossibility of dividing an epimoric into equal parts (test. A19 Huffman), we cannot tell for sure.

10　The ratio of the octave (2/1) is epimoric and multiple at the same time.

11　As far-fetched as this argument may sound today, some ancient thinkers did take this sort of coincidence very seriously; see, e.g. Euc. [Sectio canonis] 149.14–17 Jan.

12　Ptolemy takes the presence of non-epimoric ratios as inconsistent with Archytas' declared goal 'to preserve what follows the principles of reason [logos] not only in the concords but also in the divisions of the tetrachords, believing that a commensurable relation between the differences is a characteristic of the nature of melodic intervals' (Ptol. Harm. 30.10–13 Düring, trans. A. Barker). One cannot be sure, however, whether or not Ptolemy's words reflect Archytas' intentions faithfully in the first place. Even if they do, one could charge Archytas with incoherence only if the expression 'a commensurable relation between the differences (to summetron tôn hyperochôn)' referred to superparticularity, which is far from sure. A convincing discussion of Archytas' divisions is in Hagel 2010, 171–82.

13　Pl. Resp. 531b8–c4. See Barker 1978.

14　Pl. Resp. 530b–531d.

15　See Meriani 2003, 109–13.

16　Aristox. Harm. 27–11.

17　Pl. Resp. 531A: 'some affirm that they can hear a note between and that this is the least interval and the unit of measurement, while others insist that the strings now render identical sounds' (trans. P. Shorey, adapted).

18　Aristox. Harm. 7.32 (the verb is katapyknoō, 'to make denser').

19　The important epistemological differences between Euclid's Elements and Aristoxenus' axiomatisation of harmonics cannot be expounded here. See the masterly discussion of Barker 2007, 203–4.

20　Such is the fascinating thesis of Barker 2007, 215–28.

21　Aristox. Harm. 32.26.

22　See Barker 2007, 208–13.

23　In ancient arithmetic theory of ratios, 8/3 belongs in fact to the category of 'mutiple superpartients' (pollaplasiepimereîs) for its greater term contains the lesser twice plus two parts of the lesser itself. In particular, since 8 = (3 x 2) + (3 x 2/3), the ratio is to be defined as 'double-sesquithird' (diplasiepiditritos), cf., e.g. Nicomachus, Introductio arithmetica 1.23.

24　Ptol. Harm. 6.3–25 Düring. See also Plut. De E apud Delphos 389d–e; Boethius, De mus. 2, p. 259.10–13 Friedlein. More detail in Barbera 1984. The eleventh is silently omitted also by the author of the Division of the Canon (see below): Barker 2007, 387.

25　Ptol. Harm. 14.1–10 Düring; Porph. In Ptol. Harm. 135.15–136.26 Raffa = 107.15–108.21 Düring (= Archyt. test. A17 Huffman). Huffman 2005, 435–6 suggests that Archytas is drawing on Philolaus here.

26　Barker 1989, 35, n. 29 proposes an interesting explanation for this procedure involving pre-Aristotelian acoustic theory; however, expounding the topic would go far beyond the aims of this chapter.

27　Thphr. fr. 716 Fortenbaugh ap. Porph. In Ptol. Harm. 75.4–79.29 Raffa = 61.16–65.15 Düring.

28 This is but a crude overview of Theophrastus' extant doctrine on music. For fuller discussions, see Barker 1985; Sicking 1998; Fatuzzo 2009.

29 Ptol. *Harm.* 9.6–15 Düring.

30 Aristox. *Harm.* 32.18–29.

31 Ptolemaïs in Porph. *In Ptol. Harm.* 28.8–21 Raffa = 23.24–24.5 Düring. Ptolemaïs' fragments are edited by Thesleff 1965, 242–3.

32 Porph. *In Ptol. Harm.* 31.16–32.7 Raffa = 26.6–25 Düring.

33 There is no consensus on the authorship, date, and unity of the work. I shall assume here, with Andrew Barker, that at least its bulk dates from the beginning of the third century CE. For further detail, see Barker 2007, 364–410; thorough bibliographical references in Creese 2010, 133 n. 3.

34 See the groundbreaking work of Creese 2010, which has reshaped our understanding of the relevance of the monochord to ancient harmonics.

35 There are in fact scant pieces of evidence for the monochord being used as a musical instrument (see, e.g. Ptol. *Harm.* 66.6–67.20 on the disadvantages of playing melodies on the monochord; 67.21–68.14 Düring on a new technique introduced by Didymus the Musician).

36 Euc. [*Sectio canonis*] prop. 14. Six tones = $(9/8)^6$ = 531,441/262,144, which is a shade bigger than the 2/1 ratio of the octave. See also Ptol. *Harm.* 25.1–26.14 Düring.

37 Euc. [*Sectio canonis*] prop. 18.

38 For a partial attempt to reconstruct this debate, see Raffa 2013, where I argue that the issue concerned particularly the commentators of Plato's *Timaeus*.

39 Porph. *In Ptol. Harm.* 113.1–8 Raffa = 91.4–10 Düring.

40 Ptol. *Harm.* 70.7–74.3 Düring. A fascinating hypothesis on Eratosthenes' method is in Creese 2010, 196–206.

41 Ptol. *Harm.* 10.6–8 Düring; Porph. *In Ptol. Harm.* 104.16–21 Raffa = 84.26–9 Düring.

42 Porph. *In Ptol. Harm.* 107.4–9 Raffa = 86.19–24 Düring.

43 Ibid., 163.8–10 Raffa = 125.20-22 Düring.

44 Ibid., 117.19–24 Raffa = 95.13–17 Düring.

45 The epithet may hint at this Panaetius being younger than the more famous philosopher of Rhodes (second century BCE).

46 Panaetius Iunior *ap.* Porph. *In Ptol. Harm.* 80.7–82.3 Raffa = 65.21–67.9 Düring.

47 Ptol. *Harm.* 3.1–6.13 Düring. See Barker 2004, 14–32.

48 Ptol. *Harm.* 17.27–19.15 Düring.

49 Ibid., 26.3–27.13 Düring.

50 Ibid., 83.1–85.34 Düring. On the *helikōn*, see Barker 2009.

51 Ptol. *Harm.* 13.6–7 Düring.

52 Ibid., 14.2–15.2 Düring.

53 Ptol. *Harm.* 33.1–37.20 Düring. For further detail, see my commentary in Raffa 2002, 352–61.

54 See Ptol. *Harm.* 3.20–4.7 Düring.

55 Porph. *In Ptol. Harm.* 13.16–16.4 Raffa = 13.25–15.28 Düring.

56 Clem. Al. *Protr.* 1.5.1–2. I am going to discuss this passage in more detail in a forthcoming publication. Here, the translation 'garbage' echoes the language of the early Church Fathers.

13 Ancient Greek Historiography of Science

Leonid Zhmud

UNCERTAIN ORIGINS

There is some uncertainty among historians of science as to when the history of science first appeared. Unlike the old historical debate over the origin of mathematics or astronomy, the origin of the history of science has never been widely discussed or properly considered, and the interested reader will find a variety of starting points which reflect the professional preoccupations of historians. One is in the twentieth century with George Sarton, another in the nineteenth century with William Whewell, and yet another in the eighteenth century with Joseph Priestley. Thus, Helge Kragh regards Priestley's *The History and the Present State of Electricity* (1767) as the best example of the history of science in the age of the Enlightenment, which 'saw history as an instrument for progress in the battle against the old feudal order. Only the recent development was worthy of interest while the past was generally regarded as irrational and inferior.'[1] Following this path in his immensely popular constructivist history of science, Jan Golinski refers to Priestley as the pioneer of the history of science:

> When it began, during the eighteenth-century Enlightenment,
> it was practised by scientists (or 'natural philosophers') with an
> interest in validating and defending their enterprise. They wrote
> histories in which the discoveries of their own day were presented
> as the culmination of a long process of advancing knowledge and
> civilization.[2]

In fact, Priestley's overview of the experiments conducted by his seventeenth- and eighteenth-century predecessors did not pretend to be a history of science. If it did it would have been exceptional, for most histories of science at that time dealt not with its recent development but with its ancient past. Montucla's classic history of mathematics was mostly devoted to the pre-modern period, considering Thoth the Egyptian to be the inventor of mathematics.[3] An astronomical pendant to

Montucla's history, Bailly's great work[4] started from Atlas and Zoroaster as the first astronomers and ended with early Hellenistic astronomy. Obviously, both works borrowed their framework from the early modern historiography of science, which is, regrettably, poorly known outside the specialists' milieu.[5] Interestingly, even contemporaries sometimes appeared not to be aware of its existence. The French mathematician Pierre Rémond de Montmort wrote in 1713 to Nicolas Bernoulli:

> It would be desirable if someone wanted to take the trouble to instruct us how and in what order the discoveries in mathematics have followed themselves, one after another, and to whom should we be obliged for them ... What a pleasure it would be to see the union, the connection between methods, the linkage between the different theories, beginning from the earliest time up to our own, where this science has been brought to such a high degree of perfection.[6]

If Rémond de Montmort had gone to a good library, he would have found that his wish had been granted many times over. Bulky Latin volumes by learned humanists, polymaths, and scientists, general histories of the progress of knowledge and histories of the individual disciplines, dissertations on the specific problems, and the like regularly appeared during the seventeenth century and earlier.[7] So when, in 1605, Francis Bacon put forward an analogous proposal for a history of mathematics, 'it was already out-of-date: discussions of the history of mathematics had been rife on the continent and in England throughout the previous century'.[8]

In the seventeenth century, when Archimedes and Hippocrates were topical as never before, most writings in the history of science were directly focused on antiquity, with much less attention paid to the immediate past. The closer we approach the Renaissance the clearer it becomes that the historiography of science appeared, or rather was revived, as the history of Greek science. Indeed, to return to ancient science after so many centuries; to edit and translate Euclid, Apollonius, Archimedes, Ptolemy, and Pappus; to understand 'who was who' in ancient science – all this urgently demanded at least a general historical picture of Greek mathematics and astronomy which presented its achievements chronologically. The question put by Rémond de Montmort was even more topical for Renaissance scientists and humanists, yet even by this time it already had a very long history. A closer look at historiographical exercises of that time reveals their marked continuity with the ancient tradition, on both the formal and the thematic level.

The distinguished mathematician and astronomer Christoph Clavius opened his Latin edition of Euclid's *Elements* (1574) with a *Prolegomena* based on ancient authors. A section entitled *Inventores mathematicarum disciplinarum* presented a condensed overview of the history of the quadrivium.[9] Each mathematical science had developed very gradually, rather than achieving perfection at the outset. Arithmetic was invented by the Phoenicians, developed further by Pythagoras, and amplified by the Arabs; music came from Hermes, Thamyras, Linus, and others; geometry originated in Egypt and Thales transferred it to Greece (see below, p. 280). Clavius' long list of Greek geometers is partly taken from Proclus' commentary to the first book of the *Elements* (see below, p. 277), and partly compiled by himself. For astronomy, some authorities start with Atlas, others with the Chaldeans, yet others with the Egyptians or Babylonians. What is reflected in Clavius' short exposé – and in hundreds of similar works before and after him – is ancient discussions on the origin of sciences and arts and the quest for the 'first discoverers' (*prōtoi heuretai*). This trend, which was already present in classical Greek thought, gave rise to two different but related genres: heurematography, which treated most different elements of culture as discoveries (*heurēmata*), and the history of science.

IN SEARCH OF THE FIRST DISCOVERERS

Originally the quest for *prōtoi heuretai* as a sort of intermediary link between the past and the present had little to do with history. It was rather a rationalisation of the mythical past, the more so because the *heuretai* themselves were often legendary and mythical figures. Still, from the seventh century BCE onwards, interest in first discoverers in the absolute sense, meaning those who invented metallurgy, agriculture, or writing, was stimulated by attention to innovations in poetry, music, technology, etc. and to the question of priority in their creation. As a result, almost every element of culture came with time to be regarded as someone's discovery.

The *prōtoi heuretai* are first mentioned in a fragment of *Phoronis*, an epic poem of the early sixth century BCE. It identifies the Idaean Dactyls, the mythical dwarfish blacksmiths, as the Phrygian sorcerers who first invented 'the art of the wise Hephaestus' (*Scholia in Apollonium Rhodium* 102.3–9). Their blacksmithery is thereby transferred from the divine sphere into the human one, while its discovery is attributed to the neighbours of the Greeks. Thus, we find here the germs of two important tendencies that were to be developed later: first, the gradual and incomplete replacement of gods by semi-divine/heroic figures and subsequently by humans, and second, the Greeks' tendency to assign inventions, including their own, to Oriental neighbours. The process of replacement was not a linear one, because in Homer, Hesiod, and even before them, the Greek gods were represented not as the *prōtoi heuretai* but as the 'donors of goods' and as the patrons of crafts that they had taught to humans. It is only after the fame of the human inventors had spread throughout the Greek world, that Hermes turned into the inventor of the lyre and the art of making fire, Palamedes was credited with the invention of measures, weights, and the alphabet, and Prometheus was associated with the appearance of astronomy and arithmetic.[10]

Both of the above-mentioned tendencies were developed by Hecataeus and, later, by Herodotus, whose influence on later literature proved decisive. In Herodotus, Greek gods and heroes never figure as *prōtoi heuretai*, discoveries usually being attributed to 'barbarian' nations. Egyptians invented geometry and laid the foundations for calendar astronomy, whereas two important astronomical instruments, the gnomon and *polos*, as well as the division of the day into twelve hours, came from Babylon (2.4, 109). After Herodotus, the idea that geometry originated in Egypt and astronomy in Babylon (or in Egypt) became firmly established in ancient literature, passing into medieval and early modern historiography. On the whole, by the turn of the fifth century BCE, when heurematography created its own particular genre, a kind of cataloguing of discoveries under the standard title *On Discoveries (Peri heurēmatōn)*,[11] Greek thought had already acquired a persistent tendency to associate a considerable share of its own civilisation with the influence of neighbours, especially Oriental neighbours. The genre of heurematographic writings survived until the end of antiquity and later provided a model for Arabic and European writers.[12]

FROM ART (*TECHNĒ*) TO SCIENCE (*EPISTĒMĒ*)

Though the framework of heurematography allowed discussion of the origin of arts and sciences, it was utterly unsuitable for writing their real history. The emerging historiography of different arts continued the traditional quest for *prōtoi heuretai*, yet went far beyond a list of random discoveries. It arranged discoveries chronologically and conceived their sequence as a sign of progress – an idea first formulated by Xenophanes:

> The gods did not reveal to men all things in the beginning, but in the course of time, by searching, they find out better.[13]

When Glaucus of Rhegium (late fifth century BCE) in his *On the Ancient Poets and Musicians* undertook the first attempt to systematise the early history of poetry and music, he started from Musaeus (fr. 1 Lanata) and wrote mainly about who invented what, often resorting to chronology to resolve questions of priority. Unlike heurematography, Glaucus' history in addition to *prōtos heuretēs* was also aware of *deuteros* (fr. 2) – an important innovation that contains *in nuce* the motive of improving the first discoveries and finally bringing them to perfection.

A history of medicine constructed in the Hippocratic treatise *On Ancient Medicine* (late fifth century BCE) was presented as successive attempts to find the true method of medicine: very soon the whole of medicine would be found, as at present it was a τέχνη based on knowledge (*epistēmē*), which, in turn, was obtained by research and discovery (*zētēsis* and *heuresis*). These notions, known from Xenophanes' dictum, imparted to *technē* a certain dynamic quality, which caused it to be viewed, especially by the Sophists, as systematic 'research', 'discovery', or 'invention' of new things, knowledge, or skills. As the famous teacher of rhetoric Isocrates boasted, 'progress is made, not only in τέχναι, but in all other activities through those ... who have the courage constantly to change anything that is not as it should be',[14] which is to say people like himself. Such people were first discoverers not in the absolute but in the relative sense, having found something new in rhetoric, music, or astronomy.

Isocrates' coeval Archytas of Tarentum, a Pythagorean mathematician and philosopher, presents in *On Sciences* (*Peri tōn mathēmatōn*) his views on scientific method using the same notions *zētēsis* and *heuresis*: 'Discovering without research is difficult and (happens) seldom, by research it is easy and practicable, but without knowing (how) to research it is impossible to research' (47 B 3). Archytas' Pythagorean predecessors (οἱ περὶ τὰ μαθήματα) obviously possessed such a method, being praised by him for their discoveries and true insight in astronomy, geometry, arithmetic, and harmonics (B 1). The first two sciences of the quadrivium appeared in Ionia in the early sixth century BCE, and their names, geometry and astronomy, are attested in Herodotus, Philolaus, and Aristophanes.[15] The names of two Pythagorean sciences, arithmetic and harmonics, appear first (though not yet firmly established) in the fragments of Archytas himself (B 1–3). It is with Archytas that the word *mathēmata* acquires terminological significance and designates a particular group of kindred mathematical disciplines (B 1), as we know it, for example, from Plato's *Republic*. By the turn of the fifth century, four basic *mathēmata* were formed, received their names and their specialists – geometers, astronomers, arithmeticians (Pl. *Euthyd.* 290c1) – and were regarded as evolving with time.

The last notion, it should be noted, is far from self-evident even in those cultures which witnessed undeniable progress in mathematics and astronomy. When Berossus (third century BCE) decided to acquaint the Greeks with Babylonian history and culture, he affirmed that a primeval beast, Oannes, 'gave men the knowledge of letters and sciences and crafts of all types ... In general, it taught men everything that is connected with a civilised life. From that time nothing further has been discovered' (BNJ 680 F 1b). In Greece such a view had already been abandoned by the archaic period. The Greek term for progress, ἐπίδοσις, was probably first applied to *mathēmata* in the Platonic Academy. A fourth-century Academic, quoted by Philodemus, says:

> at this time *mathēmata* were also greatly advanced, with Plato being the architect of this development ... In this way, the general theory of proportions and research on definitions reached their peak, as Eudoxus and his students completely revised the old theory of Hippocrates of Chios. Especially great progress (*epidosis*) was made in geometry, as (at that time) the methods of analysis and of diorism were discovered.[16]

This condensed overview of the development of mathematics clearly belongs to a person knowledgeable about its past and present, but for the history of mathematics his general perspective is too Platocentric. Though Plato was not an 'architect of *mathēmata*', as some Academics wished to see him,[17] he was an admirer and advocate of exact sciences; he valued mathematics highly for its ability to provide irrefutable knowledge and improve the human soul. *Mathēmata*, earlier constituting a special group among *technai* (Archytas 47 B 4), in Plato came to be regarded as a paradigm of *epistēmē* that does not serve any end but knowledge itself (*Res.* 525c–d). The final step into the classification of sciences was taken by Aristotle, who while still in the Academy produced his division of *epistēmai* into three kinds: practical, for example ethics and politics; productive, or arts and crafts (τέχναι); and theoretical. Later, relying on Plato's tripartite division of being into Forms, mathematical, and corporeal objects, Aristotle subdivided theoretical sciences into mathematics, physics, and theology.[18] Thus, in Aristotle *mathēmata* began to constitute a special branch of theoretical sciences, which he regarded as the most exact. They continued to be regarded this way until the end of Antiquity, at least among the specialists. As Ptolemy stated at the beginning of the *Syntaxis*,

> The first two divisions of theoretical philosophy should be
> called guesswork rather than knowledge: theology because of its
> completely invisible and ungraspable nature, physics because of the
> unstable and unclear nature of the matter … only mathematics can
> provide sure and unshakable knowledge to its devotees, provided
> one approaches it rigorously. For its kind of proof proceeds by
> indisputable methods, namely arithmetic and geometry.[19]

HISTORY OF KNOWLEDGE IN THE LYCEUM

The historical development of mathematics, unlike its philosophical implications, was a comparatively minor concern for Plato and his students, except for Aristotle, whose range of interests was richer and more varied than that of his colleagues at the Academy. History in general, and the history of knowledge in particular, owes him much more than any other ancient philosopher, both conceptually and for the specific historiographical studies which he wrote or initiated. He was fully aware of the historical character of such human accomplishments as the state, art, philosophy, and the sciences, and he endeavoured to reveal the inner logic of their development. By analogy with the teleological conception of development in nature, he viewed society, culture, and its individual branches as evolving from a primitive state to a perfect one. For many things this state of perfection was thought to have already been achieved or almost achieved. Tragedy, for example, had already attained its perfection, society had found its best and final state in the *polis*, and philosophy, whose early ideas were as immature as childish speech, would soon be completed.[20] Peripatetic studies in the history of knowledge by Theophrastus, Eudemus, and Meno were cast in the concepts and categories of Aristotle's thought and relied on his conception of the progress of knowledge.

Furthermore, the obvious division of labour and close coordination between Theophrastus and Eudemus allows us to speak of the *historiographical project* of the Lyceum, which aimed to collect, systematise, and analyse in a preliminary way material which was related, in the first instance, to the theoretical sciences. The degree of Aristotle's involvement in the project is hard to determine for certain; at the very least, he must have prompted the Peripatetics to undertake research into the history of different theoretical sciences, if not distributed it among his students. What is incontrovertible is that individual parts of the project, which embraces Theophrastus' doxographical compendium *Opinions of the Physicists* (*Physikōn doxai* in sixteen or eighteen books), Eudemus' three histories of *mathēmata* (*History of Geometry* in four books, *History of Arithmetic* in two books, *History of Astronomy* in two books), and his history of theology,[21] correspond to the division of the theoretical sciences into mathematics, physics, and theology. The material of each science was, in turn, arranged in a way designed as far as possible to avoid duplication, for example between mathematical and physical astronomy, physics and theology, physics and medicine, and so on. Meno's *Medical Collection* (*Iatrikē synagōgē*), dealing with medical theories of the fifth and fourth centuries, was close to physical doxography in its methods of organising material.[22]

According to Aristotle, each theoretical science had its own experts: physicists, mathematicians, theologians. Theophrastus' doxography was devoted *exclusively* to the opinions of the physicists as a distinctive group, which included most of the Presocratic philosophers, several Sophists, and Plato as an author of the *Timaeus*. The subject matter of the *Physikōn doxai* corresponded to what Aristotle understood by an 'inquiry about nature' (*peri physeōs historia*) covering fundamental principles, notions, and categories of physics (matter, causes, space, time, void, etc.) as well as its separate branches (astronomy, meteorology, psychology, physiology, and embryology). The treatise was organised systematically; within the chapters devoted to specific problems, the main 'units' consisted of the theories of individual philosophers, which were collected into groups according to their similarity (if this was relevant) and were often, though not always, arranged in chronological order. The opening chapter, for example, started with Thales and ended with Plato, presenting philosophers in two series, ordered by chronology and school affiliation: Milesians – Anaxagoras – Archelaus and Xenophanes – Eleatics – Atomists – Diogenes of Apollonia – Metrodorus.[23]

The exclusive criteria of the *Physikōn doxai* meant that it ignored the opinions of those who were counted as theologians, mathematicians (mathematical astronomers), or doctors. Eudemus' theologians, which is to say the authors of early mythical cosmogonies and theogonies (Orpheus, Homer, Hesiod, Pherecydes),[24] constituted the same exclusive group not overlapping with the physicists. Therefore, no physicist figures in the *History of Theology*, and none of the theologians are mentioned in the *Opinions of the Physicists*. In contrast, Eudemus' histories of geometry, astronomy, and arithmetic dealt not with the opinions of mathematicians and astronomers as a specific group, but with mathematical and astronomical discoveries, which could also have been made by those whom the Peripatetics regarded as physicists – Thales, Anaximander, Anaxagoras, and others. Observing the borders between mathematical and physical astronomy which had been drawn by Aristotle, Eudemus and Theophrastus distributed astronomical material in the following way. Eudemus limited his *History of Astronomy* to the purely mathematical aspects of this science, while the astronomical division of the *Physikōn doxai* treated opinions belonging to both physical (for example, the nature of the sun and moon, etc.) and mathematical astronomy (the form of celestial bodies, their order, size, etc.), but *only* those that came from the physicists. Such typical *mathēmatikoi* as Hippocrates of Chios or Archytas do not figure in Theophrastus' work. Finally, Meno's *Medical Collection*, as the title implies, contained not opinions of the doctors as a professional group, but *medical theories* about the origins of diseases. For this reason, Meno could legitimately include in his work ideas on this subject coming from the physicists Hippo, Philolaus, and Plato, though all his other personages were doctors.

EUDEMUS' HISTORIES OF EXACT SCIENCES

The epistemological status of knowledge preserved in different theoretical sciences was very uneven. The *theologoi* reasoned not rationally but mythically (Arist. *Metaph.* 1000a18); the *physikoi* left behind both true and false opinions which, collected by Theophrastus, showed the difficult path to the truth finally revealed in Aristotle's physical teaching. It is only the contributions of the *mathēmatikoi* which represented that kind of knowledge which was considered to be true and unshakable, both by themselves and by most philosophers of the time. In this sense Eudemus' histories of the exact sciences were an epistemologically privileged part of the project. They were written most probably in the 320s BCE, when Eudemus, a friend of Theophrastus and a devoted student of Aristotle, whom he closely followed in his *Physics*, stayed at the Lyceum. After Aristotle's death he returned to Rhodes, where he continued to study and to teach.

Of the quadrivium of mathematical sciences, harmonics was the only one on the history of which no Peripatetic work was written. One reason for this may have been that Aristoxenus, the main expert on music in the Lyceum, though he was a student of the Pythagoreans, opposed their mathematical approach to harmonics. But since mathematical harmonics was closely connected to Pythagorean arithmetic, Eudemus could have treated problems related to it in the *History of Arithmetic*, as follows from the only fragment of this treatise, preserved by Porphyry:

> For Eudemus makes clear in the first book of the *History of Arithmetic* that they demonstrated the ratios of concordant intervals through the *pythmenes*, saying of the Pythagoreans the following word for word: '(They said) moreover that it turned out that the ratios of the three concords, of the fourth, the fifth and the octave, taken in the first numbers (*en prōtois*), belong to the number nine. For 2 and 3 and 4 are nine.'[25]

Eudemus' histories of geometry and astronomy aroused more interest among late antique authors and have come to us in nine and seven fragments, respectively. Only a few of the fragments are long verbatim quotations, for example fr. 140 on squaring the lunes by Hippocrates, or extensive excerpts, for example the so-called catalogue of geometers in which twenty mathematicians are mentioned (fr. 133). The named fragments are to be supplemented by quite extensive evidence, whose Eudemian authorship is long accepted or can be established with a considerable degree of certainty.[26]

Among the different ways of systematising the vast material which he collected, Eudemus has chosen the chronological method, using it very skilfully. The catalogue of geometers, compiled probably by Porphyry and transmitted by Proclus (fr. 133), reveals that the *History of Geometry* contained chronological indications concerning practically all the mathematicians mentioned in it.[27] Their accuracy differs according to the information which was available to Eudemus.

Sometimes it confines itself to a chronological sequence: Pythagoras comes after Mamercus, a brother of Stesichorus. From the fifth century on this information becomes more detailed: Neoclides and his student Leon were younger than Leodamas, Eudoxus 'was a little younger' than Leon, Athenaeus 'lived in the same time' as Eudoxus' students. In effect, what we have in this work are not just separate chronological references, but a series, or scale, connecting all geometers from Thales to Eudemus' own time. This seems to be Eudemus' unique achievement. Aristotle was also concerned with making cultural events datable: he compiled the list of Olympic victors, the victors in musical agones in Delphi, and in dramatic agones at the Dionysia and Lenaea.[28] Yet he could use previous lists (for example, that of Olympic victors by Hippias of Elis) and official records, whereas Eudemus had to rely mostly on his historical acumen. The idea that science is 'a collective enterprise of researchers in successive generations' is not only characteristic of the modern age,[29] but was fully shared by the first historian of Greek science.

Since Eudemus typically presented the contributions of mathematicians and astronomers as discoveries, the formula *prōtos heuretēs* occurs, in full or abridged, in practically every fragment of his histories. Here is, for example, a short and regrettably error-ridden excerpt from the first book of the *History of Astronomy* (fr. 145), structured very similarly to the catalogue of geometers and titled in the later sources 'Who discovered what in mathematics?':

> Eudemus relates in his *Astronomies* that Oenopides first discovered
> the obliquity of the zodiac and the duration of the Great Year;
> Thales the eclipse of the sun and the fact that the sun's period
> with respect to the solstices is not always the same; Anaximander
> that the earth is suspended in space and moves about the middle
> of the cosmos; Anaximenes that the moon receives its light from
> the sun and how it is eclipsed. And others discovered in addition
> to this that the fixed stars move round the immobile axis that
> passes through the poles, whereas the planets move round the axis
> perpendicular to the zodiac; and that the axis of the fixed stars
> and that of the planets are separated from another by the side of a
> (regular) pentadecagon, i.e., 24°.

In order to reinstate the original meaning of the text, distorted during transmission, we need to move Oenopides to the end of the list, where he chronologically belongs; relate to him the measurement of the obliquity of ecliptic, assigned here to some anonymous astronomers; change Thales' 'discovery' of the solar eclipse to its prediction; correct the entry on Anaximander's earth that did not move but rested in the middle of the cosmos, and finally, replace Anaximenes with Anaxagoras, who was the first to offer correct explanations for lunar and solar eclipses (cf. fr. 147). The remaining fragments of the *History of Astronomy* are related to Thales' prediction of the solar eclipse (fr. 143–4), Anaximander's account of the sizes and distances of the planets and the discovery of their order by the Pythagoreans (fr. 146), and Eudoxus' theory of homocentric spheres (fr. 148) and its modifications by his pupil Callippus (fr. 149), whom Aristotle and Eudemus must have known personally.

Now we can better see the perspective of Eudemus' work. From the earlier periods of astronomy, he selected the major discoveries which constituted an integral part of contemporary mathematical astronomy or appeared significant in its progress to the state of perfection. It is worth recalling that Aristotle perpetuated in the *Metaphysics* (1073b17-1074a37) the kinematic model of Eudoxus and Callippus, adding to it the retrograde spheres and prime mover. Obviously, this could have been done only to the system he conceived as the final word of astronomy. Eudemus also relied on the expert knowledge of scientists, in accordance with which he sorted out and assessed the historical evidence. He carefully distinguished, for example, between Anaximander's 'first account' of the sizes and distances of the planets, long outdated by the late fourth century, and the Pythagorean discovery of the order of the planets accepted by the contemporary specialists. Thus, his approach to the scientific past was basically the same as that of the modern history of science, which still remains the history of those methods and results, whose significance is acknowledged by the contemporary scientific community. As Nick Jardine aptly put it:

> Against the objection that such an approach commits anachronism of selection to the extent that it picks out scenes, agendas and doctrines ancestral to those of our sciences, the proper response is surely: so be it! The very existence of history of science as a discipline depends upon such selective anachronism, and there is nothing historically improper in attending to the causal processes that have given rise to our sciences.[30]

Admittedly, the teleological progressivism that Eudemus shared with Aristotle was an idealised construction. Yet in defence of Eudemus it should be said that he did not focus only on the scientific successes of the past and ignored all the failures, but recorded, for example, an unsuccessful attempt to square a circle (fr. 139–40). This famous geometric problem aroused much interest in Athens (Ar. *Av.* 1004–10); it attracted both mathematicians, such as the brilliant Hippocrates of Chios (*fl.* 440–430 BCE), who demonstrated the possibility of squaring several crescent-shaped figures (lunes), and philosophers and sophists – Anaxagoras, Antiphon, and Bryson. Aristotle not infrequently referred to the problem, considering all the attempts to solve it as being unsuccessful.[31] Eudemus includes in his histories mathematical examples mentioned by Aristotle; in the case of Antiphon he follows his teacher's judgement and specifies it: Antiphon tried to square the circle by successively doubling the number of sides of the inscribed regular polygon, so that they will eventually coincide with the circle. Thereby, he did not admit the basic principles (ἀρχαί) of geometry, in particular, that geometrical magnitudes are infinitely divisible.[32] Unlike Aristotle, however, who accused Hippocrates of having committed a logical mistake by squaring the circle with the help of lunes, Eudemus found no fault with him. He records in great detail all four quadratures of lunes by Hippocrates, testifies that the specialists found them correct, but nowhere asserts that the latter claimed to have squared the circle by squaring the lunes.[33] He seemed tacitly to correct Aristotle at this point, as Theophrastus often did.

In agreement with the historiographical pattern of his day, Eudemus assigned the invention of geometry to the Egyptians and that of arithmetic to the Phoenicians. Thales was the first to bring geometry to Greece and discovered many things in it himself, treating some of them more generally and some more empirically (fr. 133). Eudemus' view of Thales as the originator of both Greek geometry and astronomy (fr. 144: *prōtos astrologēsai*) must reflect a well-known tradition: in Aristophanes both sciences are related to Thales' name (*Nub.* 178–9; *Av.* 1003–4). Still earlier, Xenophanes (21 B 19), Heraclitus (22 B 38), and Herodotus (1.74) testified that he was engaged in astronomy, which brings us closer to Thales' own times. We may assume then that Eudemus' choice of Thales was not determined by Aristotle's decision to start natural philosophy from Thales, but relied on the earlier sources.

Conspicuously, Eudemus speaks of the first Greek geometer in great detail, referring to four propositions attributed to him. One of them Thales was the 'first to prove' (Eucl. 1 def. 17), another he was the 'first to learn and state' (1.5), and a third the 'first to discover' (1.15). Regarding the last theorem, about the equality of the triangles that have one side and two angles equal (1.26), Eudemus says that Thales simply 'knew', since he must have used it to determine the distances of ships from the shore (fr. 134). Though this detailed information evidently derives from an early mathematical text, many historians of science have denied and continue to deny either that Thales had studied geometry at all, or that he proved any theorem, or that his proofs might have been known to Eudemus. A case can no doubt be made regarding Greek geometry as starting with Hippocrates, from whom an extended fragment on squaring the lunes is preserved. But though some scholars believe that squaring the lunes can be seen as the starting point of Greek geometry,[34] it seems preferable to follow Eudemus who transmitted that very text, but named five geometers before Hippocrates: Thales, Mamercus, Pythagoras, Anaxagoras, and Oenopides of Chios (possibly a teacher of Hippocrates).

Let us recall that Mamercus, who comes between Thales and Pythagoras, was born in southern Italy, and did not emigrate to it, as the Samian Pythagoras did. It is thus reasonable to infer that Thales' geometry must have reached Italy in a written form, even if we do not have direct evidence for this. There is no reason why it could not have been written back in the sixth century BCE, when Pythagoras, according to Heraclitus, derived all his wisdom from certain *syngraphai* (22 B 129), which is to say writings in prose.[35] To these general considerations one can add an important textual argument. Eudemus says that Thales 'was the first to notice and assert that angles at the base of any isosceles are equal, though in a somewhat archaic fashion he called the "equal" angles "similar"' (*archaikōteron de tais isas homoias proseirēkenai*).[36] Now, Hippocrates had already called the equal angles ἴσας (fr. 140, p. 60.6 Wehrli), so that the text available to Eudemus, where theorems attributed to Thales were written down, must go back to the first part of the fifth century, if not earlier. This seriously increases the chances that at least some propositions *and* their proofs mentioned by him stem from Thales, though possibly not all.

Thus, Eudemus substantiates the attribution to Thales of his fourth theorem by asserting that the method Thales used to determine the distances of ships from the shore *presupposes* the use of this theorem (fr. 134). We might be dealing with a mere reconstruction, possibly a fallacious one, but no history of mathematics can dispense with reconstructions. The very way in which Eudemus explains his reasoning reveals his conscious approach to the sources. His sensitivity to problems of terminology shows up also in the case of Oenopides, who called the perpendicular in the archaic manner gnomon-wise, since the gnomon also stands at right angles to the horizon (Procl. *In primum Euclidis*, 283.7–8). Generally, Eudemus' tendency to distinguish carefully between 'archaic' and 'modern' usages reveals him as a reliable historian of science, who could shorten and simplify his source (as all historians do), but did not manipulate it intentionally. Specifically, his remark that clearly presupposes the existence of Oenopides' written text reiterates the point that Hippocrates was heir to an established tradition of mathematical writing and did not represent 'the first generation of Greek mathematical authors'.[37]

HISTORY OF KNOWLEDGE AFTER THE LYCEUM

The historiography of science emerged in Greece not when it became necessary for the scientists, as happened in the Renaissance, but when it became possible. Aristotle's encyclopedic horizon and keen interest in the origins of human knowledge, on the one hand, and Eudemus' scientific competence and historical skill, on the other, constituted a unique constellation. Subsequently, though, unlike the other historiographical genres emerging in the Lyceum, such as biography, doxography, and the history of culture, the history of science was not carried forward by others, and especially not in the professional community. If the history of exact sciences had been as attractive to mathematicians and astronomers as doxography was to philosophers, we would have known of other attempts to emulate or advance it. But we do not. Eudemus' histories of *mathēmata* were written by a philosopher for philosophers, and in order to continue it one probably needed not just a new Eudemus, but a new Aristotle. Much of what was done in the early Lyceum had to wait until the early modern period in order to be continued.

The philosophical schools of Hellenism did not fully share the cognitive ideals of the classical period: their attitude towards mathematics and astronomy was more or less indifferent, sceptical, and even hostile. Epicurus denied the validity of mathematics and mathematical astronomy, and attacked the school of Eudoxus at Cyzicus as 'enemies of Greece'.[38] Posidonius of Apamea and his students' studies in exact sciences turned out to be only a short episode in the history of Stoicism; later Stoics returned to their usual natural philosophy.[39] The Neopythagoreans, Peripatetics, Middle Platonists, and then Neoplatonists became more and more interested in *mathēmata*, though not in their history in the sense of independent research and discovery. The larger part of the evidence on the history of science survived in various introductions and commentaries, for example, in Dercyllides, Nicomachus, Adrastus, Theon of Smyrna, Porphyry, Iamblichus, Proclus, and Simplicius. Still more valuable from this point of view are the works of commentators and systematisers of mathematical sciences, such as Hero of Alexandria, Menelaus, Sosigenes, Sporus, Pappus, and Eutocius.[40] But even those late writers who used Eudemus' histories did not try to continue them and include later developments. Thus, the author of the catalogue of geometers, after having reached the last generation covered by Eudemus, briefly mentions Euclid, Archimedes, and Eratosthenes and then stops (Procl. *In primum Euclidis*, 68.6–7). What a contrast with the *History of Geometry* in four books!

Eratosthenes, the only Hellenistic scientist and philosopher who definitively knew the *History of Geometry*, employed its material in the fictitious plot of his dialogue *Platonicus*: Plato, the 'architect of *mathēmata*', sets the problem of doubling the cube to Archytas, his student Eudoxus, and Eudoxus' student Menaechmus.[41] Needless to say that Eudemus did not mention Plato in connection with this problem. Revealingly, Eratosthenes was the only person who applied the historical approach to a science outside the quadrivium, namely to geography, which was also partly mathematised in antiquity. At the very beginning of his *Geography* he gave a concise historical introduction: Anaximander was the first to draw the map of the earth, while Hecataeus was the first to write a prose work on geography and also drew a geographical map (Strabo 1.11.9). After them came Hellanicus of Lesbos, Damastes of Sygeum, Democritus, Eudoxus, and Dicaearchus. At some further point Eratosthenes set forth his predecessors' views on the form of oecumene, combining Eudemus' scheme of *prōtos heuretēs* with Theophrastus' method of exposition and criticism of the *doxai*:

> The ancients mapped the habitable world as circular, with Greece placed in the middle, and Delphi in the middle of it; for they said it held the navel of the world. It was Democritus, a man of great experience, who first realized that the world is elongated, with its length half as much again as its breadth; Dicaearchus the Peripatetic agreed with him. Eudoxus made the length double the breadth, but Eratosthenes more than double.[42]

Eratosthenes' overview was continued by Posidonius and preserved in a condensed form by Agathemerus (third century CE). None of them obviously reached the level of Eudemian histories, which remained the starting and the highest point of this genre in antiquity.

The fate of doxography was rather different.[43] While Theophrastus' monumental *Physikōn doxai* remained unsurpassed, in the middle of the first century BCE a school of Posidonius produced its revised and updated version in six books, the so-called *Vetusta placita*. Around 100 CE an otherwise unknown Aetius condensed it to five books and his epitome generated a rich offspring.[44] Since Posidonius' concept of *physikē* was much broader than that of Aristotle, doxography came to include also opinions of theologians, astronomers (sometimes astrologers), and doctors, both classical and Hellenistic. Thus, in Aetius we find the *doxai* of seven astronomers – Oenopides, Eudoxus, Aratus, Aristarchus, Eratosthenes, Hipparchus, and Seleucus – and of two astrologers – Berosus and Epigenes of Byzantium. Fairly often *mathēmatikoi* figure as a separate category of specialists, to whom the astronomical *doxai* are ascribed, for example on the motion of the planets from the west to the east (2.16.2–3), on the distance between the earth and the moon (2.31.2), and so on. All of the astronomers and doctors whose names appear in the doxographical sources dependent on the *Vetusta placita* lived before 100 BCE. This means that the anonymous compiler of this compendium was the last to care about updating the earlier doxographical tradition, and his followers merely abridged it.

It is symptomatic of the decline of serious interest in the history of science that the popular versions of the origin of *mathēmata* in the Orient and their transmission to Greece came to the foreground. The question of what happened next has almost never been raised in this context. Already in the classical period it was widely agreed that geometry originated in Egypt and was brought to Greece by either Thales or Pythagoras. More complicated is the origin of astronomy, which, according to the three main versions, derived from Egypt (with Thoth-Hermes as *prōtos heuretēs*),[45] Babylon and Phoenicia,[46] or Greece. The last version added to the classical inventors of astronomy, Palamedes and Prometheus, two Hellenistic ones, Atlas and Endymion.[47] In addition to the traditional Greek *prōtoi heuretai* of arithmetic and counting, Palamedes and Prometheus, we hear also about the Egyptians and Phoenicians.[48] Porphyry sets forth the version which had the widest currency: the Greeks (which is to say Pythagoras) borrowed geometry from Egypt, astronomy from Babylon, and arithmetic from Phoenicia (*Plot.* 6).

The new Oriental version of *inventio artium* began to emerge when the Hellenised Jews advanced their own view of the origin of sciences. Alexander Polyhistor (first century BCE) says, referring to the Jewish historians, that Chaldaean astronomy was invented by Abraham while he stayed in Babylonia; later he transferred it to the Phoenicians and Egyptians.[49] Josephus Flavius tells a slightly different story: astronomy and arithmetic were invented by the Chaldaeans, and Abraham taught these sciences to the Egyptians, who in turn passed them over to the Greeks (*AJ* 1.167–8). It is only natural that this view was vigorously promoted by the early Christian Greek writers. Clement of Alexandria, Eusebius, and Theodoret supported it with a wealth of material borrowed from the catalogues of discoveries: both philosophy and nearly all the arts and sciences were invented by the 'barbarians', the most ancient of whom were the Jews.[50] Widely accepted in Byzantium, this 'biblical' version determines the general view of the historical path of science in early modern historiography: from the Jews through the Egyptians and the Babylonians to the Greeks, and from the Greeks, either directly or through the intermediary of the Arabs, to modern times. This is the view that we find in Christoph Clavius' *Inventores mathematicarum disciplinarum* (see above, p. 270) and in most other Renaissance historians of science. But when these *eruditi* passed from the mythical prehistory to the real history of Greek mathematics, their most reliable source remained the catalogue of geometers deriving, via Proclus and Porphyry, from the first historian of Greek science Eudemus of Rhodes.

NOTES

1 Kragh 1987, 3, 5.
2 Golinski 1998, 2.
3 Montucla 1758. It was only his successor, J. Laland, who brought his history to the modern period.
4 Bailly 1775.
5 For a selected bibliography, see Zhmud 2006. See also Dauben and Scriba 2002, and a thematic section 'Histories of Science in Early Modern Europe' in *Journal of the History of Ideas* 67 (2006): 33–104.
6 Pfeiffer 2002, 6.
7 See, e.g. Biancani 1615; Deusing 1640; Voss 1650; Dechales 1674; Baldi 1707.
8 Popper 2006, 88–9.
9 Clavius 1611, 4–5.
10 Stesich. fr. 213 Page; *Hymn. Hom. Merc.* 24–5, 108–9; Aesch. *PV* 457–8.
11 See Kaldellis 2007; Paradiso 2008. The Academic Heraclides Ponticus wrote *On Discoveries* (fr. 152 Wehrli); Aristotle also was interested in the subject (fr. 924

Gigon), and his successors Theophrastus (fr. 728–34 FHSG) and Strato (fr. 144–7 Wehrli) left special writings on discoveries.

12 Atkinson 2007.

13 21 B 18, trans. by W. Guthrie.

14 *Evagoras* 7, trans. by La Rue van Hook.

15 Hdt. 2.109; Philolaus 44 A 7a; Ar. *Nub.* 200–1.

16 Dorandi 1991, 126–7. Young Aristotle in the *Protrepticus* also enthusiastically praised brisk progress in mathematics (fr. 53 Rose).

17 See Zhmud 2006, 82–9.

18 Arist. *Metaph.* 1025b–1026a, 1063b36–1064b6. Cf. *Top.* 145a14–18, 157a10; *Eth. Nic.* 1140a2–3.

19 Ptol. *Syn. Math.* 6.11–21, trans. G. Toomer. On this, see also Chapter 10 by Taub in this volume.

20 *Eth. Nic.* 1098a23; *Poet.* 1449a15; *Pol.* 1252a26, 1264a3; *Metaph.* 993a15.

21 The only fragment of this work (fr. 150), preserved by Damascius, does not contain a title, but was rightly related to the *History of the Divine* in six books, listed among Theophrastus' works (251 no. 2 FHSG).

22 On ancient medical doxography, see van der Eijk 1999; Manetti 2011.

23 For details, see Zhmud 2013.

24 The theogonies of the Babylonians, Persian Magi, Sydonians, and Egyptians were treated separately. On Aristotle's theologians, see *Metaph.* 983b29, 1000a9, 1071b27, 1091a34; Palmer 2000.

25 Porph. *In Ptol. Harm.* p. 114 Düring = fr. 142. *Pythmenes*, or the 'first numbers', are the ratios of the concordant intervals expressed in their lowest terms (2:1, 3:2, 4:3).

26 See Zhmud 2006, 169–79, 228–38. Most of this evidence is included in the forthcoming edition: Stork et al. in prep.

27 Some of them, such as Mamercus, Neoclides, Leon, Theudius, Athenaeus, and Hermotimus, are otherwise unknown.

28 Fr. 615–17 Rose = fr. 408–14 Gigon. He also compiled (probably with the help of his students) the so-called Διδασκαλίαι, an extensive list of all the tragedies, comedies, and satyr plays performed at artistic festivals, dating them by the names of the Athenian archons (fr. 415–62 Gigon).

29 Niiniluoto 2015.

30 Jardine 2004, 274.

31 Arist. *Cat.* 7b31; *An. pr.* 69a30–4; *An. post.* 75b40–1; *Soph. el.* 171b13–172a8; *Ph.* 185a16–17; *Eth. Eud.* 1226a29.

32 Eudem. fr. 140, p. 59, 9–12 Wehrli. He passes over Bryson in silence, for his construction was similar to that of Antiphon.

33 Lloyd 1987a.

34 Netz 2004.

35 To the sixth-century συγγραφαί belong, for example, two technical treatises (Vitr. 7, praef. 12), the work on music by Lasus of Hermione (18 A 3 DK; Aristox. *Harm.*, 7.19–10), the interpretation of the Homeric poems by Theagenes of Rhegium (8 A 2 DK), the voyages of Scylax (*FGrHist* 709) and Euthymenes (*FGrHist* 647), and the philosophical treatises of Anaximander and Anaximenes, the first one with astronomical drawings and a geographical map. For more detail, see Zhmud 2017.

36 Procl. *In primum Euclidis elementorum librum commentarii*, 251.2–3, trans. G. Morrow. The Eudemian origin of these words is widely accepted.

37 Thus Netz 2004, 263.

38 Epicurus fr. 117, 163, 227, 229 Usener. Sedley 1976. The mathematician Polyaenus of Lampsacus, whom Epicurus converted to Epicureanism, wrote a special treatise on the fallacy of geometry as a whole.

39 A partial exception is Posidonius' follower Cleomedes, whose work *On the Orbits of the Heavenly Bodies* includes some glimpses of mathematical astronomy and geography.

40 Knorr 1986; Cuomo 2000.

41 Eratosthenes also used the *History of Geometry* in his letter to King Ptolemy III on the problem of doubling the cube (Eutocius, *In Archimedis De sphaera et cylindro*, 88.3–96.9). See Knorr 1986.

42 Eratosth. fr. 2C1 Berger = Pos. fr. 200a E–K = Agathemerus, *Geographiae informatio*, 1.2, trans. I. Kidd.

43 For a more detailed overview, see Zhmud 2013.

44 For Aetius, see Mansfeld and Runia 1997–2009.

45 Isoc. *Bus.* 22–3; Pl. *Phdr.* 274c7–d2; Hecataeus of Abdera (*FGrHist* 264 F 15); Diog. Laert. 1.11.

46 [Pl.] *Epin.* 986a3–4; Strabo 16.2.24; Diog. Laert. 1.11; Clem. Alex. *Strom.* 1.16.74.

47 Atlas: Pseudo-Eupolemus *ap.* Euseb. *Praep. Evang.* 9.17.9; Diod. Sic. 1.3.60, 4.27; Diog. Laert. Prooem. 1. Endymion: Mnaseas *ap. Scholia in Apollonium Rhodium*, 265.10, 275.22.

48 Isoc. *Bus.* 28; Pl. *Phdr.* 274d1–2, *Leg.* 747a–c; Eudem. fr. 133; Aristox. fr. 23; Strab. 16.2.24; Procl. *In primum Euclidis elementorum librum commentarii*, 65.3–4.

49 Alex. Polyh. *FGrHist* 273F19a; Eupolemus *FGrHist* 724 F1–2; Artapan *FGrHist* 726F 1.

50 Clem. Alex. *Strom.* 1.15.72–16.77; Euseb. *Praep. Evang.* 10.1.1–7, 10.4.17, etc.

Bibliography

ANCIENT AND MEDIEVAL AUTHORS

This list does not pretend to be comprehensive. Works that appear rarely are, for the most part, detailed where they occur. Works judged to be familiar to the presumed readers of this volume are not always indicated. For Greek and Latin texts, readers may wish to consult the editions specified in *The Oxford Classical Dictionary*, 4th edn, ed. S. Hornblower, A. Spawforth, and E. Eidinow (Oxford, 2012). In some cases items are included to direct the reader to a particular edition or translation.

Collections

Barker, A., 1989 *Greek Musical Writings, vol. II: Harmonic and Acoustic Theory* (Cambridge University Press).

Deichgräber, K., 1930/65 *Die griechische Empirikerschule: Sammlung der Fragmente und Darstellung der Lehre* (Weidmann).

Diels, H., 1952 *Die Fragmente der Vorsokratiker*, 6th edn, rev. W. Kranz (Weidmann) (abbreviated as DK).

Duffy, J. M. et al., 1997 *Commentary on Hippocrates'* Epidemics VI, *fragments. Commentary of an Anonymous Author on Hippocrates'* Epidemics VI, *fragments. Edition, Translation, and Notes by J. M. Duffy. John of Alexandria. Commentary on Hippocrates'* On the Nature of the Child. *Edition and Translation by T. A. Bell, D. P. Carpenter, D. W. Schmidt, M. N. Sham, G. I. Vardon, L. G. Westerink* (Akademie Verlag).

Graham, D. (trans. and ed.), 2010 *The Texts of Early Greek Philosophy* (Cambridge University Press).

Halleux, R. and Schamp, J., 1985 *Les lapidaires grecs. Lapidaire orphique. Kéygmes lapidaires d'Orphée. Socrate et Denys. Lapidaire nautique. Damigéron-Evax (traduction latine). Texte établi et traduit par R. Halleux et Jacques Schamp* (Les Belles Lettres).

Helmreich, G., Marquardt, J. and Mueller, I. (eds.), 1884–93 *Scripta Minoram*, 3 vols. (Teubner).

Kirk, G. S., Raven, J. E., and Schofield, M., 1957 *The Presocratic Philosophers: a Critical History with a Selection of Texts* (Cambridge University Press) (abbreviated as KRS).

Laks, A. and Most, G. W. (trans. and eds.), 2016 *Early Greek Philosophy*, 9 vols. (Harvard University Press, Loeb Classical Library).

Rome, A., 1931–43 *Commentaries de Pappus et de Théon d'Alexandrie sur l'Almagest*, 3 vols. (Biblioteca Apostolica Vaticana).

Taylor, C. C. W. (trans.), 1999 *The Atomists: Leucippus and Democritus. Fragments: a Text and Translation with a Commentary* (Toronto).

Thesleff, H., 1965 *The Pythagorean Texts of the Hellenistic Period*, Acta Academiae Aboensis, ser. A. Humaniora, vol. 30, no. 1.

Abū'l-'Abbās al-Faḍl ibn Ḥātim al-Nairīzī

Lo Bello, A., 2003 *Gerard of Cremona's Translation of the Commentary of al-Nayrizi on Book I of Euclid's Elements of Geometry* (Brill).

Anaxagoras

Curd, P., 2007 *Anaxagoras of Clazomenae: Fragments. Text and Translation with Notes and Essays* (University of Toronto Press).

Anonymus Londiniensis

Manetti, D. (ed.), 2011 *Anonymus Londiniensis. De medicina* (De Gruyter).

Apollonius of Perga

Decorps-Foulquier, M. and Feberspiel, M., 2008–10 *Apollonius de Perge, Coniques: Text grec et arabe établi, traduit et commenté*, vols. I.2, II.2 (de Gruyter).

Heath, T., 1896 *Apollonius of Perga* (Cambridge University Press).

Heiberg, J. L., 1891–3 *Apollonii Pergaei quae graece exstant cum commentariis antiquis*, 2 vols. (Teubner).

Rashed, R., 2008–10 *Apollonius de Perge, Coniques: text grec et arabe établi, traduit et commenté*, vols. I.1, II.1–2, III, IV (Arabic text) (De Gruyter).

Rashed, R. and Bellosta, H., 2010 *Apollonius de Perge. La section des droits selon des rapports* (De Gruyter).

Toomer, G. T., 1990 *Apollonius: Conics, Books V to VII: the Arabic Translation of the Lost Greek Original in the Version of the Banū Mūsā* (Springer-Verlag).

Archimedes

Clagett, M., 1976 *Archimedes in the Middle Ages, vol. II: Translations from the Greek by William of Moerbeke*, 2 parts (American Philosophical Society).

Heath, T., 1912 *The Works of Archimedes* (Cambridge University Press).

Heiberg, J. L. and Stamatis, E. S., 1972 *Archimedis opera omnia, 3 vols.* (Teubner).

Aristarchus

Berggren, J. L. and Sidoli, N., 2007 'Aristarchus': *On the Sizes and Distances of the Sun and the Moon*: Greek and Arabic Texts', *Archive for History of Exact Sciences* 61: 213–254

Heath, T., 1913 *Aristarchus of Samos* (Clarendon Press).

Aristophanes

Henderson, J. (trans.), 1998 *Aristophanes: Clouds, Wasps, Peace* (Harvard University Press; Loeb Classical Library).

Aristotle

Barnes, J. (ed.), 1984 *The Complete Works of Aristotle: the Revised Oxford Translation*, 2 vols. (Princeton University Press).

Detel, W., 1993 *Aristoteles: Analytica Posteriora* (Akademie Verlag).

Hardie, R. P. and Gaye, R. K. (trans.), 1984 'Physics', in J. Barnes (ed.), *The Complete Works of Aristotle; the Revised Oxford Translation*, vol. I (Princeton University Press), pp. 315-446.

Kullmann, W. (trans.), 2007 *Aristoteles: Über die Teile der Lebenwesen*, in H. Flashar (ed.), *Aristoteles Werke in deutscher Übersetzung*, vol. XVII/I (Akademie Verlag).

Lee, H. D. P. (trans.), 1952 *Aristotle: Meteorologica* (Harvard University Press, Loeb Classical Library).

Lennox, J. (trans.), 2002 *Aristotle: On the Parts of Animals I–IV* (Clarendon Press).

Peck, A. L. (trans.), 1942 *Aristotle: Generation of Animals* (Harvard University Press).

Ross, W. D. (ed.), 1924 *Aristotle's Metaphysics: a Revised Text with Introduction and Commentary* (Clarendon Press).

Ross, W. D. (ed.), 1936 *Aristotle's Physics: a Revised Text with Introduction and Commentary* (Clarendon Press).

Ross, W. D. (ed.), 1961 *Aristotle: De Anima* (Clarendon Press).

Shields, C. (trans.), 2016 *Aristotle: De Anima* (Clarendon Press).

Webster, E. H. (trans.), 1931 *Aristotle: Meteorology*, in *The Works of Aristotle*, vol. III, ed. W. D. Ross (Clarendon Press).

Williams, C. J. F., 1982 *Aristotle's De Generatione et Corruptione* (Clarendon Press).

Diogenes Laertius

Hicks, R. D., 1925 *Lives of Eminent Philosophers*, 2 vols. (Harvard University Press, Loeb Classical Library).

Diophantus

Sesiano, J., 1982 *Books IV to VII of Diophantus' Arithemetica* (Springer).

Tannery, P. (ed.), 1893 *Diophantus Alexandrini Opera Omnia* (Teubner).

Empedocles

Inwood, B., 2001 *The Poem of Empedocles*, revised edn (University of Toronto Press).

Wright, M. R., 1995 *Empedocles: the Extant Fragments* 2nd edn (Bristol Classical Press).

Epicurus

Inwood, B. and Gerson, L. P. (trans.), 1998 *The Epicurus Reader: Selected Writings and Testimonia* (Hackett).

Euclid

Menge, H., 1896 *Euclidis Opera Omnia*, vol. 6VI (Teubner).

Taisbak, C. M., 2003 *Euclid's Data* (Museum Tusculanum Press).

Eudemus of Rhodes

Stork, P., Dorandi, T., and van Ophuijsen, J. M. (eds.), in prep. *Eudemus of Rhodes: the Sources, Text and Translation.*

Wehrli, F. (ed.), 1969 *Eudemus von Rhodos. Texte und Kommentar* (Schwabe).

Euripides

Nauck, A. (ed.), 1902 *Euripidis Tragoaediae, vol. III: Perditarum tragoediarum fragmenta.* Teubner.

Galen

De Lacy, P. (ed.), 1992 *Galeni De semine, edidit, in linguam Anglicam vertit, commentatus est Ph. De Lacy* (Akademie Verlag).

De Lacy, P. (ed.), 2005 *Galeni De placitis Hippocratis et Platonis, edidit, in linguam Anglicam vertit, commentatus est Ph. De Lacy* (Akademie Verlag).

Helmreich , G. (ed.) 1907–9 *Galenou Peri chreias moriōn IZ* = *Galeni De usu partium libri XVII.*

May, M. T. (trans.) 1968 *On the Usefulness of the Parts of the Body* (Cornell University Press).

Nutton, V., 1999 *Galeni De propriis placitis, edidit, in linguam Anglicam vertit, commentatus est V. Nutton* (Akademie Verlag).

Walzer, R. (trans.) 1985, *On Medical Experience*, in M. Frede and M. Walzer (trans.) *Galen: Three Treatises on the Nature of Science* (Hackett) (abbreviated as Walzer).

Geminus

Evans, J. and Berggren, L., 2006 *Geminos's Introduction to the Phenomena* (Princeton University Press).

Georgios Pachymeres (1242–1310)

Telelis, I., 2012 *Georgios Pachymeres: Philosophia, Book 5, Commentary in Aristotle's Meteorologica: Prolegomena, Text, Indices* (Academy of Athens; Vrin).

Heraclides of Pontus

Schutrumpf, E. (ed.), 2008 *Heraclides of Pontus: Texts, Translation, and Discussion* (Transaction).

Herodotus

de Selincourt, A. and Marincola, J. M. (trans.), 2003 *Herodotus: Histories* (Penguin).

Hesiod

Most, G. (trans.), 2007 *Hesiod: Theogony, Works and Days* (Harvard University Press).

Hippocrates

Festugière, A.-J. (trans.), 1948 *Hippocrate, l'ancienne medicine* (Klincksieck).
Jones, W. H. S. (trans.), 1923 *Hippocrates*, vol. I (Heinemann).
Jouanna, J. (ed. and trans.), 1990 *Hippocrate l'ancienne medicine* (Les Belles Lettres).
Jouanna, J. (ed. and trans.), 2003 *Hippocrate: Des vents – de l'art* (Les Belles Lettres).
Schiefsky, M. (trans.), 2005. *Hippocrates on Ancient Medicine* (Brill).

Lucian

Harmon, A. M. (trans.), 1961 *Lucian in eight volumes*, vol. IV (Harvard University Press, Loeb Classical Library).

Menelaus of Alexandria

Krause, M., 1936 *Die Sphärik von Menelaos aus Alexanderien in der Verbesserung von Abū Naṣr Manṣūr b. ʿAlī b. ʿIrāq* (Weidmannsche Buchhandlung).
Sidoli, N. and Kusuba, T., 2014 'Al-Harawī's Version of Menelaus', *Sphaerics', Suhayl* 13: 149–212.

Meno

Manetti, D. (ed.), 2010 *Meno: Anonymus Londiniensis: De medicina* (Akademie Verlag).

Nemesius

Sharples, R. W. and van der Eijk, P. J., 2008 *Nemesius: On the Nature of Man* (Liverpool University Press).

Nicolaus Damascenus

Drossaart Lulofs, H. J. and Poortman, E. L. J., 1989 *Nicolaus Damascenus De Plantis: Five Translations* (North-Holland).

Pappus of Alexandria

Hultsch, F., 1876 *Pappi Alexandrini Collectionis, 3 vols.* (Berolini).
ver Eecke, P. (trans.) 1933 *La collection mathématique* (Desclée de Brouwer).

Philoponus

Hayduck, M., 1897 *Ioannis Philoponi in Aristotelis De anima libros commentaria* (Reimer).
Kupreeva, I., 2011 *Philoponus: On Aristotle Meteorology, 1.1–3* (Bloomsbury).
Kupreeva, I., 2012 *Philoponus: On Aristotle Meteorology 1.4–9,12* (Bloomsbury).

Plato

Burnet, J. (ed.), 1900–7 *Platonis Opera*, 5 vols. (Clarendon Press).
Cooper, J. and. Hutchinson, D. S (eds.), 1997 *Plato: Complete Works* (Hackett).

Cornford, F. M. (trans. and comm.), 1975 *Plato's Cosmology: the Timaeus of Plato* (Library of Liberal Arts).

Croiset, A. and Bodin, L. (ed. and trans.), 1955 *Platon: Gorgias, Menon* (Les Belles Lettres).

Dalfen, J. (trans.), 2004 *Platon: Gorgias* (Vandenhoeck and Ruprecht).

Dodds, E. R. (ed.), 1959 *Plato: Gorgias* (Oxford University Press).

Grube, G. M. A. (rev.) and C. D. C. Reeve (trans.), 1997 *Republic*, in *Plato: Complete Works*, ed. J. M. Cooper, associate ed. D. S. Hutchinson (Hackett).

Irwin, T. (trans.), 1979 *Plato: Gorgias* (Clarendon Press).

Lamb, W. R. M. (trans.), 1932 *Plato: Lysis, Symposium, Gorgias* (Harvard University Press, Loeb Classical Library).

Lee, D., 2008 *Plato, Timaeus and Critias* (Penguin).

Schleiermacher, F. (trans.), 1804–28 *Platons Werke* (Berlin).

Slings, S. R. (ed.), 2003 *Platonis Respublica* (Clarendon Press).

Zeyl, D. J. (trans.) 1997 *Plato: Timaeus*, in *Plato: Complete Works*, ed. J. Cooper, associate ed. D. S. Hutchinson (Hackett).

Pliny the Elder

Rackham, H. (trans.), 1950 *Pliny: Natural History, vol. V: Books 17–19* (Harvard Universaity Press).

Porphyry

Wilberding, J. (trans.), 2011 *Porphyry: To Gaurus on How Embryos are Ensouled and On What is in our Power* (Bristol Classical Press).

Proclus

Friedlein, G. (ed.), 1873 *Procli Diadochi in Primum Euclidis Elementorum Librum Commenatarii* (Teubner).

Morrow, G. R. (trans.), 1970 *Proclus: a Commentary on the First Book of Euclid's Elements* (Princeton University Press).

Steel, C. (trans.), 2007 *Proclus on Providence* (Cornell University Press).

Pseudo-Aristotle

Furley, D. J. (trans.), 1955 'Pseudo-Aristotle: De Mundo', in *Aristotle: On Sophistical Refutations, On Coming-to-Be and Passing-Away, On the Cosmos* (Heinemann), pp. 333–430.

Thom, J. C. (ed.), 2014 *Cosmic Order and Divine Power: Pseudo-Aristotle, On the Cosmos* (Mohr Siebeck).

Ptolemy

Berggren, J. L. and Jones, M., 2000 *Ptolemy's Geography: an Annotated Translation of the Theoretical Chapters* (Princeton University Press).

Goldstein, B. R. (ed.), 1967 'The Arabic Version of Ptolemy's *Planetary Hypotheses*', *Transactions of the American Philosophical Society* 57: 3–55.

Heiberg, J. L., 1898–1903 *Claudii Ptolemaei: Opera quae exstant omnia, vol. I, Parts I and II, Syntaxis Mathematica* (Teubner).

Heiberg, J. L., 1907 *Claudii Ptolemaei opera quae exstant omnia, vol. II, Opera astronomica minora* (Teubner).

Robbins, F. E. (ed. and trans.), 1940 *Tetrabiblos* (Harvard University Press, Loeb Classical Library).

Sidoli, N. and Berggren, L., 2007 'The Arabic Version of Ptolemy's *Planisphere* or *Flattening the Surface of the Sphere*: Text, Translation, Commentary', *SCIAMVS* 8: 37–139.

Toomer, G. T., 1984 *Ptolemy's Almagest* (Springer).

St Gregory of Nyssa

Roth, C. P. (trans.), 1993 *St Gregory of Nyssa: The Soul and the Resurrection*, Popular Patristics Series 12 (Saint Vladimir's Seminary Press).

Seneca

Hine, H. M. (trans.), 2010 *Seneca: Natural Questions* (University of Chicago Press).

Sextus Empiricus

Bury, R. G. (trans.), 1949 *Sextus Empiricus in Four Volumes: volume IV. Against the Professors* (Harvard University Press, Loeb Classical Library).

Simplicius

Diels, H. (ed.), 1882 *Simplicii in Aristotelis Physicorum libros quattuor priores commentaria* (Reimer).

Fleet, B., 1997. *Simplicius: On Aristotle's Physics 2* (Cornell University Press).

Hagen, C. (trans.), 1994 *Simplicius: On Aristotle Physics 7* (Duckworth).

Heiberg, J. L. (ed.), 1894 *Simplicius In Aristotelis De caelo commentaria* (Reimer).

Mueller, I. (trans.), 2005 *Simplicius: On Aristotle: On the Heavens, 2.10–14* (Duckworth).

Theodosius

Czinczenheim, C., 2000 Edition, traduction et commentaire des *Sphériques* de Théodose, PhD dissertation, University of Paris IV.

Kunitzsch, P. and Lorch, R., 2010 *Theodosius, Sphaerica: Arabic and Medieval Latin Translations* (Steiner).

Theon of Smyrna (Mathematical knowledge useful for reading Plato)

Dupuis, J. (ed. and trans.), 1892; repr. 1966 *Théon de Smyrne, philosophe platonicien: exposition des connaissances mathématiques utiles pour la lecture de Platon* (Hachette).

Hiller, E., 1878 *Theonis Smyrnaei Philosophi Expositio rerum mathematicarum ad legedum Platonem utilium* (Teubner).

Theophrastus

Daiber, H. (trans.), 1992 The *Meteorology* of Theophrastus in Syriac and Arabic Translation, in W. W. Fortenbaugh and D. Gutas (eds.), *Theophrastus: his Psychological, Doxographical, and Scientific Writings* (Transaction).

Fortenbaugh, W. W., Huby, P. M., Sharples, R. W., and Gutas, D. (eds.), 1922 *Theophrastus of Eresus: Sources for his Life, Writings, Thought, and Influence, Pt. 1–2* (Brill) (abbreviated as FHSG).

Sider, D. and Brunschön, C. W. (eds.), 2007 *Theophrastus of Eresus: On Weather Signs* (Brill).

Vegetius

Milner, N. P. (trans.), 1996 *Vegetius: Epitome of Military Science*, revised 2nd edn (Liverpool University Press).

Reeve, M. D. (ed.), 2004 *Vegetius: Epitoma rei militaris* (Oxford University Press).

Xenophanes

Lesher, J. H., 1992 *Xenophanes of Colophon: Fragments* (University of Toronto Press).

MODERN AUTHORS

Acerbi, F., 2007 *Euclide, Tutte le opere*. Bompiani.

Acerbi, F., 2010 *Il silenzio delle sirene. La storia matematica greca antica* (Carocci).

Acerbi, F., 2011a 'The Language of the "Givens": its Form and its Use as a Deductive Tool in Greek Mathematics', *Archive for History of the Exact Sciences* 65: 119–53.

Acerbi, F., 2011b *La sintassi logica della matematica greca*. Archives-ouvertes.fr, Sciences de l'Homme et de la Société, Histoire, Philosophie et Sociologie des sciences. hal.archives-ouvertes.fr: hal-00727063.

Acerbi, F., 2012 'I codici stilistici della matematica greca: dimonstrationi, prodedure, algorithmi', *Quaderni Urbinati di Cultura Classica* NS 101: 167–214.

Ackrill, J. L., 1972/3 'Aristotle's Definition of *Psuche*', *Proceedings of the Aristotelian Society* 73: 119–33.

Allen, J., 2001 *Inference from Sign: Ancient Debates about the Nature of Evidence* (Oxford University Press).

Althoff, J., 2018 'Aristotle, the Inventor of Natural Science', in P. T. Keyser and J. Scarborough (eds.), *Oxford Handbook of Science and Medicine in the Classical World* (Oxford University Press), pp. 236–56.

Andersen, Ø., 1976 'Aristotle on Sense-Perception in Plants', *Symbolae Osloenses* 51(1): 81–6.

Anscombe, G. E. M., 1971 'Causality and Determination', Inaugural Lecture at Cambridge University; repr. in *Metaphysics and the Philosophy of Mind* (University of Minneapolis Press, 1981).

Anton, J. P. (ed.), 1990 *Science and the Sciences in Plato* (Caravan Books).

Asper, M., 2009 'The Two Cultures of Mathematics in Ancient Greece', in E. Robson and J. Stedall (eds.), *The Oxford Handbook of the History of Mathematics* (Oxford University Press), pp. 107–32.

Atkinson, C., 2007 *Inventing Inventors in Renaissance Europe* (Mohr Siebeck).

Aujac, G., 1984 'Le langage formulaire dans la géométrie grecque', *Revue d'Histoire des Sciences* 37: 97–109.

Avigad, J., Dean, E., and Mumma, J., 2009 'A Formal System for Euclid's *Elements*', *Review of Symbolic Logic* 2: 700–68.

Bailly, J. S., 1775 *Histoire de l'astronomie ancienne depuis son origine jusqu'à l'établissement de l'École d'Alexandrie* (Les Freres Debure).

Bajri, S., Hannah, J., and Montelle, C., 2015 'Revisiting Al-Samaw'al's Table of Binomial Coefficients: Greek Inspiration, Diagrammatic Reasoning and Mathematical Induction', *Archive for History of Exact Sciences* 69: 537–76.

Baldi, B., 1707 *Cronica de' matematici overo Epitome dell' istoria delle vite loro* (A. A. Montecelli).

Baltes, M., 1996 'Γέγονεν (Platon, Tim. 28 B 7). Ist die Welt real enstanden oder nicht?', in K. Algra, P. van der Horst, and D. Runia (eds.), *Polyhistor: Studies in the History and Historiography of Ancient Philosophy* (Brill), pp. 76–96.

Barbera, A., 1984 'The Consonant Eleventh and the Expansion of the Musical Tetractys', *Journal of Music Theory* 28(2): 191–223.

Barker, A., 1978 'Σύμφωνοι ἀριθμοί: A Note on *Republic* 531C 1–4', *Classical Philology* 73: 337–42.

Barker, A., 1985 'Theophrastus on Pitch and Melody', in W. W. Fortenbaugh et al. (eds.), *Theophrastus of Eresus: On his Life and Works* (Transaction Books), pp. 289–324.

Barker, A., 2004 *Scientific Method in Ptolemy's Harmonics* (Cambridge University Press).

Barker, A., 2007 *The Science of Harmonics in Classical Greece* (Cambridge University Press).

Barker, A., 2009 'Ptolemy and the Meta-Helikon', *Studies in the History and Philosophy of Science* 40: 344–51.

Barnes, J., 1971/2 'Aristotle's Concept of Mind', *Proceedings of the Aristotelian Society* 72: 101–14.

Barney, R., 2012 'History and Dialectic (*Metaphysics* A3, 983a24–984b8)', in C. Steele (ed.), *Aristotle's Metaphysics Alpha: Symposium Aristotelicum* (Oxford University Press), pp. 153–88.

Beere, J., 2009 *Doing and Being: an Interpretation of Aristotle's Metaphysics Theta* (Oxford University Press).

Berggren, J. L. and Van Brummelen, G., 2000 'The Role and Development of Geometric Analysis in Ancient Greece and Medieval Islam', in P. Suppes, J. M. Moravcsik, and H. Mendell (eds.), *Ancient and Medieval Traditions in the Exact Sciences* (CSLI Publications), pp. 1–31.

Bernal, M., 1992 'Animadversions on the Origins of Western Science', *Isis* 83: 596–607.

Bernard, A. and Christianidis, J., 2012 'A New Analytical Framework for the Understanding of Diopantus', *Arithmetica* I–III', *Archive for History of Exact Sciences* 66: 1–69.

Berryman, S., 2002a 'Democritus and the Explanatory Power of the Void', in V. Caston and D. W. Graham (eds.), *Presocratic Philosophy: Essays in Honour of Alexander Mourelatos* (Ashgate), pp. 183–91.

Berryman, S., 2002b 'Galen and the Mechanical Philosophy', *Apeiron* 35: 235–53.

Berryman, S., 2003 'Ancient Automata and Mechanical Explanation', *Phronesis* 48: 344–69.

Berryman, S., 2005 'Necessitation and Explanation in Philoponus' Aristotelian Physics', in R. Salles (ed.), *Metaphysics, Soul, and Ethics: Themes from the Work of Richard Sorabji* (Clarendon Press).

Berryman, S., 2007 'Teleology without Tears: Aristotle and the Role of Mechanistic Conceptions of Organisms', *Canadian Journal of Philosophy* 37: 357–70.

Berryman, S., 2009 *The Mechanical Hypothesis in Ancient Greek Natural Philosophy* (Cambridge University Press).

Berryman, S., 2010 'The Puppet and the Sage: Images of the Self in Marcus Aurelius', *Oxford Studies in Ancient Philosophy* 38: 187–209

Berryman, S., 2014. 'Review of Jean De Groot, *Aristotle's Empiricism: Experience and Mechanics in the 4th Century BC*', *Aestimatio*, 11: 248–52.

Berryman, S., 2016 'Review of Jean De Groot, Aristotle's Empiricism: Experience and Mechanics in the 4th Century BC', *Aestimatio* 11 (https://jps.library.utoronto.ca/index.php/aestimatio/article/view/26427).

Betegh, G., 2012 " 'The Next Principle" (*Metaphysics* A 3–4, 984b8–985b25)', in C. Steele (ed.), *Aristotle's Metaphysics Alpha: Symposium Aristotelicum* (Oxford University Press), pp. 105–40.

Betegh, G., 2013 'On the Physical Aspect of Heraclitus' Psychology: With New Appendices', in D. Sider and D. Obbink (eds.), *Doctrine and Doxography: Studies on Heraclitus and Pythagoras* (De Gruyter), pp. 225–61.

Biancani, G., 1615 *De natura mathematicarum scientiarum tractatio, atque clarorum mathematicorum chronologia* (Bartolomeo Cochi, Geronimo Tamburini).

Bodnar, I., 2005 'Teleology across Natures', *Rhizai* 2: 9–29.

Bogen, J. and Woodward, J., 1988 'Saving the Phenomena', *Philosophical Review* 97(3): 303–52.

Boudon-Millot, V., 2008 'La naissance de la vie dans la théorie médicale et philosophique de Galien', in L. Brisson, M.-H. Congourdeau, and J.-L. Solère (eds.), *L'embryon: formation et animation. Antiquité grecque et latine, traditions hébraïque, chrétienne et islamique* (Vrin), pp. 79–94.

Bourgey, L., 1953 *Observation et experiénce chez les médecins de la collection Hippocratique* (Vrin).

Bowen, A. C., 2002 'The Art of the Commander and the Emergence of Predictive Astronomy', in C. J. Tuplin and T. E. Rihll (eds.), *Science and Mathematics in Ancient Greek Culture* (Oxford University Press), pp. 76–111.

Boyer, C. B., 1987 *The Rainbow: from Myth to Mathematics* (Princeton University Press).

Brentjes, S., 1994 'Textzeugen und Hypothesen zum arabischen Euklid in der Überlieferung von al-Haggag b. Yusuf b. Matar (zwischen 786 und 833)', *Archive for History of Exact Sciences* 47: 53–92.

Brisson, L., M.-H. Congourdeau, and J.-L. Solère (eds.), 2008 *L'embryon: formation et animation. Antiquité grecque et latine, traditions hébraïque, chrétienne et islamique* (Vrin).

Broadie, S., 1987 'Nature, Craft and *Phronesis* in Aristotle', *Philosophical Topics* 15: 35–50.

Broadie, S., 2004 '*On Generation and Corruption* I.4: Distinguishing Alteration – Substantial Change, Elemental Change, and First Matter in *GC*', in F. De Haas and J. Mansfield (eds.), *Aristotle's On Generation and Corruption I* (Oxford University Press), pp. 123–50.

Bryan, J., 2012 *Likeness and Likelihood in the Presocratics and Plato* (Cambridge University Press)

Bunbury, E. H., 1883 *A History of Ancient Geography among the Greeks and Romans from the Earliest Ages till the Fall of the Roman Empire*, 2nd edn, 2 vols. (John Murray) (reprinted 1959, Dover).

Burnyeat, M. F., 1992 'Is an Aristotelian Philosophy of Mind Still Credible? (A Draft)', in M. Nussbaum and R. Rorty (eds.), *Essays on Aristotle's De Anima* (Oxford University Press), pp. 15–26.

Cambiano, G., 2012 'The Desire to Know (*Metaphysics* A 1)', in C. Steele (ed.), *Aristotle's Metaphysics Alpha: Symposium Aristotelicum* (Oxford University Press), pp. 1–47.

Cameron, A., 1990 'Isidore of Miletus and Hypatia: On the Editing of Mathematical Texts', *Greek, Roman and Byzantine Studies* 31: 103–27.

Capelle, W., 1912 'Μετέωρος – μετεωρολογία', *Philologus* 71: 414–48.

Capelle, W., 1922 'Zur Hippokratischen Frage', *Hermes* 57: 247–65.

Capelle, W., 1997 'Epiphenomenalisms, Ancient and Modern', *Philosophical Review* 106: 309–63.

Carone, G. R., 2005 *Plato's Cosmology and its Ethical Dimensions* (Cambridge University Press).

Caston, V., 1997 'Epiphenomenalisms, Ancient and Modern', *Philosophical Review* 106: 309–63.

Caston, V., 2005 'The Spirit and the Letter: Aristotle on Perception', in R. Salles (ed.), *Metaphysics, Soul, and Ethics: Themes from the Work of Richard Sorabji* (Oxford University Press).

Caston, V. and Graham, D. W. (eds.), 2002 *Presocratic Philosophy: Essays in Honour of Alexander Mourelatos* (Ashgate).

Charles, D., 1991 'Teleological Causation in the *Physics*', in L. Judson (ed.), *Aristotle's Physics: a Collection of Essays* (Oxford University Press).

Charles, D., 2008 *Aristotle on Meaning and Essence* (Clarendon Press).

Charles, D., 2012 'Teleological Causation', in C. Shields (ed.), *The Oxford Handbook of Aristotle* (Oxford University Press), pp. 227–66.

Charlton, W., 1970 *Aristotle Physics Books I and II: Translated with Introduction, Commentary, Note on Recent Work and Revised Bibliography* (Clarendon Press).

Christianidis, J., 2007 'The Way of Diophantus', *Historia Mathematica* 34: 289–305.

Christianidis, J. and Oaks, J., 2013 'Practicing Algebra in Late Antiquity: the Problem-Solving of Diophantus of Alexandria', *Historia Mathematica* 40: 127–63.

Clavius, C., 1611 'In disciplinas mathematicas prolegomena,' in C. Clavius, *Opera Mathematica*, vol. I (by Reinhard Eltz, at the expense of Anthony Heirat).

Collingwood, R. G., 1945/78 *The Idea of Nature* (Oxford University Press).

Connell, S. M., 2016 *Aristotle on Female Animals: A Study of the Generation of Animals* (Cambridge University Press).

Cooper, J., 1982 'Aristotle on Natural Teleology', in M. Schofield and M. C. Nussbaum (eds.), *Language and Logos* (Cambridge University Press), pp. 197–222.

Cooper, J., 2004 'Method and Science in *On Ancient Medicine*', in J. Cooper, *Knowledge, Nature and the Good: Essays on Ancient Philosophy* (Princeton University Press) (reprinted from H. Linneweber-Lammerskitten and G. Mohr (eds.), *Interpretation and Argument* (Königshausen and Neumann), pp. 3–42).

Cooper, J., 2012 'Conclusion – and Retrospect (Metaphysics A10)', in C. Steele (ed.), *Aristotle's Metaphysics Alpha: Symposium Aristotelicum* (Oxford University Press), pp. 333–64.

Copenhaver, B., 1998 'The Occultist Tradition and its Critics', in D. Garber and M. Ayers (eds.), *The Cambridge History of Seventeenth-Century Philosophy*, vol. I (Cambridge University Press), pp. 454–512.

Cordero, N., 2010 'The "*Doxa* of Parmenides" Dismantled', *Ancient Philosophy* 30: 231–46.

Cornelli, G., McKirahan, R., and Macris. C. (eds.), 2013 *On Pythagoreanism* (De Gruyter).

Cornford , F. M. (trans. and comm.), 1975 *Plato's Cosmology: the Timaeus of Plato* (Library of Liberal Arts).

Couprie, D., 2002 'The Discovery of Space: Anaximander's Astronomy,' in D. Couprie, R. Hahn, and G. Naddaf, *Anaximander in Context: New Studies in the Origins of Greek Philosophy* (SUNY Press).

Creese, D., 2010 *The Monochord in Ancient Greek Harmonic Science* (Cambridge University Press).

Crowley, T. J., 2008 'Aristotle's So-Called Elements"', *Phronesis* 53: 223–42.

Cunningham, A. and Williams, P., 1993 'De-Centring the "Big Picture": "The Origins of Modern Science" and the Modern Origins of Science', *British Journal for the History of Science*, 26(4): 407–32.

Cuomo, S., 2000 *Pappus of Alexandria and the Mathematics of Late Antiquity* (Cambridge University Press).

Cuomo, S., 2007 *Technology and Culture in Greek and Roman Antiquity* (Cambridge University Press).

Cuomo, S., 2019 'Mathematical Traditions in Ancient Greece and Rome', *HAU: Journal of Ethnographic Theory* 9(1) (Special issue: *Science in the Forest, Science in the Past*) : 75–85

Curd, P., 2001 'Why Democritus was not a Skeptic', in A. Preus (ed.), *Before Plato* (SUNY Press), pp. 149–69.

Curd, P., 2004 *The Legacy of Parmenides: Eleatic Monism and Later Presocratic Thought* (Parmenides Publishing).

Curd, P., 2013 'The Divine and the Thinkable: Toward an Account of the Intelligible Cosmos,' *Rhizomata* 1: 217–47.

Curd, P., 2016 'Presocratic Philosophy', *The Stanford Encyclopedia of Philosophy* (Winter 2016 edition), ed. Edward N. Zalta, https://plato.stanford.edu/archives/win2016/entries/presocratics/.

Curd, P. and Graham, D. (eds.), 2008 *The Oxford Handbook of Presocratic Philosophy* (Oxford University Press).

Dauben, J. W. and Scriba, C. J. (eds.), 2002 *Writing the History of Mathematics: its Historical Development* (Birkhäuser).

Dechales, C. F. M., 1674 *Cursus seu mundus mathematicus. Pars I. Tractatus proemialis, de progressu matheseos et illustribus mathematicis*, vol. I (Anissonios, Joan. Posuel and Claud. Rigaud).

De Groot, J., 2014 *Aristotle's Empiricism: Experience and Mechanics in the 4th Century BC* (Parmenides Publishing).

De Haas, F., 1997 *John Philoponus' New Definition of Prime Matter* (Brill).

De Haas, F., 1999 'Mixture in Philoponus: an Encounter with a Third Kind of Potentiality,' in J. M. M. H. Thijssen and H. A. G. Braakhuis (eds.), *The Commentary Tradition on De generatione et corruptione: Ancient, Medieval, and Early Modern* (Brepols).

De Young, G., 1981 The Arithmetical Books of Euclid's Elements in the Arabic Tradition, PhD Dissertation, Harvard University.

De Young, G., 2005 'Diagrams in the Arabic Euclidean Tradition: a Preliminary Assessment', *Historia Mathematica* 32: 129–79.

Decorps-Foulquier, M., 1999 *Recherches sur les Coniques d'Apollonios de Pergé et leurs commentateurs grecs: Histoire de la transmission des Livres I–IV* (Klincksieck).

Deichgräber, K., 1930/65 *Die griechische Empirikerschule: Sammlung der Fragmente und Darstellung der Lehre* (Weidmann).

Dekker, E., 2013 *Illustrating the Phaenomena: Celestial Cartography in Antiquity and the Middle Ages* (Oxford University Press).

Des Chene, D., 2001 *Spirits and Clocks: Machine and Organism in Descartes* (Cornell University Press).

Detienne, M. and Vernant, J.-P., 1974 *Les ruses de l'intelligence: la mètis des Grecs* (Flammarion).

Deusing, A., 1640 *De astronomiae origine, ejusdemque ad nostram usque aetatem progressu* (Hardwijk).

Dicks, D. R., 1970 *Early Greek Astronomy to Aristotle* (Cornell University Press).

Dijksterhuis, E. J., 1961. *The Mechanization of the World Picture*, trans. C. Dikshoorn (Oxford University Press).

Diller, H, 1932 ''Οψις ἀδήλων τὰ φαινόμενα', *Hermes* 67: 119–43.

Diller, H, 1952 'Hippokratische Medizin und attische Philosophie', *Hermes* 80: 385–409.

Diller, H., 1964 'Ausdrucksformen des methodischen Bewusstseins in den Hippokratischen Epidemien', *Archiv für Begriffsgeschichte* 9: 133–50.

Donini, P., 2008 'Psychology', in R. J. Hankinson (ed.), *The Cambridge Companion to Galen* (Cambridge University Press), pp. 184–209.

Dorandi, T., 1991 *Filodemo. Storia dei filosofi: Platone e l'Academia* (Bibliopolis).

Drachmann, A. G., 1958 'How Archimedes Expected to Move the Earth', *Centaurus*, 5: 278–82.

Drachmann, A. G., 1963 *The Mechanical Technology of Greek and Roman Antiquity: a Study of the Literary Sources* (Munksgaard).

Dufour, R., 2004 *Chrysippus. Oruvre Philosophique*, 2 vols. (Les Belles Lettres).

Duhem, P., 1969 *To Save the Phenomena: an Essay on the Idea of Physical Theory from Plato to Galileo*, trans. E. Doland and C. Maschler (University of Chicago Press) Originally published as 'ΣΟΖΕΙΝ ΤΑ ΦΑΙΝΟΜΕΝΑ, Essai sur la notion de theorie physique de Platon a Galilee' in *Annales de philosophic chretienne* vol. 79/156 (ser. 4 V1), reprinted 1908 by A. Hermann et Fils.

Dunn, F., 2005 'On Ancient Medicine and its Intellectual Context', in P. J. van der Eijk (ed.), *Hippocrates in Context* (Brill), pp. 49–67.

Ebrey, D., 2007 Aristotle's Motivation for Matter, PhD dissertation, UCLA.

Ebrey, D., 2014 'Making Room for Matter: Material Causes in the *Phaedo* and the *Physics*', *Apeiron* 47: 245–65.

Ebrey, D., 2015 'Blood, Matter, and Necessity', in D. Ebrey (ed.), *Theory and Practice in Aristotle's Natural Science* (Cambridge University Press).

Ebrey, D., n.d. 'The Definition of Matter in *Physics* I', unpublished paper.

Engroff, J. W., 1980 The Arabic Tradition of Euclid's Elements: Book V, PhD dissertation, Harvard University.

Evans, J., 1998 *The History and Practice of Ancient Astronomy* (Oxford University Press).

Evans, J., 1999 'The Material Culture of Greek Astronomy', *Journal for the History of Astronomy* 30: 237–307.

Evans, J., 2003 'The Origins of Ptolemy's Cosmos', in *Cosmology through Time: Ancient and Modern Cosmologies in the Mediterranean Area*, ed. S. Colafrancesco and G. Giobbi (Mimesis), pp. 123–32.

Evans, J., 2016 'Images of Time and Cosmic Connection', in A. Jones (ed.), *Time and Cosmos in Greco-Roman Antiquity* (Princeton University Press), pp. 143–69.

Falcon, A. (2005), *Aristotle and the Science of Nature: Unity without Uniformity* (Cambridge University Press).

Fatuzzo, C., 2009 'Il pensiero musicale di Teofrasto', in D. Castaldo, D. Restani, and C. Tassi (eds.), *Il sapere musicale e i suoi contesti: da Teofrasto a Claudio Tolemeo* (Longo), pp. 21–39.

Federspiel, M., 1995 'Sur l'opposition défini/indéfini dans la langue des mathématiques grecques', *Les Études Classiques* 63: 249–93.

Federspiel, M., 1999 'Notes critiques sur le livre II des Coniques d'Apollonius de Pergè, Première partie', *Revue de Études Greques* 112: 409–43.

Feeney, D., 2008 *Caesar's Calendar: Ancient Time and the Beginnings of History* (University of California Press).

Feke, J., 2009 Ptolemy in Philosophical Context: a Study of the Relationships between Physics, Mathematics, and Theology, PhD dissertation, University of Toronto.

Feke, J., 2012 'Ptolemy's Defense of Theoretical Philosophy', *Apeiron* 45: 61–90.

Feke, J., 2018 *Ptolemy's Philosophy: Mathematics as a Way of Life* (Princeton University Press).

Feyerabend, P., 1985 'The Methodology of Scientific Research Programs', in P. Feyerabend, *Problems of Empiricism, vol. II: Philosophical Papers* (Cambridge University Press), pp. 202–30.

Fowler, R. L., 1997 'Polos of Akragas: Testimonia', *Mnemosyne* 50: 27–34.

Foxhall, L., 1998 'Natural Sex: the Attribution of Sex and Gender to Plants in Ancient Greece', in L. Foxhall and J. Salmon (eds.), *Thinking Men: Masculinity and its Self-Representation in the Classical Tradition* (Routledge), pp. 57–70.

Frede, M., 1987 'The Original Notion of Cause', in M. Frede, *Essays in Ancient Philosophy* (Clarendon Press), pp. 125–50.

Frede, M., 1990 'An Empiricist View of Knowledge: Memorism', in S. Everson (ed.), *Epistemology: Companions to Ancient Thought 1* (Cambridge University Press), pp. 225–50.

Frede, M., 1992 'On Aristotle's Conception of Soul', in M. C. Nussbaum, A. Oksenberg, and R. Rorty (eds.), *Essays on Aristotle's De Anima* (Clarendon Press), 93–107.

Frede, M., 2003 'Experience in the Ancient "Empiricists"', Δευκαλίων 21: 23–44.

Freeland, C., 1990 'Scientific Explanation and Empirical Data in Aristotle's *Meteorology*', *Oxford Studies in Ancient Philosophy* 8: 67–102.

Frey, C., 2007, 'Organic Unity and the Matter of Man', *Oxford Studies in Ancient Philosophy* (Summer): 167–204.

Frey, C., 2015a 'From Blood to Flesh: Homonymy, Unity, and Ways of Being in Aristotle', *Ancient Philosophy* 35: 1–20.

Frey, C., 2015b 'Two Conceptions of Soul in Aristotle', in D. Ebrey (ed.) *Theory and Practice in Aristotle's Natural Science* (Cambridge University Press), pp. 137–60.

Frey, C., Fritsch, B., Rinner, E., and Graßhoff, G., 2013 '3D Models of Ancient Sundials: a Comparison', *International Journal of Heritage in the Digital Era* 2: 361–73.

Fritscher, B., 2006 'Meteorology', in H. Cancik and H. Schneider (eds.), *Brill's New Pauly: Encyclopaedia of the Ancient World: Antiquity*, vol. VIII, pp. 796–800.

Fritscher, B., 2008, 'Meteorology', in M. Landfester (ed.), *Brill's New Pauly: Encyclopaedia of the Ancient World: Classical Tradition*, vol. III, pp. 536–40.

Furth, M. 1988 *Substance, Form, and Psyche: an Aristotelean Metaphysics* (Cambridge University Press).

Gabbey, A., 2001 'Mechanical Philosophies and their Explanations', in C. Lüthy, J. E. Murdoch, and W. R. Newman (eds.), *Late Medieval and Early Modern Corpuscular Matter Theories* (Brill), pp. 441–66.

Gee, E. R. G., 2013 *Aratus and the Astronomical Tradition* (Oxford University Press).

Gelber, J., 2010 'Form and Inheritance in Aristotle's Embryology', *Oxford Studies in Ancient Philosophy* 39: 183–212.

Georgi, L., 1982 'Pollination Ecology of the Date Palm and Fig Tree: Herodotus 1.193.4-5', *Classical Philology* 77: 224–8.

Gibbs, S. L., 1976 *Greek and Roman Sundials* (Yale University Press).

Gill, M. L., 1989 *Aristotle on Substance: the Paradox of Unity* (Princeton University Press).

Gill, M. L., 2009 'The Theory of the Elements in *De Caelo* 3 and 4', in A. C. Bowen (ed.), *New Perspectives on Aristotle's De Caelo* (Brill), pp. 139–62.

Goldstein, B., 1997 'Saving the Phenomena: the Background to Ptolemy's Planetary Theory', *Journal for the History of Astronomy* 28: 1–12.

Golinski, J., 1998 *Making Natural Knowledge: Constructivism and the History of Science* (Cambridge University Press).

Gotthelf, A., 1976 'Aristotle's Conception of Final Causality', *Review of Metaphysics* 30(2): 226–54.

Gotthelf, A., 2012a 'Aristotle as Scientist: a Proper Verdict (with Emphasis on his Biological Works)' in A. Gotthelf, *Teleology, First Principles, and Scientific Method in Aristotle's Biology* (Oxford University Press), pp. 371–98.

Gotthelf, A., 2012b *Teleology, First Principles, and Scientific Method in Aristotle's Biology* (Oxford University Press).

Gotthelf, A. and Lennox, J., 1987/2000 *Philosophical Issues in Aristotle's Biology* (Cambridge University Press).

Gourinat, J.-B., 2008 'L'embryon végétatif et la formation de l'âme selon les stoïciens', in L. Brisson, M.-H. Congourdeau, and J.-L. Solère (eds.), *L'embryon: formation et animation. Antiquité grecque et latine, traditions hébraïque, chrétienne et islamique* (Vrin), pp. 59–77.

Graham, D. W., 1994 'The Postulates of Anaxagoras', *Apeiron* 27: 77–131.

Graham, D. W., 2008a *Explaining the Cosmos: the Ionian Tradition of Scientific Philosophy* (Princeton University Press).

Graham, D. W., 2008b 'Leucippus's Atomism', in P. Curd and D. Graham (eds.), *The Oxford Handbook of Presocratic Philosophy* (Oxford University Press).

Graham, D. W., 2013 *Science before Socrates: Parmenides, Anaxagoras, and the New Astronomy* (Oxford University Press),

Graham, D. W., 2014 'Philolaus', in C. Huffman (ed.), *A History of Pythagoreanism* (Cambridge University Press), pp. 46–68.

Granger, H., 1985 'The *Scala Naturae* and the Continuity of Kinds', *Phronesis* 30: 181–200.

Grant, E., 2007 *A History of Natural Philosophy: From the Ancient World to the Nineteenth Century* (Cambridge University Press).

Graßhoff, G., 2010 'Babylonian Meteorological Observations and the Empirical Basis of Ancient Science', in G. J. Selz and Klaus Wagensonner (eds.), *The Empirical Dimension of Ancient Near Eastern Studies* (LIT Verlag), pp. 33–48.

Graßhoff, G., 2012 'Globalization of Ancient Knowledge: From Babylonian Observations to Scientific Regularities', in J. Renn (ed.), *The Globalization of Knowledge in History* (Max Planck Institute), pp. 175–90.

Graßhoff, G., 2017 'Living According to the Seasons: the Power of *parapēgmata*', in M. Formisano and P. van der Eijk (eds.), *Knowledge, Text and Practice in Ancient Technical Writing* (Cambridge University Press), pp. 200–16.

Graßhoff, G., Rinner, E., Schaldach, K., Fritsch, B., and Taub, L., 2016 *Ancient Sundials* (Edition Topoi: http://repository.edition-topoi.org/collection/BSDP).

Graver, M., 1999 'Commentary on Inwood', *Proceedings of the Boston Area Colloquium of Ancient Philosophy* 15: 44–56.

Gregorić, P. and Grcić, F., 2006 'Aristotle's Notion of Experience', *Archiv für Geschichte der Philosophie* 88: 1–30.

Gregory, A., 2013 *The Presocratics and the Supernatural: Magic, Philosophy and Science in Early Greece* (Bloomsbury).

Grene, M., and Dupew, D., 2004 *The Philosophy of Biology: an Episodic History* (Cambridge University Press).

Gros, P., 2006 'Un probème de la science Hellénistique', in *Vitruve et la tradition des traités d'architecture: fabrica et ratiocinatio* (École Français de Rome), pp. 437–46.

Hagel, S., 2010 *Ancient Greek Music: a New Technical History* (Cambridge University Press).

Hamm, E., 2016 'Modelling the Heavens: *Sphairopoiia* and Ptolemy's *Planetary Hypothesis*', *Perspective on Science* 24: 416–24.

Hankinson, J., 1989 'Galen and the Best of All Possible Worlds', *Classical Quarterly* 39: 206–27.

Hankinson, J., 2003 'Philosophy and Science', in D. Sedley (ed.). *Cambridge Companion to Greek and Roman Philosophy* (Cambridge University Press), pp. 271–99.

Hankinson, J., 2008 'Reason, Cause, and Explanation in Presocratic Philosophy', in P. Curd and D. Graham (eds.), *The Oxford Handbook of Presocratic Philosophy* (Oxford University Press), pp. 434–57.

Hankinson, J., 2013 'Lucretius, Epicurus, and the Logic of Multiple Explanation', in D. Lehoux, A. D. Morrison, and A. Sharrock (eds.), *Lucretius: Poetry, Philosophy, Science* (Oxford University Press), pp. 69–98.

Hankle, H., 1874 *Zur Geschichte der Mathematik in Alterthum und Mittelalter* (Teubner).

Hannah, R., 2001 'From Orality to Literacy? The Case of the Parapegma', in J. Watson (ed.), *Speaking Volumes: Orality and Literacy in the Greek and Roman World* (Brill), pp. 139–59.

Hannah, R., 2009 *Time in Antiquity* (Routledge).

Hannah, R., 2013 *Greek and Roman Calendars: Constructions of Time in the Classical World* (Bloomsbury).

Hardy, G. and Totelin, L. M. V., 2016 *Ancient Botany* (Routledge).

Harig, G. and Kollesch, J., 1982 'Die Konstituierung der Biologie als einer selbständigen Disziplin', in F. Jürß (ed.), *Geschichte des Wissenschaftlichen Denkens im Altertum* (Akademie Verlag).

Hasper, P. S. and Yurdin, J., 2014 'Between Perception and Scientific Knowledge: Aristotle's Account of Experience', *Oxford Studies in Ancient Philosophy* 47: 117–47.

Heath, T., 1921/81 *A History of Greek Mathematics*, 2 vols. (Cambridge University Press; Dover reprint).

Heilen, S. and Greenbaum, D. G., 2016 'Astrology in the Greco-Roman World', in A. Jones (ed.), *Time and Cosmos in Greco-Roman Antiquity* (Princeton University Press), pp. 123–42.

Heinimann, F., 1961 'Eine vorplatonische theorie der *techne*', *Museum Helveticum* 18: 105–30.

Hellmann, G., 1908 'The Dawn of Meteorology', *Quarterly Journal of the Royal Meteorological Society* 34: 221–32.

Henry, D., 2005 'Embryological Models in Ancient Philosophy', *Phronesis* 50: 1–42.

Henry, D., 2013 'Optimality and Teleology in Aristotle's Natural Science', *Oxford Studies in Ancient Philosophy* 45: 225–64.

Henry, D., 2015 'Substantial Generation in *Physics* I.5–7', in M. Leunissen (ed.), *Aristotle's Physics: a Critical Guide* (Cambridge University Press), pp. 44–61.

Henry, D., 2019 *Aristotle on Substantial Generation* (Cambridge University Press).

Holberg, J. B., 2007 *Sirius: the Brightest Diamond in the Night Sky* (Springer).

Høyrup, J., 1996 'The Formation of a Myth: Our Mathematics – Greek Mathematics', in C. Goldstein, J. Gray, and J. Ritter (eds.), *Mathematical Europe: History, Myth, Identity* (Éditions de la Maison des sciences de l'homme), pp. 103–19.

Huffman, C., 1993 *Philolaus of Croton: Pythagorean and Presocratic* (Cambridge University Press).

Huffman, C., 2005 *Archytas of Tarentum: Pythagorean, Philosopher and Mathematician King* (Cambridge University Press).

Huffman, C., 2014 *A History of Pythagoreanism* (Cambridge University Press).

Hünemörder, C. and Pingel, V., 1999 'Koralle', in H. Cancik and H. Schneider (eds.), *Der neue Pauly Enzyklopädie der Antike Altertum, Band 6. Iul-Lee* (J. B. Metzler), p. 731.

Hunter, Virginia J., 1982/2017 *Past and Process in Herodotus and Thucydides* (Princeton University Press).

Hussey, E., 1991 'Aristotle's Mathematical Physics: a Reconstruction', in L. Judson (ed.), *Aristotle's Physics: a Collection of Essays* (Oxford University Press), pp. 213–42.

Inwood, B., 2005 *Reading Seneca: Stoic Philosophy at Rome* (Oxford University Press).

Jackson, D. E. P., 1980 'Towards a Resolution of the Problem of τὰ ἑνὶ διαστήματι γραφόμενα in Pappus' Collection Book VIII', *Classics Quarterly* 30: 523–33.

Jacques, J.-M., 2008 'Andokudēs', in P. T. Keyser and G. L. Irby-Massie (eds.), *The Encyclopedia of Ancient Natural Scientists: the Greek Tradition and its Many Heirs* (Routledge).

Jaeger, M., 2008 *Archimedes and the Roman Imagination* (University of Michigan Press).

Jardine, N., 1979 'The Forging of Modern Realism: Clavius and Kepler against the Sceptics', *Studies in History and Philosophy of Science Part A* 10(2): 141–73.

Jardine, N., 2004 'Etics and Emics (Not to Mention Anemic and Emetics) in the History of the Sciences', *History of Science* 42: 261–78.

Johansen, T. K., 2004 *Plato's Natural Philosophy: a Study of the Timaeus-Critias* (Cambridge University Press).

Johansen, T. K., 2009 'From Plato's Timaeus to Aristotle's De Caelo: the Case of the Missing World Soul', in A. C. Bowens and C. Wildberg (eds.), *New Perspectives on Aristotle's De Caelo* (Brill), pp. 9–29.

Johansen, T. K., 2010 'Should Aristotle have Recognised Final Causation in Plato's Timaeus?', in R. Mohr (ed.), *Plato's Timaeus Today* (Parmenides Publishing), pp. 179–200.

Johansen, T. K., 2014 'Why the Cosmos needs a Craftsman: Plato's Timaeus 27d5–29b', *Phronesis* 59: 297–320.

Johansen, T. K., 2015 'The Two Kinds of End in Aristotle: the View from the De Anima', in D. Ebrey (ed.), *Theory and Practice in Aristotle's Natural Science* (Cambridge University Press), pp. 119–36.

Johansen, T. K., 2016 'Parmenides' Likely Story', *Oxford Studies in Ancient Philosophy* 50: 1–29.

Johnson, M. R., 2005 *Aristotle on Teleology* (Oxford University Press).

Johnson, M. R., 2009 'The Aristotelian Explanation of the Halo', *Apeiron* 42(4): 325–57.

Johnson, M. R., 2015 'Aristotle's Architectonic Sciences', in D. Ebrey (ed.), *Theory and Practice in Aristotle's Natural Science* (Cambridge University Press), pp. 163–86.

Johnson, M. R., 2019 'Aristotle on *Kosmos* and *Kosmoi*', in P. Horky (ed.), *Cosmos in the Ancient World* (Cambridge University Press), pp. 74–107.

Jones, A., 1994 'Peripatetic and Euclidean Theories of the Visual Ray', *Physis* 31 NS: 47–76.

Jones, A., 2015 'Theon of Smyrna and Ptolemy on Celestial Modelling in Two and Three Dimensions', in V. De Risi (ed.), *Mathematizing Space* (Trends in the History of Science) (Springer), pp. 75–103.

Jones, A., 2016 'Translating Greek Astronomy: Theon of Smyrna on the Apparent Motions of the Planets', in A. Imhausen and T. Pommerening (eds.), *Translating Writings of Early Scholars in the Ancient Near East, Egypt, Greece, and Rome: Methodological Aspects with Examples* (De Gruyter), pp. 465–505.

Jones, A., 2017 *A Portable Cosmos: Revealing the Antikythera Mechanism, Scientific Wonder of the Ancient World* (Oxford University Press).

Jones, A., 2018 'Greco-Roman Astronomy and Astrology', in A. Jones and L. Taub (eds.), *Cambridge History of Science, vol. I: Ancient Science* (Cambridge University Press), pp. 374–401.

Jones, A. and Taub, L. (eds.) 2018. *The Cambridge History of Science, vol. I: Ancient Science* (Cambridge University Press).

Judson, L., 2005 'Aristotelian Teleology', *Oxford Studies in Ancient Philosophy* 29: 341–66.

Kahn, C., 1960 *Anaximander and the Origins of Greek Cosmology* (Columbia University Press; reprinted Hackett, 1994).

Kahn, C., 1979 *The Art and Thought of Heraclitus* (Cambridge University Press).

Kahn, C., 1997 'Greek Religion and Philosophy in the Sisyphus Fragment', *Phronesis* 42: 247–62.

Kahn, C., 2003 'Writing Philosophy: Prose and Poetry from Thales to Plato', in H. Yunis (ed.), *Written Texts and the Rise of Literate Culture in Ancient Greece* (Cambridge University Press), pp. 139–61.

Kaldellis, A., 2007 'Skamon of Mytilene (476)', in I. Worthington (ed.), *Brill's New Jacoby Online* (Brill).

Kalligas, P., 2016 'Platonic Astronomy and the Development of Ancient *Sphairopoiia*', *Rhizomata* 4: 176–200.

Keyser, P. T., 1998 'Orreries, the Date of [Plato] *Letter* 11, and Eudoros of Alexandria,' *Archiv für Geschichte der Philosophie* 80: 241–67.

Kidd, I. G., 1988 *Posidonius, vol. II: the Commentary* (Cambridge University Press).

Kidd, I. G., 1992 'Theophrastus' *Meteorology*, Aristotle, and Posidonius', in W. W. Fortenbaugh and D. Gutas (eds.), *Theophrastus: his Psychological, Doxographical, and Scientific Writings* (Transaction Books), pp. 294–306.

King, H. R., 1956 'Aristotle without Prime Matter', *Journal of the History of Ideas*, 17: 370–89.

Kirk, G. S., Raven, J. E., and Schofield, M., 1983 *The Presocratic Philosophers: a Critical History with a Selection of Texts*, 2nd edn (Cambridge University Press) (abbreviated as KRS).

Knorr, W., 1978 'Archimedes and the Pre-Euclidean Proportion Theory', *Archives Internationals d'Histoire des Sciences* 28: 183–244.

Knorr, W., 1986 *The Ancient Tradition of Geometric Problems* (Birkhäuser).

Knorr, W., 1989 *Textual Studies in Ancient and Medieval Geometry* (Birkhäuser).

Knorr, W., 1990 'Plato and Eudoxus on the Planetary Motions', *Journal for the History of Astronomy*, 21(4): 313–29.

Knorr, W., 1994 'Pseudo Euclidean Reflection in Ancient Optics: a Re-examination of Textural Issues Pertaining to the Euclidean *Optica* and *Catoptrica*', *Physis* 31 NS: 1–45.

Knorr, W., 1996 'The Wrong Text of Euclid: On Heiberg's Text and its Alternatives', *Centaurus* 38: 208–76.

Kragh, H., 1987 *An Introduction to the Historiography of Science* (Cambridge University Press).

Krizan, M.,2013 'Elemental Structure and the Transformation of the Elements in *On Generation and Corruption* 2.4', *Oxford Studies in Ancient Philosophy* 45: 195–224.

Kühn, J.-H., 1956 *System- und Methodenprobleme im Corpus Hippocraticum* (Wiesbaden).

Kuhn, T., 2012 *The Structure of Scientific Revolutions*, 4th edn (University of Chicago Press).

Kullmann, W., 1974 *Wissenschaft und Methode: Interpretationen zur aristotelischen Theorie der Naturwissenschaft* (De Gruyter).

Kullmann, W., 1998 *Aristoteles und die moderne Naturwissenschaft* (Philosophie der Antike Bd. 5) (Steiner).

Kullmann, W. and Föllinger, S., 1997 *Aristotelische Biologie: Intention, Methoden, Ergebnisse* (Franz Steiner Verlag).

Kühnert, F., 1961 *Allgemeinbildung and Fachbildung in der Antike* (Akademie-Verlag).

Laks, A., 2006 *Introduction à la 'philosophie présocratique'* (Presses Universitaires de France).

Laks, A. 2008 'Speculating about Diogenes of Apollonia', in P. Curd and D. Graham (eds.), *The Oxford Handbook of Presocratic Philosophy* (Oxford University Press), pp. 353–64.

Laks, A. and Louguet, C. (eds.), 2002 *Qu'est-ce que la philosophie présocratique?* (Presses Universitaires du Septentrion).

Lang, H. S., 1998 *The Order of Nature in Aristotle's Physics: Place and the Elements* (Cambridge University Press).

Le Meur, G., 2012 'Le rôle des diagrammes dans quelques traités de la Petite astronomie', *Revue d'Histoire des Mathématiques* 18: 157–221.

Lehoux, D., 2004 'Observation and Prediction in Ancient Astrology', *Studies in History and Philosophy of Science* 35: 227–46.

Lehoux, D., 2007 *Astronomy, Weather, and Calendars in the Ancient World: Parapegmata and Related Texts in Classical and Near-Eastern Societies* (Cambridge University Press).

Lennox, J. 1980 'Aristotle on Genera, Species, and the "More and the Less"', *Journal of the History of Biology* 13: 321–46.

Lennox, J. 1985 'Plato's Unnatural Teleology', in D. J. O'Meara (ed.), *Platonic Investigations* (Catholic University of America Press), pp. 195–218.

Lennox, J. 1987 'Divide and Explain: the *Posterior Analytics* in Practice', in A. Gotthelf and J. Lennox (eds.), *Philosophical Issues in Aristotle's Biology* (Cambridge University Press), pp. 90–119.

Lennox, J. 1998 'The Disappearance of Aristotle's Biology: A Hellenistic Mystery', *Apeiron* 27/4: 7–24 (reprinted in Lennox 2001a, pp. 110–26).

Lennox, J. (ed.), 2001a *Aristotle's Philosophy of Biology: Studies in the Origins of Life Science.* (Cambridge University Press).

Lennox, J. (ed.), 2001b 'Kinds, Forms of Kinds, and the More and the Less in Aristotle's Biology', in Lennox, *Aristotle's Philosophy of Biology* (Cambridge University Press), pp. 339–59.

Leroi, A. M., 2015 *The Lagoon: How Aristotle Invented Science* (Viking Penguin).

Lettinck, P., 1999 *Aristotle's Meteorology and its Reception in the Arab World* (Brill).

Liewert, A., 2015 *Die meteorologische Medizin des Corpus Hippocraticum* (Walter de Gruyter).

Lloyd, A. B., 1988 *Herodotus: Book 2, Commentary 99–182* (Brill).

Lloyd, G. E. R., 1966 *Polarity and Analogy: Two Types of Argument in Early Greek Thought* (Cambridge University Press).

Lloyd, G. E. R., 1973 *Greek Science after Aristotle* (Norton Books).

Lloyd, G. E. R., 1979 *Magic, Reason, and Experience: Studies in the Origin and Development of Greek Science* (Cambridge University Press).

Lloyd, G. E. R., 1987a 'The Alleged Fallacy of Hippocrates of Chios', *Apeiron* 20: 103–28.

Lloyd, G. E. R., 1987b *The Revolutions of Wisdom: Studies in the Claims and Practice of Ancient Greek Science* (University of California Press).

Lloyd, G. E. R., 1991a *Methods and Problems in Greek Science: Selected Papers* (Cambridge University Press).

Lloyd, G. E. R., 1991b 'Saving the Appearances', in *Methods and Problems in Greek Science: Selected Papers* (Cambridge University Press), pp. 248–77 (originally published in *Classical Quarterly* 28 (1978), 202–22).

Lloyd, G. E. R., 1991c 'The Invention of Nature', in *Methods and Problems in Greek Science: Selected Papers* (Cambridge University Press), pp. 417–34.

Lloyd, G. E. R., 1992 'Methods and Problems in the History of Ancient Science: the Greek Case', *Isis* 83: 564–77.

Lloyd, G. E. R., 1996 *Aristotelian Explorations* (Cambridge University Press).

Lloyd, G. E. R., 2006 'Diogenes of Apollonia: Master of Ducts', in M. M. Sassi (ed.), *La construzione del discorso filosofico nell' età dei Presocratici/The Construction of Philosophical Discourse in the Age of the Presocratics* (Edizioni della Normale), pp. 237–57.

Lloyd, G. E. R., 2009 *Disciplines in the Making* (Oxford University Press).

Lloyd, G. E. R. and Vilaça, A., 2019 *Science in the Forest: Science in the Past*, special issue of *HAU: Journal of Ethnographic Theory* (University of Chicago Press).

Long, A. A. (ed.), 1999a *The Cambridge Companion to Early Greek Philosophy* (Cambridge University Press).

Long, A. A. (ed.), 1999b 'The Scope of Early Greek Philosophy', in A. A. Long (ed.), *The Cambridge Companion to Early Greek Philosophy* (Cambridge University Press), pp. 1–21.

Long C. P., 2006 'Saving "Ta Legomena": Aristotle and the History of Philosophy', *Review of Metaphysics* 60(2): 247–67.

Lonie, I. M., 1969 'On the Botanical Excursus in *De Natura Pueri* 22–27', *Hermes* 97: 391–411.

Lorch, R., 2001 'Greek–Arabic–Latin: the Transmission of Mathematical Texts in the Middle Ages', *Science in Context* 14: 313–31.

Lorenz, H., 2007 'The Assimilation of Sense to Sense-Object in Aristotle', *Oxford Studies in Ancient Philosophy* 23: 179–220.

Louis, P., 1955 'Le mot ἱστορία chez Aristote', *Revue de Philologie* 81: 39–44.

Lovejoy, A., 1948/60 *Essays in the History of Ideas* (Johns Hopkins Press/Capricorn Books).

McCoy, J. (ed.), 2013 *Early Greek Philosophy: The Presocratics and the Emergence of Reason* (The Catholic University Press of America)

McKirahan, R., 2011 *Philosophy before Socrates*, 2nd edn (Hackett).

Magdelaine, C., 2000 'Le corail dans la littérature médicale de l'Antiquité gréco-romaine au Moyen-Age', *Travaux du Centre Camille Jullian* 25: 239–53.

Manders, K., 2008 'The Euclidean Diagram (1995)', in P. Mancosu (ed.), *The Philosophy of Mathematical Practice* (Oxford University Press), pp. 80–133.

Mansfeld, J., 1992 'PERI KOSMOU: a note on the history of the title,' *Vigiliae Christianae*, 46: 391–411.

Mansfeld, J., 1998 *Prolegomena Mathematica: From Apollonius of Perga to the Late Neoplatonists* (Brill), pp. 160–81.

Mansfeld, J., 1999 'Sources', in A. A. Long (ed.), *The Cambridge Companion to Early Greek Philosophy* (Cambridge University Press), pp. 22–44.

Mansfeld, J., 2010a 'Epicurus Peripateticus', in J. Mansfeld and D. T. Runia (eds.), *Aetiana: the Method and Intellectual Context of a Doxographer* (Brill), pp. 237–54.

Mansfeld, J., 2010b '*Physikai doxai* and *problêmata physica* in Philosophy and Rhetoric: from Aristotle to Aetius (and Beyond)', in J. Mansfeld and D. T. Runia (eds.), *Aetiana: the Method and Intellectual Context of a Doxographer* (Brill), pp. 33–98.

Mansfeld, J., 2011 'Aristotle on Anaxagoras in Relation to Empedocles in *Metaphysics* A', *Philologus* 155: 361–6.

Mansfeld, J., and Runia, D.. 1997–2009, *Aetiana: the Method and Intellectual Context of a Doxographer*, 2 vols. (Brill).

Mansfeld, J. et al., 2016 *Eleatica 2012: Melissus between Miletus and Elea* (Academia Verlag).

Marciano, M. L. G., 2006 'Indovini, *magoi* e *meteorologoi*: interazioni e definizioni nell'ultimo terzo del V secolo a.C.', in M. M. Sassi (ed.), *La costruzione del discorso filosofico nell'età dei Presocratici* (Edizioni della Normale).

Marmodoro, A., 2015 'Anaxagoras' Qualitative Gunk', *British Journal for the History of Philosophy* 23: 402–22.

Marmodoro, A., 2017 *Everything in Everything: Anaxagoras's Metaphysics* (Oxford University Press).

Marsden, E. W., 1969. *Greek and Roman Artillery: Historical Development* (Oxford University Press).

Marsden, E. W., 1971 *Greek and Roman Artillery: Technical Treatises* (Oxford University Press).

Martin, A. and Primavesi, O., 1999 *L'Empédocle de Strasbourg* (De Gruyter).

Mayr, O., 1986 *Authority, Liberty and Automatic Machinery in Early Modern Europe* (Johns Hopkins University Press).

Mendell, H., 1998 'Reflections on Eudoxus, Callippus and their Curves: Hippopedes and Callippopedes', *Centaurus* 40: 177–275.

Mendell, H., 2007 'Two Traces of Two-Step Eudoxan Proportion Theory in Aristotle', *Archive of History of Exact Sciences*: 3–37.

Menn, S., 2002 'Aristotle's Definition of Soul and the Programme of the *De Anima*', *Oxford Studies in Ancient Philosophy* 22: 83–139.

Meriani, A., 2003 'Teoria musicale e antiempirismo nella *Repubblica* di Platone', in *Sulla musica greca antica. Studi e ricerche* (Guida), pp. 82–113.

Meyer, M. F., 2015 *Aristoteles und die Geburt der biologischen Wissenschaft* (Springer).

Miller, D. P., 2017 'The Story of "Scientist": the Story of a Word', *Annals of Science* 74(4), 255–61.

Mittelstraß, J., 1963 *Die Rettung der Phänomene* (Walter de Gruyter).

Montucla J.-E., 1758 *Histoire des mathématiques*, vol. I (Chez Henri Agasse); 2nd edn 1798.

Mosshammer, A., 1981 'Thales' Eclipse', *Transactions of the American Philological Association* 111: 145–55.

Mourelatos, A. P. D., 1980 'Plato's "Real Astronomy": *Republic* 527D–531D', in J. P. Anton (ed.), *Science and the Sciences in Plato* (Caravan Books), pp. 33–73.

Mourelatos, A. P. D., 2005 'The Ancients' Meteorology: Forecasting and Cosmic Natural History', *Rhizai* 2:279–91.

Mourelatos, A. P. D., 2008a 'The Cloud-Astrophysics of Xenophanes and Ionian Material Monism', in P. Curd and D. Graham (eds.), *The Oxford Handbook of Presocratic Philosophy* (Oxford University Press), pp. 134–68.

Mourelatos, A. P. D., 2008b *The Route of Parmenides*, revised and expanded edn (Parmenides Publishing).

Mourelatos, A. P. D., 2013 'Parmenides, Early Greek Astronomy, and Modern Scientific Realism', in J. McCoy (ed.), *Early Greek Philosophy: the Presocratics and the Emergence of Reason* (Catholic University Press of America), pp. 91–112.

Mourelatos, A. P. D., 2014 'The Conception of *eoikōs/eikōs* as Epistemic Standard in Xenophanes, Parmenides, and Plato's Timaeus', *Ancient Philosophy* 34: 169–91.

Mueller, I., 1980 'Ascending to Problems: Astronomy and Harmonics in *Republic* VII', in J. P. Anton (ed.), *Science and the Sciences in Plato* (Caravan Books), pp. 103–21.

Mueller, I., 1981 *Philosophy of Mathematics and Deductive Structure in Euclid's Elements* (MIT Press).

Mugler, C., 1959 *Dictionnaire historique de la terminologie géométrique des grecs* (Gautier-Villars).

Murdoch, J. E., 2001 'The Medieval and Renaissance Tradition of *Minima Naturalia*', in C. Lüthy, J. E. Murdoch, and W. R. Newman (eds.), *Late Medieval and Early Modern Corpuscular Matter Theories* (Brill), pp. 91–132.

Murschel, A., 1995 'The Structure and Function of Ptolemy's Physical Hypotheses of Planetary Motion', *Journal for the History of Astronomy* 26: 33–61.

Myres, J. L., 1953 *Herodotus: Father of History* (Clarendon Press).

Naddaf, G., 2005 *The Greek Concept of Nature* (State University of New York Press).

Negbi, M., 1995 'Male and Female in Theophrastus' Botanical Works', *Journal of the History of Biology* 28: 317–32.

Netz, R., 1999a 'Proclus' Division of the Mathematical Proposition into Parts: How and Why was it Formulated?', *Classical Quarterly* 49: 282–303.

Netz, R., 1999b *The Shaping of Deduction in Greek Mathematics: a Study in Cognitive History* (Cambridge University Press).

Netz, R., 2004 'Eudemus of Rhodes, Hippocrates of Chios and the Earliest Form of a Greek Mathematical Text', *Centaurus* 46: 243–86.

Netz, R., 2009 *Ludic Proof* (Cambridge University Press).

Netz, R., 2012 'The Texture of Archimedes' Writings: Through Heiberg's Veil', in K. Chemla (ed.), *The History of Mathematical Proof in Ancient Traditions* (Cambridge University Press), pp. 163–205.

Netz, R., and Noel, W., 2007 *The Archimedes Codex: Revealing the Secrets of the World's Greatest Palimpsest* (Da Capo Press).

Netz, R., Noel, W., Wilson, N., and Tchernetska, N. (eds.), 2011 *The Archimedes Palimpsest*, 2 vols. (Cambridge University Press).

Neugebauer, O., 1953 'On the "Hippopede" of Eudoxus', *Scripta Muthematica* 19: 225–9.

Neugebauer, O., 1975 *A History of Ancient Mathematical Astronomy*, 3 vols. (Springer Verlag).

Niiniluoto, I., 2015 'Scientific Progress', in E. N. Zalta (ed.), *The Stanford Encyclopedia of Philosophy* (Summer 2015 Edition). http://plato.stanford.edu/archives/sum2015/entries/scientific-progress/.

Nussbaum, M. C., 1986 'Saving Aristotle's Appearances', in *The Fragility of Goodness* (Cambridge University Press), pp. 240–63 (a longer version of M. C. Nussbaum, 1982 'Saving Aristotle's Appearances', in M. Schofield and M. C. Nussbaum (eds.), *Language and Logos* (Cambridge University Press), pp. 267–94).

O'Brien, D., 1981 *Theories of Weight in the Ancient World: Four Essays on Democritus, Plato and Aristotle, vol. I: Democritus, Weight and Size: an Exercise in the Reconstruction of Early Greek Philosophy* (Brill).

Osborne, C., 1987 'Empedocles Recycled', *Classical Quarterly* 37: 24–50.

Owen, G. E. L., 1961 'Tithenai ta phainomena', in S. Mansion (ed.), *Aristote et les problemes de methods: communications presentées au Symposium Aristotelicum tenu à Louvain du 24 août au 1er septembre 1960* (Louvain), 83–103; reprinted in G. E. L. Owen, *Logic, Science and Dialectic: Collected Papers in Greek Philosophy*, ed. Martha Nussbaum (Cornell, 1986), pp. 49–62.

Palmer, J., 2000 'Aristotle on the Ancient Theologians', *Apeiron* 33: 181–205.

Palmer, J., 2009 *Parmenides and Presocratic Philosophy* (Oxford University Press).

Panagiotou, S., 1975 'Aristotle's *De anima*, 424 b3', *Symbolae Osloenses* 50(1): 47–53.

Paradiso, A., 2008 'Simonides (ὁ γενεαλόγος) (8)', in I. Worthington (ed.), *Brill's New Jacoby Online*, http://referenceworks.brillonline.com/entries/brill-s-new-jacoby/simonides-8-a8.

Pease, A. S., 1927 'The Loves of the Plants', *Classical Philology* 22: 94–8.

Pease, A. S., 1933 'Notes on Ancient Grafting', *Transactions and Proceedings of the American Philological Association* 64: 66–76.

Pellegrin, P., 1982 *La classification des animaux chez Aristote, statut de la biologie et unité de l'aristotélisme* (Les Belles Lettres).

Pellicer, A., 1966 *Natura: étude sémantique et historique du mot latin* (Presses Universitaires de France).

Peters, F. E., 1967 *Greek Philosophical Terms: a Historical Lexicon* (New York University Press).

Pfeiffer, J., 2002 'France', in J. W. Dauben and C. J. Scriba (eds.), *Writing the History of Mathematics: its Historical Development* (Birkhäuser), pp. 3–44.

Pierris, A. (ed.), 2005 *The Empedoclean Kosmos: Structure, Process and the Question of Cyclicity* (Institute for Philosophical Research).

Pingree, D., 1992 'Hellenophilia versus the History of Science', *Isis* 83: 554–63.

Pohlenz, M., 1918 'Das zwanzigste Kapitel von Hippokrates *de prisca medicina*', *Hermes* 53: 396–421.

Pohlenz, M., 1953 'Nomos und Physis', *Hermes*: 418–38.

Popper, K., 1998 *The World of Parmenides: Essays on the Presocratic Enlightenment* (Routledge).

Popper, N., 2006 '"Abraham, Planter of Mathematics": Histories of Mathematics and Astrology in Early Modern Europe', *Journal of the History of Ideas* 67: 87–106.

Pottier, E., 1887 'Corallium ou Curalium', in C. V. Daremberg and E. Saglio (eds.), *Dictionnaire des antiquités grecques et romaines d'après les textes et les monuments, contenant l'explication des termes qui se rapportent aux mœurs, aux institutions, à la religion, aux arts, aux sciences, au costume, au mobilier, à la guerre, à la marine, aux métiers, aux monnaies, poids et mesures, etc. etc., et en général à la vie publique et privée des anciens*, vol. I, part 2 (Hachette), pp. 1503–4.

Powers, N., 2009 'The Natural Theology of Xenophon's Socrates', *Ancient Philosophy* 29, 249–66.

Price, D. J. de Solla, 1957 'Precision Instruments: to 1500', in C. Singer, E. J. Holmyard, A. R. Hall, and T. I. Williams (eds.), *A History of Technology*, vol. III (Oxford University Press), pp. 582–619

Price, D. J. de Solla, 1974 *Gears from the Greeks: the Antikythera mechanism, a Calendar Computer from ca. 80 BC* (American Philosophical Society).

Primavesi, O., 2008 'Empedocles: Physical and Mythical Divinity', in P. Curd and D. Graham (eds.), *The Oxford Handbook of Presocratic Philosophy* (Oxford University Press), pp. 250–83.

Radermacher, L., 1951 *Artium scriptores (Reste der voraristotelischen Rhetorik)* (R. M. Rohrer)

Raffa, M., 2002 *La scienza armonica di Claudio Toleme* (A. Sfameni).

Raffa, M., 2013 'The Debate on λόγος and διάστημα in Porphyry's *Commentary* on Ptolemy's *Harmonics*', *Greek and Roman Musical Studies* 1: 243–52.

Raffa, M., 2014 'On the Text of Theophrastus fr. 717 Fortenbaugh', *Classical Quarterly* 64: 409–10.

Rashed, R. and Papadopoulos, A., 2017 *Menelaus' Spherics: Early Translation and al-Māhānī/al-Harawī's Version*. De Gruyter.

Renehan, R., 1995. 'Polus, Plato, and Aristotle' *Classical Quarterly* 45: 68–72.

Riedweg, C., 2005 *Pythagoras: his Life, Teaching, and Influence* (Cornell University Press); trans. of 2002 *Pythagoras. Leben, Lehre, Nachwirkung* (C. H. Beck).

Rihll, T., 2007 *The Catapult: a History* (Westholme).

Rochberg, F., 1992 'Introduction', *Isis* 83: 547–53.

Rochberg, F., 2016 *Before Nature: Cuneiform Knowledge and the History of Science* (University of Chicago Press).

Rommevaux, S., Djebbar, A., and Vitrac, B., 2001 'Remarques sur l'histoire du texte des Éléments d'Euclide', *Archive for History of Exact Sciences* 55: 221–95.

Rood, T., 2017 'Of Sundials', *Anachronism and Antiquity* blog, Faculty of Classics, University of Oxford (https://anachronismandantiquity.wordpress.com/2017/03/31/of-sundials/).

Rose, P. L. and Drake, S., 1971 'The Pseudo-Aristotelian *Questions of Mechanics* in Renaissance Culture', *Studies in the Renaissance* 18, 65–104.

Ross, S., 1964 'Scientist: the Story of a Word', *Annals of Science* 18 (June 1962): 65–85, http://dx.doi.org/10.1080/00033796200202722.

Runia, D., 2008 'The Sources for Presocratic Philosophy', in P. Curd and D. Graham (eds.), *The Oxford Handbook of Presocratic Philosophy* (Oxford University Press), pp. 27–54.

Saito, K., 1997 'Index of the Propositions Used in Book 7 of Pappus' *Collection*', *Jinbunn Kenkyu: Journal of the Humanities, Chiba University* 26: 155–88.

Saito, K., 1998 *Girishia sugaku no tool box no fukugen*, Research Report, Sakai.

Saito, K. and Sidoli, N., 2010 'The Function of Diorism in Ancient Greek Analysis', *Historia Mathematica* 37: 579–614.

Saito, K. and Sidoli, N., 2012 'Diagrams and Arguments in Ancient Greek Mathematics', in K. Chemla (ed.), *The History of Mathematical Proof in Ancient Traditions* (Cambridge University Press), pp. 135–62.

Sambursky, S., 1962 *The Physical World of Late Antiquity* (Routledge and Kegan Paul).

Savage-Smith, E., 1985 *Islamicate Celestial Globes: their History, Construction, and Use* (Smithsonian Institution Press, Smithsonian Studies in History and Technology 46).

Schiefsky, M., 2007 'Art and Nature in Ancient Mechanics', in B. Bensaude-Vincent and W. Newman (eds.), *The Artificial and the Natural: an Evolving Polarity* (MIT Press), pp. 67–108.

Schiefsky, M., 2008 'Theory and Practice in Heron's Mechanics', in S. Roux and W. Roy Laird (eds.), *Mechanics and Natural Philosophy before the Scientific Revolution* (Springer).

Sedley, D., 1976 'Epicurus and the Mathematicians of Cyzicus', *Cronache Ercolanesi* 6: 23–54.

Sedley, D., 1982 'Two Conceptions of Vacuum', *Phronesis* 27: 175–93.

Sedley, D., 1991 'Is Aristotle's Teleology Anthropocentric?', *Phronesis* 36: 179–96.

Sedley, D., 1998a *Lucretius and the Transformation of Greek Wisdom* (Cambridge University Press).

Sedley, D., 1998b 'Platonic Causes', *Phronesis* 43: 114–32.

Sedley, D. (ed.), 2003 *The Cambridge Companion to Greek and Roman Philosophy* (Cambridge University Press).

Sedley, D., 2007 *Creationism and its Critics in Antiquity* (University of California Press).

Sedley, D., 2009 *Creationism and its Critics in Antiquity* (University of California Press).

Sedley, D., 2010 'Teleology, Aristotelian and Platonic', in J. Lennox and R. Bolton (eds.), *Being, Nature, and Life in Aristotle* (Cambridge University Press), pp. 5–29.

Sellars, W., 1975 'Autobiographical Reflections (February 1973)', in H-N. Castañeda (ed.), *Action, Knowledge, and Reality: Studies in Honor of Wilfrid Sellars* (Bobbs-Merrill), pp. 277–93.

Sezgin, F., 1974–9 *Geschichte des Arabischen Schrifttums, Bände V–VII* (Brill).

Sicking, C. M. J., 1998 'Theophrastus on the Nature of Music', in J. M. van Opuijsen and M. van Raalte (eds.), *Theophrastus: Reappraising the Sources* (Transaction), pp. 97–142.

Sider, D., 2002 Demokritos and the Weather', in A. Laks and C. Louguet (eds.), *Qu'est que la philosophie présocratique?/What is Presocratic Philosophy?* (Presses Universitaires du Septentrion), pp. 287–302.

Sidoli, N., 2005 'Heron's *Dioptra* 35 and Analemma Methods: an Astronomical Determination of the Distance between Two Cities', *Centaurus* 47: 236–58.

Sidoli, N., 2014 'Research on Ancient Greek Mathematical Sciences, 1998–2012', in N. Sidoli and G. Van Brummelen (eds.), *From Alexandria, through Baghdad: Surveys and Studies in the Ancient Greek and Medieval Islamic Mathematical Sciences in Honor of J. L. Berggren* (Springer), pp. 25–50.

Sidoli, N., 2015 'Mathematics Education', in W. M. Bloomer (ed.), *A Companion to Ancient Education* (Blackwell), pp. 387–400.

Sidoli, N. and Saito, K., 2009 'The Role of Geometrical Construction in Theodosius' *Spherics*', *Archive for History of Exact Sciences* 63: 581–609.

Sidoli, N. and Saito, K., 2012 'Comparative Analysis in Greek Mathematics', *Historia Mathematica* 39: 1–33.

Simms, D. L., 1995 'Archimedes the Engineer,' *History of Technology* 17: 45–111.

Sisko, J., 2005 'Anaxagoras and Recursive Refinement', *Ancient Philosophy* 25: 239–45.

Snell, B., 1924 *Die Ausdrücke für den Begriff des Wissens in der vorplatonischen Philosophie* (Weidmann).

Sorabji, R. R. K., 2002 'Latitude of Forms in Ancient Philosophy', in C. Leijenhorst, C. Lüthy, and J. M. M. H. Thijssen (eds.), *The Dynamics of Aristotelian Natural Philosophy from Antiquity to the Seventeenth Century* (Brill), pp. 37–63.

Steel, C. (ed.), 2012 *Aristotle's Metaphysics Alpha: Symposium Aristotelicum* (Oxford University Press).

Störig, H., 1965 *Kleine Weltgeschichte der Wissenschaft* (Kohlhammer).

Stothers, R., 1979 'Ancient Aurorae', *Isis* 70: 85–95.

Stothers, R., 2009 'Ancient Meteorological Optics', *Classical Journal* 105: 27–42.

Taisbak, C. M., 2014 'An Archimedean Proof of Heron's Formula for the Area of a Triangle: Heuristics Reconstructed', in N. Sidoli and G. Van Brummelen (eds.), *From Alexandria, through Baghdad: Surveys and Studies in the Ancient Greek and Medieval Islamic Mathematical Sciences in Honor of J. L.Berggren* (Springer), pp. 189–99.

Talbert, R., 2017. *Roman Portable Sundials* (Oxford University Press).

Tannery, P., 1876 'Note sur le systeme astronomique d'Eudoxe', *Memoires de la Societe des sciences physiques et naturelles de Bordeaux* 1: 441–449 (1893 reprint in *Memoires Scientifiques* (Gauthier-Villars), vol. 1, pp. 1–11).

Tannery, P., 1883 'Seconde note sur le systeme astronomique d'Eudoxe', *Memoires de la Societe des sciences physiques et naturelles de Bordeaux* 5: 129–47 (1893 reprint in *Memoires Scientifiques* (Gauthier-Villars), vol. 1, pp. 317–38).

Tatarkiewicz, W., 1963 'Classification of the Arts in Antiquity', *Journal of the History of Ideas* 24: 231–40.

Taub, L., 1993 *Ptolemy's Universe: the Natural Philosophical and Ethical Foundations of Ptolemy's Astronomy* (Open Court).

Taub, L., 1997 'The Rehabilitation of Wretched Subjects', *Early Science and Medicine*, 2: 74–8.

Taub, L., 2002 'Instruments of Alexandrian Astronomy: the Uses of the Equinoctial Rings', in C. Tuplin (ed.), *Science in Ancient Greece* (Oxford University Press).

Taub, L., 2003 *Ancient Meteorology* (Routledge).

Taub, L., 2009 'Cosmology and Meteorology', in J. Warren (ed.), *The Cambridge Companion to Epicureanism* (Cambridge University Press), pp. 105–24.

Taub, L., 2010 'Translating the *Phainomena* across Genre, Language and Culture', in A. Imhausen and T. Pommerening (eds.), *Writings of Early Scholars in the Ancient Near East, Egypt and Greece: Zur Übersetzbarkeit von Wissenschaftssprachen des Altertums* (De Gruyter), pp. 119–38.

Taub, L., 2017 *Writing Science in Greco-Roman Antiquity* (Cambridge University Press).

Teller, P., 2010 '"Saving the Phenomena" Today', *Philosophy of Science* 77: 815–26.

Theiler, W., 1924 *Zur Geschichte der teleologischen Naturbetrachtung bis auf Aristoteles* (Füssli; 2nd edition 1965, Walter de Gruyter).

Thibodeau, P., 2011 *Playing the Farmer: Representations of Rural Life in Vergil's Georgics* (University of California Press).

Thom, J. C. (ed.), 2014 *Cosmic Order and Divine Power: Pseudo-Aristotle, On the Cosmos* (Mohr Siebeck).

Thomas, R., 2000 *Herodotus in Context: Ethnography, Science and the Art of Persuasion* (Cambridge University Press).

Thomson, J. O., 1948 *History of Ancient Geography* (Cambridge University Press).

Todd, R. B., 1972 '*Epitêdeiotês* in Philosophical Literature: Towards an Analysis', *Acta Classica* 15: 25–35.

Tortzen, C. G., 1991 'Male and Female in Peripatetic Botany', *Classica et Mediaevalia* 42: 81–110.

Tozer, H. F., 1964 *A History of Ancient Geography* (Biblo and Tannen).

Trépanier, S., 2004 *Empedocles: an Interpretation* (Routledge).

Turner , A. J. 1994 *Mathematical Instruments in Antiquity and the Middle Ages: an Introduction* (Vade-Mecum Press).

Tybjerg, K., 2003 'Wonder-making and Philosophical Wonder in Hero of Alexandria', *Studies in History and Philosophy of Science Part A* 34: 443–66.

Tybjerg, K., 2005 'Hero of Alexandria: between Theory and Practice', in A. Schürmann (ed.), *Physik/Mechanik* (Franz Steiner Verlag).

van der Eijk, P. J. (ed.), 1999 *Ancient Histories of Medicine: Essays in Medical Doxography and Historiography in Classical Antiquity* (Brill).

Vegetti, M., 1993 'I nervi dell' anima', in J. Kollesch and D. Nickel (eds.), *Galen un das Hellenistische Erbe: Verhandlungen des IV. Internationalen Galen-Symposiums* (Franz Steiner), pp. 63–77.

Vetter, B., 2015 *Potentiality: From Dispositions to Modality* (Oxford University Press).

Vitrac, B., 2012 'The Euclidean Ideal of Proof in *The Elements* and Philological Uncertainties of Heiberg's Edition of the Text', in K. Chemla (ed.), *The History of Mathematical Proof in Ancient Traditions* (Cambridge University Press), pp. 69–134.

Vitrac, B., n.d. *Quand? Comment? Pourquoi les textes mathématiques grecs sont-ils parvenus en Occident*, www.academia.edu/32567771/Quand_Comment_Pourquoi_les_textes_math%C3%A9matiques_grecs_sont-ils_parvenus_en_Occident.

Vlastos, G., 1975 *Plato's Universe* (University of Washington Press).

Vlastos, G., 1980 'The Role of Observation in Plato's Conception of Astronomy', in J. P. Anton (ed.), *Science and the Sciences in Plato* (Caravan Books), pp. 1–31.

von Staden, H., 1982 'Hairesis and Heresy: the Case of the Haireseis Iatrikai', in B. F. Meyers and E. Sanders (eds.), *Jewish and Christian Self-Definition III* (Fortress Press), pp. 76–100.

von Staden, H., 1992 'Affinities and Elision: Helen and Hellenocentrism', *Isis* 83: 578–95.

von Staden, H., 1996 'Body and Machine: Interactions between Medicine, Mechanics, and Philosophy in Early Alexandria', in J. Walsh and T. F. Reese (eds.), *Alexandria and Alexandrianism* (J. Paul Getty Museum), pp. 85–106.

Voss, G. J., 1650 *De universae matheseos natura et constitutione liber, cui subjungitur chronologia mathematicorum* (Amsterdam).

Walker, T., 2012 *Plants: a Very Short Introduction* (Oxford University Press).

Watson, W., 1751 'An Account of a Manuscript Treatise, Presented to the Royal Society, Intituled, Traité du corail, contenant les nouvelles découvertes, qu'on a fait sur le corail, les pores, madrepores, scharras, litophitons, éponges, et autres corps et productions, que la mer fournit, pour servir à l'histoire naturelle de la mer; That is to Say, A Treatise upon Coral, and Several Other Productions Furnish'd by the Sea, in Order to Illustrate the Natural History Thereof, by the Sieur de Peyssonnel, M. D. Correspondent of the Royal Acad. of Sciences of Paris, of That of Montpelier, and of That of Belles Lettres at Marseilles; Physician-Botanist, Appointed by His Most Christian Majesty in the Island of Guadalupe, and Heretofore Sent by the King to the Coasts of Barbary for Discoveries in Natural History. Extracted and Translated from the French by Mr. William Watson, F. R. S.', *Philosophical Transactions of the Royal Society* 47: 445–69.

Whewell, W., 1840 *The Philosophy of the Inductive Sciences Founded upon their History*, 2 vols. (J. and J. J. Deighton).

White, S. A., 2002 'Thales and the Stars', in V. Caston and D. W. Graham (eds.), *Presocratic Philosophy: Essays in Honour of Alexander Mourelatos* (Ashgate), pp. 3–18.

White, S. A., 2008 'Milesian Measures: Time, Space, and Matter', in P. Curd and D. Graham (eds.), *The Oxford Handbook of Presocratic Philosophy* (Oxford University Press), pp. 89–133.

Whiting, J., 1992 'Living Bodies', in M. C. Nussbaum and A. O. Rorty (eds.), *Essays on Aristotle's De Anima* (Clarendon Press), pp. 75–92.

Wietzke, J., 2017 'The Public Face of Expertise: Utility, Zeal and Collaboration in Ptolemy's *Syntaxis*', in J. König and G. Woolf (eds.), *Authority and Expertise in Ancient Scientific Culture* (Cambridge University Press), pp. 348–73.

Wilberding, J., 2008 'Porphyry and Plotinus on the Seed', *Phronesis* 53: 406–32.

Wilberding, J., 2014 'The Secret of Sentient Vegetative Life in Galen', in P. Adamson, R. Hansberger, and J. Wilberding (eds.), *Philosophical Themes in Galen* (Institute of Classical Studies), pp. 249–68.

Wilberding, J., 2015 'Neoplatonists on the Causes of Vegetative Life', in A. Marmodoro and B. D. Prince (eds.), *Causation and Creation in Late Antiquity* (Cambridge University Press), pp. 171–85.

Williams, G. D., 2012 *The Cosmic Viewpoint: a Study of Seneca's Natural Questions* (Oxford University Press).

Williams, R. 1976/83 rev. edn *Key Words: a Vocabulary of Culture and Society* (Oxford University Press).

Wilson, M., 2013 *Structure and Method in Aristotle's Meteorologica: a More Disorderly Nature* (Cambridge University Press).

Wöhrle, G. (ed.), 2014 *The Milesians: Thales*; translation of 2012 German version with additional material by R. McKirahan (De Gruyter).

Wright, L., 1973 'Functions', *Philosophical Review* 82: 139–68.

Wright, M. R., 2008 'Presocratic Cosmologies', in P. Curd and D. Graham (eds.), *The Oxford Handbook of Presocratic Philosophy* (Oxford University Press), pp. 413–33.

Yavetz, I., 1998 'On the Homocentric Spheres of Eudoxus', *Archive for History of Exact Sciences* 52: 221–78.

Zeller, E., 1897 *Aristotle and the Earlier Peripatetics* (Longmans, Green).

Zhmud, L., 1998 'Plato as "Architect of Science"', *Phronesis* 43: 211–44.

Zhmud, L., 2005 '"Saving the Phenomena" between Eudoxus and Eudemus', in G. Wolters and M. Carrier (eds.), *Homo Sapiens und Homo Faber: Festschrift für J. Mittelstrass* (De Gruyter), pp. 17–24.

Zhmud, L., 2006 *The Origin of the History of Science in Classical Antiquity* (De Gruyter).

Zhmud, L., 2012 *Pythagoras and the Early Pythagoreans*, trans. K. Windle and R. Ireland (Oxford University Press).

Zhmud, L., 2013 'Die doxographische Tradition', in H. Flashar, D. Bremer, and G. Rechenauer (eds.), *Die Philosophie der Antike. Frühgriechische Philosophie* (Schwabe), pp. 150–74.

Zhmud, L., 2017 'Heraclitus on Pythagoras', in E. Fantino, U. Muss, C. Schubert, and K. Sier (eds.), *Heraklit im Kontext* (De Gruyter), pp. 173–87

Zhmud, L. and Kouprianov, A., 2018 'Ancient Greek *Mathēmata* from a Sociological Perspective: a Quantitative Analysis', *Isis* 109(3): 445–72.

Index Locorum

The abbreviations here generally follow those in the *Oxford Classical Dictionary* (4th edition).

BNJ =   *Brill's New Jacoby*, I. Worthington (ed.) (2006–)
DK =   H. Diels and W. Kranz, *Die Fragmente der Vorsokratiker* (Diels–Kranz, *Vorsokr.*)
fr. =   fragment; the name(s) in brackets following indicate the editor(s)

General Index

OTHER VOLUMES IN THE SERIES OF CAMBRIDGE

COMPANIONS *(continued from page ii)*